Ferrari: The Grand Prix Cars

(New Edition)

34
30

Ferrari: The Grand Prix Cars

(New Edition)

Alan Henry

Hazleton Publishing, Richmond, Surrey

The author would like to thank the following for their help, advice, information and assistance: Kathy Ager, Michele Alboreto, Cliff Allison, John Barnard, Gerhard Berger, Ann Bradshaw, Tony Brooks, Piero Lardi-Ferrari, Paul Frère, Mauro Forghieri, Graham Gauld, Franco Gozzi, Mike Greasley, Ann Henry, Innes Ireland, Denis Jenkinson, Stefan Johansson, Niki Lauda, Doug Nye, Victor Pigott, Harvey Postlethwaite, Nigel Roebuck, Jody Scheckter, John Surtees, Patrick Tambay, Mike Tee, David Tremayne, Brenda Vernor and Nigel Wollheim.

Also to William Kimber & Co. Ltd. for permission to quote from Mike Hawthorn's two books *Challenge Me the Race* and *Champion Year.*

This second edition published in 1989 by Hazleton Publishing, 3 Richmond Hill, Richmond, Surrey TW10 6RE.

ISBN: 0-905138-61-9

First edition published in 1984.

Printed in Holland by drukkerij de Lange/van Leer b.v., Deventer. Typesetting by C. Leggett & Son Ltd., Mitcham, Surrey, and First Impression Graphics Ltd., Richmond, Surrey.

Cover photographs by Nigel Snowdon and Fotovantage.

Colour Photography by:
Peter Coltrin
Graham Gauld
Geoffrey Goddard
LAT Photographic
Franco Lini
Phipps Photographic
Nigel Roebuck
Nigel Snowdon

Black & White Photography by:
Jesse Alexander
Diana Burnett
Bernard Cahier
Edward Eves
Graham Gauld
Geoffrey Goddard
Alan Henry
International Press Agency
Denis Jenkinson
LAT Photographic
Franco Lini
Rene Maestri
Phipps Photographic
Pirelli
Cyril Posthumous
Nigel Roebuck
Nigel Snowdon
Keith Sutton

DISTRIBUTORS

USA
Motorbooks International,
PO Box 2, 729 Prospect Av.,
Osceola, Wisconsin 54020

New Zealand
David Bateman Ltd.,
PO Box 65062,
Mairangi Bay,
Auckland 10

Australia
Technical Book & Magazine Co.,
289-299 Swanston Street,
Melbourne, Victoria 3000

UK and Other Markets
Osprey Publishing Ltd.
59 Grosvenor Street,
London W1X 9DA

(frontispiece)

Where it all started. Prince Igor Troubtezkoy's Ferrari 166 heads Tazio Nuvolari's Cisitalia in the rain-soaked 1948 Monaco Grand Prix. Prince Igor's outing in this race marked the start of a long path – it was the first Ferrari entry of any sort in a Grand Epreuve, an international Grand Prix of established standing. This 166 later passed into the ownership of Englishman Dudley Folland.

Contents

Marlboro

Foreword:
Gerhard Berger

There are those who have said my decision to join the Ferrari team was a purely romantic one and, to a great extent, I admit that is the case. There is so much tradition and prestige bound up in the business of being a Ferrari driver that I felt it was an opportunity I couldn't miss; rightly or wrongly, I thought there would always be another chance of driving for some of the other top constructors. My three Grand Prix victories for the team have produced an enormous sense of satisfaction. Driving for Ferrari is something special, with a very particular, almost intangible feel about it. I think Alan Henry has captured some of that elusive mystique in this second edition of this comprehensive AUTOCOURSE marque history.

Introduction

"Where Fiat takes the Ferrari legend after his passing is a matter of absorbing fascination for everybody who has even a fleeting interest in the complex, colourful world that is Grand Prix racing . . ."

Those words were contained in the last sentence of the first edition of this book when it was published in the summer of 1984. At the time Enzo Ferrari was 86 years old, still dynamic and far from frail. Although I wrote those words, I somehow believed that this extraordinary, driven, melodramatic legend would live for ever.

In common with all my contemporary colleagues, I was very aware that Enzo Ferrari had been a vital cornerstone of motor racing long before I first put pen to paper and, to judge by the way in which he ruled his domain, it seemed he would probably outlast us.

I was admitted to his presence but once. A few days prior to the 1986 Italian Grand Prix a group of English journalists was invited to make a detour to Maranello, where we would be received by Mr. Ferrari. Even the cynical downed tools to be there.

Although he was then 88 years old and entered the room assisted by his son, Piero Lardi, we were all struck by the aura of power he radiated. Unquestionably, the man was *somebody*. Yet his patrician image was an illusion: he came from the humblest of backgrounds. The force of his personality had been moulded, developed and honed with the passing of the years. His very existence, the fact that he was a survivor from the pioneering days of the sport, ensured that others would respect him almost as an icon, viewed with awe from afar, the prisoner of his own image.

There is no other marque in Grand Prix racing today that stirs the passions in the way Ferrari does. The groundswell of enthusiasm for the team's cars, exploits and tradition transcends the political machinations of the moment. Yet, as one follows the course of the team's history, time after time the same torrid scenario repeats itself, Enzo Ferrari falling out with key people within his team at crucial moments. Yet to strip away this façade of eccentricity would be to destroy part of the legend.

In my researches I have talked to many Grand Prix drivers who have been members of the Ferrari squad over four decades. All have affectionate memories of their spell driving for "the Old Man" – although I suspect that time has put a soft focus on their recollections. Those who have been through the Maranello mill more recently, such as the articulate Michele Alboreto, give the impression that leaving the team was a bit like getting early parole from a prison sentence!

Enzo Ferrari was a theatrical gambler who played for high risks, never believing he could come unstuck. Having built up his Scuderia in the 1930s with support from Alfa Romeo, he had no hesitation in turning his back on the famous concern after a major dispute with the management. He walked out of the door in 1939. Twelve years later, Froilan Gonzalez would drive a Ferrari 375 to victory in the British Grand Prix at Silverstone, beating the Alfa Romeo 158s fair and square. Immediately afterwards Ferrari sent a telegram to the Alfa management, the contents of which have passed into motor racing folklore. It read, "I still feel for our Alfa the adolescent tenderness of first love."

Privately, Ferrari must have simply relished putting it over his former employers. Moreover, when Alfa withdrew at the end of 1951, the stage was clear for Ferrari to fashion an identity based on continuity and solidity, layer upon layer of half-truth, speculation and rumour being added to the lustrous sheen of Enzo Ferrari's image as the decades passed.

Enzo Ferrari at Maranello in September 1986 on the occasion of a press conference for visiting British journalists. Marco Piccinini is on the left, Piero Lardi-Ferrari on the right.

His life was not without tragedy. After the death of his son Dino, from nephritis, a kidney ailment, on June 30, 1956, Ferrari was left to grieve for the heir who was to have taken up the torch. Only when Dino's mother Laura died in 1978 would Piero Lardi, Enzo's illegitimate son, be acknowledged as a member of the Ferrari dynasty.

Ferrari's relationships with his drivers were complex and confusing. He never believed in permitting them to become too comfortable, regarding keen rivalry between his men as the key to their retaining a competitive edge. All too frequently, of course, this either led to drivers seeking alternative employment or over-reaching themselves with tragic consequences. Yet he was never predictable. Some drivers he went out of his way to pamper, such as Surtees, Amon and Ickx, yet none of them stayed the course. He could fall out with just about anybody if he had a mind to and, even in the late evening of his life, became embroiled in a major row with Piero Lardi, ousting him from his position in the racing division, pushing him "across the road" to the production car plant.

This titanic man died on Sunday August 14, 1988, closing an historic chapter in the history of Italian motor racing and car making. Almost by accident, or so it seems, Ferrari also became the manufacturer of the world's most exclusive and desirable road cars, even if he saw them merely as a means of bankrolling his motor racing, always his first love. The company was brought to the verge of bankruptcy by this business philosophy, but the shrewd Gianni Agnelli of Fiat stepped in with a discreet financial safety net in 1969.

The last decade has seen the fortunes of Ferrari's Grand Prix cars waver, only occasional flashes of brilliance punctuating a series of generally disappointing performances. Yet the belief that Maranello has the power and will to turn the corner, to make things better, has led a succession of drivers to turn to the Prancing Horse in the hope of improving their results, making their name and winning a World Championship.

I like to think that this second edition of *Ferrari: The Grand Prix Cars* rules off neatly the end of two eras. The 1988 season marked both the end of the turbos in Formula 1 and the passing of the man who gave his name to the most romantic of all racing organizations. The way in which Fiat shape the team's future will indeed be fascinating, yet without Enzo Ferrari it cannot be expected to radiate the dynastic idiosyncrasies that have captured our imagination for so many years.

Alan Henry
Tillingham
Essex
January, 1989

Section I: Getting the show on the Grand Prix road: The V12 trail-blazers, 1948-51

Chapter 1
A supercharged start against Alfa Romeo

Ferrari's first major international Grand Prix success came at Berne's Bremgarten circuit in 1949 where Ascari's 125, pictured here, scored a convincing win in the Swiss Grand Prix. Team-mate Villoresi backed him up splendidly with second place, a victory made easy by the temporary absence of Alfa Romeo from the racing scene that year.

When one examines the technically refined, immensely complex Ferrari F1/87/88C of 1988 and considers the computer-age technology which has been harnessed to translate its design into reality, it is sometimes very difficult to remember that the Scuderia Ferrari edged into the Grand Prix arena at a time when the world had a very different look about it. The continuity which has been Ferrari's great strength had its seeds in the pre-World War Two Alfa Romeo Grand Prix development and Enzo Ferrari's very own Formula One cars came into being at a time when Europe was staggering to recover from six years of destruction and mayhem. Motor racing as a sport flickered back into life once more in 1946, eventually to become one of the most prestigious, publicized and heavily promoted 'commercial sports' by the start of the 1980s. Of course, on the way to its multi-million dollar status, Grand Prix racing was to have its ups and downs, Ferrari's Formula 1 efforts mirroring these changing circumstances from time to time. But, at the end of the day, the red cars from Maranello were always there . . .

Enzo Ferrari, born near Modena in 1898, by his own admission harboured boyhood ambitions to be an opera singer, sports writer and a racing driver – in that order. The personal history of this canny, cunning, often charming self-made man, who indeed became a racing driver of no mean ability before retiring in 1932 when his wife Laura gave birth to their only child, a son named Alfredino, has been exhaustively chronicled by many commentators. His contribution to the Alfa Romeo racing effort between the Wars is legend. The Scuderia Ferrari built and ran what amounted to the Alfa Romeo factory cars from 1929 through until 1938 and his close relationship with Gioacchino Colombo, the man who designed the historic supercharged Alfa 158 which finally made its racing début during Ferrari's final season in partnership with the Milanese manufacturer, led Colombo to join Enzo's new Scuderia as a consultant immediately after the war.

Ferrari split with Alfa Romeo under a cloud after a major policy disagreement over the way in which the marque's future racing plans should be handled. This disagreement, primarily with Alfa Romeo director Ugo Gobbato, was compounded by the arrival of Spanish engineer Wilfredo Ricart – and it's abundantly clear that the practical, down-to-earth Enzo took an instant dislike to Gobbato's protégé.

'. . . With sleek, oiled hair and smart clothes that he wore with a somewhat levantine elegance, Ricart affected jackets with sleeves that came down far below his wrists and shoes with enormously thick rubber soles. When he shook hands, it was like grasping the cold, lifeless hand of a corpse.' Uncompromising stuff! Ricart later went to work after the War for the Spanish Pegaso company, for

Surrounded by a crowd of fascinated onlookers, the first unpainted Ferrari 125 Grand Prix car is seen after tests in Turin's Valentino Park during the summer of 1948. Nino Farina stands behind the car in his linen helmet: he was to drive one of the three Ferrari entries in the Italian Grand Prix on this circuit at the start of September. This car, however, was eventually allocated to Bira for the race.

whom Ferrari also reserved some crushingly acid remarks in his memoirs.

The heart of Ferrari's disagreement with Alfa revolved round the Milan manufacturer's intention to re-enter racing under its own name in 1938, the newly established *Alfa Corse* organization absorbing the Scuderia Ferrari and transferring the new 158 Grand Prix car operation back from Modena to its Portello base in Milan. From this point onwards it was only really a matter of time before Enzo Ferrari's autocratic attitude found itself stifled by Alfa Romeo's new approach and he went his own way. When Ferrari finally split with Alfa during 1939, he was bound by a clause in his terms of severance which forbade his becoming involved in any motor racing activities, save with an Alfa Romeo, for a period of four years. But Ferrari's connections with Alfa over all those years had made him some trusted, crucially important friends and associates. Those people would become absolutely vital to Enzo Ferrari over the next few years as his ambitious mind formulated plans for designing and building cars of his own.

By the end of 1939, less than a year after the Alfa Romeo split, Enzo Ferrari was preparing the first design for his own cars. Late in 1939 he was approached by two competitors who wanted him to build them cars for the 1940 (and as it turned out, the last Pre-War) Mille Miglia road race. Working from the old Scuderia Ferrari premises on Modena's Viale Trento Trieste, a new company, *Auto Avio Construzioni*, was formed and these two cars were completed from a design pencilled by Alberto Massimino, whose association with Ferrari would last another 35 years up until his death in 1975. Massimino was born in Turin in 1895 and, having obtained an engineering diploma abroad, he joined Fiat's special engineering department in 1924. In 1928 he quit Fiat to take a post on the aero

engine staff of the *Stablimenti Farina*, later rejoining Fiat's own aero engine department where he was in charge from 1931 to '37. He joined Ferrari in 1938 and was destined to stay with him until 1943, after which he directed the technical staff of Alfieri Maserati, later resuming his association with Ferrari as an engineering consultant from 1952 onwards.

The Massimino-designed eight-cylinder "Tipo 815s", as these first Ferraris were simply named, were built for a young aspiring ace called Alberto Ascari (son of the great Antonio Ascari) and the Marchese Lotario Rangoni Machiavelli di Modena, a well-heeled local aristocrat who was sadly destined to die in a wartime bomber crash. Having established himself as a car manufacturer, Ferrari's preoccupation then became to survive the War in which Fascist Italy found itself engulfed later in 1940. Sustaining his tiny business by doing specialist machine tool work during those dark days, including impressively high quality sub-contract work to demanding specifications, Enzo Ferrari eventually in 1943 moved his base out of Modena and built a new facility on a piece of land he already owned near a tiny village called Maranello. He had already determined to get himself swiftly involved once again in motorsport, an ambitious decision bearing in mind the shortages and material supply problems in those austere post-War days.

The initial funding of the Ferrari company is a matter shrouded in the mists of history, but it is fairly clear that Enzo was a shrewd businessman who didn't allow his enthusiasm for motor cars and racing to compromise his hard financial sense. It's clear that his wartime machine tool business was reasonably profitable and it has been speculated that his wife Laura had family money from an early stage which helped significantly: there were also the industrial sources and contributions from ambitious, wealthy privateer racing drivers who were associated with the Scuderia Ferrari from its early days. One thing quickly became clear; Enzo Ferrari liked to do a job properly and spared no expense to achieve that goal.

Massimino was but one of the 'old guard' from the Alfa Romeo days that Ferrari relied upon during the formative years of his new company. But one should also quickly mention the name of Luigi Bazzi in connection with Ferrari's pioneering days. The man who conceived the fearsome twin-engined Alfa Romeo

Raymond Sommer's Ferrari 125 splashes through the rain on its way to third place in the 1948 Italian Grand Prix held on Turin's Valentino Park circuit. He is about to be lapped by the winning Alfa Romeo 158 of Jean-Pierre Wimille.

"Bimotore" in the 1930s, Bazzi joined Alfa Romeo as early as 1922 after a spell with Fiat's experimental department and became Enzo's right-hand man in 1933. He joined the new Ferrari company after the War and was available as a valued technical guiding hand well into the 1960s, assisting and advising some of the more prominent engineers who later joined the company. He gained a reputation for smoothing any technical wrinkles with unobtrusive efficiency. Bazzi and Ferrari became close friends early in their relationship and when Enzo recruited former Fiat designer Vittorio Jano in the early 1920s, it was largely on the strength of his trusted colleague's advice. Jano, of course, was to become responsible for the design of the historic P2 and monoposto Alfa Romeos in the early 1930s and would later become associated as a consultant to Ferrari in the wake of the Scuderia's take-over of the Jano-designed Lancia D50s mid-way through 1955. Other early associates included Eduardo Weber, whose company's carburetters would be seen equipping many Ferrari cars in the years that followed.

The first Ferrari cars to appear post-War stepped out on to a fragile international motor racing stage which seemed to have no clear-cut future. Clearing up the debris of a World war left motorsport fairly low on the list of people's priorities, but as Europe dusted itself down and surveyed the destruction of the past six years' madness, so the first flickers of racing enthusiasm began to be nurtured in the dying embers of the conflict. Prior to the War a change in the Formula A (what amounted to Formula One) regulations had been planned for 1941, altering the rules to 4.5-litres unsupercharged or 1½-litres supercharged, so the newly titled *Federation Internationale de l'Automobile*, as the sport's governing body, quickly adopted these regulations for anybody who felt ready to participate. Alfa Romeo's fantastic 158s had allegedly spent much of the war walled-up in an Italian cheese factory and were ready to pick up where they fleetingly started in 1938, and while Mercedes-Benz and Auto Union could hardly be expected on the scene at this stage, there were some old French Talbots, the odd Delahaye, some pre-War British ERAs and Italian Maseratis from which one could reasonably cobble together some sort of starting grid.

In the wake of the first Ferrari sports cars, the marque's first Grand Prix cars finally made their first public appearance in 1948. However, it should be mentioned as a footnote that the 60-degree type 125, 1498cc non-supercharged Ferrari 125 sports car made its first race appearance in practice for the Piacenza event on May 11, 1947. Two examples were on hand, one driven by Franco Cortese, the other by Dr. Nino Farina. Unfortunately Farina managed to crash his during practice and Cortese retired with a seized fuel pump.

By the start of 1948, the 125 engines were bored and stroked out to just under 2-litres (or 166cc per cylinder) and the famous type 166 Ferrari was born. The development of this machine is not strictly relevant to this volume, but it should be recorded that the very first Ferrari entry in a *Grand Epreuve*, an established, classic Grand Prix event, was a 166 (with its cycle-style wings removed) in the Monaco Grand Prix on May 16, 1948. Prince Igor Troubetzkoy, perhaps better known for his marriage to Woolworth heiress Barbara Hutton, ran a private 166 in this event, proceeding steadily until he crashed at the chicane on lap 58. Although this was no Grand Prix car, it could honestly be said that the Ferrari marque's Grand Prix career began at this race . . .

Throughout the summer of 1948, competitors such as Leslie Brooke, Count Soave Besana, Monaco "hero" Troubetzkoy, Raymond Sommer and Nando Righetti, campaigned 166 Ferraris in various secondary "Formula One" events, but Maranello's red letter day arrived with the Italian Grand Prix, held in Turin's Valentino Park, on September 5, 1948. It was the occasion of the race début of the supercharged, Ferrari 125 designed for former Alfa man Gioacchino Colombo.

Colombo's 60-degree V12 had oversquare dimensions of 55 x 52.5mm, bore and stroke, for a total capacity of 1496.77 cc. It had an aluminium alloy crankcase and cylinder block and single chain-driven overhead camshafts on each of its detachable cylinder heads. The crankshaft ran on seven main bearings and the engine employed a single Weber 50WCF carburettor and a single-stage

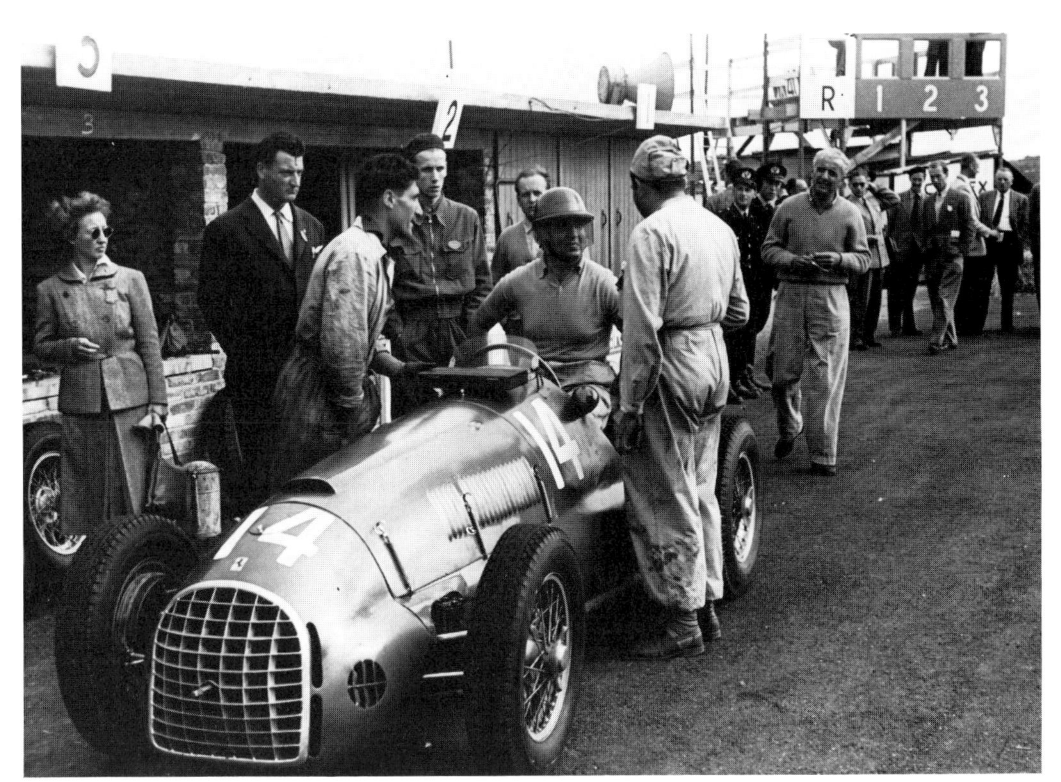

Pit scene during practice for the 1949 Zandvoort Grand Prix with Alberto Ascari listening to some words of advice from French verteran Phillippe Etancelin. In the background Luigi Villoresi can be seen strolling towards the car. Ascari's 125 retired from this race with stub axle failure, but Villoresi finished second behind Bira's Maserati.

Roots-type supercharger, running at 1.22 times the crankshaft speed, helped boost the power output to a claimed 225bhp at 7000rpm.

A great deal of thought and consideration went into the design of Ferrari's first Grand Prix car, Enzo admitting that he had for a long time had an almost romantic attraction towards V12 engines stemming from seeing pictures of early Packards at Indianapolis. However, there were some far more practical engineering reasons behind the decision to opt for a 12-cylinder configuration. Colombo's choice of ultra-short stroke dimensions offered potential for much higher rev. limits than the arch-rival Alfa Romeo eight-cylinder unit, and had the advantages of reduced bearing loads, a stiffer crankcase and a lighter, lower cylinder block. The V12 also scored in the two crucial areas of stress criteria: mean piston speed and piston acceleration, both of which would be significantly lower than the Alfa 158. The cars from Milan were developing their peak power at around 8000rpm in 1948 with a mean piston speed of 3675 ft/min. while the single stage Ferrari 125 produced its peak power at 7500rpm with a mean piston speed of 2584 ft/min. Clearly, the Alfa Romeo was approaching the limit of its development potential, but the Ferrari had more to come.

An uncomplicated tubular chassis frame formed the basis of the car, the main longerons being of oval section, and there was a box-section front cross member and a welded tubular upper structure on which the aluminium body panels were carried. The five-speed gearbox was in unit with the clutch housing, the power being transmitted via an open driveshaft to the differential. Transverse leaves eventually provided the springing medium all round by the start of the 1949 season, but early 125s had this system only at the front, torsion bars being employed in conjunction with a swing-axle arrangement at the rear. Unequal length wishbones were used at the front and Houdaille, vane-type shock absorbers were employed all-round. These first Ferrari 125s had a rather unprepossessing, dumpy appearance and with their relatively short wheelbase of 2160mm (85.1in) they quickly earned a reputation as being rather skittish and difficult to handle.

Alberto Ascari's revised 125 in the paddock at Monza prior to its debut victory in the 1949 Grand Prix of Europe. Not only did the car feature Lampredi's two-stage supercharged version of Colombo's 1497cc V12 engine (an "unclad" example of which is seen below) but had slightly longer wheelbase and wider track as well as a modified front radiator grille. The very English looking gentleman in the blazer standing behind the 125's left rear wheel is BRDC official Desmond Scannell.

After tests earlier in the summer with Nino Farina at the wheel, three such cars were fielded for the Valentino Park race driven by Raymond Sommer, Prince Bira and Farina himself. The event was held in difficult conditions of pouring rain, and although Jean-Pierre Wimille's Alfa Romeo 158 emerged victorious, the Ferraris didn't disgrace themselves by any means. Sommer only lost out in a battle for second place to Luigi Villoresi's Maserati by a matter of feet, although Bira retired with transmission trouble and Farina slid into a straw bale, damaging the front end of his 125.

Farina made up for this disappointment by scoring a win for the 125 Grand Prix car in the Garda race on September 24, but the *Grand Premio Autodromo* at Monza was a failure for the new Ferraris. Although both Sommer and Farina started from the second row of the starting grid, Farina retired from fourth place with transmission failure, while his unfortunate French team-mate had a sudden asthma attack which obliged him to pull in and retire whilst holding a respectable third place. Completing that first season, the trio of 125s contested the *Grand*

Premio de Penya Rhin at Barcelona's Pedralbes circuit, Bira retiring with transmission failure whilst in the lead, Farina going out with a similar failure whilst fourth, and local tyro José Pola breaking the engine of his loaned machine.

For the 1949 season Ferrari concentrated a great deal of time and effort towards improving not only the 125's reliability, but also its precarious handling qualities which certainly held the attention of all its early drivers. He also took the opportunity of selling two cars to non-factory sources: one went to English privateer Peter Whitehead, the other to crusty British engine bearing magnate Tony Vandervell. This latter car was to become the very first "Thinwall Special", a competition test bed for Vandervell's thinwall bearings as well as a car which laid the ground for the development of the splendid Vanwalls which, ten years later, would drive Enzo Ferrari's cars into the ground. From little acorns . . .

In 1949 Alfa Romeo withdrew from the Grand Prix arena, worried about potential opposition from Ferrari and the long-awaited BRM V16. As things turned out, the troubled BRM project wasn't destined to get off the ground until 1950, so Ferrari was to have the stage pretty well to himself, particularly as he had been able to defuse the Maserati opposition by signing up two of their leading exponents, Alberto Ascari and Luigi Villoresi, for 1949. The deaths of Jean-Pierre Wimille, Achille Varzi and Count Trossi had also been persuasive factors behind the Alfa Romeo withdrawal, although 1949 was to be but a brief interlude of domination for Ferrari as his former masters would return to the scene in 1950.

Milan's favourite son, Alberto Ascari was born into a racing family: his father Antonio had been a member of the Alfa Romeo Grand Prix team and was killed in the 1925 French Grand Prix when his son was only eight. Alberto's career began on motorcycles and he competed in the 1940 Mille Miglia in the aforementioned '815' before the War interrupted his racing aspirations. By the end of the War Ascari had a wife and children and briefly considered giving up racing for good. Villoresi persuaded him otherwise. They resumed together on Maseratis in 1948 and now they were Maranello men together . . .

Opening Ferrari's 1949 record, Peter Whitehead took his 125 to sixth in the Sanremo Grand Prix, two places behind Felice Bonetto's 166 "sports car", while Sommer's works 125 retired. Whitehead's entry for the rain-soaked Jersey road race was made under the Scuderia Ferrari banner as far as the paper work was concerned and he finished seventh in this contest, daunted by the still-precarious handling of the 125 on the treacherous surface. Sharing the car with Dudley Folland, Whitehead finished eighth in the British Grand Prix at Silverstone on May 14, but the début of Vandervell's first "Thinwall Special" ended in near-disaster when Ken Richardson took over the wheel from Raymond Mays, only to spin into the spectator enclosure at Abbey Curve and lightly injure several spectators. The race was won by Baron Emmanuel de Graffenried at the wheel of a Maserati entered by Enrico Plate, after which the Vandervell-owned Ferrari 125 was returned to Italy with the firm assurance from Vandervell himself that he wasn't at all satisfied with his purchase!

By the time the factory Ferraris appeared at Spa-Francorchamps for the Belgian Grand Prix on June 19, they had been revised with the aforementioned transverse leaf spring replacing the torsion bars at the rear, and it seemed as though Luigi Villoresi was going to score a well-earned victory for Maranello after the Maseratis of Fangio and Farina went out in the early stages of the race. Unfortunately the high fuel consumption of the supercharged 125s was to prove their undoing and Villoresi was unable to make up sufficient time to win after a fuel stop, finishing fifty seconds behind the plodding, lorry-like 4.5-litre French Talbot driven by uninspired gentleman Louis Rosier, which had gone through non-stop. Ascari was third, Whitehead fourth. Back at Maranello, Enzo Ferrari started thinking seriously . . .

Morale was boosted when Ascari and Villoresi finished first and second in the Swiss Grand Prix at Bremgarten on July 3, Farina's pole position Maserati being the only machine to get on terms with the cars from Maranello. On July 17, Ferrari was given more food for thought when another lumbering old 4.5 Talbot, this time handled by Louis Chiron, grasped a late-race triumph in the *Grand Prix de France* at Reims-Gueux, although on this occasion it must be admitted that the Ferrari works team was represented only by a single 125 for Villoresi which succumbed to a seized front brake whilst battling for the lead with Fangio's Maserati. None the less, Whitehead might well have saved Ferrari's day had his gearbox not jammed in fourth, causing him to drop from first to third place on the very last lap.

The season progressed with Villoresi winning at Zandvoort and then both he and Ascari getting embroiled in a fierce battle with Farina's Maserati at both the *Daily Express* Silverstone Trophy meeting, where Ascari won, and the Lausanne Grand Prix, where Farina dealt out a convincing defeat to Alberto by a margin of more than a minute. It was clear that Maranello needed more power to defeat the Maserati 4CLT/48s and Ferrari's new designer Aurelio Lampredi responded with a two-stage supercharged version of the Ferrari 125 which made its début in the 1949 Italian Grand Prix at Monza.

The revised engines not only incorporated two Roots-type blowers, mounted one above the other on the front of the engine, but there were now twin overhead camshafts on each bank of six cylinders, a Weber 50WCF carburettor, the compression ratio had been increased from 6.5 to 7.0:1 and the claimed power output was now 290bhp at 7500rpm. Further, to make the car more pleasant and progressive to drive, the wheelbase had been lengthened to 2380mm (93.7in) and the rear track increased by two inches. Ascari led this 313-mile race from start to finish at the wheel of one of these new two-stage 125s, Villoresi's second such car retiring from second place after 27 laps with gearbox trouble. The single-stage 125s of Sommer, Bonetto and privateer Whitehead were no match for the new 306bhp, so-called Maserati-Milanos driven by Farina and Piero Taruffi: it was therefore a shame that the temperamental Farina, despite leading all the single-stage Ferraris, retired from the race in a temper because he wasn't able to keep up with Ascari or Villoresi!

The 1949 season was rounded off by Peter Whitehead taking a good victory in the 220-mile Czechoslovakian Grand Prix at Masaryk, inheriting a relatively easy triumph after the Maseratis of Farina, Parnell and Bira all crashed. Phillippe Etancelin's old Talbot came through to take second place ahead of Franco Cortese's Formula 2 V12 Ferrari.

News that Alfa Romeo would be bursting back on to the international scene in 1950 with the tremendously strong driving team of Farina, Juan-Manual Fangio and Luigi Fagioli prompted Ferrari to reappraise his whole approach to the business of Formula One. There would be added interest attaching to Grand Prix racing with the instigation of a formal World Championship contest from the start of the 1950 season and the 4.5-litres normally aspirated/1½-litre supercharged category was intended to continue until the end of 1953. Eventually, although encouraged by the initial performance from his two-stage supercharged 125 V12, Ferrari was on the verge of opting for a major change in technical direction. He was going to abandon the supercharged route and opt for a 4.5-litre normally aspirated V12 . . .

Section I: The V12 trail-blazers, 1948-51

Chapter 2 Lampredi's big V12 defeats the Alfas – the build-up to an emotional moment for Maranello

By the time Maranello's two-stage supercharged 125 V12 was nudging the 300bhp barrier at the end of 1949, rumours were rife that Alfa Romeo was coaxing around 335bhp from the supercharged straight-eight in preparation for their return to the fray, although the amount of alcohol-laced fuel they were using was destined to be tremendous, the Alfa consumption eventually dropping to below 2 mpg, which meant that they had to run the races with enormously heavy fuel loads and were obliged to stop frequently. As far as Ferrari was concerned, it was becoming increasingly clear that the supercharged road was a path to nowhere in the long-term, and his view that Maranello should concentrate on a normally aspirated 4½-litre V12 was one to which Aurelio Lampredi, one of his newly-recruited engineers, also subscribed.

Arguably second only to Mauro Forghieri in his contribution to the Ferrari marque's technical fortunes, Aurelio Lampredi was born on June 16, 1917 at Livorno, the son of a machine shop superintendent. After starting out his career as a draughtsman in the Livorno Naval yards, he progressed to the engineering department of the Piaggio aircraft company and from there to Le Reggiane aircraft concern at Reggio Emilia. At this last-mentioned location he was involved on a variety of ambitious projects such as an 18-cylinder, inverted W-configuration engine which had such subtleties as three-stage supercharging and direct fuel injection. On the recommendation of his seniors, who pointed him out to Ferrari, Lampredi moved to Maranello in September 1946 when he was 29 years old. He was given the title of junior designer, but wasn't happy working under Colombo, so left in early 1947 to join the Isotta Fraschini company. By the end of 1947 Ferrari successfully wooed Lampredi back to Maranello and he became increasingly responsible for the development of the early V12 designs, honing Colombo's concepts to a fresh competitive edge. Colombo gradually visited Maranello less and less frequently until he severed his links with Ferrari in 1949, leaving Lampredi in full command of the engine development department.

Although Lampredi directed the two-stage supercharged 125 development, he and Ferrari quickly agreed that the normally aspirated route offered far more potential. One needed some 220-235bhp per litre from a supercharged unit to be in the Grand Prix ball park and Lampredi reckoned that it would be a much easier task to develop 80bhp per litre from a 4½-litre V12 to be competitive. And there wouldn't be so many pit stops for fuel either . . . remember the old Talbots!

By the start of the 1950 season, however, Ferrari was still relying on his type 125s. Now developing around 315bhp at 7500rpm, their handling had been improved by the development of a de Dion rear end with a four-speed gearbox in unit with the final drive, although this version didn't appear until the Swiss Grand

SERVICIO
16
A Pirelli con simpatia y admiracion
Juan M Fangio

Making his reputation: Juan-Manuel Fangio used this 2-litre 166-engined 125 to finish second to Alberto Ascari's in the Peron Trophy at Buenos Aires's Palermo Park circuit in December, 1949. Entered by the Automobil Club Argentina, this car was painted light blue with a bright yellow bonnet, the country's national racing colours.

Prix at Bremgarten in June, 1950. By this time Lampredi's first normally aspirated V12 was on the road and the subject of considerable development attention. The works supercharged cars were destined to win no more Formula One races during 1950, although Villoresi scored second places at Zandvoort, Pau and Sanremo, and Ascari was second at Monaco. Whitehead managed an encouraging victory in the Ulster Trophy at Dundrod, however. Following his unsettling experiences with the first Ferrari 125 "Thinwall Special", Tony Vandervell acquired the long-chassis machine which had been used by Villoresi at Zandvoort and entered it for Alberto Ascari to drive in the *Daily Express* Trophy race at Silverstone on August 26: while Whitehead's similar car finished third in this event, Ascari spun off the road and the second "Thinwall Special" ended its début race as quickly and ignominiously as the first.

The début of Lampredi's normally aspirated Grand Prix engine was in the Belgian Grand Prix at Spa-Francorchamps on June 18, 1950. The 60-degree V12 unit, initially dubbed 275 because it first appeared in 3.3-litre form, had a bore and stroke of 72 x 68mm for a total capacity of 3322.34cc. This engine had grown, via a 2560cc interim version, from the 166 Formula 2 engine which had been raced throughout 1949 with considerable success. Like the supercharged V12 the engine had a seven main bearing crankshaft, but unlike Colombo's original unit, Lampredi's engine had the aluminium cylinder heads/block cast as one with a separate alloy crankcase. Single chain driven overhead camshafts on each head drove two valves per cylinder and twin magnetos were driven from the rear of those camshafts. Running with three Weber 42DCF carburettors, a single sparking plug per cylinder and a 10.0: 1 compression ratio, the power output was claimed as an impressive 280bhp at 7000rpm.

The Lampredi V12 ran reliably on its first race outing installed in a long-chassis car with swing axle rear suspension, but Ascari didn't find it particularly quick when compared against the Alfa Romeos and he could only finish the Belgian race a distant fifth. The car was withdrawn from the French Grand Prix at Reims-Gueux because it was absurdly off the pace during practice, but when the team appeared at the *Grand Prix des Nations* at Geneva on July 30, a further enlarged 80 x 68mm, 4101.6cc engine appeared, now developing 320bhp at 7000rpm. It was installed in a new chassis built round rectangular-section main members connected by tubular cross members with a welded upper structure for the aluminium body panels to be mounted on. Whilst a transverse leaf spring

A week before his unfortunate Geneva accident, Villoresi is seen here at Zandvoort on his way to second place in the Dutch Grand Prix in this single stage supercharged 125.

Luigi Villoresi's 125 V12 came to this sorry end during the 1950 Grand Prix des Nations at Geneva. The car skidded into the crowd, killing four and injuring 27. Villoresi was lucky to escape with a broken leg . . .

worked at the front in conjunction with unequal-length wishbones, there was a de Dion rear end similar to that employed on Villoresi's supercharged 125 earlier in the season at Bremgarten. The de Dion tube ran in a slot on the final drive casing and there was a four-speed gearbox in unit with the final drive, a transverse rear leaf spring and twin parallel links to control the rear wheels' fore/aft movement.

This was now getting pretty serious, for the big V12 Ferraris were in a position to ruffle the Alfa Romeo feathers in a big way. Ascari went straight into the lead with the type 340 Ferrari, to be gradually overhauled and dealt with by Fangio's Alfa Romeo. Unfortunately, near the end of the race Villoresi crashed his older swing axle car quite badly and Ascari's 4.1-litre V12 blew a head gasket, so although Alfa Romeo emerged from this contest in 1-2-3 formation there was some worrying writing on the wall for Enzo Ferrari's former employers to read.

Finally, on September 3, Lampredi's V12 came to a full flower from the point of view of its technical specification when two new cars were fielded for the Italian Grand Prix at Monza to the full 80 x 74.5mm, 4493.73cc planned capacity. Developing 330bhp at 7000rpm, they were fitted with larger triple choke Weber 42DCF carburettors but retained the same chassis specification as the car raced by Ascari at Geneva. Villoresi hadn't recovered from his unfortunate accident, so Ferrari test driver Dorino Serafini was recruited into the Grand Prix team for this important race. The Ferrari factory twosome was backed up by the stalwart privateer Whitehead, but ranged against Maranello's ranks was a quartet of Alfas, including two more powerful de Dion type 159s handled by Farina and Fangio, plus a trio of regular 158s for Fagioli, Taruffi and Consalvo Sanesi.

Fangio just squeezed his Alfa on to pole position with a 1m 58.6s lap, but Ascari managed 1m 58.8s and there was nobody else below the two minute barrier. At the start of the contest it was Farina who established himself in the lead, but the Alfa Romeo was unable to pull away from the 4.5-litre Ferrari so, bearing in mind that the supercharged cars from Portello were scheduled to stop twice, and the Ferrari only once, the race should have theoretically been in the bag for Maranello. But it wasn't to be. Although Ascari got through to lead for two glorious laps, his engine failed after 22 laps and the Ferrari challenge seemed broken. Nothing daunted, Ascari later took over Serafini's V12 and, despite gear changing problems, climbed up from sixth place to second at the chequered flag, just over a minute behind Farina's victorious Alfa Romeo. Maranello had now underlined that it

Proving the point. Alberto Ascari scored a convincing victory in the 1950 Penya Rhin Grand Prix at Barcelona's Pedralbes circuit.

Another new Argentinian! At the wheel of this supercharged 166 Formule Libre car, José-Froilan Gonzalez built himself quite a reputation by beating the Mercedes-Benz team in both the Peron Cup and Eva Peron Cup races held at Buenos Aires's Costanera circuit early in 1951.

could compete quite openly with Alfa Romeo and have no fear of being humiliated. It was now only a matter of time.

Farina's Monza success had clinched the World Championship title for the hard-driving Doctor, so Alfa Romeo chose not to contest the *Grand Premio de Penya Rhin* at Barcelona on October 28. Ferrari fielded a pair of 4.5-litre cars for Ascari and Serafini with a 4.1-litre for Taruffi in a race made interesting only by the European débût of the BRM V16. Under a blisteringly hot sun, the trio of Ferrari V12s went straight into the lead and ran non-stop to finish 1-2-3 after 194 scorching miles. The BRM challenge was over in the now-customary embarrassing confusion almost before it had started, so apart from a brief spin by Taruffi, there was nothing to take the edge off Ferrari's complete and utter control of the race. In a distant fourth place was Etancelin's plodding Talbot . . . the car which helped germinate the notion of a big, non-supercharged V12 in Enzo Ferrari's mind to start with!

By the start of the 1951 season, Tony Vandervell had taken delivery of a single-plug-per-cylinder 4½-litre V12 engine which was installed in the old Thinwall LWB 125 chassis, about now extensively revised with a de Dion rear end. It was to be somehow appropriate that Vandervell should go on to enjoy some encouraging, and technically worthwhile, results with this 4½-litre V12 since it was the 375 engine which firmly established Ferrari's use of Vandervell thinwall shell bearings rather than the thicker babitted bearings as used on the 125 and 166.

As far as the Ferrari factory opposition was concerned, for what was destined to be Alfa Romeo's swansong, the engineers at Portello had boosted the eight-cylinder supercharged engine's output to a staggering 410/420bhp, but Ferrari knew his car was going to be starting races in rather lighter trim and would still undergo fewer pit stops, so the Lampredi V12 could afford to lag slightly behind this figure. The main improvement to the single-cam, two valves-per cylinder 375 V12 for 1951 was the addition of twin plug ignition which Lampredi and Bazzi hopefully developed together. Initial test bed figures indicated that this had boosted the output to 380bhp at 7500rpm, a single magneto now being mounted on the front of the engine and the compression ratio upped to 12.0:1. There were also improved brakes with stiffer drums and backplates for 1951, so the big, brutal-looking type 375 with its distinctive "cheese-cutter" radiator grill stood poised to establish a brilliant reputation at the start of the 1951 season.

Luigi Villoresi opened the 1951 European international season with a win in the Syracuse Grand Prix at the wheel of this works 375.

With rain glistening on Bremgarten's treacherous wet pavé, Piero Taruffi thrusts his 4½-litre V12-engined Ferrari 375 into an early second place ahead of Nino Farina's Alfa Romeo on the opening lap of the 1951 Swiss Grand Prix. Taruffi drove superbly to finish second behind Juan-Manuel Fangio's Alfa – which has already disappeared, in the lead, out of this picture . . .

On the driver front, Ascari and Villoresi were retained, while Piero Taruffi was also on the books, but his duties as Gilera motorcycle Grand Prix team chief engineer made him a busy man and it was the pressure of this work that was eventually to introduce a famous and historic name to the ranks of works Ferrari Formula 1 drivers. In this connection, it should be remembered that, as the engineers and mechanics toiled at Maranello to prepare the new cars for the World Championship season, in far away Argentina events of considerable long-term significance were being enacted. Mercedes-Benz had resurrected a trio of 1939 two-stage supercharged W163 cars for the formule libre races at the start of the season, the 45 lap Peron Cup at Costanera, Buenos Aires, on February 18 and the similar distance Eva Peron Cup held a week later on the same circuit. The German marque was treating this project as a pilot programme, testing the temperature of the water in preparation for a future return to the sport. But in both races the menacing silver cars from Stuttgart were comprehensively blown off by a 2-litre supercharged Ferrari 166 driven by a tubby, sweating, dramatic and tremendously spectacular Argentinian who, as Enzo Ferrari was later to observe, got himself into such a lather at the wheel of a racing car that one was tempted to wonder why he ever raced at all! His name was José Froilan Gonzalez, the "Pampas Bull".

Prior to the World Championship opener in Switzerland, there was the customary round of non-title contests in Europe which the Ferrari factory team attended. On March 11 Villoresi won at Syracuse after Ascari's dominant 375 retired near the end and the team then missed Pau before appearing at Sanremo on April 22 where Ascari handled the 24-plug 375 on its race début. In the absence of the Alfas, Alberto scored an easy victory, the Scuderia's luck spoilt when Villoresi dropped out in the closing stages after sliding into a straw bale and damaging his car's radiator.

Ferrari missed the International Trophy meeting at Silverstone, but Alfa Romeo did attend the English race and, in monsoon conditions the contest was prematurely halted after a mere six laps – by which time Reg Parnell in the "Thinwall Special" was galloping away from the Portello cars and was thus awarded a nominal, if hardly significant, victory.

It has also to be said that the opening round of the World Championship, the Swiss Grand Prix at Berne's Bremgarten circuit, wasn't totally conclusive. Ascari had been painfully burnt on the arm in the Genoa Formula 2 race and was well off-form when it came to handling the Grand Prix machine. Although it was possible, if equipped with their maximum auxiliary tanks, for the Alfa Romeos to go through non-stop, it was Fangio's supercharged car which led throughout in this rain-soaked event – apart from the fact that he made a routine pit stop. With Ascari off the pace, feeling badly out of sorts, and Villoresi sliding off the road in the blinding spray, it was left to Taruffi to maintain the honour of the Prancing Horse, a feat he performed quite admirably with a splendid charge through to second place ahead of Farina's ill-handling Alfa.

From Berne it was on to Spa-Francorchamps for the Belgian Grand Prix where Ascari, Villoresi and Taruffi all had 24-plug V12s at their disposal. With the race being run over a distance of 315 miles, both Ferrari and Alfa Romeo would have to make a single pit stop apiece, so the non-supercharged philosophy was effectively negated at this event. The brilliant Fangio took his Alfa 159 round in 4m 25s to take pole position, slicing 9.1s off Farina's pole time from the previous year, and although Villoresi briefly sprinted ahead at the start, Farina and Ascari soon displaced him at the front of the pack. As the race settled down, Farina and Fangio outdistanced the 4½-litre Ferraris, and although the Argentinian lost all chance of victory when a wheel jammed on its hub during a pit stop, Farina drove in a manner befitting a reigning World Champion and won by almost three minutes from Ascari with Villoresi third.

Notwithstanding these temporary setbacks for Maranello, it was clear that Ferrari was hovering on the brink of that psychologically-crucial first victory over its arch-rivals. The battle hotted up, in every sense of the word, at the French Grand Prix at sun-soaked Reims-Gueux on July 1, a race extended to 77 laps (603.7km/374.91 miles) just to make sure that Ferrari would have to stop for fuel as well, and although Alfa Romeo emerged from this event with its honour intact, there were to be no more imperious demonstration runs for the Portello cars. This was hand-to-hand fighting, the outcome also affected by mechanical failure and driver fatigue in the sweltering conditions. Taruffi was faced with something of a clash of loyalties prior to this race as he was also supposed to be in Belgium for the motorcycle Grand Prix with Gilera, but the problem was resolved when he was taken ill and, although fit enough to journey to Belgium, was clearly not sufficiently well to take his place in a Formula 1 cockpit. Thus, Gonzalez was recruited to join Ascari and Villoresi in the factory 375s.

From the word go, Ascari pitched in hard against Fangio's Alfa 159, only for gearbox failure to sideline the best-placed Ferrari after a mere nine laps. But magneto trouble had already delayed Sanesi's Alfa and now afflicted Fangio's car as well, so Farina and Villoresi hurtled ahead into the leading two places. When veteran Luigi Fagioli brought his Alfa in to refuel on lap 24, Fangio resumed the race at the wheel of his car while, on lap 34, Ascari similarly commandeered Gonzalez's Ferrari 375 and the battle really began for second place. When Fangio made another pit stop and Farina's leading 159 threw a tyre tread, Ascari surged into the lead, only to be displaced by the hard-driving Fangio when he stopped the 375 for fuel and brake adjustments in the second half of the race. That allowed Fangio to sail home victorious ahead of Ascari, Villoresi and Reg Parnell in the 4½-litre "Thinwall Special".

Luigi Villoresi's 375 is pushed out to the startline at Reims-Gueux for the 1951 Grand Prix of Europe in which he finished third.

Then, at the bleak airfield wastes of Silverstone, history was finally enacted on July 14. Gonzalez was still in the team for the British Grand Prix and, despite the fact he was only allocated a 12-plug 1950 375, he stunned all onlookers by sweeping round the converted airfield track in 1m 43.4s, for a 100mph lap of the circuit which was good enough to take pole position by a full second over Fangio's Alfa. The big heavy 159s hadn't got sufficient straights at Silverstone on which to get fully wound up and Gonzalez consolidated his place at the front of the field in the early stages, gradually to be hauled in by the determined Fangio. But the Ferrari and Alfa were amazingly closely-matched on this summer afternoon, and although Fangio got ahead, Gonzalez, "a fat dark little man, bare arms at full length," clawed his way back on to the Alfa Romeo's tail and retook the lead on lap 38. He then pulled confidently away from his compatriot, arms flailing and his bulk brimming over the cockpit sides . . .

On lap 60 Gonzalez pulled in for his routine stop and clearly expected to hand over to Ascari whose car had retired with gearbox trouble four laps earlier. He made to climb out of the cockpit, but Alberto merely grinned, put a reassuring hand on his shoulder and indicated that he should stay aboard the Ferrari. His lead intact, Froilan Gonzalez accelerated back into the fray and, at the chequered flag, had a 50s advantage over Fangio's second-placed Alfa Romeo. It was the culmination of a 13 year contest with Alfa Romeo, Enzo Ferrari's efforts and persistence paying off against his former employers. It was an unashamedly emotional moment for the Commendatore who sent an historic telegram to Alfa Romeo's Managing Director expressing "that I still feel for our Alfa the adolescent tenderness of first love . . ." But, make no mistake, the mould of Formula One racing had been broken for good that July afternoon, the Alfas being beaten for the first time since the inaugural post-war French Grand Prix at St. Cloud in 1946.

Aspirations for the successful quickly change. Having got his first Grand Prix triumph over Alfa Romeo out of the way, it quickly became apparent to Ferrari that there was a chance of actually snatching the 1951 World Championship. At the first post-War Championship German Grand Prix at the Nürburgring on July 29, a quartet of 24-plug 375s was fielded for Ascari, Villoresi, Gonzalez and Taruffi. Practice was dominated by the V12 Ferraris and, thanks to the fact that Fangio's Alfa Romeo had to make one more pit stop than the Maranello cars, Ascari came out of the race a clear, comfortable winner with Fangio's interloping

Alberto Ascari's Ferrari 375 chasing Fangio's Alfa Romeo for all it's worth during the 1951 Grand Prix of Europe at Reims-Gueux. This car's gearbox eventually wilted under the strain, but Ascari took over Gonzalez's similar 375 to finish second in the end.

Momentous achievement! José-Froilan Gonzalez's older 12-plug Ferrari 375 finally defeated the Alfas fair and square in the 1951 British Grand Prix at Silverstone. At his last pit stop, Ascari declined to take over the car, feeling that Gonzalez deserved some thanks for handing over his 375 at Reims a fortnight earlier.

Alfa in second place ahead of a sea of Ferraris in the order Gonzalez, Villoresi and Taruffi. Alfa was now the one who could be regarded as the outsider . . .

Prior to the crucially important Italian Grand Prix at Monza, Ferrari entered cars at both the non-title Pescara and Bari races. Gonzalez won the former race in the absence of Alfa Romeo opposition, but Portello fielded entries at Bari and Fangio emerged the winner, albeit only after Ascari's 375 caught fire after a carburettor problem and Villoresi's machine seized its engine. Gonzalez finished second at Bari ahead of Piero Taruffi at the wheel of a brand new, 2490cc four-cylinder Ferrari prototype . . . but that, as Part 2 of this book will explain in some detail, is very much another story.

To counter the growing attacks from Ferrari, Alfa Romeo fielded an improved, more powerful 159M for the Italian Grand Prix at Monza and Maranello responded by fielding no fewer than five 375s; 24-plug versions for Ascari, Villoresi, Gonzalez and Taruffi and a 12-plug machine for Francisco "Chico" Landi, the Brazilian privateer who was keen to buy one for the 1952 season. Landi had also been allowed a few laps in the four-cylinder prototype during practice, but Ferrari had decided he should use one of the V12s for the race itself.Brazil's President Vargas eventually presented Landi with a Government purchased 375 during the following winter's South American series.

Although Fangio bagged pole position, Ascari and Gonzalez joined him on the front row and from the start, Alberto was drawn into a murderous cut-and-thrust confrontation with the Alfas of Fangio and Farina. Alfa ranks were depleted early on with de Graffenried and Farina out before the 10 lap mark, and when Fangio's car threw a tyre tread on lap 13, Ascari settled down to consolidate an advantage he was never to lose. Farina later took over Bonetto's sole surviving 159 and screamed home to a vain third place behind Ascari and Gonzalez, but with Villoresi and Taruffi sandwiching him in fourth and fifth positions, this was truly Alfa Romeo's Waterloo.

With a single World Championship Grand Prix remaining at the end of 1951, the Spanish race at Barcelona on October 20, Ferrari could theoretically grasp the title from Alfa Romeo. What's more, having trounced the Alfas on three successive occasions, there was every reason to feel confident about Maranello's prospects. Perhaps rather foolishly in retrospect, Ferrari decided to experiment over Pirelli tyre sizes for this crucial race, opting for 16-in. diameter wheels all round rather than the 17-in diameter rims they had used for much of the season and which were also employed by the Alfa team. Despite the fact that Ascari comfortably qualified for pole position in 2m 10.59s ahead of Fangio (2m 12.27s) and Gonzalez (2m 14.01s), and led from the start, the 375s quickly began throwing tyre treads. By lap 14 all four cars had been in the pits for fresh rubber and the race was effectively lost. The Alfas could make their routine stops for fuel content in the knowledge that they had a sufficient cushion over the Ferraris to maintain their advantage to the finish. Although Gonzalez, driving in his customary feverish style, managed to pull up to second place at Farina's expense when the Alfa made its final fuel stop, Fangio was a dominant winner by the margin of almost a minute, thereby clinching his first World Championship title by 31pts to the 25pts of Ascari. It was a triumphant season's finale for Alfa, but the end of the road for the 159s . . .

In the absence of any financial support from the Government, Alfa Romeo announced that it would be withdrawing from racing at the end of 1951 and, bearing in mind the BRM team's somewhat irregular and haphazard approach, entering some races and not others, the prospects for the current Formula 1 regulations looked pretty sparse by the start of 1952.

It was difficult to see just how many events would be run for Formula 1 cars in 1952, but the final straw which resulted in the World Championship being staged to Formula 2 regulations came as the result of a rather convoluted sequence of events. At the start of the season Fangio had returned home to South America where he had participated at the wheel of a 2-litre supercharged Ferrari 166 in a series of seven events, six of which he had managed to win. They were the Sao Paulo Grand Prix at Interlagos, the Boavista Grand Prix at Rio, the two Buenos Aires Grands Prix and the two Piriapolis events in Uruguay.

Back in Europe, the start of the European Formula 1 season was awaited with a mixture of anticipation and trepidation, the Turin Grand Prix opening proceedings at Valentino Park on April 6. For much of the winter BRM had been down at Monza carrying out a series of development tests and the Turin organizers, to whom many other European races were looking for a lead, felt hopeful than the English V16s would attend. Suddenly, the BRM boys received a message from base to pack up and return home as Fangio and Gonzalez were coming to test the cars at the Folkingham airfield in Lincolnshire as a possible prelude to signing for the team. This they did, so the Turin organizers were left with only a handful of 4½-litre Ferraris on their hands out of the ranks of current Grand Prix cars. That little disappointment was all the CSI needed to rubber stamp a World Championship for Formula 2 cars. Fangio did *sign* for BRM, but only for the handful of non-title events. He signed for Maserati to contest the World Championship, but his season was abruptly terminated when, after driving down from Paris overnight following a hurried flight from Northern Ireland where he'd been driving the BRM at Dundrod, he crashed badly in the Autodrome Grand Prix at Monza, breaking vertebrae in his neck. He was out of action for the remainder of the season.

Into the swing of things! A month after Gonzalez's victory at Silverstone, the ebullient South American notched up another triumph for the Ferrari 375 in the Pescara Grand Prix. Here Villoresi leads Ascari and Gonzalez away from the line, but only Gonzalez survived to the finish.

As the World Championship contests for the next couple of seasons became dominated by four-cylinder Formula 2 Ferraris, the old 4½-litre cars eked out a twilight existence in the handful of Formula 1 races still left on the calendar, many of which were simply British national libre events which the organizers continued to stage as a patriotic sop to the tardy BRM project.

That Valentino Park race *did* eventually take place on April 6, 1952, Ascari and Nino Farina driving 390bhp 24-plug V12s installed in new chassis frames strengthened by a triangular array of small-diameter tubes mounted on the regular chassis members. These cars were intended for that year's Indianapolis 500 race where Ascari's "works" entry was destined to be only one of four 4½-litre V12s to qualify. He made a reasonable impression in the American classic before a hub seized, a wire wheel collapsed and he skated to a halt on the infield. His performance in the Turin "warm up" race was rather better: he was leading comfortably until he retired with a split fuel tank three laps from the finish. Farina went out with gearbox trouble leaving Villoresi to win with an earlier-engined "Indy special" 375, ahead of Taruffi's 2½-litre four-cylinder prototype. It should also be mentioned that Peter Whitehead contested this Turin race with his blown 125, Rudolf Fischer had his 2½-litre V12 and his Ecurie Espadon team-mate Peter

Hirt handled a 2-litre V12 Formula 2 machine. A mixed bag of challengers from Maranello, all of which had contributed, or were about to contribute, to the team's successful racing history.

The three other Indianapolis entries had a mixed time at the Brickyard. Although the Grant Piston Ring entry qualified, team driver Johnnie Parsons opted to drive an Offenhauser-engined machine in the race, Johnny Mauro failed to qualify his machine and Bill Vukovich, who tried Howard Keck's third car, also opted for an Offy-engined roadster for the 500.

After that, the Maranello factory team fielded the 375 on a mere two occasions, sending a single car to England for Villoresi to handle in the libre events at Silverstone and Boreham. At Silverstone, where the unreliable BRMs also appeared, Villoresi finished second to Vandervell's "Thinwall Special", and at Boreham the works car won with Chico Landi's private machine in second place.

In the non-title Albi Grand Prix on June 1, the private 375s of Louis Rosier and Landi cruised home in convincing 1-2 formation in the absence of any really serious opposition, so it was really left to the green-liveried "Thinwall" to produce a series of demonstration runs in English domestic events which were morale-boosting, of technical assistance to Tony Vandervell in his plans for the long-term Vanwall project, but of little significance in the overall pattern of international racing.

By the start of the 1953 season, Formula 1 racing in the old style had virtually disappeared from the international calendar, but there were still some fleeting outings from the 4½-litre V12s. Ascari handled one in the formule libre Buenos Aires Grand Prix on February 1, retiring with a major engine breakage early in the race, and he reappeared at the wheel of that machine at Albi on May 31 where Louis Rosier also fielded his private car.

This event was a curious F1/F2 *mélange* of a race with Farina in the "Thinwall"

Overleaf: Twilight days. Luigi Villoresi on his way to second place in a Formule Libre race at the Silverstone Grand Prix meeting in 1952, such races providing the only scope for such machines now that the World Championship catered for Formula 2. On the same visit to England, he also managed a win at Boreham in this machine.

joining in, the BRM V16s present for Fangio, Gonzalez and Ken Wharton plus a selection of Formula 2 machinery. Rosier won the first heat at the wheel of a four-cylinder F2 Ferrari and was third in the second heat. The second heat also saw an explosive confrontation between the tyre-smoking, ear-shattering V16 BRMs which made one realize just how sensational Grand Prix racing might have been in the early 1950s if the Bourne team had got its act together more promptly and efficiently. Fangio and Ascari briefly hurtled down the tree-lined straights, Ferrari and BRM side-by-side, steering up the camber towards each other in order to stay on course at speeds of up to 170mph! It was stirring stuff, but all too quickly over. The BRMs' prodigious appetite for rubber was their undoing and, in the final, with Fangio retiring and Wharton crashing, it was left for a delayed Gonzalez to hurtle home second behind Rosier's old 4½-litre Ferrari . . . Ascari's works machine retired after that early second-heat spurt with a leaking gearbox and couldn't contest the final.

Unquestionably, of course, the "Thinwall Special" was one of the most interesting Ferrari 4½-litre Formula 1 derivatives and Tony Vandervell's team continued racing this car right through until the end of 1954 on the British national scene, although by that time the car bore little resemblance to any other 375 to come out of the Maranello factory. However, early in the 4½-litre car's career its owner became concerned about its braking capability and encountered some resistance when he asked Ferrari to supply their latest brakes for use on the "Thinwall". It seems that Enzo Ferrari was a little concerned that Vandervell might be transmitting information he picked up from Maranello across to the BRM team, one of whose leading lights Vandervell had been in the early years. The English industrialist assured Ferrari that he was no longer in any way associated with BRM, having decided to go his own way with a separate Grand Prix project, but the suspicion was still there so Vandervell decided to press on with his own Girling three-shoe adaptation, although he was clear his own mind that disc brakes must be the path to follow for the future.

In retrospect, it was all too obvious that Vandervell was squeezing every bit of knowledge out of that Ferrari 4½-litre engine, considering experiments with revised carburation, different pistons and other ancillary equipment. For the 1952 season the "Thinwall" was rebuilt again, this time round one of the longer Indianapolis chassis frames, although it was still effectively an evolutionary product stemming from the original twin stage supercharged car. Taruffi used it to win the Ulster Trophy race at Dundrod and a Silverstone formule libre event supporting the British Grand Prix later in the summer, while Hawthorn drove it at Turnberry and Farina handled it at both Goodwood and Charterhall towards the end of the season.

Throughout 1953 Vandervell's team was hard at work finalizing the design of the 2-litre Vanwall special which would eventually lead to the World Championship winning car in 1958. None the less, there was still plenty of potential left in the old 4½-litre "Thinwall Special" which appeared for its first outing at Goodwood on April 6, the Easter Meeting, equipped with Goodyear-inspired disc brakes. Farina then handled it at Albi, as briefly mentioned, where it retired after an oil pipe broke, but the Italian doctor won the libre race at Silverstone with it on July 18 at the British Grand Prix meeting. He then retired at Charterhall on August 15 and the car's final outing was at Goodwood on September 26, when Ferrari hero Mike Hawthorn won a couple of libre events in impressive style.

By 1954, Vandervell's attention was firmly focussed on the new four-cylinder Vanwall special and the old 4½-litre "Thinwall" took something of a back seat. But it still had four outings in British libre events, all in the hands of new English rising star Peter Collins who won two of those races, at Snetterton and Goodwood, developing his talent as an aspiring Grand Prix driver. And it was Enzo Ferrari who would eventually reap the benefit of Collins's early experience in the "Thinwall Special".

Before the 4½-litre finally finished its career, it was to participate in a few more

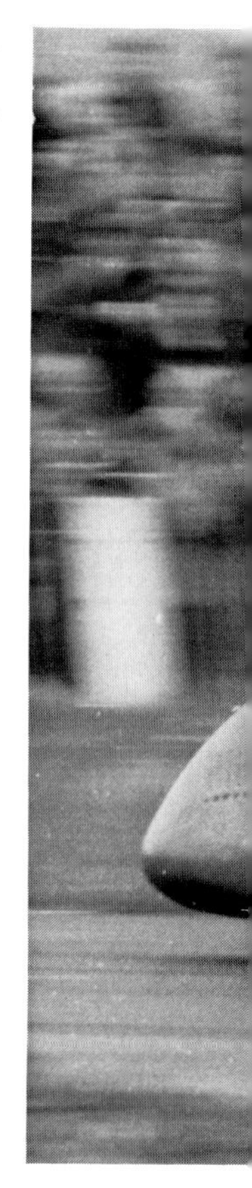

Very special! No history of Ferrari's Grand Prix cars would be complete without reference to Tony Vandervell's Thinwall Specials which helped provide the English bearing magnate's team with the experience to build the Ferrari-beating Vanwalls. This is Reg Parnell at the wheel of Vandervell's 4½-litre V12 Thinwall on his way to victory in the 1951 Festival of Britain Trophy at Goodwood.

unsuccessful assaults on the Indianapolis 500, but none of these outings were memorable. In 1954 Villoresi was entered by Luigi Chinetti's wife Marion in the 500, but didn't appear to drive. The final big V12 derivative was the superb 4.1-litre machine used by the supremely brave Luigi Musso in the 1958 Trophy of Two Worlds at Monza where, sharing with Phil Hill and Mike Hawthorn it finished third in a mind-blowing confrontation against the Indianapolis regulars, although that is outside the scope of this volume.

SUNDAY EXPRESS
HAVOLINE
LUCAS
16
17

Section II: Formula 2 domination of two World Championships

The heyday of Alberto Ascari

Silverstone, 1952, with the 500s of Farina (No.16) and Taruffi (No.17) being pushed out to the starting grid. The bulges on the bonnet for the longer carburetter intakes are well shown in this shot. Ascari's 500 won the race from Taruffi, while Farina had persistent plug trouble and could only manage sixth.

Enzo Ferrari's early insistence that his firm's initial V12 engine should have more than one possible application paid off very quickly indeed. We have already seen that the first *Grand Epreuve* outing by a Maranello car was by one of the "two-seater" 166 machines in the 1948 Monaco Grand Prix and the next step was to install one of these normally aspirated 60 x 58.8mm, 1995cc engines into a 125 chassis for Formula 2 racing. Ferrari's initial approach to the 2-litre Formula 2 category in 1948 had been patchy to say the least: he had got more than sufficient work on his hands developing the supercharged Grand Prix V12. But in 1949 the V12 166 single seaters, now producing 155bhp on three Weber 32DCF carburetters, were fielded in many races by both the factory and several important private entrants.

Between them, Ascari and Villoresi managed to win every race the works Formula 2 cars entered for in 1949 and the trend continued throughout the 1950 season during which the 166s were based round a long-chassis with a de Dion rear end replacing the earlier swing axle arrangement. In supercharged guise the 166s also dominated the early 1950 libre races in Argentina, a feat which they repeated the following winter (when Gonzalez made his name) and their success in this prestigious international single seater second division continued through much of 1951 as well.

As far as Formula 1 was concerned, the 4½-litre unsupercharged/1½-litre supercharged rules were scheduled to continue until the end of 1953 and detailed consideration was being given by the FIA to the introduction of a 2½-litre Formula 1 at the start of 1954. During the 1951 season Ferrari had produced the 2560cc V12 "interim" engine on the way to developing the type 375, and although this unit had never been part of the factory's mainstream effort, it was raced quite regularly by works-assisted Swiss privateer Rudi Fischer's Ecurie Espadon as well as Dorino Serafini.

However the crucial date to remember in connection with the proposed 2½-litre Formula 1 is September 2, 1951 when Piero Taruffi appeared in a 2490cc *four-cylinder* Ferrari in the Bari Grand Prix. Although it was only another fortnight before a 2-litre version of this unit made an appearance in the Modena Grand Prix, Taruffi's outing was of more long-term importance. It was the start of the pure Lampredi era as far as Ferrari single seaters were concerned. It was also a race to which Stirling Moss had been invited to drive the new car — he arrived to find that it had been given to Taruffi with no warning or explanation. Stirling was not amused!

Whilst Lampredi certainly can take the credit for the normally aspirated 4½-litre V12, one tends to associate the V12 configuration with Colombo, even

Greater than Fangio? The essence of Formula 2 Grand Prix racing in 1952/53 is epitomized by this shot of Alberto Ascari's Ferrari 500 heading for victory in the 1953 Belgian Grand Prix at Spa-Francorchamps. The type 500 was a trim, compact car with lines as well-balanced as the "Squalo's" were stumpy and ugly.

though he didn't stay on long enough at Maranello to deserve all of the credit even for the long-term development of the supercharged car. But when Lampredi introduced his four-cylinder engine, it seemed as though all the technical groundwork between 1948 and '50 had been summarily thrown out of the drawing office window. Although Lampredi knew that the four-cylinder engine would have a longer stroke and bigger piston area than a corresponding V12, he set less store by these priorities than did his predecessor. He felt that the torque characteristics would be much improved and, perhaps every bit as important, he knew that a four-cylinder engine would be significantly lighter than the V12. The figures that have been quoted are a reduction of total engine weight from 400 lbs to 348 lbs, a reduction in the number of moving parts by some 65 per cent and an estimated increase in the power-to-weight ratio of up to 15 per cent. As history would relate, Lampredi's calculations would be spot-on as far as a 2-litre Formula 2 car was concerned, but the theories behind this dramatic change of technical direction would be stretched unrealistically when it came to fielding a competitive 2½-litre unit.

Just prior to opting for the four-cylinder route, Lampredi planned a twin o.h.c. version of his V12, but this was eventually shelved. If the single-cylinder Norton motorcycle engine could be tuned to produce 100bhp per litre, then so, thought Lampredi, could his four-cylinder unit.

The two versions initially prepared were the 90 x 78mm, 1984.85cc Formula 2

unit and the 94 x 90mm, 2498.32cc derivative. The engine was based round a light alloy crankcase, the crankshaft supported by five Thinwall bearings, and the twin overhead camshafts were driven by a train of gears taken off the nose of the crankshaft. Initially the magnetos were mounted horizontally at the front of the engine and a two-plugs-per-cylinder arrangement was employed. In order to guarantee an effective gas and water seal, the four steel cylinder liners were screwed into recesses surrounding the combustion chambers. On two Weber 50 DCO carburetters, the first four-cylinder Formula 2 engine developed almost 170bhp at 7500rpm as compared to the 155/160bhp of the admittedly s.o.h.c. 2-litre V12.

The chassis was an uncomplicated tubular affair based round oval-section main longerons with tubular cross members and a welded upper structure to support the beaten aluminium body panels: in short, the mixture much as before. The suspension at the front consisted of unequal-length wishbones working in conjunction with a transverse leaf spring, while there was a de Dion arrangement with universally jointed drive shafts and parallel radius rods and a transverse leaf spring again at the rear. Transmission was by means of a multi-plate clutch to a crash four-speed gearbox mounted in unit with the ZF final drive. Houdaille vane-type shock absorbers were fitted all round and hydraulic brakes were employed with finned alloy drums. The Formula 2 car was, logically, dubbed the type 500, reflecting the individual capacity of each cylinder, and on its début in the 1951 Modena event, Ascari and Villoresi used two of these machines to completely dominate both practice and the race. Unfortunately Villoresi retired shortly after half distance with engine trouble, but Ascari went on to win convincingly with a new lap record under his belt. Interestingly, second place fell to Gonzalez at the wheel of an older 166 V12.

Prior to the start of the 1952 season, the Ferrari 500s underwent a number of detail improvements. Four Weber 45DOE single choke carburetters were fitted and the compression ratio raised from 11.5 to 12.0:1, the power output being boosted to around 170bhp at 7200rpm. The exhaust system was also modified and the bodywork slightly revised. Ready to race, the cars weighed in at 560kg, had a wheelbase of 85.1in (2160mm) and were fitted with centre-lock Boranni wire wheels shod with Pirelli rubber.

With the imminent demise of the 4½-litre Formula 1 as a viable proposition for European race organizers, there followed an almost unseemly haste for promoters to switch their events to Formula 2 status. This meant that the Ferrari

The revised exhaust on the 1953 type 500 is shown off in this shot of Ascari heading to victory in the Pau Grand Prix over the splendid street circuit in South West France.

Hawthorn in the ascendant. Early in the 1953 French Grand Prix at Reims-Gueux, the brilliant Englishman's 500 hurtles across the cornfields of the Marne with team-mate Piero Taruffi in close company. At the end of this race, Hawthorn was to pip Fangio's Maserati to score the first of three Grand Prix career victories . . .

500s were racing virtually every weekend of the season, the seven-event official World Championship series looking rather insignificant when compared with the enormous list of non-title contests, including the prestigious *Grand Prix de France* series. Ascari, Villoresi and Taruffi could usually be seen at the wheel of works cars in addition to Nino Farina and, occasionally, French driver André Simon. Ranged against them were the new Colombo-designed six-cylinder Maseratis, scheduled to be handled by Fangio, Gonzalez and Felice Bonetto, plus the six-cylinder French Gordinis which would be entrusted to Robert Manzon and former motorcycle ace Jean Behra.

There were four major non-title races on the European calendar before the Swiss Grand Prix opened the World Championship struggle. Three of them were won by Alberto Ascari, the brilliant Italian heading a Maranello 1-2-3- at Syracuse on March 16 in front of Taruffi and Farina, while at Pau on April 14 he led French privateer Louis Rosier's 500 across the line. On April 27 Ascari survived to win the Marseilles Grand Prix on the Parc Borely circuit, a race made notable for Farina's indiscipline, the veteran Italian refusing to acknowledge Ascari's team leader status. The opening phase of this event was highlighted by a battle between the two Ferrari works cars and it's indicative of Farina's determined, uncompromising approach to motor racing that he couldn't even take things easy after Ascari made a stop for new tyres, leaving him the race apparently in the bag. Shortly before the end of this three-hour contest, Farina slid off the road, lightly damaging his 500 against the straw bales, and allowing Ascari through to a lucky victory!

The factory didn't contest the BRDC International Trophy race at Silverstone, but Rudi Fischer's new 500 finished fourth with Peter Whitehead's old 125-based V12 fifth. Finally, the 153-mile Naples Grand Prix at Posillipo on May 11 saw Farina and Taruffi representing the factory and finishing in convincing 1-2 formation.

Berne's Bremgarten circuit saw the first World Championship round take place on May 18, many observers making the point that these 2-litre cars looked distinctly less than spectacular on this superb track where supercharged Alfa 159s and 4½-litre Ferrari 375s had battled it out the previous year. That might well have been the case, but there was never to be any going back to those halcyon days and the spectators were treated to a Ferrari demonstration run. Farina, Taruffi and Simon represented the Maranello works team as Ascari was away competing at Indianapolis and Villoresi was recovering from the effects of a road accident. Farina led initially before being sidelined with magneto failure, so it was then left to Taruffi to lead through to the finish ahead of Rudi Fischer's private machine. Farina briefly took over Simon's second-place works 500, but this also succumbed to magneto failure, while Rosier crashed spectacularly in his private car, being flung out on to the circuit but surviving with cuts and bruises.

On May 25 the Paris Grand Prix at Montlhery fell to Taruffi's works car while Rudi Fischer's private 500 was busy at the Nürburgring on the same day, dealing out a defeat to Stirling Moss's HWM in the Eifelrennen. On June 8 the works 500s appeared for the Autodrome Grand Prix at Monza sporting a number of minor detail improvements, including long inlet trumpets on the carburetters which gave rise to a bulge in the right-hand side of the bonnet, and longer nose sections. This was the race in which they would face up to the new six-cylinder Maserati A6GCMs for the first time on the European scene, these rivals from Modena to be driven by Fangio, Gonzalez and Bonetto. It was widely speculated that these machines might well be the ones to break Ferrari's Formula 2 stranglehold, but Maserati's morale received a shattering set-back in the first of the event's two 35-lap heats. As previously mentioned, Fangio had travelled by road from Paris after competing in the previous day's Ulster Trophy at Dundrod. Exhausted, he started on the back row of the Monza grid without practising and crashed badly on the second lap. He was out of action for the rest of the season with those neck injuries – and Maserati's challenge was significantly blunted.

At the end of this Monza race the Maserati team had been well and truly defeated, with Farina winning the two-part race on aggregate from Simon and Fischer. Gonzalez's Maserati retired from the first heat with ignition trouble and Bonetto's from the second with fuel pump trouble. Villoresi's Ferrari retired in the first heat with a bent valve while Ascari, battling fiercely with "team-mate" Farina, dropped out of the second heat with a seized camshaft.

On June 22 the World Championship contest continued with the *Grand Prix d'Europe* at Spa-Francorchamps, Ascari taking pole position from Farina and Taruffi. The only serious opposition on this occasion came from Behra's Gordini which briefly slipped ahead to lead the field on the opening lap, but from then on it was Ascari all the way in confident style, the Italian running the gauntlet of a brief rain shower to come home a dominant winner. Into second place came Farina ahead of Robert Manzon and a spindly little British-entered Cooper-Bristol handled by an enthusiastic, blond-haired Englishman who was driving in his first overseas race. His name, to be recalled a few months later in Maranello, was Mike Hawthorn . . .

On June 29, Ferrari confidence received something of a knock at the non-title Reims Grand Prix where Jean Behra's Gordini out-ran Ascari's works 500 in highly impressive style, Alberto being forced into the pits with overheating problems early in the chase after slipstreaming the French car too closely. Naturally, there were those detractors who were quick to suggest that the Gordini's 2-litre engine might not be all it appeared, but in the immortal words of

Ascari again. Alberto's type 500 leads the similar cars of Villoresi and Farina into Tarzan at the start of the 1953 Dutch Grand Prix, another victory for the reigning World Champion.

Mandy Rice-Davies "they would say that, wouldn't they?" Just to rub in the point, Behra never allowed Farina's second-place Ferrari 500 to get anywhere near him and, while Ascari sprinted back to third after letting Villoresi share his car, Bira rounded off Gordini's joy day on home soil with a fine fourth.

For the French Grand Prix at Rouen-les-Essarts a week later, there were a number of fresh modifications to be seen on the factory 500s, including the re-positioning of the magnetos vertically at the front of the engine, driven directly from the front of the crankshaft rather than the camshafts. The engines were mounted further back within the chassis and were now rated at 175bhp at 7500rpm. In this guise the 500s had the race to themselves, finishing 1-2-3 in the order Ascari, Farina, Taruffi. Two weekends later Ascari put on an equally convincing demonstration in the 249-mile/400km British Grand Prix at Silverstone, this time with Taruffi second and Farina a distant sixth after a time-consuming pit stop to change sparking plugs and adjust the magneto in order to get rid of a misfire. Mike Hawthorn's Cooper-Bristol finished third in the Englishman's home Grand Prix, a performance which gave him more excellent press in Italy.

Alberto Ascari was well on his way to becoming World Champion by now, his smooth and stylish approach, matched with just the right amount of fire, was paying dividends. With Fangio out of action, there was no doubt that he had become the best driver in the business and there were those who considered him the equal, even superior, of the gifted Argentinian. The only criticism levelled at Ascari was that he probably wasn't at his best in a tight corner, preferring to set a blistering pace from the start to get clear of any potential challengers. Truly, in the manner of Jim Clark who was to follow him in the next decade, Ascari was a man who liked to control races from the front.

On August 3 at the Nürburgring, he won his fourth *Grand Epreuve* of the season, albeit narrowly from Farina on this occasion, with Fischer third and Taruffi fourth. The Swiss privateer had only overtaken the third works car in the closing stages of the race as Taruffi slowed with a broken de Dion tube. Mike Hawthorn surprised Maranello's runners in the first World Championship Dutch Grand Prix at Zandvoort on August 17 by getting his Cooper-Bristol on to the front row of the grid in amongst the 500s. There was no way he could stay with the Ferraris once the race got under way, even on what most people regarded as a medium-speed circuit, but he finished fourth behind Ascari, Farina and Villoresi. There was no ignoring the blond boy from Farnham . . .

The final Grand Prix victory of Nino Farina's distinguished career was at the Nürburgring in 1953 at the wheel of this type 500. Ascari was out of luck on this occasion, losing a front wheel on his own car and then blowing up the engine of the 500 he took over from Villoresi.

Despite problems with a carburetter blockage, Alberto Ascari won the 1953 Swiss Grand Prix at Bremgarten with this type 500.

It was important that Maserati showed its new car's potential in front of an Italian crowd at Monza for the Italian Grand Prix on September 7, so the decision was taken to run Gonzalez's machine with a light fuel load from the start, hoping he could build up sufficient an initial advantage. From the start, Gonzalez forced his twin-plug A6GCM through into the lead from the second row, the rival Modena marque having missed much of the season's racing programme following the disaster to Fangio and only returning to the scene at the Nürburgring. Although this wasn't a really fair comparison, it was clear that the Maserati was obviously not something to be ignored, even though Froilan dropped back to fifth spot after an absurdly long pit stop for fuel at the end of lap 37. This left Ascari serenely running home to score his sixth World Championship victory of the year while Gonzalez battled his way back to second place at the chequered flag, ahead of Villoresi and Farina.

The Ferrari type 500, in the hands of factory drivers or privateers equipped with the slightly less-powerful engines which peaked at 6500rpm, had run riot across the European racing calendar throughout 1952. Whether in the most exalted and prestigious *Grand Epreuve* surroundings of Bremgarten, Monza or the Nürburgring, or bitterly fighting non-Championship battles at such long-abandoned racing venues as Comminges, La Baule-Escoublac, Modena, Posillipo or Les Sables d'Olonne, the dumpy, yet well-balanced looking, little four-cylinder Ferrari had written itself a glowing page of racing history. Alberto Ascari was World Champion and riding the crest of a wave of popularity and acclaim. What's more, that Ferrari roller-coaster would continue in this successful vein throughout the following year.

Before the end of the 1952 season, Ferrari had invited Mike Hawthorn for a test with a view to his joining the Scuderia's 1953 line-up. This was scheduled to take place in the shape of an entry in the non-title Modena Grand Prix, but the Englishman rather blotted his copybook by up-ending his own Cooper-Bristol (which had been brought along for Roy Salvadori to drive) during an unplanned test run! Enzo Ferrari was obviously won over by young Mike's open, easy-going personality as much as by his prowess behind the wheel, because this unfortunate little episode wasn't to stand between Hawthorn and a full-time Ferrari Grand

Prix drive. He was signed up to partner Ascari, Villoresi and Farina for the 1953 season.

Thus started one of the most remarkable, enduring relationships that Enzo Ferrari was ever to enjoy with one of his employees. The son of a former motorcycle racer Leslie Hawthorn, Mike was born in Mexborough, Yorkshire, on April 10, 1929 but his family moved south to Farnham, Surrey in order that Leslie could be close to Brooklands. Hawthorn Senior established the Tourist Trophy Garage in that pleasant rural town and, shortly after the War, both father and son began racing Rileys regularly in British national events. A friend of the family, Bob Chase, purchased the Cooper-Bristol in which he made his name and attracted Ferrari's attention. Mike was a bluff, outgoing and gregarious individual, but his extrovert personality concealed the fact that he suffered a serious kidney ailment which would almost certainly have prevented him from living beyond middle age had he not tragically died in a road accident, after his retirement, at the age of 29. This kidney problem made him ineligible for the national service so many of the national newspapers accused him of "dodging", and those same areas of the popular press also accused him of being "unpatriotic" driving for a European racing team. These were rather simplistic times . . .

The start of the 1953 season saw the type 500's power output boosted to 180bhp, but there were only minor exhaust system and bodywork alterations to be seen as outward indications of the work carried on at Maranello over the winter. Ranged against the Maserati team, Ascari opened the season by dominating the Argentine Grand Prix at the Buenos Aires Autodrome on January 18, Villoresi finishing second ahead of Gonzalez's Maserati. Sadly, this was a tragic event for Farina crashed into a group of spectators wandering on to the circuit, which was disgracefully marshalled and controlled, and no fewer than ten people lost their lives in this disaster. It was a harrowing, exhausting, scorching début for young Mike Hawthorn who finished a worthy fourth on his Ferrari Grand Prix début, responding to pit signals from his team manager and easing off just when it seemed as though he might be in a position to challenge the third-place Maserati.

The team's first European appearance was at Syracuse on March 22, an event which it should have won easily in the absence of works Maserati entries. In the event, although the four 500s dominated the opening stages, Villoresi retired with a broken valve spring, Ascari lost a lot of time in the pits with hub trouble and eventually took over Hawthorn's car only to retire that 500 with valve spring failure. This left Farina on his own in the lead, but he too succumbed to the same problem on lap 60, the legacy of a faulty batch of valve springs, so de Graffenried's Platé-Maserati took a lucky win from Louis Chiron's Osca.

On April 6 Ferrari sent its works team to the Pau Grand Prix where Hawthorn blotted his copybook again during practice by spinning and lightly damaging his 500 – he felt better when Ascari did exactly the same thing! Ascari took pole position from Farina with Hawthorn on the inside of the second row. Farina led initially but couldn't keep his temperament under control and spun off, buckled a wheel and stalled the car. That left Ascari to an easy victory from Hawthorn.

After Ascari notched up another victory at Bordeaux on May 3, Mike Hawthorn's biggest success yet came in the BRDC International Trophy at Silverstone the following Saturday. Mike won his heat comfortably and was holding an initial second place in the final when de Graffenried, who initially led, was signalled that he'd incurred a 60s penalty for a jump-start. The Swiss driver retired his Maserati in disgust, leaving Hawthorn to speed home to a splendid victory. Just to round off the Ferrari team's popular excursion to Britain, Mike's 500 was retained for the following week's Ulster Trophy at Dundrod in which Hawthorn also won his heat and the final. It was an encouraging prelude to the serious business of the World Championship Grand Prix season which continued in Europe with the Dutch race at Zandvoort on June 7.

Maintaining his reputation, World Champion Ascari took pole position for this race ahead of Fangio's Maserati and Farina, with Villoresi and Gonzalez sharing row two. Even though the seaside circuit had been recently resurfaced, there was

Classic pose. Ascari ready for the off at the wheel of a Ferrari 500.

still a great deal of trouble with sand and gravel blowing across it, so many teams experimented with gauze covers to protect the cockpit screens and carburetter intakes. In this event Ascari was simply in a class of his own yet again, completing the 90-lap race non-stop despite a leaking exhaust manifold troubling him in the closing stages. Farina was a second with Gonzalez a splendid third, breaking up the symmetry of a Ferrari 1-2-3 result by beating Hawthorn back into fourth.

Villoresi, Farina and Hawthorn were still in the cars they used in Holland when practice began for the Belgian Grand Prix at Spa-Francorchamps, third round of the Championship, but Ascari used the car which had been the team spare at Zandvoort, its bigger "4½-litre" brakes now replaced by normal Formula 2 brakes again. But this car and Farina's 500 were fitted with a new carburetter set-up, a pair of 50DO4 double choke Webers replacing the previous system of four separate carburetters. These were mounted rigidly to the chassis by means of a steel framework, the intakes joined to the cylinder head by rubber tubes, preventing the vibration of the engine adversely affecting the fuel-feed system.

For this race Fangio was on pole with Gonzalez on the outside of the front row, Maserati providing the bread for a Ferrari sandwich with Ascari between them. Villoresi and Farina shared the second row with Hawthorn in the middle of row three. From the start, it looked as though the Ferrari 500 was finally going to be beaten fair and square by the other Italian manufacturer for Gonzalez hurtled into an immediate lead, pulling away even from his team-mate while Fangio, in turn, was pulling away from Ascari. Clearly the Maseratis had the legs of their arch-rivals on this occasion, but their joy was to be short-lived: Gonzalez ground to a halt at Stavelot on lap 12 and Fangio was in the pits two laps later, both cars with engine failure. Ascari sailed through to yet another easy victory from Villoresi and Onofre Marimon's Maserati, Hawthorn only managing fifth place after a pit stop to deal with a split fuel line. Fangio took over Johnny Claes's Maserati and tore back through the field to reach third place before crashing heavily at *Stavelot*, fortunately without injury.

The non-Championship *Grand Prix de Rouen* saw Farina and Hawthorn trying the 2½-litre Lampredi four-cylinder engine installed in the 500 chassis, the two Ferraris finishing this demonstration run in that order with local celebrity "Phi-Phi" Etancelin's lumbering 4½-litre Talbot three laps down in third place at the finish.

Then, on July 5, came what turned out to be one of the all-time classic Grand

Prix events, the 1953 French round of the Championship over 60 laps of the yet-again revised 8.347km road circuit in the flat, sun-scorched Marne countryside. However, what was to be variously described as the Race of the Age or Duel of the Century very nearly didn't come to pass. Why? Well, not only had the *Automobile Club de Champagne* spent all this money on circuit alterations, reputed to be around £100,000, but they also determined to steal some of Le Mans's thunder by staging a 12-hour sports car epic starting at midnight on the Saturday and finishing a few hours before the start of the Grand Prix, at midday on Sunday.

Owing to a bureaucratic interpretation and application of the rather unfortunate regulations, the Umberto Maglioli/Piero Carini 4½-litre Ferrari coupé was withdrawn from the race after the organizers had announced that no more times would be recorded for it after it had infringed, allegedly, a minor regulation about when the competing cars were permitted to turn their lights off in the early dawn. Enzo Ferrari reacted by threatening to withdraw his Formula 2 cars from the Grand Prix, but eventually decided against that course of action. In truly dramatic style, however, the 500s were the last competitors to be wheeled out to the grid, keeping everybody in suspense until the last possible moment.

This was destined to be an epic Maserati/Ferrari confrontation and Gonzalez's six-cylinder Maserati galloped into an immediate lead as the Modena team's "hare", running with a light fuel load once again and planning to make a pit stop. In his wake the other red cars from the two famous Italian marques weaved and jinked their way round the circuit in frenetic style, Ascari, Villoresi, Bonetto, Hawthorn, Farina and Marimon all locked together in a terrific confrontation.

Eventually, after 30 laps, Gonzalez came in to refuel, but he just failed to get back into the fray before Fangio and Hawthorn raced through wheel-to-wheel. From this point onwards the main issue was between the young Englishman and the established Argentinian, Ferrari and Maserati running side-by-side down the long straights on many laps with each driver crouched down low behind their windscreens, coaxing the last ounce of speed from their cars. It was only going to be sorted out on the very last lap and with Fangio's first gear proving difficult to engage, the Argentine driver was clearly set for trouble on the relatively slow Thillois right-hander which led out on to the final run up to the flag. On that nail-biting last lap Hawthorn timed everything just right, slicing up the inside of his rival as Fangio fumbled for a gear, the Englishman sprinting for the line to win his first Grand Prix triumph by a scant second. Behind Fangio the order was Gonzalez (Maserati), Ascari (Ferrari), Farina (Ferrari) and Villoresi (Ferrari). After the fright they had experienced at Spa, Maranello had reconfirmed its supremacy and Mike Hawthorn had become the first of Britain's golden crop of post-War racing talent to win a *Grand Epreuve*.

On July 18, Ascari was back on top form to win the British Grand Prix at Silverstone from Fangio, Farina, Gonzalez and Hawthorn. Mike's efforts in his home race were highlighted by an absolutely *enormous*, grass-cutting spin at Woodcote right in front of the main grandstand. It clearly held the young Englishman's attention, spoiling his day after starting from second place on the grid: he made a long pit stop to rectify a fuel leak before resuming the chase.

Gonzalez was out of action following a sports car accident for the German Grand Prix at the Nürburgring on August 5, so this 18 lap, 410.58km race was without one of Maserati's strongest runners. Ascari was in charge quite brilliantly until he came into view minus his right front wheel and coasted to a halt on the right front hub. That left Farina to collect victory ahead of Fangio's Maserati, Hawthorn and Bonetto's Maserati: Ascari sprinted back through the field to fourth place, with Hawthorn almost in sight, but having established a new Formula 2 record in 9m 56s (137.78kph), the engine wilted and finally expired under the strain. It was to be Farina's last Grand Prix victory . . .

There were only two races left to run in the World Championship arena by this stage and the Maserati opposition was really hotting up, a factor which could no longer be underestimated. Just to emphasize the reality of this situation, Fangio

Four cylinder exponent. Hands in pockets, Aurelio Lampredi chats to Mike Hawthorn and Harry Schell at Monza in 1953. Lampredi's four-cylinder engines may have dominated the 2-litre category, but when stretched beyond to 2.5-litres in 1954 they suffered a dramatic decline . . .

took pole position for the Swiss Grand Prix at Bremgarten on August 23, just squeezing in ahead of the Ferrari 500s of Ascari and Farina. When it came to the 65 lap contest, however, Ascari seemed virtually certain to wrap up this race as well in overwhelmingly confident style. He accelerated straight into the lead where he stayed for 39 laps before spluttering into the pits, a carburetter jet having become blocked by an obstruction. His mechanics took a mallet to the offending component, a few well-aimed blows clearing the blockage, and Ascari hurtled back into the thick of the battle. Although his early delay had allowed Farina and Hawthorn to establish themselves firmly in first and second places, such was the pace of Ascari's recovery that he overhauled both his team-mates before the chequered flag to score another worthy triumph and clinch his second World Championship title.

With the new 2½-litre Formula 1 beckoning for 1954, Ferrari used the Italian Grand Prix at Monza as the opportunity for him to début his new challenger for the following season, the distinctively-styled "Squalo". This new chassis was intended to supersede the type 500 for the start of the new Grand Prix era and it made its first appearance at the Italian race fitted with a small capacity 93 x

34

The other end of the spectrum. As well as the factory cars, private owners also enjoyed success in type 500 Formula 2 cars. With Kurt Adolff's ex-Ecurie Espadon 166 languishing in the ditch at the bottom of the banking, Jacques Swaters's Ecurie Francorchamps 500 holds off Rodney Nuckey's Cooper-Bristol on its way to victory at Berlin's spectacular Avusring, 1953.

73.5mm, 1997.11cc version of Lampredi's "other" four-cylinder design. The new car was based round a much shorter wheelbase than the type 500, constructed round a small-tube spaceframe, with double wishbone and transverse leaf front suspension. A de Dion rear end was employed with a transverse leaf spring mounted quite high above the rear axle line and the main fuel tanks were slung on panniers on either side of the cockpit, giving the car a distinctive "waisted" appearance.

The new four-cylinder engine had its valves set at a 100-degree angle to each other in the cylinder head and had the crankcase/cylinder block cast as one rather than the head/block. The special twin Weber carburetters, mounted on the chassis, were unchanged, as were the twin magnetos driven from the timing gears and mounted low at the front of the chassis, supplying the twin-plugs per cylinder. Unfortunately, although the Squalo looked much sleeker than its predecessor, the fact that Ascari could only manage a 2m 5s lap with it as opposed to the 2m 3s best with his regular 500 hardly promised well for the future.

At the end of the day Maglioli and Carini drove a pair of these new 2-litre machines, thereby qualifying Maranello for the special 7 million lire prize for the constructor who fielded *two* brand new cars at Monza – Maserati only fielded a single new A6. Up at the front of the field Ascari took pole position with his type 500 from Fangio's Maserati, Onofre Marimon's similar Argentine-backed car, Farina, Bonetto, Villoresi and Hawthorn. Again this was a Reims-style cut-and-thrust battle with Ascari pulling every trick in the book to keep in front of Fangio, for Juan-Manuel was absolutely set on winning this, the final *Grand Epreuve* to count for the World Championship.

Marimon actually forced his Maserati into the lead on the opening lap, but the race, almost inevitably, settled down into a battle between Ascari and Fangio for most of the afternoon. In the end Marimon, who'd been delayed by a pit stop to deal with a damaged water radiator, got himself embroiled once more in the battle for the lead, even though he was actually three laps behind. In his enthusiasm to aid his compatriot Fangio, Marimon sparked off a last corner *débâcle* in which he and Ascari spun off the road, much to Alberto's thinly-disguised annoyance, and Fangio dodged through to score Maserati's sole Grand Prix triumph in two year's endeavour. Farina, who was in with that leading bunch, wound up a slightly-delayed second while the Ferrari 500s of Villoresi and Hawthorn came pounding home to take third and fourth places. Maglioli's Squalo trundled home a less-than-impressive eighth, four laps behind, while Carini's similar car failed to last the distance.

Thus the era in which Formula 2 held sway on the World Championship stage came to an exciting and spectacular end, Ferrari's last-race defeat perhaps anticipating leaner times to come for the Prancing Horse. Immediately after Monza Ferrari made one of his public, frequent, but hardly serious threats to withdraw his team from racing, but none the less team manager Nello Ugolini simply smiled when Mike Hawthorn queried this announcement, telling the innocent Englishmen to come down to Maranello and sign his contract for the following year. He did, but Ascari didn't – and there were difficult years ahead for the Commendatore and his team . . .

EEDO
4

Section III: 2½-litre heyday, 1954-60:

A time of trial and error

Chapter 1
Lampredi's dream gives way to Lancia's

The blistered paint on the Squalo's bonnet and the dejected expression on Froilan Gonzalez's face mark the end of the bulky Argentinian's efforts to get in amongst the victorious Mercedes-Benz W196s in the 1954 French Grand Prix at Reims-Gueux.

AT the end of the Formula 2 "interregnum", despite having carried out a lot of work on engine development, Ferrari could hardly be said to find itself in a strong position at the start of the new 2½-litre Formula 1. In fact the 1954 season produced precious few indications of the success the marque would later enjoy under these regulations. On the driver front Alberto Ascari had moved across to the fledgling Lancia Grand Prix team – a great mistake, as it turned out – but Mike Hawthorn had been signed up again following his epic victory over Fangio at Reims the previous summer, while Farina, Umberto Maglioli and Froilan Gonzalez (who'd returned from Maserati) were also on the books. The team wasn't short on driving talent; the problem was, quite simply, one of giving them the tools to do the job properly!

On the car front, Ferrari opened the season by taking 2½-litre-engined versions of the old, but successful, Formula 2 machines to the opening Grand Prix in Buenos Aires. The full 2½-litre version of the type 553 "Squalo", (shark), which had made its first public appearance in 2-litre form at Monza the previous autumn, was held back for further development as it still didn't look as promising as the older cars. The 1953 type 500 chassis were dubbed type 625 when fitted with the 2½-litre engines, and opened the season fitted with a 94 × 90mm unit directly derived from the 2-litre engine which had proved so dominant over the two previous seasons. The engine retained a one-piece block and head assembly and had gear-driven camshafts with the twin magnetos mounted horizontally on the front of the crankcase, feeding two sparking plugs per cylinder. The two Weber 50DCOA carburetters were positioned on a bracket mounted to the chassis frame on the right-hand side and were coupled to the engine by a rubber pipe in order to minimize problems caused by vibration.

The 625's chassis was unchanged from the previous year's Formula 2 car, and front suspension was by means of double wishbones and transverse leaf spring, while a transverse leaf spring was also employed at the rear in conjunction with a de Dion assembly, twin radius arms locating it in a fore and aft plane. A total of six cars was retained by the Maranello factory, while one was rebuilt over the winter for sale to Frenchman Maurice Trintignant, thus joining the similarly "updated" machines retained by Ecurie Francorchamps, Louis Rosier and Reg Parnell.

In the Argentine Grand Prix Ferrari fielded Farina, Hawthorn and Gonzalez, knowing full-well that there would be no challenge from his most feared potential rivals Mercedes-Benz and Lancia, neither of whom was ready with their new cars. Fangio was thus loaned to Maserati for his home Grand Prix and, indeed, triumphed on his home ground after a controversial protest from Ferrari, which centred round the number of mechanics permitted to work on the Maserati during a pit stop, was rejected by the stewards. Farina finished a distant second ahead of Gonzalez, with Trintignant's private car fourth, but the 625s were clearly no match for the 1951 World Champion at the wheel of a Maserati 250F. There was a sliver of consolation for Ferrari when Trintignant's private 625 won the non-Championship Buenos Aires Grand Prix at the same venue a fortnight later, beating the Farina/Gonzalez 625 into second place, but there wasn't a surfeit of optimism within the team as it faced the start of the European racing season.

On April 11, the Syracuse Grand Prix took place over the Sicilian road circuit and Ferrari fielded a pair of 625s (for Gonzalez and Farina) and a couple of substantially revised type 553s for Hawthorn and Trintignant. The 553 chassis was basically of the same spaceframe construction as had been seen at Monza the previous year, but the wheelbase was 2½in. longer and the pannier fuel tanks had been supplemented by one in the tail of the car. Transverse leaves continued to provide the springing medium all round, at the front working in conjunction with small double wishbones, while a de Dion assembly was featured at the rear. The four-speed gearbox and differential were in unit, mounted to the chassis frame, the drive passing under the differential unit to reduction gears and then up to the crownwheel and pinion, thence to the two rear wheels by means of universally jointed drive shafts.

The four-cylinder engine had a 100 × 79.5mm bore/stroke for a total capacity of 2497.56cc, and followed the Formula 2 unit's design with 100-degree angle between the inlet and exhaust valves. Two sparking plugs per cylinder were again employed, these fired from two magnetos mounted low down on the front of the engine adjacent to the water pump. Two double choke Weber 58 DCOA3 carburetters were employed and the power output was claimed at 240bhp at 7500rpm, a 5bhp increment over the engines powering the old 625s.

As much as anything, the problems encountered by the early 553s could be put down to driver resistance against their handling characteristics. Time and again throughout Ferrari's history cars with all their weight concentrated within the wheelbase would be received with a degree of caution by a significant number of the team's drivers. In 1954 it was the type 553, in 1955 it would be the Lancia-Ferrari D50, in 1973 it would be the prototype 312B3 and in 1975 it would be the 312 *transversale* – all offered very high levels of adhesion, but coupled with a sudden loss of control if those limits were over-stepped by the driver. In 1954, Farina, in particular, just refused to adapt his driving style to accommodate the 553's peculiarities. Gonzalez was rather more prepared to adapt, but Hawthorn frankly didn't think much of the early 553 "Squalo" and Ferrari designer Aurelio Lampredi waged an internal battle for much of the season in an effort to get his drivers to alter their styles. At the end of the day, all things considered, he was unsuccessful in this quest.

At Syracuse there was quite a practice battle between the four Ferrari drivers, but the race was something of a disaster for the new type 553. Hawthorn's 625 glanced a wall, rupturing its fuel tank and bursting into flames. Gonzalez stopped his "Squalo" to go to his team-mate's assistance and although he managed to help Mike from his burning car, he indirectly compounded the disaster when his "parked" 553 rolled gently down a slope into the 625 and both cars were completely burnt out! As some consolation, Farina won the race in his 625, but Hawthorn was to spend several weeks in hospital recovering from his unpleasant burns.

On May 9 Gonzalez won the non-title Bordeaux Grand Prix at the wheel of a 625 and the 553 didn't appear again until a single car arrived at Silverstone for the International Trophy meeting on May 11. Gonzalez was entrusted with the new car on this occasion and he won his heat with ease in the pouring rain. Unfortunately, although he won the final as well, he was obliged to "commandeer" Trintignant's 625 to achieve this success after the "Squalo" seized its engine whilst being warmed up in the paddock.

The World Championship season continued at Spa-Francorchamps on June 20 (there was no F1 Monaco Grand Prix in 1954) where Farina (recovered from his accident in the Mille Miglia) and Gonzalez handled the 553s, again revamped with their engines moved forward slightly in the chassis, the resultant change in weight distribution intended to make the cars feel slightly more progressive when driven close to the limit of adhesion. Gonzalez was increasingly confident about the 553, but Farina still had his reservations despite the fact that they both got on the front row alongside Fangio's pole-winning Maserati. Hawthorn and Trintignant stuck to the old 625s for this race.

The team's challenge was badly blunted when Gonzalez's 553 suffered engine troubles on the opening lap, trickling into the pits to retire after the Argentinian had burst away into the lead from the start. Fangio was thus allowed to triumph in the 36 lap contest, winning by over 20s from Trintignant despite easing off in the closing stages. Moss's 250F finished third while Gonzalez took over Hawthorn's 625 (to finish fourth) on lap 20 after the Englishman had been badly affected by gases from a cracked exhaust pipe. Prior to his retirement with a trifling ignition problem, Farina had actually managed to poke his type 553 into the lead ahead of Fangio, but his retirement on the 15th lap allowed Fangio's Maserati to have an easy run for the balance of the race distance.

The Ferrari 553 might well have been demonstrating vastly improved form, but on July 4 a massive new factor was injected into Formula 1 equation when the teams arrived for the *Grand Prix de l'ACF* at Reims-Gueux. This was the fantastic, historic Mercedes-Benz comeback for which Fangio had been "kept warm" at the wheel of the Maserati at the start of the season. The high-technology eight-cylinder cars from the Daimler-Benz AG rewrote the parameters of contemporary Grand Prix car performance over the next two years, although it would be incorrect to say that they were dominant or unbeatable. In fact, as their achievements fade into historical perspective, the fact that the Mercedes team was hamstrung by the political necessity to have German drivers on the team compromised its efforts quite significantly. However, they did have the great Fangio in their armoury and that was to prove their ace card. What's more, just to increase the pressure on Ferrari, Ascari and Villoresi were released by Gianni Lancia to drive Maseratis in this event. The Formula 1 Lancia still wasn't ready, so there was no point in keeping these two men sitting on the sidelines twiddling their thumbs.

Fangio and Karl Kling made the Reims event a demonstration run for the Mercedes W196s, but Gonzalez got his 553 in amongst them during the early stages and actually held second place behind Kling on the opening lap. He then dropped back to third before succumbing to engine failure on the super-fast, sun-drenched circuit. The same fate also befell Hawthorn and Trintignant, so Robert Manzon's private 625 was left to uphold the marque's honour. Finishing third a lap behind the triumphant German cars. There were only six finishers after this gruelling race in which 21 competitors lined up to take the start. Farina, it should be recalled, was out of action again, recuperating from another accident in a sports Ferrari the previous weekend at Monza!

By this stage if was clear that the 553 programme spelt short-term trouble for the Ferrari team. The car had showed intermittent promise, but the middle of a crowded Grand Prix season was not the time to be carrying out a test and development programme, so the whole technical programme was revised after the team's mechanical disasters at Reims. It was decided to employ the good-handling 625 chassis, which was popular with the team's drivers, and equip it with a "hybrid" four-cylinder engine which incorporated features from both the regular 625 unit and the new 553. This employed the crankcase and bottom end of the earlier engine, with twin magnetos driven horizontally from the front of the crankcase, but with a new head and cylinder block assembly from the 553 engine employing the 100-degree valve angle and having the new engine's 100 × 79.5mm dimensions. Installing this engine into the older chassis called for some minor alterations including a new bonnet to accommodate the larger Weber 58DCOA3 carburetters, and a new steering box. These interim cars made their first race appearance at the *Grand Prix de Rouen-les-Essarts* on July 11 where they were driven by Hawthorn and Trintignant, the two cars completely dominating this

Ferrari's new challenger for the 2½-litre Formula 1 was the type 553 "Squalo" developed by Lampredi: despite being the subject of much development work neither the chassis, nor its four cylinder engine could ever really match the multi-cylinder challengers from Mercedes-Benz or Maserati.
Senior Ferrari mechanic Stefano Meazza (later to move to Bugatti) casts an almost quizzical glance over a 553 in the Syracuse pits prior to the 1954 race. Standing behind the type 553 is one of the trusty 625s which stepped into the breach so effectively.

The rear end of a 1955 "Super Squalo" (now dubbed type 555) photographed at Turin, showing clearly the tubular framework at the rear, the oil and petrol tanks in the tail and the final drive unit, with its detachable cover to enable the reduction gearing to be changed.

non-title race with the Frenchman winning after the crankshaft broke on Hawthorn's machine. Despite this unexpected mechanical failure, this latest model "cocktail" looked pretty promising.

In fact, revenge for Maranello came suddenly and rather unexpectedly. The streamlined Mercedes-Benz cars were certainly *not* suited to Silverstone, (funny how times change: in those days it was regarded as quite a slow circuit, by the 1980s it was one of the very quickest tracks on the Grand Prix calendar) and Gonzalez put on a splendid demonstration at the wheel of one of the 625/553s to win handsomely. It was three years since he'd previously won the British Grand Prix at that same venue and then, as now, his compatriot Juan-Manuel Fangio had been his biggest rival from the point of view of sheer driving talent. However, in pure motor racing terms, Gonzalez's two Silverstone Grand Prix victories were as different as chalk from cheese. In 1951 his 4½-litre Ferrari represented the bright-eyed newcomer, sweeping away the old guard in the form of the 1½-litre supercharged Alfa Romeos. By 1954, the Ferrari 625 could really be considered in the same light as the Alfa 159 three years earlier. Gonzalez's 1954 victory was a morale-boosting interlude, not a change in the fundamental Formula 1 trend. Notwithstanding this victory for Maranello, Mercedes-Benz had got them on the run.

Ferrari decided to stick with the re-engined 625 for the German Grand Prix (where the engines were built up based on 735S crankcases) at the Nürburgring on August 1, practice for which was marred by the fatal accident to popular Argentinian Onofre Marimon who crashed his Maserati 250F going down to *Wehrseifen*. This tragedy deeply affected Gonzalez, who was a close personal friend of his unfortunate compatriot, and although Froilan got the jump on the now open wheeled Mercedes W196s at the start, hurtling through from his position on the second row, he eventually dropped away from the leading bunch. In fact Gonzalez led that first lap until the start of the long return straight up the *Tiergarten*, when Fangio sailed past. Hawthorn retired on lap four, leaving Gonzalez to battle alone with the Mercedes of Fangio, Hermann Lang and Kling, but by lap seven, depressed over recurring thoughts of Marimon's practice accident, Gonzalez was out of touch with them and losing ground fast. Eventually a subdued "Pampas Bull" handed his car over to Hawthorn and Mike brought it through to a good second place, Lang having spun and stalled, while Kling dropped to fourth behind Trintignant after a lengthy stop to tend damaged suspension on his W196. Fangio was thus left to win his third Grand Prix of the season unchallenged.

For the remainder of the 1954 season, Ferrari's Grand Prix challenge continued in the same vein with the 553 being kept very much on the sidelines as the 625 chassis continued in the front line of racing activity. Gonzalez continued to keep the team's morale running at an optimistic level by placing his 53/54 car on pole for the Swiss Grand Prix at Bremgarten, but Fangio's Mercedes-Benz went away easily once the race started, to score another impressive victory. Gonzalez was left to battle with Moss's Maserati, eventually taking his Ferrari through to finish second after Stirling retired with loss of oil pressure, while Hans Herrmann completed the "Ferrari sandwich" by coming home third in his Mercedes. Hawthorn and Trintignant both succumbed to engine malfunctions. Modifications tried for this meeting included a high tail-fairing on the car eventually driven by Gonzalez, but initially tried by Hawthorn. Robert Manzon blotted his copybook fairly comprehensively by crashing one of the 553s during practice while Umberto Maglioli drove the other '54 car steadily through to seventh place, which at least proved that a "Squalo" could finish a race without falling apart!

For the Italian Grand Prix at Monza, Ferrari *really* decided to stir things up for this most important race of the year! Despite having undergone extensive testing, including some successful runs at Monza, Gianni Lancia still hadn't given the green light for his Formula 1 D50's race début, so he agreed to loan Alberto Ascari to drive for the Prancing Horse. Regarded as an equal to Fangio in terms of sheer talent, Ascari had been biting his finger nails to the bone throughout much of the 1954 season as he watched Fangio race away to the World Championship. Thus, the prospect of re-establishing his pre-eminent 1952/53 reputation in front of his home crowd was something to which he looked forward with considerable relish. The fact that Ferrari's decision to put Ascari into one of his cars at Monza caused a degree of dissent and irritation amongst his other drivers mattered not one jot to the Old Man. These were desperate times which called for desperate remedies; and Enzo thrived on this sort of confrontation, anyway.

No fewer than six cars were fielded at Monza, Ascari's being yet another model variation of the 625 fitted with a 553 model engine, while Hawthorn and Trintignant had similar chassis fitted with the first version of the "hybrid" engine which made its début at Rouen. Manzon had a similar machine entered as a semi-works challenger, Maglioli drove an original specification 625 and only Gonzalez was fielded in a "pure" 553 "Squalo". Fangio took pole position with Ascari alongside and Moss completing the front row for Maserati, a line-up which presaged a fantastic battle in front of the thousands of screaming Italian fans. Kling, Gonzalez and Villoresi were on the second row and it was Kling who catapulted away into the lead when the starter's flag was dropped.

Kling kept ahead for a short while, but the pressure of running in amongst the "high rollers" on a circuit as fast as Monza quickly took its toll and the German made a slight, heart-stopping, error on one of the faster corners and dropped back to fifth. That left Fangio out in front, but Ascari was out to underline that he had lost none of his old driving prowess during his enforced lay-off waiting for the Lancia. By lap 10 he had not only worked his way through into the lead, but opened out a six second advantage over the streamlined Mercedes-Benz which had Moss and Gonzalez scrambling all over it, looking for a way through. The jinx which seemed to follow the "Squalo" around the Grand Prix circuits of the World struck again on lap 17 when Gonzalez retired with gearbox trouble, and from that point onwards the crowd was treated to some magnificent motor racing in the grand manner as Fangio gradually chiselled his way into Ascari's advantage. But Stirling Moss also came into the picture, driving his Maserati 250F with the brilliance that was to be his trademark for so many years and, by the time Ascari's Ferrari finally wilted under the strain, retiring with a broken valve after 49 stupendous laps, it was Moss, not Fangio, who swept imperiously through into the lead. Only after 68 laps, when a cracked oil pipe scuppered Stirling's chances as victory was within his grasp, did Fangio go through to score another triumph by over a lap from Hawthorn. Gonzalez took over Maglioli's 625 and continued storming round in his irrepressible style to wind up third at the chequered flag. It seemed as though Maranello, if not quite taking a step in the right direction, was perhaps on the verge of ascertaining in *which* technical direction the team should actually make its next move.

Trintignant (No.18) and Hawthorn (No.16) sandwiching Jean Behra's Gordini on the front row of the grid for the non-Championship 1954 Rouen Grand Prix, where the Ferrari 625s were fitted with "hybrid" 625/553 engines for the first time. Trintignant won comfortably, but his English team-mate retired. Gonzalez's unloved type 553 (No.14) is about to be swamped by a couple more Gordinis from its place on the second row . . .

Mike Hawthorn recounted what happened after the Italian Grand Prix, prior to the final race on the World Championship calendar at Barcelona: "All this time Ferrari had been working hard to cure the faults of the Squalo, which had proved so disappointing, and we assembled at Monza to try a new version, with coil spring front suspension instead of the transverse leaf spring. It was improved out of all recognition and had become a very nice little car. Maglioli and I spent some time driving it round, and then Gonzalez, who was recovering after his Dundrod accident, said he would like to try it. He had only done a few laps when the de Dion tube broke just as he was going round the *Curva Grande*. We heard the engine note die away and rushed round to find the car stopped after a hectic series of swerves with one back wheel at a very peculiar angle. . .

"The car was repaired and sent out to Barcelona for me to drive in the Spanish Grand Prix, with one of the old type fitted with a Squalo engine for Trintignant."

This revised car became dubbed the type 555, but that race, held round 80 laps of the spectacular Pedralbes road circuit on October 24, saw another car of far more long-term significance to Ferrari make its competition début. It was the long-awaited 4 o.h.c. Lancia V8 D50, two examples of which were fielded for Ascari and Villoresi.

Gonzalez hunched over the wheel of his type 553 on the way to victory in one of the International Trophy heats at Silverstone, 1954. The 553's engine seized, however, while it was being warmed up prior the the final and he switched to a 625 to win that event.

It is appropriate to dwell on the original Lancia D50 at some length, for reasons that will soon become apparent in the text of this volume. "The whole conception of the Lancia Grand Prix car was one of normal Grand Prix design but with great attention paid to detail, excellent finish on the mechanical parts and a keen eye to weight saving," wrote Denis Jenkinson shortly after the D50's racing début. The design of the car had been approved in principle back in August 1953, Gianni Lancia leaving his chief designer Vittorio Jano to draw on his experience with the D-series sports cars in order to finalize the Formula 1 machine's configuration.

Thanks to a somewhat convoluted sequence of events, described in this section, the Lancia D50 project would eventually pass into the control of the Ferrari team and rescue the Prancing Horse from a mammoth hole dug, in effect, by Lampredi's four-cylinder cars. After a year of speculation and testing, the Lancia D50 finally emerged to do battle in that race at Barcelona. One can only imagine the frustration which nagged at 35-year old Ascari throughout 1954: the previous two years had seen him win the World Championship title for Ferrari, establishing a dominant and crushing style with which he reeled off so many victories. Recently he'd been forced to sit and ruminate as arch-rival Fangio demonstrated Teutonic engineering prowess quite brilliantly, sweeping to his second World Championship title with a Mercedes-Benz. Now Ascari could *really* exact his revenge – or so it

18
16

21

Mike Hawthorn, seen here unusually wearing goggles and with scarf trailing in the slipstream, practises his 625 for the 1954 German Grand Prix at the Nürburgring In this race the car broke its engine and he took over Gonzalez's machine to finish second.

seemed at the time.

The Lancia D50's gestation period was so long and protracted that certain contemporary magazines began making unkind comparisons between it and the British BRM project – something of a national joke by this stage. There was even speculation from *Motor Sport's* Denis Jenkinson that the car might well employ 4WD, a very well-reasoned, but unfortunately inaccurate hypothesis. After all, the project had been under development for more than a year prior to the D50's race début and the prototype car had first turned a wheel within the courtyard of Lancia's competitions department, on Turin's Via Caraglio, on February 8, 1954. Just over two weeks earlier, on January 21, Ascari and Villoresi had signed their Lancia contracts, and while test driver Giuseppe Gillio, and then Ascari, took the D50 out on Turin's Caselle airport for tests in mid-February, another eight months were to pass before the car raced. Ascari kept his hand in, of course, driving Lancia sports cars, winning the Mille Miglia in a 3.3-litre D24 which kept his respected name in the public eye.

The D50's chassis frame was built out of small diameter tubing and a box-like tubular structure formed the driver's cockpit in the centre section. From this centre section, two small diameter tubes ran forward at the lowest level to the front suspension structure, also of small diameter tubing, which formed a smaller box structure at the front of the car. Between the bulkhead ahead of the cockpit and

Evening the score: Gonzalez used this 625 to triumph in the 1954 British Grand Prix at Silverstone, trouncing the unsuitable aerodynamic Mercedes entries on the bleak airfield circuit.

the front suspension cross members sat the 73.6 × 73.1mm, 2487cc, 90-degree V8 engine, itself mounted on an angle of 12-degrees within the chassis with the propellor shaft running to the left alongside the driver's seat in order to help keep the overall package as low as possible.

On either side of the engine at either end, there were two cast-in lugs which attached to the two main frame structures, thus employing the engine as a semi-stressed unit, doubling, in effect, as the upper tube in a complete spaceframe. Front suspension was by means of equal-length, double tubular wishbones and a thin transverse leaf spring, while inboard shock absorbers were operated by rocker arms extending from each top wishbone. The D50 had a de Dion rear end, the de Dion tube itself being of welded construction to combine strength with lightness, working in conjunction with a transverse leaf spring, twin radius arms and inboard shock absorbers operated by rocker arms.

Long, distinctive pannier tanks were fitted alongside the chassis within the wheels, giving the Lancia D50 a distinctive and functional appearance that could in no way be confused with any of its contemporary Formula 1 rivals. The right-hand tank contained exclusively fuel, while the left-hand one carried fuel towards the rear and an oil cooler towards the front. The V8 engine had twin overhead camshafts on each bank, driven by a train of gears from the front of the crankshaft, and the magnetos ran from the rear end of each inlet camshaft,

Mercedes beater? The Jano- designed Lancia V8 engine, semi-stressed in the D50 chassis. With the plug leads off, the two-plugs per cylinder arrangement can be clearly seen, as can the distinctive pannier fuel tanks situated within the wheelbase.

supplying sparks for eight plugs on each bank of four cylinders. Four downdraught Solex double choke carburetters nestled within the vee of the engine and 260bhp at 8200rpm was quoted as the Lancia's power output.

At 1367 lbs (620kg), the D50 was one of the lightest Grand Prix cars of its time. The Mercedes-Benz W196 scaled 1587 lbs (720kg) in aerodynamic trim and 1521 lbs (690kg) in open-wheeled form; the Ferrari 625s weighed in at 1433 lbs (650kg) and the 553 "Squalo" was just over 1300 lbs (590kg). It had originally been intended to début the car in the French Grand Prix at Reims at the same time as the Mercedes-Benz W196, but the D50 wasn't quite ready and the programme was further delayed after Ascari crashed heavily during tests at Monza on July 9 and badly damaged one of the cars. Eventually Gianni Lancia gave his approval for the car's racing début after Ascari managed a 1m 56.0s lap at Monza – more than three seconds quicker than Fangio's best in the streamlined Mercedes during the Grand Prix weekend. It can therefore be said that Ascari's subsequent performance at Barcelona was not such a great surprise, bearing in mind the D50's power-to-weight ratio and what Ascari personally was out to prove!

The concentration of the D50's weight within the wheelbase predictably endowed the car with high levels of adhesion, requiring a sensitive touch on fast corners – something which Ascari was quite capable of supplying, even if similar characteristics were too much for Farina with the original Ferrari 553!

At Barcelona Ascari took pole position quite easily from Fangio and was pulling away in the lead convincingly between laps four and seven, making two seconds a lap on his pursuers, before retiring with what was officially described as clutch trouble. Hawthorn had put his coil sprung type 553 Ferrari on the front row of the grid behind the Lancia and Fangio's Mercedes and, after Ascari's retirement, the Englishman became embroiled in a close battle for the lead with his team-mate Trintignant's 625 and Harry Schell's Maserati 250F which was demonstrating tremendous form.

Hawthorn recalled, "On lap 22 I got into the lead but Harry came back and something had to be done to shake him off. I saw my chance while coming round a left-hand bend leading into a shortish straight which ended in a right-hand corner; I kept well to the left down the straight, which gave me the right approach to the right-hander and Harry came up on my right. We were both going as fast as we could and I decided to leave my braking until the last possible moment because, knowing Harry's volatile temperament, I expected he would try and hang on even longer. I crammed my brakes hard on just in time to take the corner, but sure enough, Harry kept going and the last I saw of him he was motoring at high speed

straight into the straw bales. . .

"The Squalo was going beautifully, while the Mercedes was giving trouble and Fangio was struggling on, covered in oil and black dust. . . The pit signalled each lap to tell me what the gap was between Fangio and I, but towards the end the Mercedes began to trail a smokescreen and was beaten into second place by Musso's Maserati. So I won my second Grand Prix for Ferrari, Ugolini kissed me on both cheeks and I got a fantastic reception from the crowd."

Trintignant's Ferrari 625 and Villoresi in the other Lancia D50 were also retirements at Barcelona, but the outcome of the race was none the less quite significant. It finally proved that the hitherto troublesome Ferrari 553 could be massaged into a Grand Prix winner and it underlined that Lancia's new D50 would be a most formidable weapon with which to tackle the 1955 season. In the long-run, however, neither of the "signs" indicated by that 1954 Spanish Grand Prix result ever fully manifested itself in hard reality. Before much longer, there were to be some unbelievable twists and turns of fate within the world of Italian motor racing.

For 1955 opposition to Ferrari was further consolidated when Mercedes-Benz signed Stirling Moss to partner Fangio.

As far as Maranello was concerned, Mike Hawthorn was lost from the line-up (albeit briefly, as it was to work out!) as he felt that driving for the British based

At the start of the 1955 season, the Lancia D50s seemed set to realize the promise demonstrated by Ascari at Barcelona the previous autumn. Here Ascari's D50 (No.6) awaits to start the Naples Grand Prix at Posillipo from pole position. In the absence of any works Ferraris, Alberto won comfortably from the Maserati 250F of Luigi Musso.

Twilight for the 625s: the continued unreliability and lack of driver acceptance of the type 555 "Super Squalos" meant that the 625s raced on well into 1955. Left, a shirt sleeved Umberto Maglioli, driving relief for Farina, heads for third place in the sweltering Argentine Grand Prix at Buenos Aires. Below, kicking up the dust and scowling with displeasure, a below-par Mike Hawthorn is seen on the 625's last championship outing, the 1955 British Grand Prix at Aintree. Feeling unwell, the Englishman handed this machine over to Eugenio Castellotti to take through to sixth place.

Vanwall team would enable him to devote more time to his family's Farnham garage business following the death of his father in a road accident earlier in 1954. Trintignant and Farina formed the core of Ferrari's driver line-up and the fact that the even *further* revised Squalo was held back from the season's first race in Buenos Aires on January 30 meant that these "reliable", rather than inspired, drivers would have to drive cars which mirrored similar qualities.

Ranged against the Mercedes-Benz W196s and Lancia D50s, Ferrari's Argentine challenge centred round two-year-old 625 chassis which were now sporting coil spring and wishbone front suspension as successfully tried on the 553 at Barcelona. The de Dion rear end was retained, but the transverse leaf spring was repositioned above the differential and a five-speed gearbox was also installed. In typically torrid Argentine summer weather, the revamped 625s with their 100 × 79.5mm engines were no match for the Mercedes/Fangio combination and Juan-Manuel raced to another victory in conditions which saw temperatures of 52°C (125°F!) recorded. Moss made it a W196 one-two, but Trintignant did a good job of squeezing out Kling to prevent a Stuttgart 1-2-3!

Once the European international season got under way, Ferrari took a deep breath yet again – and wheeled out the updated 553, now dubbed the 555 and nicknamed the "Super Squalo". This further revised version of Hawthorn's Barcelona winner made its first appearance at Turin's *Grand Prix del Valentino* on March 27, built round a completely new chassis frame which used smaller diameter tubing built up on the two main longerons, forming a secondary "superstructure" which carried the body, fuel tanks and final drive. Farina tried it once again in practice, but the experienced Italian elder statesman was far too set in his ways to adapt to its handling quirks and took a 625 for the race. At the end of the day, the best-placed Ferrari was Harry Schell's 625, three laps down in fifth place, and with Ascari, Villoresi and Castellotti scoring a tremendous 1-2-3 success the writing was very clearly on the wall for Ferrari. It spelt "LANCIA" and nobody at Maranello was very pleased about this state of affairs, to say the least!

After the Turin fiasco Ferrari missed the Pau Grand Prix in Central southern France, a race almost won by Ascari after another crushing demonstration from the Lancia D50, and when two type 555s turned up for the Bordeaux Grand Prix on April 24, both cars retired from the 123 lap, 302km race on the "T-shaped" road circuit. Trintignant had brake troubles and Farina's 555 broke its gearbox, thereby leaving the way open for another humiliating defeat, this time a Maserati 1-2-3-4 headed by Jean Behra. Ferrari once more returned to his lair to fume quietly after these two defeats, at the same time working his technical staff at a ferocious pace in preparation for Monaco. The fact that Lancia notched up another victory during his short absence from the Italian domestic scene, Ascari's D50 bagging the Naples Grand Prix on May 8 from Luigi Musso's Maserati, did little to improve the highly-charged atmosphere at Maranello.

Frankly, however, Ferrari's Formula 1 effort was, at this time, busy going nowhere. It seemed honestly unbelievable that the team still had to hedge its bets with the old 625 in the Monaco classic on May 22 – and even more amazing when Trintignant's smooth, reliable style rewarded this technically outclassed car with another Grand Prix victory. Two 625s had been taken to the Mediterranean street circuit, modified only by the addition of bigger brakes, the other car being driven by Farina. Two 555s were on hand and were entrusted to Harry Schell and Piero Taruffi for this race. From the start, Monaco had looked as though it would be another Mercedes-Benz demonstration run – the fastest Ferrari was Trintignant's 625 down on the fourth row!

However, despite Fangio and Moss quickly assuming 1-2 formation, the Argentinian's W196 broke its transmission at half distance (50 laps) and Moss vanished from the lead on lap 81 when the engine failed. Ascari's Lancia D50 would have taken the lead if it had completed the lap it was on, but as Stirling's Mercedes coasted into the pits to retire, Ascari was hurtling into the harbour! He'd apparently locked up his Lancia's brakes as he went into the chicane, shot off the road and disappeared in a shower of spume and spray amidst the yachts and motor boats. Shaken, but unhurt, the Italian was rescued by frogmen (positioned there for just such an unlikely eventuality!) and was left to dry himself as Trintignant steadily cruised on to an unexpected victory. Castellotti's D50 finished second from the Behra/Perdisa Maserati 250F and the doggedly plodding Farina.

Schell's type 555 blew its engine apart spectacularly while Taruffi became so fed

Emotional moment. The formal handing over of the Lancia team assets to Ferrari took place in front of Italian Automobile Federation officials in the summer of 1955. Moustachioed Ferrari team manager Mino Amarotti can be seen in the group standing by two of the Lancia D50s (one still unpainted), immediately below the 'S' of the Scuderia Lancia lettering on the transporter.

up with his similar machine that he came into the pits and handed it over to the team's reserve driver Paul Frère to see if he could make any sense of it. Frère, an intelligent and perceptive driver who wasn't the quickest man around but understood chassis behaviour, had earlier attempted to make some helpful suggestions to Ing. Amarotti in a quest to improve the 555's handling.

"That car was a real beast to handle round Monaco," recalled Frère, "as it just wanted to plough straight on at the two tight hairpins. I hinted that it might be a good idea to disconnect the front anti-roll bar, but Amarotti was responsible for technical matters at the races and I'm sure he was really upset by my suggestion. He did not want to take the responsibility for modifying something which was part of the original design – for which he was not responsible. If he *had* taken my advice and then something had gone wrong, he most certainly would have been held responsible for it back at the factory. He just wasn't prepared to do it."

By the time the Formula 1 circus reassembled at Spa for the 36 lap Belgian Grand Prix on June 5, its world had been touched by an ironic tragedy. Ascari, who had emerged from that watery excursion at Monaco with little more than a cut nose and bruises, had been killed a few days later in a banal testing accident at the wheel of Castellotti's sports Ferrari at Monza. For Lancia it was a shattering body-blow following so closely on that year of expense and endeavour developing

the D50 design: now, when it seemed as though they were on the verge of great success, one of their most crucial assets had been snatched away.

Gianni Lancia had originally not wanted to field his team at Spa, but Eugenio Castellotti begged him to make available a single D50 for the Belgian race which the team owner eventually did. Clearly in a highly emotional, hyped-up state of mind, Castellotti was obviously out to "win this one for Alberto's memory" and there were more than a few worried faces in the pits as the volatile Italian set off to practise on this spectacularly quick track. But Eugenio did a fine job for the Turin marque, planting the D50 on pole position during the first day's practice and retaining it through the second after rain thwarted Fangio's Mercedes counter-attack.

Ferrari brought a trio of type 555s to this race, along with a lone 625, and the Super Squalos ended the weekend on a quite optimistic note with Farina and Frere coming home third and fourth behind the Fangio-Moss Mercedes steamroller. Castellotti's Lancia efforts were impressive during the race: he hung on well in third place for 15 laps before the Italian V8 expired.

By this time, financial problems were weighing heavily on Gianni Lancia's shoulders in addition to his sorrow over the death of his number one driver. After the Spa race he decided that he was faced with no real alternative but to withdraw from Grand Prix racing and the Lancia company eventually passed into the control of Cav. Carlo Pesenti, a rich Italian cement magnate. But this sad decision was by no means to mark the end of the Lancia D50's racing career.

On the basis that every misfortune can provide a corresponding streak of good luck to somebody else, a deal was struck whereby Fiat stumped up an amazing £30,000 a year, (or thereabouts), for Ferrari to take over the D50 project and continue the Formula 1 fight for the honour of Italy against the might of Germany. Enzo Ferrari must have thought it was Christmas, and he played the emotional aspect of the situation for all it was worth, painting a picture of his team as a tiny little organization fighting on behalf of its country against the complete German industrial machine. This wasn't *quite* the case, of course, but Fiat obviously felt the project was worthwhile!

On July 26, 1955 the formal hand over of six D50s, spares, drawings, tools and a host of other equipment took place before representatives of the Italian Automobile Federation. Vittorio Jano and Luigi Bazzi moved across to Maranello with the D50 project and, all in all, bearing in mind the pressure of competition against the four-cylinder Formula 1 Ferraris in 1955, this free hand-out could hardly have been more timely. In reality, it could also be regarded as a massive vote of no-confidence in Lampredi's cars, and he left Ferrari to join Fiat on the road car side shortly afterwards after making an abortive attempt to salvage his reputation by designing an experimental two-cylinder Grand Prix engine and a six-cylinder to replace the 555. The two-cylinder unit was conceived on the basis that if a four-cylinder developed lots of torque for use on tight circuits, then this would be even better. It seems a somewhat idiosyncratic approach in retrospect, but Ferrari was obviously ready to be convinced by Lampredi, for this 118 × 114mm, 2493cc vertical twin cylinder unit, with four valves per cylinder, was actually built in prototype form. Whether it would have reliably realized its claimed 175bhp at 4800rpm is another matter: Lampredi's other design, the 82.4 × 78mm, in-line six cylinder engine never progressed beyond the drawing board.

Meanwhile, the type 555s were still struggling. At the Dutch Grand Prix, held at Zandvoort on June 19, Fangio and Moss enacted another 1-2 demonstration run with the open-wheeled Mercedes W196s. Castellotti and Hawthorn were now included within the Ferrari ranks, the Italian having simply been recruited when Lancia withdrew, while Hawthorn's availability came as a result of his getting involved in a disagreement with Tony Vandervell at Spa. He agreed that it would be best if he left the Vanwall team and had actually accepted an offer from Lancia shortly before they withdrew. He was welcomed into the Ferrari fold once again, for although Enzo might not have appreciated his defection at the end of the previous season, he needed all the good drivers he could get his hands on in the

Process of evolution. After the takeover of the Lancia D50s, Ferrari quickly altered its design in line with his own theories. On the left, an "original" D50 with its fuel carried in the side panniers. On the right, the vestigial panniers are now faired in between the wheels and contain only the exhaust pipes. The fuel had been moved to a tail tank, with a reserve tank attached to the side of the main chassis frame.

middle of 1955.

Hawthorn's reacquaintance with the revised Super Squalo didn't leave him unduly impressed, but he got the 555 on to row two and held fifth place during the early stages of the race before a quick pit stop to investigate a troublesome gear-change dropped him to seventh. Castellotti was fifth, but Trintignant retired with gearbox problems.

Unfortunately, by this time there were only two World Championship Grands Prix left on the international calendar. A few weeks earlier Pierre Levegh's Mercedes-Benz hurtled into the crowd at Le Mans, this tragedy not only killed more than 80 onlookers, it also resulted in the sudden cancellation of the French, German, Swiss and Spanish Grands Prix. In due course, three of those races were to return to the international calendar, but that was the end of all serious motor racing in Switzerland.

For the British Grand Prix at Aintree on July 6, there was some more Ferrari back-tracking as the trusty 625s were dragged into the limelight yet again. It was felt that the older cars would be more at home on the "tight" Liverpool circuit, but they were never remotely in the hunt on a day which saw Fangio allow Moss to win his home Grand Prix for Mercedes-Benz. With the German cars filling the first four places, it was left for Ferrari and Maserati to jostle over the crumbs: in Maranello's case that meant sixth place for Hawthorn, who was feeling unwell, and thus handed his 625 over to Castellotti in the second half of the race.

The Italian Grand Prix at Monza on September 11 saw the return to the scene of the Lancia D50's, now dubbed Lancia-Ferrari by most observers of the scene, even though this nomenclature quickly became a source of considerable irritation to the Commendatore, who would have liked the car's Lancia parentage buried once and for all. It was frustrating to have one's team honour saved by what amounted to a free hand-out of bankrupt stock from another manufacturer and the Lancia name was a perpetual reminder that the Turin firm had been able to produce a far better car at its first attempt in Formula 1 than Ferrari had managed with all his accumulated experience.

Although the Lancia D50s were to quickly become regarded as the Ferrari team's front-line cars, the Super Squalos were to demonstrate much-improved form at Monza. Whilst Jano worked away on his D50 project, former Maserati and Alfa Romeo engineer Alberto Massimino helped sort out the type 555's handling quirks and, equipped with a new five-speed gearbox, the Super Squalo had developed into quite a pleasant car by the time it appeared for what was its final race. But it was now pretty clear that 2-litres had been about the limit for Lampredi's four-cylinder engine in terms of obtaining the maximum possible specific output, and the 2.5-litre four-cylinder Ferrari was raced only once again after the 1955 Italian Grand Prix.

Frankly,however, that Monza race was a fiasco. There were three powerful Lancia-Ferraris on hand for Farina, Castellotti and Villoresi, plus a trio of further-modified Super Squalos for Hawthorn, Trintignant and Umberto Maglioli. The D50s were fast, competitive with the Mercedes-W196s and obviously capable of giving Italy a win on home ground – except that there was one major problem. The D50 had been designed in conjunction with Pirelli tyres and now it had to run on rubber from the Belgian Englebert company, to whom Ferrari was contracted, the V8-engined machines were throwing treads left, right and centre on the bumpy Monza bankings.

Castellotti summoned up all his reserves of patriotic courage to qualify his D50 fourth on the inside of row two, but the decision was eventually made to withdraw the Lancia-Ferraris from the race. Some consideration was given to running them on Pirelli rubber, but Englebert's representatives began murmuring about legal action and the whole idea quietly died a death. Race officials permitted Castellotti to start from his second row position in a substitute spare Super Squalo and, determined to do well on home ground, the Italian drove magnificently in front of an adoring, ecstatic crowd. He got that Super Squalo in amongst the Mercedes-Benz squad during those opening laps and, driving his heart out, finally finished a stupendous third. Fangio and Taruffi took the first two places for Mercedes, while Hawthorn's Super Squalo retired with broken gearbox mountings after Mike had spent many laps wrestling with a worrying vibration. Maglioli was sixth, Trintignant eighth, while the withdrawal of the D50s left Farina and Villoresi without a drive.

The season was rounded off by Hawthorn and Castellotti turning up to drive their Englebert-shod Lancia-Ferraris in the Oulton Park Gold Cup, Mike taking pole during practice but being beaten conclusively in the race by Stirling Moss who had been loaned a Maserati 250F for the occasion. Admittedly Mike had been feeling unwell again, this time through after-effects of tonsilitis, but he outclassed his team-mate who suffered steering problems and could only finish seventh.

Experimental handful. Just to check out that he was on the right lines, Ferrari fitted a Lancia V8 engine to this type 555 Squalo for the 1956 Argentine Grand Prix. Olivier Gendebien wrestled the beast to fifth place, but wasn't impressed . . .

Section III: 2½-litre heyday, 1954-60

Chapter 2
Fangio's Ferrari Championship

With Mercedes-Benz withdrawing from the Formula 1 scene at the end of 1955, Juan-Manuel Fangio found himself thrown together with Ferrari for 1956. It was to be a successful year-long relationship, but one which seldom gave rise to much personal warmth away from the circuits. The bare, historical facts of the matter record that Fangio became World Champion for the fourth time at the wheel of a Lancia-Ferrari in 1956. But he didn't get on with Enzo Ferrari on a personal level and it's not really clear why.

"At the end of 1955 I considered the possibility of retiring," Fangio was later to reflect, "but the Argentine Government had fallen during the summer and there were great changes going on in my country. In fact things began to go not-so-well in Argentina, so I decided to postpone my retirement for another year. As Mercedes-Benz had withdrawn, I returned to Europe to race with Ferrari in 1956, but I wasn't very happy about it.

"Since I first raced in Europe I had always been in a team opposing Ferrari. Now I was joining him, with Castellotti, Musso and Collins. But he would never say who was to be number one driver, although the younger men told me 'Juan, you are the leader'.

"Ferrari was a hard man. His team raced in every category and his drivers drove always for *him*. He wanted victory primarily for his cars and this suited my attitude, because I never raced solely for myself, but for the team as a whole. But a driver must have a good relationship with his mechanics and I found this rather difficult to achieve within the Ferrari team. I suppose it was because I had been their opposition for so many years and now here I was as their driver."

Notwithstanding the fact that Ferrari had Fangio on his team strength for 1956, there was some pretty strong potential competition with Moss at Maserati and both BRM and Vanwall making obvious progress. Over the winter therefore, Ferrari gave a great deal of thought to the best chassis/engine combination it could concoct from the enormous amount of equipment at its disposal. At the end of the day it proved to be a continuation of the Lancia-Ferrari development, but not before a whole host of new ideas were tried in Argentina at the start of the year.

Only Ferrari and Maserati made the trip to Buenos Aires for the first Grand Prix of the season on January 22, both BRM and Vanwall waiting for the start of the European season before opening their 1956 challenges. Ferrari fielded one "standard" D50 for Castellotti and a slightly modified car with a much larger tail fuel tank, small reserve tank in the panniers and exhaust pipes exiting through the rear section of the panniers for Luigi Musso. Fangio was allocated a car to this latter specification, but also fitted with a re-positioned rear transverse leaf spring above the rear axle assembly (rather than below it, as on the original Lancia)

The Modena airfield circuit was the scene of most of Ferrari's testing in the fifties and sixties. Here Ferrari mechanics Cassani (left) and Parenti, tend lovingly to a Lancia-Ferrari D50 early in 1956.

incorporating vane-type Houdaille shock absorbers at the rear instead of the original telescopic ones. There were also longitudinal bracing tubes on either side of the engine bay as Ferrari didn't like the semi-stressed engine installation. This proved to be the most successful "recipe" to emerge from the Argentine experimentation and all subsequent Lancia-Ferrari derivatives evolved from this concept.

Just to cross-check that he was making progress in the correct direction, a straightforward type 555 Super Squalo was on hand for new recruit Peter Collins and a fearsome Lancia V8-engined Super Squalo with which Olivier Gendebien wrestled his way gamely home to fifth place. At the end of the day Fangio won his home Grand Prix, but suffered engine trouble with his originally allocated car and had to take over Musso's machine during the course of the race. Behra was second for the Maserati works team with Hawthorn, driving the Owen Organization's Maserati 250F in the absence of the BRM he'd signed to drive that season, finishing third.

Fangio sealed his new partnership with Ferrari by taking another victory in the non-Championship Mendoza Grand Prix on February 5, before the team headed back to Europe for an intensive racing schedule which began at Syracuse on April 15. For that domestic Italian race, Ferrari fielded four D50s, all to the successful "Argentine" specification, but one featuring even more modifications with the panniers dispensed with and the reserve tanks fitted to the chassis frame directly. Full-width bodywork was fitted to "fair in" the gaps between the wheels and it looked outwardly as though the panniers were still contained within the bodywork: they were not, in fact, and the bodywork between the wheels contained nothing but exhaust pipes.

Fangio drove this new model to victory at Syracuse, although he says that Musso had found out that the new Argentine government was making things financially difficult for him and persuaded his team-mates to let him win without much trouble because he was "in need of the money". Musso finished second at Syracuse ahead of Collins, while Castellotti blotted his copybook by spinning into retirement, damaging his D50's steering against a brick wall.

Up to this point in the season Ferrari hardly seemed able to make a wrong move. In addition to his Formula 1 successes, his cars had won sports races at Agadir, Dakar and Sebring as well as prestigious home triumphs in the Giro Sicilia and the Mille Miglia. But on the weekend of May 5/6, 1956, it all went badly wrong. . .

That weekend, Ferrari divided his forces. He sent Fangio and Collins to Silverstone for the BRDC International Trophy on Saturday, and local tyros Musso and Castellotti to Naples for the 60-lap 13th *Gran Premio Napoli* at the Posilippo circuit on Sunday. The two machines at Silverstone were fitted with separate fuel tanks and, while great things were naturally expected from the two Ferrari drivers, the fast-rising Vanwalls were now becoming serious threats which couldn't be ignored. What's more, with Moss loaned from Maserati to handle a Vanwall at Silverstone, the English cars' chances were further enhanced. Moss qualified on pole flanked by team-mate Harry Schell and Hawthorn's BRM was third before Fangio squeezed on to the outside of row one.

Fangio managed to get off the line first, but Hawthorn was almost immediately through in the BRM and when Mike retired on lap 14 it was Stirling's Vanwall which was sitting in second place, ready to take over at the front. Moss's precision driving was more than a match for Fangio on this occasion and by the time his Lancia-Ferrari's clutch failed on lap 21, the World Champion was almost a full minute adrift. Despite taking over Collins's car, clutch failure intervened again for the Argentinian and Moss sailed on to lap the field.

However, the Lancia-Ferraris went down with Fangio fighting to an honourable defeat at Silverstone – at least by the standards of the débâcle which was enacted the following day 1500 miles away in sun-soaked Italy. Ferrari's two entries at this race included an "all-enclosed" Lancia-Ferrari with new independent rear suspension, allotted to Castellotti, while Musso drove a regular car. The independent rear suspension didn't find much favour with Castellotti and, when it came to the race, he was in to retire with no oil pressure after a mere two laps. Musso, who had started from pole, got as far as lap 37 in the lead only to suffer engine failure and return to the pits on foot. Victory fell to Robert Manzon's French Gordini!

On May 13, the 100 lap Monaco Grand Prix saw what most people regarded as an uncharacteristically ragged performance by the great Fangio, but one which Juan-Manuel himself regards as "possibly my greatest drive . . . perhaps even better than the Nürburgring in 1957." Ferrari produced five cars to be shared between Fangio, Musso, Castellotti and Collins, two of which had separate side-pods and three fully faired-in bodywork. Although Fangio managed to take pole for this gruelling race, Moss thrust his works Maserati 250F into an immediate lead at the start and sped confidently away to one of the most masterly triumphs of his career. To quote Denis Jenkinson in *Motor Sport*, when confronted with the sight of the jostling, weaving, jousting colourful pack jinking its way through the sunlit streets at the end of the first lap, "everybody seemed to be going completely mad, except Moss, who was well out on his own, looking smooth and relaxed. . ."

Fangio spun going into *Ste. Devote* on lap two, and in an untypically inconsiderate return to the fray managed to send not only Schell's Vanwall into retirement, but also Luigi Musso's Lancia-Ferrari into the straw bales and out of the race! The battle then settled down with Collins in second place and a ruthless Fangio elbowing his way back into contention, treating team-mates and rivals alike in the most uncompromising style when it came to overtaking them. During the course of this seemingly frantic recovery, he hit a wall at *Tabac* with the right rear wheel, breaking the location of the de Dion tube with the result that when he took

At the wheel of a Lancia-Ferrari D50 taken over from team-mate Luigi Musso, Fangio heads for victory in the 1956 Argentine Grand Prix at Buenos Aires. Note that the filler cap in the tail hadn't been closed properly at a pit stop.

left-hand corners, there was only the strength of the rear suspension radius rods locating it. This drama made the car's handling distinctly odd and, having "used up" this car, Fangio came in and handed what was left of his Lancia-Ferrari to Castellotti: after a brief rest he then took over Collins's second-place car to take through to the finish, working himself up into a crescendo of gifted effort and setting the race's fastest lap on the 100th and final tour. He finished a mere 6.1s behind Moss, with Behra third for Maserati and Castellotti's tattered Lancia-Ferrari "wreck" struggling home fourth!

For the Belgian Grand Prix at Spa on June 3, all five Lancia-Ferraris featured full-width bodywork and it was here that the Moss/Fangio battle really got into its stride, the young Englishman now capitalizing on everything he'd learned alongside the Old Man the previous year when they'd been together at Mercedes-Benz. The Lancia D50 had been on pole position the previous year thanks to Castellotti's brave effort, the Italian managing a 4m 18.1s lap, so when Fangio started out with a 4m 17.4s in 1956, everybody sat up and took very serious notice. Then Moss responded with a 4m 14.7s in his Maserati, but Fangio put the whole issue beyond debate with a 4m 10.7s – and then a stupendous 4m 09.8s to throw pole position well beyond the aspirations of his rivals!

With BRM not entering this race, Hawthorn got himself into a bit of a personal muddle, having tacitly accepted offers from both Maserati and Ferrari for Spa, so he eventually deemed it tactful to accept neither drive and withdrew from the meeting. This allowed Paul Frere to take the place of the injured Luigi Musso and the Belgian certainly impressed everybody once the race got under way.

At the start of the race Moss took the lead from Castellotti and Fangio, but by lap five Fangio was through into a lead he kept all the way to lap 24 in the 26 lap event when he coasted to a halt at Stavelot with transmission trouble. Moss by this time had lost a wheel and taken over Perdisa's 250F, so the net result was a win for the conscientious Collins – who had already relinquished his car twice to Fangio prior to the Belgian Grand Prix and was to do so again before the end of the year – while Frere was a good second and Moss third.

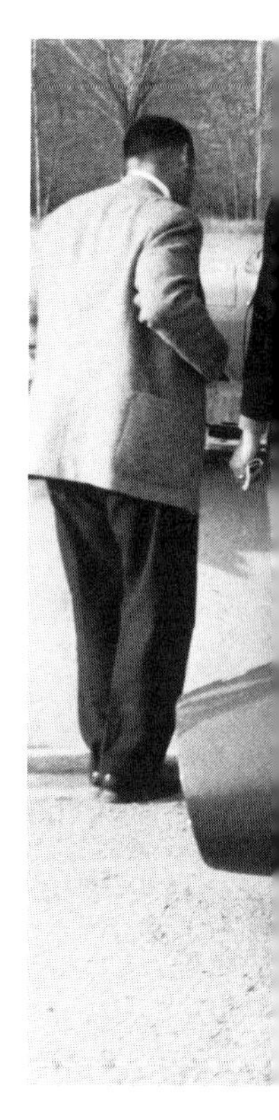

Peter Collins prepares to climb into a Lancia-Ferrari D50 for some laps round Modena, Spring, 1956.

Looking back on the Lancia-Ferrari D50s, Frere tends to feel that they would have been better cars if they'd been left in their original Lancia guise – without pandering to the whims of the drivers by compromising their high road holding ability in an effort to make them more progressive-handling. "I rather agree with those who say that Ferrari's revamping of the Lancia D50 was mechanical heresy," he recalled, "after all, the side tanks of the original D50 which maintained the weight distribution little altered over a race distance were certainly a better solution than having most of the fuel hanging out at the back. When all these cars were handed over to Ferrari the design was very new, and I think that if Jano had been allowed to go ahead with his original development, the D50 might have become a better and longer-lasting machine than the Ferrari version." The fact that the cars were so modified despite the fact that Jano had been retained as a design consultant perhaps points to some friction and disagreement between the former Lancia designer and established Ferrari engineer, Vittorio Bellentani.

There was another fright awaiting the Lancia-Ferraris on the super-fast Reims-Gueux circuit on July 1, the champagne country road circuit which had previously been used for the French Grand Prix two years earlier. Reims is the home of speed, and the aerodynamically efficient Frank Costin-designed profiles of the Vanwalls were clearly set to reap some worthwhile benefits on this high-speed track. Mike Hawthorn and Colin Chapman joined Schell in the Vanwall line-up for this race, but a practice collision between the first-mentioned pair of drivers meant that only Hawthorn joined Schell to race against the Lancia-Ferraris in the Grand Prix. Maranello fielded D50 derivatives handled by Fangio, Castellotti, Collins, Olivier Gendebien and the extrovert Spanish aristocrat, "Fon" de Portago (Musso was still convalescing from his Nürburgring sports car shunt).

Five Lancia-Ferraris were on hand including a specially-developed "streamliner" with all-enveloping bodywork which was tried by Castellotti during practice,

but proved so "spooky" in cross-winds that the Italian driver hurriedly brought it back into the pits. It later re-emerged with its tail fairing removed, and although it felt more comfortable, it wasn't any quicker than the regular cars so it was shelved for the remainder of the weekend.

Fangio, Castellotti and Collins wrapped up the front row, but Schell was lurking behind them on the second row alongside a gap where his team-mate Chapman should have been. Giving impetus to the proceedings was the fabulous £10,000 first prize put up by BP, and at the end of the opening lap it was the trio of of Shell-fuelled Lancia-Ferraris of Castellotti, Fangio and Collins leading the field with Schell in furious pursuit from fourth place. On lap two, sadly, the best-placed Vanwall dropped back with gearbox problems, losing second, and eventually the Franco-American driver missed a gear and crept in to retire after lap six with a badly damaged engine.

This left Mike Hawthorn in fourth place with the other Vanwall, but he was very tired after driving the 12-hour sports car race for Jaguar and was quickly dropping out of contention. On lap 11 Vanwall called him in and Schell took over: he resumed, driving brilliantly, some 42s behind the Lancia-Ferrari threesome. Thanks to an amazing lack of attention on the part of Ferrari's pit crew, Maranello's drivers were lulled into thinking that Schell was a full lap behind: there was no warning forthcoming because the Italian pit hadn't noticed that Hawthorn had been called in to give his car to his team-mate!

On lap 20 he was only 28s behind the Lancia-Ferrari threesome and, by lap 28 he was right on the Italian cars' tail, they now realized that he was on the same lap as them and the battle royal began! The three Italian cars pulled every trick in the book to block Schell's Vanwall, running side-by-side on the straights, easing off slightly whilst running two-abreast, but the English car was obviously a match for the Lancia-Ferraris and Fangio, Castellotti and Collins had their work cut out in a big way. Schell actually managed to get himself briefly up to second place behind

Precarious proposition. Eugenio Castellotti tries out the "streamlined" Lancia-Ferrari D50 during practice for the 1956 French Grand Prix at Reims-Gueux. It proved a real handful in crosswinds and wasn't used in the race.

Fangio, but once the Lancia-Ferraris began working together as a team there was really nothing he could do. It was a great day for British motor racing enthusiasts, but it ended on lap 38 when Schell's Vanwall pulled into the pits with a broken ball joint on the linkage to the fuel injection pump.

Hardly had Fangio breathed a sigh of relief than he was in trouble with a split fuel line, so on lap 40 he pulled into the pits for attention. In typically vague and uncertain style, the Ferrari pit wasn't showing its drivers which lap they were on, but Collins was keeping his eye out for rival pit signals and was ahead at the lap 50 mark – at which point it was ordained whoever was ahead would stay there until the end. Thus Collins won from Castellotti, Behra's Maserati and the brilliant Fangio who came hurtling back after his pit stop to set the fastest lap of the race before the finish.

By this time Jano had revamped the dimensions of the Lancia-designed V8 to 76 × 68.5mm for a total capacity of 2487cc, the engine now producing in the region of 280bhp, 20bhp more than the best four-cylinder Super Squalo had ever done. But the Lancia-Ferrari chassis still hadn't really developed into a particularly progressive machine to handle and this point was emphasized pretty dramatically during the British Grand Prix at Silverstone, a 101 lap event held in dry, dull summer weather on July 14. Fangio wasn't feeling particularly well either, and pictures taken at the time show a joyless scowl on his face for the entire race.

"I had a fever," he later explained, "the doctors didn't want me to race, but the organizers insisted, so they gave me a pill and I waited for the fever to go down. It

did and I raced, but afterwards I felt dead. It was the first and only time I won in England."

As much as for Fangio's hard-fought victory, this race will be remembered for the impressive performance of the four-cylinder BRMs during the opening stages. Hawthorn and Brooks accelerated into the lead at the start, and although Fangio quickly caught and passed Brooks, he found himself falling foul of the Lancia-Ferrari's unpredictable handling and himself spun at Becketts. Moss then got into his stride with the pole-winning works Maserati 250F, pushing through to second place and eventually demoting Hawthorn from the lead after 15 laps. This made the order Moss-Hawthorn-Salvadori (driving brilliantly at the wheel of the Gilby Engineering Maserati)-Fangio, but the Argentinian, surprisingly, wasn't even making much ground on the Englishman immediately in front of him.

Hawthorn retired after 23 laps with grease oozing out of a transmission joint and this left Moss in complete control of the situation. Brooks made a quick pit stop to fix a troublesome throttle linkage and then resumed only to up-end the BRM at Abbey Curve and be carried off to hospital with a broken jaw, cuts and abrasions: the BRM, which had suffered a mechanical malfunction, burnt itself out in the middle of the track "which was the best possible thing that could happen to that particular motor car," according to Brooks. This experience was to have a salutary long-term effect on his approach to race driving: thereafter he adopted an intelligently prudent attitude towards dealing with damaged or mechanically suspect cars – a factor which was to influence his behaviour as a Ferrari driver three years later. Possibly, it would cost him a World Championship. . .

Later in the race Salvadori found himself delayed by a broken tank retaining strap, dropping from contention before eventually retiring his Maserati with fuel starvation problems. So it seemed that Stirling Moss would cruise home easily to his second straight British Grand Prix win, for Fangio's Lancia-Ferrari was clearly in no position to challenge his Maserati. Alas, on lap 69 Moss dropped from the lead after suffering a sudden loss of power, pulled into the pits for attention and eventually resumed a lap and a half behind Fangio in second place, but ahead of Collins who had retired his original Lancia-Ferrari with engine trouble and taken Fon de Portago's car which felt much more powerful and nicer-handling than his original mount.

Obviously Moss wasn't going to win, but after a brief further stop for more oil,

Team formation. Fangio leads Castellotti and Collins through Thillois during the early stages of the 1956 French Grand Prix. Few pictures taken of Fangio during that season show him smiling much . . .

the Maserati's gearbox broke with only eight laps to go and Stirling was to be denied even a helping of World Championship points. So Fangio was thus allowed a convincing victory ahead of team-mate Collins, Behra's Maserati and Jack Fairman's Connaught. Portago was put into Castellotti's car at a late stop after the Italian had pulled in to have a wheel examined after he'd damaged it during a spin. The car had damaged an axle, however, and de Portago didn't make it to the finish, stopping just before the line before pushing the car past the flag at the end of the race.

After the débâcle for BRM and Vanwall at Silverstone, Ferrari and Maserati were left to wage an all-Italian battle in the German Grand Prix at Nürburgring on August 5, only the interloping Gordinis of André Milhoux and Robert Manzon breaking up their ranks in a small way. There were five Lancia-Ferraris on hand for Fangio, Collins, Castellotti, Portago and Musso (making his return to the cockpit after his shunt during the 1000kms sports car race at this circuit earlier in the year). All five cars were to "standardized" specification first seen at Syracuse.

The Lancia-Ferrari squad encountered a bit of a set-back on the first day when de Portago found himself baffled by his slow lap times until it became apparent that his car's chassis had fractured at the rear end adjacent to the shock absorber mountings. That meant stripping all the other four cars for inspection and welding on gusset plates to prevent the problem repeating itself – this was the D50's first visit to the 'Ring, of course.

After the disappointment over the car's handling on the wide open spaces at Silverstone, the Lancia-Ferraris were just the job round the twisting Nürburgring, the V8 engine's torque characteristics being spot-on for this difficult track. Fangio qualified on pole with a 9m 51.2s, a mere 0.2s faster than Collins – phenomenally close by the standards of the day – while Castellotti did a 9m 54.4s and, although Moss squeezed his Maserati on to fourth place, he couldn't break the ten minute barrier.

Collins made a frantic getaway at the start, but Fangio was quickly through into the lead with Moss moving up to challenge Collins until they got round as far as *Döttinger-Hohe*, from which point the two Lancia-Ferraris streaked away from the Maserati as they came back along the undulating straight towards the start/finish area. Castellotti had an early spin down to the tail of the field as he tried to displace Moss from second place, and from that moment onwards it looked as though the race would turn out to be a Fangio-Collins demonstration run.

Amongst the other Lancia-Ferrari drivers there was a good deal of swapping around, with Castellotti coming in to retire with loss of power due to a faulty magneto. He was instructed to take over from Musso, who obviously wasn't having a particularly happy time with his recently-healed arm, and when Luigi was called in to hand over to his compatriot he arrived in the pit lane at precisely the same time that Collins drew up, nearly unconscious from a fuel leak caused by the handbrake cable chafing through a fuel line!

For a few moments there was a delightfully Italian pantomime enacted in the Ferrari pit as Castellotti mistakenly jumped into Collins's car then, realizing his error, jumped out just as quickly and climbed into Musso's machine. Meanwhile de Portago had driven through to a comfortable fourth place, so after a short while in the pits to recover, Collins took over the Spaniard's car and moved up to third place. Unfortunately Collins's enthusiasm got the better of him as he strove to get on to terms with Moss's second-place Maserati and he spun off into the trees at *Hatzenbach*, emerging unhurt but unhappy from the damaged Italian machine.

With Castellotti spinning and stalling the car he'd taken over from Musso, there was now only one Lancia-Ferrari in the race, but it was in the right position and the meticulous Fangio broke the lap record as he won by almost a minute from his former Mercedes team-mate, now troubled with transmission bothers on his Maserati. As an interesting footnote, after the race de Portago, whether through pique that Collins had wasted the fruits of his labours, or simply through good-humoured mischief, told Peter that he ought to have pushed the Lancia-Ferrari back on to the circuit. In order to informally settle this dispute, the

British win! The chequered flag comes down for Peter Collins as the Englishman triumphs in the 1956 French Grand Prix by a matter of yards over team-mate Eugenio Castellotti.

two of them went off round the circuit to examine Fon's hypothesis a little further, only to find that it needed Peter's Ford Zephyr, a tow rope and many helping hands to retrieve the wayward Lancia-Ferrari!

On September 2, there were six Lancia-Ferraris on hand for the Grand Prix d'Europe at Monza with the usual five drivers nominated for their regular machines plus amiable German aristocrat Wolfgang von Trips who was brought along as the team's reserve driver. It was intended that von Trips should race the spare car if it survived practice intact, but he crashed heavily during practice at *Curva Grande*, fortunate to emerge unhurt from what was a huge accident. The rather crestfallen newcomer walked back to the pits and explained that the car suddenly veered out of control . . . a remark which prompted indulgent smiles from most of his team colleagues! The wrecked Lancia-Ferrari was shoved into one of the garages and not seriously examined until the Tuesday after the race. If only somebody had taken the trouble to look at it, closely, prior to the race, another Ferrari fiasco on home ground might well have been avoided.

The race turned into a repeat of the 1955 catalogue of disasters since Englebert *still* seemed unable to produce a sufficiently durable tyre that would withstand the strain of running round the bumpy Monza bankings. This time there were no Super Squalos to fall back on and Ferrari's cause was hardly aided by an irresponsible, blindly nationalistic battle between Castellotti and Musso which ended after only five laps with both cars coming into the pits with thrown left rear tyre treads. This battle for the lead arose *despite* the fact that both Fangio and Collins had experienced similar problems during practice and in the face of prudently generous suggestions from Fangio that they take it easy and conserve the cars in the opening stages of the race since he (Fangio) wasn't unduly interested in winning the race outright.

"Before the race I took Castellotti and Musso to one side and told them that one of them should win," explained Fangio, "it was sufficient for me to finish third: I

Ignoring all entreaties from their team, Englebert tyre technicians and even Fangio, Eugenio Castellotti and Luigi Musso threw themselves into an absurd, undisciplined battle during the early stages of the 1956 Italian Grand Prix at Monza. Their rubber didn't last long . . .

would still win the Championship. I said that if they didn't force the pace too much and sat behind me, I would move over ten laps from the finish and let them race to the flag.

"But they said they wanted to run the race their way. From the start they forced the pace like madmen, locking wheels under braking and spinning their tyres everywhere. I could see that neither of them would be there at the finish . . ."

The early delays inevitably suffered by the two Italian Ferrari drivers left the battle for the lead raging between Moss's Maserati and Schell's Vanwall, with Fangio and Collins keeping their fingers crossed in third and fourth places. After their Lancia-Ferraris had been fitted with new rear tyres, Castellotti and Musso were hurtling up through the field once again, spurred on by a mixture of national pride, lack of imagination, and adrenalin, but when Castellotti spun violently off into the barrier and out of the race, the only person in the entire autodrome who seemed surprised was Eugenio himself!

On lap 19 Fangio wobbled into the pits with a broken steering arm on his Lancia-Ferrari and when Collins came in for a precautionary tyre check (after an earlier failure) on lap 35, he unhesitatingly gave his car to Fangio in order to keep open the Argentinian's Championship aspirations. It was a generous, prompt gesture which attracted a deal of attention at the time, marking out Collins as a gentleman: the fact that he was a Ferrari team driver and was obliged to obey such an instruction from his team wasn't really the point. The nice thing about Collins's attitude was his *willingness* to oblige without any sort of debate, particularly when he was in with a chance of winning the Championship himself. Luigi Musso, incidentally, had earlier declined a similar suggestion that he might hand his car over to Fangio.

Mechanical problems eventually sidelined Schell's Vanwall after another highly promising run, leaving Moss's Maserati apparently untroubled in the lead. But on lap 45 Stirling's car began to cut out (a split fuel tank was found subsequently to be the cause) and it was only thanks to the Englishman's quick reactions that he made it back to the pits. He beckoned Piotti, who was driving a private Maserati, to push him round to the pits where his tank was duly topped up!

By then Musso had swept by into the lead and it seemed, with only four of the race's 50 laps left to run, that the pendulum of changing fortunes had finally swung towards the Ferrari team at the end of the day. But coming off the South Banking, Musso felt his steering go funny: the left-hand steering arm broke, a front tyre burst and he slid right across that enormous start/finish apron and just shuddered to a halt a few inches short of the pit counter. It was a bitter disappointment for the Italian ace and as the terrified Luigi was helped from the cockpit, he had to stand and watch Moss speed home to a somewhat fortunate victory for Maserati. Into second place came Fangio while the only other Lancia-Ferrari still running was eighth; Fangio's original car, now repaired, and handled for the rest of the afternoon by the dauntlessly enthusiastic, very brave and somewhat unimaginative Castellotti who hadn't so much as turned a hair after his early brush with disaster!

Of course, the bottom line to all these disasters at Monza came a few days after the race. Back at the factory mechanics stripped down von Trips's Lancia-Ferrari and found, almost inevitably, that one of the steering arms showed firm evidence of a pre-impact failure. If only they'd lent some credence to the young German driver's explanation of his sudden loss of control, the Ferrari team might well have spared itself enormous heartache. It was understandable if they didn't set too much store by the apparent excuses of a novice Formula 1 driver, but it turned out to be an expensive and unfortunate lesson for the team to learn.

So Fangio emerged as World Champion again and the Lancia-Ferraris had managed to win five of the seven races which counted for the title. On paper it was a pretty impressive demonstration, but if one looks at the team's performance more closely it was really a rather indifferent record. Fangio's win at Buenos Aires and his crucial second places at Monaco and Monza had been achieved only by the Argentinian appropriating a second car after his first broke down, while the records of his team-mates, with the notably impressive exception of Peter Collins, weren't much to write home about. And, of course, one is bound to ask just who the Lancia-Ferrari squad was beating?

Answer? Only Maserati's works team in reality, with Stirling Moss turning out to be Fangio's most formidable rival from the point of view of driving ability. Vanwall's challenge had yet to burst into full flower, although the writing was by 1956 well and truly on the wall, but neither they nor the BRM team contested every race in the Championship. Apart from that there was just Gordini and a few quite effective Maserati privateers. At the end of the day, the world's best racing driver had won Ferrari another World Championship, but he was aided by the very low level of opposition ranged against the cars from Maranello throughout 1956.

SERVIZI
ELETTRAUTO
22

Section III: 2½-litre heyday, 1954-60

Chapter 3
Marking time as an also-ran

Crucial début. The 1957 Modena Grand Prix weekend marked the début of the "enlarged" F2 Dinos, sealing the fate of the older Lancia-Ferrari based cars. In the Modena pit lane, mechanics work on the engine of Musso's machine while Collins's car stands in the foreground.

The following season, 1957, would be very much worse for Ferrari. Fangio decided to have one glorious final year in the cockpit, but opted for what he found were more congenial surroundings at Maserati to do so. Moss left Maserati and, together with Tony Brooks, joined the Vanwall line-up to make it clear that Britain at last had a Grand Prix team worth considering. Maserati also had Jean Behra on hand as Fangio's team-mate. And Ferrari?

Well, Peter Collins had proved to the Commendatore's satisfaction that he was worth keeping in the team and this young son of a Kidderminster motor trader was joined by the easy-going Mike Hawthorn, now returning for an unparalleled *third* stint with the Prancing Horse. Given Enzo Ferrari's rather ambivalent attitude towards drivers generally, one is bound to wonder why the Old Man had such an obvious affection for Mike. It may have been because of his youthful victory at Reims back in 1953, or perhaps because of his splendid, morale-boosting triumph with the revised Squalo at Barcelona the following year – or simply because Hawthorn, a fine driver in his day, really couldn't give a damn' and enjoyed his motor racing in a straightforward, uncomplicated manner. If there wasn't his motor racing, he was just as happy loping round the family garage business in Farnham: for the blond haired Englishman, life was meant for fun and enjoyment. This apparently enabled him to sail through his Ferrari racing career on the crest of a wave of relaxed good humour. Politics didn't seem to affect him and,somehow,that whole attitude seemed to touch a sympathetic chord within the Commendatore's soul.

Eugenio Castellotti and Luigi Musso were also in the team for 1957, but the former only competed in the Argentine races before being killed in a testing accident at Modena before the start of the European season. The Italian had been under some pressure from his fiancée to retire from motor racing and, in Ferrari's opinion, was in "a confused state of mind" at the time of his fatal crash. Maurice Trintignant would eventually find his way back into the Ferrari Grand Prix line-up to replace the Italian and there were two or three other junior drivers, notably von Trips, now on the horizon.

The 1957 season opened with the Argentine Grand Prix on January 13 where six Lancia-Ferraris were fielded, three of which were built round new Maranello-made chassis frames. A great deal of engine development work had been carried out in the winter and, although the revised 80 × 62mm, 2494.8cc engine wouldn't make its début until the French Grand Prix, there was much experimentation with angled Solex carburetters on the existing engines but it was clearly becoming extremely difficult to squeeze more than 275bhp out of the basically four year old unit.

Hawthorn, Musso, Collins, Castellotti, Perdisa and Gonzalez (making a one-off reappearance) were all entered in Argentina, but the revised carburation didn't put the Lancia-Ferraris on a par with the Maseratis driven by Fangio and Moss (loaned from the non-competing Vanwall team). In the race, Collins, Musso and Hawthorn all fell victim to clutch problems while Castellotti was, as usual, going full-pelt trying to mix it with the Maseratis when his car suffered a hub breakage and lost a wheel. The result ended up as a 1-2-3-4 grand slam for Maserati with Gonzalez/de Portago taking fifth from Perdisa/Collins/von Trips. Two weeks later the Lancia-Ferraris actually performed far more respectably in the Buenos Aires City Grand Prix which was held on another variation of the circuit within the Parc Almirante Brown. Collins, who shared his machine on this occasion with F1 debutant Masten Gregory, won the second heat, but Fangio took victory on aggregate from Behra, Collins/Gregory, Hawthorn and Castellotti/Musso.

Syracuse on April 7 saw a further revised Lancia-Ferrari make its début and this car was henceforth officially referred to as the Ferrari 801, even though some serious students of motor racing history consider it to have been an extension of the Lancia-Ferrari lineage. Peter Collins was allocated this car which featured large diameter tubing below the engine in the chassis frame and the V8 itself was installed once more as a semi-stressed member (some back-tracking here!) with the longitudinal bracing tubes removed. Unequal length wishbones with coil springs were now employed at the front end and the chassis had been slightly modified to accept this revision, and close-fitting bodywork without any sort of pannier tank, vestigial or otherwise, gave the car a distinctly fresh overall appearance. The exhaust pipes were now mounted on special brackets on the outside of the chassis frame. Collins used this car to take pole position ahead of Musso and Moss's Vanwall, but the English car/driver combination seemed to be in a class of its own when the race order settled down. Unfortunately for Vanwall,

Final development. The Ferrari 801 (right), seen at Syracuse in 1957 alongside an earlier Lancia-Ferrari, was the ultimate evolutionary version of the D50 which had made its race début two and half years earlier. It was also the least successful, failing to win a single Championship Grand Prix during 1957.

Stirling had to pit before half distance with a split injection nozzle and although he went like the wind when he returned to the race he had to be content with third place behind Collins and Musso.

Ferrari missed Pau on Easter Monday as the team was busy preparing for the Naples race six days later when it was destined to field not only the Lancia-Ferrari brigade, but also a brand new car the derivatives of which were going to be as significant to the Scuderia's Grand Prix plans as the appearance of the original Lancia D50 had been, albeit indirectly, on its début two and a half years before. This was, of course, the beautiful little Formula 2 Ferrari Dino which, in 2.4-litre form, would provide Mike Hawthorn with his World Championship-winning mount the following year. The new car was built to conform with the new, unsupercharged 1½-litre Formula 2 which began at the start of the 1957 season, and the V6 engine configuration is attributed by Enzo Ferrari to his son Dino, after whom the engine was named.

It is a matter of considerable historic significance *apropos* the development of this engine just how much credit the Commendatore has retrospectively heaped on his beloved son, whose death from a combination of muscular dystrophy and nephritis in the summer of 1956 marked the greatest tragedy in Enzo Ferrari's long life. Born in 1932, Dino Ferrari was clearly marked out to take over the Ferrari company from his father and would doubtless have done so but for the debilitating illness which led to his premature death at the age of 24. He enjoyed a formal engineering training and took a degree in Switzerland before becoming involved with Ferrari engine design as what one can only describe as a collaborator with his father's engine design consultant Vittorio Jano.

In his memoirs, Enzo Ferrari states that it was Dino's idea that a V6 engine configuration should be used for the new Formula 2 car, but one is bound to conclude that Jano's enormously experienced guiding hand lay behind young

Lone effort. Luigi Musso hard at work in the 1957 Pescara Grand Prix, where his 801 was the only Maranello entry. The rear-mounted oil tank is beginning to come away in this picture . . .

Ferrari's advice to his father. Dino Ferrari quite obviously had a willing, inquisitive and active technical mind and he may well have scaled considerable heights had he developed his ability fully, but what he might have achieved had he survived must necessarily be left to the realms of conjecture. Enzo Ferrari has so publicly opened his heart on the subject of his only son that one feels bound, out of respect, to accept his assessment of Dino's contribution to the design concept of this V6 engine. However, one must always remember that Jano's enormous experience was not something that could be discounted on this particular score.

We will back-track to examine the Formula 1 Dino development a little later, but for the balance of the 1957 season Ferrari's fortunes centred round the outdated 801 which would fail to score a single Grand Prix triumph for Maranello that year. At that Naples race which saw the Dino's F2 début, Collins's 56-spec. Lancia-Ferrari used a variation of the swing-axle rear suspension tried the previous year, but this time in conjunction with coil springs, while Hawthorn had a tailor-made long chassis car available to him. This was another indication of the lengths to which Enzo Ferrari seemed prepared to go to oblige his favourite Englishman, contrasting strongly with the sarcastic response "forget your head, just put your foot down" which Phil Hill would receive a couple of years later during tests at Monza when the American driver merely asked for a higher windscreen to stop his head being buffeted around in the slipstream!

The race looked like being a demonstration run for the alcohol-fuelled Lancia-Ferraris, but Luigi Musso in the little Dino F2 (running on petrol) acquitted himself magnificently and sat splendidly in third place while Collins and Hawthorn played to the crowd. This was disrupted when Mike had to pit on lap 13 with a leaking pipe to the fuel pressure gauge spraying fuel all over him and he had to tiger like seldom before to get back to second behind Peter, only passing Musso in the new Ferrari "baby" on the very last lap, his reputation thus as enhanced as the lap record was shattered. But all this was small beer compared with the World Championship struggle ahead.

Monaco was the next stop on the programme where the first European Grand Prix was scheduled for May 19. Ferrari turned up with four designated race machines and two practice cars: two of the race cars had modified Lancia front suspension (unequal length wishbones/coil springs) and two had Super Squalo front suspension, but all four had de Dion rear ends which made one wonder precisely what had happened to the supposedly successful swing-axle arrangement seen at Naples. There was also a 1956 Lancia-Ferrari and that little jewel, the F2 Dino.

Practice saw a ferocious battle for pole between Maserati , Vanwall and Ferrari. There was a lot of swapping around between Hawthorn, Collins, von Trips and Trintignant, during the course of which Collins crashed Mike's 801 with the result that Hawthorn had to use the spare Lancia-Ferrari in the race. Fangio took pole from Collins and Moss but the race, such as it was, proved brief and memorable. Moss's Vanwall jumped into the lead at the start and stayed there until lap four when he locked up under braking for the chicane and plunged into the barriers, knocking wooden poles all over the circuit. Collins slammed into the barriers on the left-hand side of the circuit, Fangio dodged through into the lead in his Maserati, but Brooks braked hard and Hawthorn cannoned off the back of the Vanwall, ricochetting into Collins's already-damaged car at the side of the road. So that was the end of what promised to be the best Monaco Grand Prix for years: Fangio simply reeled the laps away to score a fine win over Brooks, with Gregory's Maserati 250F, Stuart Lewis-Evans's Connaught and Trintignant's Lancia-Ferrari

Stirling Moss never got a works Ferrari single seater drive, but this rare photograph shows him trying the cockpit of the little F2 Dino 156 in the pit lane at Monaco, 1957. The Ferrari mechanics' expressions indicate obvious approval!

Working hard! Mike Hawthorn's Ferrari 801 clips the apex of Melling Crossing during the 1957 British Grand Prix at Aintree, a race he might well have won had he not run over debris from Jean Behra's blown-up Maserati 250F.

following on behind. Hawthorn took over von Trips's car briefly, but found the cockpit hopelessly cramped and eventually handed it back to the German. Von Trips then survived in third place until nine laps from the end when his engine blew up comprehensively and he skated into the wall at *Massenet*!

It was quite clear that Fangio was going to take some beating with his Maserati and Ferrari fielded basically the same cars as at Monaco when the time came for the French Grand Prix at Rouen-les-Essarts on July 7. The Old Man qualified on pole more than a second faster than Behra, then came Musso's 801, Harry Schell's Maserati and Collins. The brave Luigi burst into the lead on the first lap, but on lap four Fangio went sailing through and away to what many people regard as the most dominant victory of his illustrious career, power-sliding his 250F through the plunging curves beyond the pits on this spectacular circuit with a deft brilliance that wasn't even approached by his rivals. Although the courageous Musso turned in a new lap record of 2m 22.4s on lap 65, thinking that perhaps Fangio was slowing with tyre trouble, he had to settle for second place with Collins and Hawthorn third and fourth.

Notwithstanding the fact that it was Rouen's turn for the French World Championship round, the Reims organizers still staged their Formula 1 event topped by that irresistible £10,000 first prize put up by BP. Musso, who had

proved his quality the previous weekend, drove a 1956 Lancia-Ferrari complete with the old bracing struts across the top of the engine and transverse leaf front suspension – very much the recipe which had proved so successful at Reims in the previous year's French Grand Prix. It was another weekend bonanza of motor sport, marred by the deaths of Bill Whitehouse and Herbert Mackay-Fraser in the supporting events. Fangio took pole again from Lewis-Evans, now in a Vanwall, Behra and Musso, and the race itself was highlighted by Lewis-Evans's brilliant performance on his first outing for Tony Vandervell's team: on this daunting high speed circuit the young Englishman pulled confidently away from all his rivals until he was slowed by an oil leak which blew lubricant all over the car's bonnet and the driver's goggles. As he eased back to finish third, Musso came tramping through to score a fine victory ahead of Behra's Maserati. Hawthorn retired with a cooked engine and Fangio slid off, untypically, into a very firm barrier!

The 1957 British Grand Prix at Aintree marked the historic memorable Vanwall victory scored by Stirling Moss and Tony Brooks, and again the Ferrari 801s were cast very much in a supporting role. The Maranello cars were suffering from a lot of frustrating, time-consuming understeer throughout practice, contrasting with the precisely neutral handling of the sleek Vanwalls and the reassuring dash of oversteer displayed by the Maseratis. Hawthorn's 801 was the fastest on the outside of row two, but it was Behra's Maserati which provided the strongest opposition to the Vanwalls on their home ground. When Moss's car hit trouble, the Frenchman took over at the front of the field and might well have won had his 250F's clutch/flywheel not blown to pieces on lap 69. Hawthorn was at that point poised to go through into the lead, but he punctured a tyre on the debris scattered by Behra's mortally damaged machine and he had to stop for fresh rubber. That allowed the Vanwall team to reassert its superiority and Moss went on to win in the car he'd taken over from Brooks. Hawthorn wound up third behind his team-mate Musso, but if he hadn't run over that debris he might have pushed Moss hard enough to preclude Stirling from making a precautionary late-race stop for extra fuel. Might have, might have. . .

Hawthorn drove a forceful, confident race at Aintree and followed that up with a brilliant performance at the Nürburgring in a classic German Grand Prix which saw him ranged against Fangio at his stupendous best. Fangio had managed a 9m 41.6s at the wheel of a Lancia-Ferrari during the previous year's race so there was considerable speculation as to precisely where the lap record would end up in 1957. Fangio did a 9m 25.6s for pole and then Hawthorn gritted his teeth and did a 9m 37.8s – which was second fastest – and a 9m 28.4s on the second day of

Discarded and forgotten. Enzo Ferrari has a ruthlessly unsentimental attitude towards outdated racing cars. Here, at the end of the 1957 season, this Ferrari 801, carrying von Trips's Monza race numbers, languishes in the open, unmourned and uncared for. Jano's V8s had reached the end of the road . . .

Long time Ferrari design consultant Alberto Massimino makes a point to youthful British enthusiast Graham Gauld, a contributor of several fascinating pictures in this volume. Modena Grand Prix, 1957.

practice, but that was it.

Hawthorn got away first, pursued by Collins, Mike actually turning a 9m 42.5s for his first standing start lap and then did a 9m 37.9s second time round, establishing a new lap record. But the Ferrari 801's early spurt was merely a tempting *hors d'oeuvres* when compared with the *haute cuisine* main course which was to be served up by Fangio and Maserati. By the end of lap three Fangio was in the lead (running a light fuel load and intending to stop once he'd built up a suitable advantage) and by lap eight he was almost half a minute ahead. At the end of lap 12 he came in with a 28s margin over the Ferraris of Hawthorn and Collins, and it seemed as though the Maserati team was trying to handicap him as much as they could, shambling through a disgracefully tardy 52s to change the rear wheels and top up his fuel load.

That left Hawthorn and Collins swapping places and generally having a lot of fun in the lead, and Fangio took a couple of laps to get back into his stride once he resumed the chase. But then the Ferrari advantage came tumbling down and the fun was over for the two Englishmen: lap 16 saw the gap at 33s, lap 17 it was 25.5s, lap 19 it was 13.5s and on lap 20 it was a mere two seconds. Fangio dived past Collins going into North Curve, shattering a lens in Peter's goggles as he put two wheels on the dirt. Going down to *Adenau* he elbowed his way past Hawthorn, but Mike really had his dander up by this stage and fought back magnificently, going into his final lap only three seconds behind the Maserati and, by dint of hurling his Ferrari against the scenery for most of the way round that 14-mile lap, sending clumps of grass and clods of earth flying, lost only another second to Fangio on the last tour. Collins and Musso were third and fourth with Moss a distant fifth in a Vanwall obviously unsuited to the Nürburgring on this occasion.

Hawthorn recalled this epic struggle in graphic detail: "Fangio was now driving the race of his life and pulling back about eight seconds a lap despite all that we could do. On the 20th lap he got round in a completely unheard of 9m 17.4s, to average 91.8mph on one of the most difficult circuits in the World. Peter and I did everything we could to save split seconds on those countless corners and all the time the World Champion was catching us up relentlessly.

"At the end of that magnificent record lap he was only 100 yards behind us as we passed the stands. Coming out of the South Curve he passed Peter, who fought back and got a few yards ahead again, only to be overwhelmed . . . as Peter drifted in, Fangio pulled on to the outside of the bend and went by with two wheels on the grass, showering the Ferrari with dirt and stones . . .

"It was now a straight fight between Fangio and I once again, and I was driving right on the limit as we rushed through the endless treelined curves to *Hocheichen* and on to the *Quiddelbacher Hohe*, but just as I was going into a slow left-hand corner, Fangio pulled the same trick, cut sharply inside me and forced me on to the grass and almost into the ditch . .

"As we started the last lap he had the vital yards in hand which prevented me from getting to grips on the corners and he crossed the finishing line 3.6s ahead of me. This time the race had been every bit as exciting for the drivers as for the spectators and even though Peter and I had been beaten, we enjoyed every moment of it."

That victory clinched Fangio's fifth World Championship title and was to be the last triumph of his memorable career. It was a worthy result for the Ferrari team, but back in Italy things were not going too well for the Commendatore himself who was experiencing aggravation from both the Italian Government and the ACI – mainly over the Mille Miglia catastrophe earlier in the season which had cost the life of several spectators, not to mention those of Fon de Portago and his navigator Ed Nelson, when their Ferrari had crashed in the closing stages of this classic road-racing event.

As a result of this, Ferrari didn't want to send any entries to the Pescara Grand Prix on August 18, but Musso implored him to provide at least a single 801 for him to use in this 18 lap contest round the spectacular road circuit. The Commendatore relented and Musso actually managed to lead the opening lap after which Moss surged away to a good win for Vanwall. Musso fought back gallantly, but there was simply no way: by lap 10, in any case, the oil tank split and the engine had lost all its lubricant. . . Musso's performance that day epitomized the role of the dauntless, patriotic, hard-trying Italian Ferrari driver, pulling every trick in the book to make up for a combination of car deficiency and a shortage of natural flair. Against the combination of Vanwall and Moss, he was outclassed: even the great Fangio's Maserati was more than three minutes behind Stirling at the finish.

Ferrari had patched up his relationship with the ACI in time to field four cars at Monza for the Italian Grand Prix on September 8, the final outing for the Lancia D50-derived cars. It was a rather unmemorable way for this Lancia offspring to bow out of the Grand Prix arena. Conceived and weaned at a time when European racing car manufacturers dominated Grand Prix racing, it finally bid farewell on the day that Stirling Moss incontrovertibly drove home the fact that Britain's time had arrived in Grand Prix racing by winning the Italian Grand Prix in *una macchina Inglese*.

At the end of a brutal, ferocious practice it was Vanwalls 1-2-3 on the starting grid, and although Fangio's six-cylinder 250F and Behra's 12-cylinder Maserati prototype mixed it with the Vanwalls, the Ferrari 801s could only pick up a few crumbs of comfort in the second group. Moss drove away from Fangio to win by over 40s, the Vanwall and Maserati being the only two cars on the same lap. Hawthorn got his Ferrari 801 up to third place, only to be delayed by a pit visit to deal with a split fuel pipe, so he dropped to fifth leaving von Trips third ahead of Masten Gregory's 250F.

Section III: 2½-litre heyday, 1954-60

Chapter 4 A Championship for Dino's memory

During the course of the season development work had been continuing on the 1½-litre Formula 2 Dino, although there had been precious few races held in which it could take part. Nevertheless, the little Formula 2 machine gradually evolved into a slightly larger Formula 1 machine that would re-establish Ferrari's reputation in the season that followed.

For 1958, of course, revision of the Formula 1 technical regulations, prompted by fuel companies who were anxious to make advertising capital out of their involvement in Grand Prix racing, changed the requirement for alcohol-based fuels to that for pump petrol. Inevitably, there was immediate difficulty in setting and maintaining minimum acceptable standards on a world-wide basis, so it was eventually accepted that 130-octane aviation fuel (AvGas) would be used as this was the only available fuel governed by international standards and regulations.

When Ferrari gave the go-ahead for the Formula 2 Dino engine project to proceed, he was thinking in terms of an engine which would have considerable long-term development potential – which proved most prescient. Jano finalized the V6 configuration at 65-degrees to provide sufficient room for both the twin overhead camshafts on each cylinder bank and the intake ducting required to enable the engine to breathe efficiently. In its initial guise the engine had a bore and stroke of 70 × 64.55mm for a total capacity of 1490cc, laid out in two blocks of three cylinders arranged in vee formulation on a single-piece crankshaft, the right-hand block slightly staggered in relation to its neighbour.

Each cylinder block had two overhead camshafts, chain driven from take-offs at the nose of the crankshaft which itself ran on four main bearings: these also drove the oil, fuel and water pumps. Two valves per cylinder were employed and there were two sparking plugs per cylinder, fired by twin magnetos, one on the nose of each inlet camshaft. Carburation was by means of three Weber twin choke 38DCN carburetters mounted within the vee. The engine was angled in the chassis, like the Lancia D50, in order that the driveshaft pass to the driver on its way to the transverse rear-mounted four-speed gearbox in unit with the ZF limited-slip final drive.

Running with a 9.5:1 compression ratio on straight petrol the 1.5-litre Dino's initial power output was quoted at 190bhp at 9200rpm. The chassis into which the engine was initially installed wasn't anything particularly sophisticated, its large diameter tube-based main frame resembling that employed on the 1955 Super Squalo rather than the small diameter tube round which the most recent Ferrari 801 was built. Front suspension was by means of unequal length double wishbones working with coil springs, while a de Dion rear end almost identical to the 801's layout was employed, except that the de Dion tube was central mounted at hub level. A transverse leaf spring was mounted above the rear axle line. The large fuel tank and oil tank were mounted at the rear, with reserve tank on the left-hand side of the cockpit. Visually, the new Formula 2 Ferrari was a scaled-down 801, imitating the outline of the Formula 1 car first tried by Collins at Syracuse.

After that impressive third place at Naples on its début outing, the little Formula 2 car from Maranello appeared in practice, for comparative purposes, at Monaco and then won the 37-lap Formula 2 race at Reims in Trintignant's hands the same weekend as Musso scored his victory in the Lancia-Ferrari F1 car. Sadly, later that same summer during extensive tests at Modena, the second of the Formula 2 Dinos crashed in the hands of promising young engineer Andrea Fraschetti, killing its driver. Fraschetti's place in the team was taken by burly, expansive former Alfa Romeo engineer Carlo Chiti.

The Dino V6 was progressively enlarged, "officially" to 1877cc (78.6 × 64.55mm) but, according to internal Ferrari records, to 1983.7cc (77 × 71mm). These engines developed around 220bhp and, in back-to-back tests with the Ferrari 801s at both Monza and Modena, proved to be slightly quicker. More importantly, they were much easier to drive and handled more progressively than their bigger brethren, by now outclassed.

A fortnight after the Italian Grand Prix the first two Dinos were entered in the

This distinctive shot of Hawthorn's '58 Dino 246 shows off the high mounted exhaust tail pipes to good effect and the transverse leaf spring flexing under load.

non-Championship Modena Grand Prix – the last *race* (as opposed to practice) ever attended by Enzo Ferrari in person. The cars were fitted with the "1877cc" engines and they performed very respectably against a selection of Maserati 250Fs to finish second and fourth in the two heat race in the hands of Musso and Collins respectively.

Finally, as the old Lancia-Ferrari machines were brushed aside at Maranello, prior to being dismantled, the decision was taken to enter the two Dinos at the non-Championship Moroccan Grand Prix, held at Casablanca's Ain-Diab circuit on October 27. This time there was a fairly representative selection of rival Grand Prix machines on hand and Hawthorn's Dino had a 81 × 71mm, 2195.17cc engine while Collins's car featured a 85 × 71mm, 2417.33cc version. This latter unit had a quoted power output in the region of 270bhp at 8300rpm and was to become the most successful Ferrari Dino engine configuration. Both cars showed well during practice and Collins led the race briefly before spinning on lap eight. Unquestionably, Ferrari's new order had arrived!

On the face of it, Ferrari faced the 1958 season in a particularly strong position, its 2.4-litre V6 all ready to go and properly developed to run on AvGas, while rivals such as Vanwall and BRM had plenty of work to complete adapting their big four-cylinder engines which had been specifically designed to run on an alcohol-based fuel. Less welcome from Maranello's point of view, was the reduction in Grand Prix distance from 500km (312 miles) to a mere 300km (or around two hours), a move which was to offer considerable scope for the small British specialist builders whose significantly lighter cars would now be able to run non-stop for an entire Grand Prix distance with little drama.

For the 1958 World Championship season Massimino's chassis design department produced an extensively revised frame round which the next batch of pukka Grand Prix cars were to be built. The 2417.3cc engine which Collins had used at Casablanca was fixed as the "standard" engine for the year and the new frames were built out of smaller diameter tubing than the "prototype" F2 cars, lacking the large diameter longerons which formed the basis of the original two chassis. Torsional rigidity quickly proved itself to be a problem with the new small-tube chassis and most of the 1958 team cars were built round derivations of the original frame.

As far as drivers were concerned, Mike Hawthorn, Peter Collins and Luigi Musso spearheaded the team's challenge with von Trips and Phil Hill in the background ready to move in should any misfortune befall the more experienced campaigners. The Championship season opened with the customary series of races in Argentina during January, but as the Buenos Aires race was only finally confirmed in the calendar a month before it was scheduled to take place, BRM and Vanwall declined to go as they were working flat-out converting their engines to run on AvGas. BRM actually protested through the RAC that the race should not be counted for the World Championship, although the protests were tactfully withdrawn after an English car won!

It seems the ultimate in irony, but the outcome of that Argentine Grand Prix in far-away Buenos Aires on January 15, 1958 not only sparked off the "rear-engined" revolution in Formula 1 chassis design, but it also, in effect, decreed that the Ferrari Dino 246 was obsolete as a long-term Grand Prix design from the moment it made its Championship début.

The facts of that historic event have been recounted time and again, so we will only briefly re-cap on them in this volume. Stirling Moss, on loan from the absent Vanwall team to Rob Walker's equipe, drove a 1960cc Climax-engined Cooper to close victory over Luigi Musso's Dino 246. Lulled into a false sense of security by its confidence that Moss would have to stop for fresh tyres, the Ferrari team's confidence turned first into disbelief and then to anguish as it became apparent that this tiny little "bug" was going through non-stop. Musso, with the only Dino 246 to run the distance trouble-free, had been mooning about in second place allegedly waiting for pit signals to speed up. Collins's car broke one of its F2-type driveshafts on the startline while Hawthorn had been delayed by a pit stop to debate failing oil pressure with his mechanic. When it became clear that Musso would have to go for it, there wasn't sufficient time left and the Italian failed to displace the Cooper-Climax by just over two seconds. Hawthorn was a distant third and the Ferrari pit became the scene of an acrimonious post-mortem on Musso's failure to get the job done. Luigi shouted that he hadn't been kept fully informed as to Moss's progress, but Collins knew full-well that he himself held out several pit signals to his Italian team-mate and Hawthorn, too, reckoned that Musso should have won, but the two English drivers tactfully kept their feelings to themselves.

There followed a series of non-championship outings for the Dino 246s before the World Championship series continued with the second round at Monaco on May 18. Before leaving Argentina, the two-heat Buenos Aires City Grand Prix saw a quartet of Dinos line up for the start on February 2: Collins, Hawthorn and Musso joined by von Trips/Phil Hill, the intention being that each of the nominated drivers in the fourth car should drive one heat apiece. Collins suffered another driveshaft failure on the line, a fate which befell Hawthorn at the start of the second heat after Mike had splashed away easily to win the first: Moss's Cooper-Climax challenge had evaporated at the first corner when a local hero punted him off. At the end of the day Musso finished third on aggregate behind Fangio's Maserati 250F and Carlos Menditeguy, similarly 250F-mounted. Hill didn't get a drive since von Trips crashed the car in the first heat!

The Dino 246's first race victory came at Goodwood on April 7. Hawthorn using a brand new car to win the 42-lap Glover trophy at the pleasantly rural English track on Easter Monday. This new chassis, '0003' in the Dino 246 series, was to become Hawthorn's regular car throughout the season, and it was fitted with his "personal" accessories such as an aero-screen within the perspex windscreen, four-spoke steering wheel and cut-away cockpit sides. Hawthorn was presented with victory on a plate after Jean Behra's BRM P25 slammed into the brick chicane early in the race, Mike dodging through a shower of masonry to inherit the lead!

A week later and it was Musso's turn. Ferrari turned up at Syracuse with a single 246 ranged against a horde of private Maserati 250Fs and Luigi, much to the delight of the locals, won easily. In the early stages of the Sicilian demonstration run he was pulling away from the opposition at around five seconds a lap! The third pre-European season Dino triumph allowed Collins to join in on the winning streak. Using a car built round one of the smaller-tube frames, photographic evidence of which suggested that it was flexing badly, Peter inherited a comfy lead in the Silverstone International Trophy from Behra's BRM (again!), this time the British car being sidelined when a stone thrown up by a backmarker smashed the Frenchman's goggles and cut his eye. Despite hitting some oil at Copse and bouncing along the grass verge for some distance, Peter won by a big margin from Salvadori's Cooper-Climax.

At Monaco the Dino 246 faced up to the Vanwalls for the first time and it was interesting to see that Hawthorn and Moss proved particularly evenly matched. There was a fourth car ready for this event, a lightweight 1958-spec Formula 2 machine for von Trips fitted with a 2-litre V6 for practice. At the end of the day, since none of the 246 engines failed during early training, the F2 chassis was fitted with the spare full F1 engine for the German to use in final practice. An extra 50bhp certainly held his attention!

Hawthorn was moderately happy with his car, but couldn't improve on his place on the inside of row three – it was ahead of the Vanwalls of Lewis-Evans and Moss, at least! Behra's BRM was the early pacemaker and Mike gradually worked his way to the front, helped by mechanical problems befalling the English car and several other runners. Eventually the race settled down with Moss's Vanwall in the lead and Mike a few lengths behind, the two of them trading lap records. Hawthorn finally nailed the record at 1m 40.6s (Brooks's Vanwall had secured pole with a 1m 39.8s) and when Moss's green car retired, the English Ferrari driver inherited an enormous advantage. Then, on lap 46, it went rough and cut out completely just before the tunnel. Hawthorn climbed out and took off the Dino's bonnet, but it

Prelude to disaster. The start of the 1958 French Grand Prix at Reims-Gueux with Schell's BRM and Brooks's Vanwall just briefly getting the jump on the Dino 246s of Mike Hawthorn (No.4) and Luigi Musso (No.2). Hawthorn won this race in brilliant style, but Musso crashed fatally trying to keep up with him . . .

was the son of the publisher of MOTOR SPORT magazine, photographer Michael Tee, who pointed out to the driver that the fuel pump had vibrated free and was dangling down at the front of the engine.

Hawthorn walked back to the pits and watched as the Rob Walker equipe dished out another defeat to the Ferrari team, this time Maurice Trintignant being at the wheel of the English entrant's tiny Cooper-Climax. Musso and Collins wound up second and third, both complaining about serious flat-spots which hampered the throttle response of their V6 engines, but at least Luigi emerged from the contest leading the drivers' Championship.

The Dutch Grand Prix followed at Zandvoort only a week later and Hawthorn must have been put painfully in mind of his experience in 1955 at the wheel of the precarious-handling Super Squalo. The Dino 246s might have been on the pace at Monaco, but they were frankly diabolical round Zandvoort and it was painful to see the cars from Maranello being humbled by such tiny machines as Cliff Allison's 2-litre Lotus-Climax. The Vanwall trio dominated the front row, but Hawthorn was the best Ferrari on the inside of row three again and he grappled his way from understeer to oversteer throughout the race, finally finishing an infuriated fifth with Musso seventh, the two Dino 246s split by Allison's cheeky Lotus. Collins spun off when his gearbox seized on lap 35. . .

After the race Hawthorn couldn't control his irritation, particularly as he'd been

lapped not only by Moss's winning Vanwall, but also by the BRMs of Schell and Behra which had finished second and third. Having turned his back on BRM in 1955 becaue they couldn't get their act together, this humiliation was too much. He told team manager Romolo Tavoni that the car was "quite useless" and suggested that Ferrari should do something pretty dramatic before the next race. Again, showing his considerable deference towards Hawthorn, the Commendatore didn't tell Mike to make other arrangements if he wasn't satisfied with his position, but wrote a soothing reply to a quite sharp note fired off by the Englishman on the subject, assuring his favourite driver that the factory "had been working really hard on the car and hoped that they should show their proper form at Spa . . ."

Happily the Dino 246s were much more at home on the wide open sweeps of Spa-Francorchamps and Mike qualified on pole position with a 3m 57.1s best ahead of team-mate Musso (3m 57.5s), Moss (3m 57.6s), Collins, Brooks and local ace Olivier Gendebien, who'd been loaned the fourth car for his home Grand Prix. After this splendid showing in practice, Ferrari efforts were badly compromised before the start as the Belgian race officials kept the pack waiting far too long for the starting signal and Peter's Dino was suffering from terminal overheating trouble before he'd even got away from the grid.

Moss missed a gear on the opening lap and blew the engine of his Vanwall, but Brooks was there to take over in the lead for the British team and this confident, smooth and stylish driver raced away to score a splendid win for Vandervell's team. Collins's car succumbed early on, Peter prudently switching off when it became obvious that the oil and water temperatures were never going to come down. . .

Hawthorn occupied a somewhat subdued second place for much of the race, worried that the wrecked Dino he could see in a field at Stavelot was that of his friend Collins, but when he caught sight of his fellow Englishman standing in the pits he began to get back his enthusiasm for racing and started to counter-attack at the leading Vanwall. The luckless Musso was the one who'd ended in the field, his 246 having burst a tyre whilst running at around 160mph at the end of the Masta straight: amazingly, he was only bruised and shaken. . .

In his chase behind Brooks, Hawthorn took the race's fastest lap and scored a crucial extra Championship point as a result . . . despite suffering engine failure as he accelerated down to the finishing line from the final hairpin, *La Source*. Brooks had actually taken the flag with his Vanwall's gearbox showing the first signs of seizing and, as he discussed his good fortune with Hawthorn at the bottom of the hill after the finish, Stuart Lewis-Evans wobbled past the flag to finish third in the other Vanwall, a steering arm having failed on the run down to the line. . .

The next Grand Prix was the French, scheduled for Reims-Gueux on July 6, but before that the famous Monza 500-mile challenge between Indianapolis cars and rivals from European stables took place, an event which underlined Luigi Musso's unstinting enthusiasm and bravery. Using a rather crude 4.1-litre V12, derived from the old type 375 Formula 1 chassis, Musso showed a clean pair of heels to his American rivals in the first of the three 60-lap heats round the combined road/banked circuit at Monza, the Italian machine eventually finishing third on aggregate, Hawthorn and Phil Hill also doing their stints behind the wheel. There was also a more modern Ferrari chassis on hand, fitted with a 3-litre version of the Dino V6, and this was entrusted to Phil Hill. With it, the American demonstrated that a Grand Prix drive from Ferrari was long overdue as far as he was concerned. . .

Prior to the Reims race one of those typically niggling little disputes arose by means of which Ferrari so frequently sought to put pressure on his drivers. The Commendatore had recently formed the feeling that Peter Collins's driving had lost its edge, the implication being that his recent marriage to an American girl, Louise King, had taken the edge off his racing appetite. Team manager Tavoni announced that Collins would only be driving the Dino 156 in the supporting Formula 2 race, but Peter replied that if he wasn't going to be allowed to drive in the Grand Prix then he wouldn't be driving in either race. If the Old Man had been seeking to drive a wedge between Collins and Hawthorn, always the best of friends, then he wasn't able to succeed, for Mike lined up right behind Peter on this one and Tavoni eventually relented. Peter drove in the Formula 2 race, but had to settle for a distant second place to Jean Behra's central-engined Porsche special.

During practice for the Grand Prix Hawthorn was on scintillating form, smashing Fangio's 1956 Lancia-Ferrari D50 lap record by almost two seconds to take pole on 2m 23.9s on the first day and further reducing his best lap to 2m 21.7s to consolidate his position the following evening. Musso qualified second ahead of Harry Schell's BRM with Collins on the second row with Brooks's Vanwall.

Some days, Hawthorn was unbeatable. This was one of those rare occasions where he was at his brilliant best: nobody got near him. Schell's BRM briefly galloped ahead for the first few corners, but Mike had the bit between his teeth and led the French Grand Prix on every lap, closing with a spurt that guaranteed him the important extra Championship point for fastest lap. But, according to Enzo Ferrari, the price of that triumph was too high: "I have lost the only Italian driver who mattered. . ."

The death of Luigi Musso, as he chased Hawthorn round the 11th lap of the 1958 French Grand Prix, was a stunning blow to Italian motor racing. The aristocratic Roman driver came from a family who excelled in demanding sports and, since the death of Castellotti the previous year, Luigi had been more than conscious of the responsibilities resting on his shoulders. Hard on Hawthorn's tail, Musso lost control of his Dino 246 as he swept round the dauntingly fast right-hander beyond the pits at Reims, possibly after getting off-line as he lapped a slower Maserati, and the irreparable happened in a flash.

There are many people within motor racing who have hinted at another reason for Musso's over-enthusiasm, possibly the cause of his tragic accident. The clue may well be found in Ferrari's words: "On the eve of the race, he had, in fact, received a message: a few words typed on a buff telegram that urged him to make an all-out effort." With that tantalizing £10,000 first prize still riding on the outcome of this race, success for Luigi Musso might well have enabled him to clear his reputedly considerable gambling debts. It may sound like cheap fiction, but it's widely believed to be the case . . .

Moss finished second behind Hawthorn, with von Trips third and Juan-Manuel Fangio, having his very last Grand Prix outing, fourth at the wheel of a Maserati 250F. Hawthorn, respectfully, refrained from lapping the famous Argentinian driver with whom he'd been involved in that epic battle for his first Grand Prix victory five years earlier on the same circuit.

When it came to Silverstone, venue for the British Grand Prix on July 19, many people expected the fine-handling Vanwalls to run rings round the Dino 246s, but despite the fact that the Ferraris yawed precariously between understeer and oversteer during practice, Collins rocketed through into the lead from his starting position on the second row of the grid and led from mid-way round the opening lap all the way to the chequered flag. Peter was obviously anxious to nail any doubts about his ability and Mike couldn't get near him all afternoon: after a late stop for oil, Hawthorn finished almost half a minute behind his team-mate in a Ferrari 1-2 made easy by Moss's retirement in the Vanwall, Stirling having chased Collins hard in the early stages. At the end of this race there was an incident which truly epitomized Hawthorn's easy-going attitude to motor racing. During the Grand Prix he'd noticed some friends, including Tony Rolt, quaffing beer on the infield at Becketts, so on his slowing-down lap he stopped, collected a pint of shandy and drove back to the pits brandishing the mug! Happy days. . .

Twelve months earlier the German Grand Prix had been enlivened by the battle between the Ferrari 801s of Hawthorn and Collins and Fangio's Maserati, and the 1958 battle saw the same two Ferrari drivers pitch their Dino 246s against a new foe. This time it was Tony Brooks in the sleek green Vanwall, the chassis of which seemed much more at home over the bumps and undulations than it had been in

1957. Hawthorn managed to qualify for pole, a 9m 14.0s lap aided by partial resurfacing round this most demanding circuit in the business. Brooks, Moss and Collins lined up alongside him and it was Stirling who shot away into an early lead, only to stop out on the circuit with magneto trouble on lap four.

This left Hawthorn and Collins running in close company at the front, but Mike was nursing a clutch badly overheated when he'd slipped it too much getting away from the starting grid. Brooks went on to the attack for Vanwall and by lap eight he was right with the Ferrari s, losing them in terms of sheer speed on the long straight up towards the start/finish line, but out-handling them everywhere else. On lap 11 Brooks forced his Vanwall into the lead going into North Curve and Hawthorn, in third place, sat and watched as his team-mate fought back tenaciously against the British car as they plunged down towards *Adenau*, Collins determined that Maranello shouldn't lose its second straight battle at the Nürburgring.

What happened next, in the heat of the battle, must be left to conjecture. Phil Hill, who was making his Ferrari single seater début in the Formula 2 section of this Grand Prix at the wheel of the Dino 156, feels that a combination of the fast-fading Houdaille dampers and drum brakes would have made the Formula 1 Dino a really unpredictable proposition round a circuit as demanding as the Nürburgring. Coming out of the *Pflanzgarten* dip into a climbing right-hander, chasing that Vanwall for all he was worth, Peter Collins made a slight error of judgement.

Hawthorn, watching from third place, saw the drama unfold in front of his horrified eyes. As they went into that right-hander Collins was slightly off-line, running wide to the left by little more than the width of the car. The car's left rear wheel mounted the small bank on the outside of the corner and, just as Hawthorn was mentally composing a few choice phrases to throw at his team-mate if he took Mike off as well, Peter's Ferrari suddenly flipped over and threw its driver out. . .

Hawthorn almost stopped, looking backwards to see the Dino bounce upside down in a cloud of dust, before driving on like a robot, uncaring about the race and worried sick about his friend. Before he could make it round to the accident scene again, his Dino's clutch failed for good and he was stranded out on the circuit. Brooks won the race, but a shattered Hawthorn later heard that his great friend, "Mon ami, mate, Pete", had succumbed to serious head injuries in a Bonn hospital.

Although the Ferrari Dino Formula 1 programme continued apace, there is no doubt that Collins's fatal accident marked the end of a Grand Prix era as far as the young English post-war driving pioneers were concerned. The extrovert antics of Collins and Hawthorn, though deemed excessive by some, were as a colourful counter-point to the serious, professional approach adopted by the brilliant Stirling Moss. But with Peter gone, Hawthorn drove out the balance of the 1958 season without a great deal of pleasure. It was a chore, something to be completed and then forgotten, as far as Mike was concerned. At the end of the season he would retire, World Championship or no. . .

It should be recorded that von Trips finished a fine fourth at the Nürburgring, his Dino virtually brakeless for much of the race, while Hill's F2 Dino wound up fifth in its class. Phil soon found himself promoted to the Ferrari Grand Prix team after Collins's death and was to play a crucial, if sometimes forgotten, role in securing Mike Hawthorn his Championship.

On August 24, the Portuguese Grand Prix took place at Oporto where, although Hawthorn set second fastest practice time and led initially, the Dino 246's drum brakes were no match for Moss's disc-braked Vanwall and Mike couldn't get on terms with Stirling on this occasion. After losing second place to Behra's BRM when he came into the pits to have the Ferrari's brakes adjusted, Hawthorn set a new lap record as he chased after the Frenchman. It was at this point that the Vanwall pit signalled "HAWT REC" to Stirling, indicating that Mike had set fastest lap, but Moss thought he read "HAWT REG" (Hawthorn Regular) meaning that Hawthorn wasn't making any progress.

Champion performance. Mike Hawthorn's Dino 246 on its way to second place in the 1958 Moroccan Grand Prix at Casablanca's Ain Diab road circuit. It was enough to earn Mike the Championship title, the first one for a British driver . . .

Mike eventually scrabbled past the BRM and, when Behra retired, Lewis-Evans's Vanwall took up the chase in third place. At one point Mike looked in his mirror, thought the looming Vanwall was young Stuart and began working hard to keep in front . . . but it was Moss, coming up to lap him. Stirling recalls that Mike looked so horrified at the prospect of being lapped that he dropped back behind, taking the chequered flag ahead of Lewis-Evans, who was thus one lap down in third place. But Hawthorn forgot that Stuart would have finished the race by the time he was hurrying the Ferrari round its last lap, and he shot up an escape road in his enthusiasm to keep ahead of the "imaginary" Vanwall. Mike turned the car round himself, fighting off outside assistance from officials, and toured despondently round to the pits, thinking he was last, to be told by a grinning Tavoni that he'd finished second. A protest that he'd pushed his car against the direction of traffic was rejected on the evidence of Stirling Moss, who generously and accurately pointed out that the Ferrari was on the footpath, not the track, at the time. That gesture of sportsmanship on Stirling's part was characteristic, for Moss only wanted to beat his rivals on the circuit, not on a rule book technicality.

For the Italian Grand Prix at Monza on September 7, Hawthorn insisted that his Dino 246 be fitted with disc brakes and, after some thought, the Commendatore obliged his favourite driver yet again. The Dunlop disc brakes from Peter Collins's personal road Ferrari 250GT were used and two Dunlop technicians were sent out to Maranello to oversee the project, which involved the manufacture of brand new hubs and revised Borrani wire wheels to accommodate them. There was also a slightly bigger 86mm × 71mm, 2474.54cc Dino V6 available, reputedly producing 290bhp at 8800rpm, and this was fitted to Mike's car for the start of practice. Also on the scene was the Monza 500 special chassis, raced in June with the 3-litre V6 by Phil Hill, which featured a de Dion rear end with coil springs, a portent of what was to come in 1959.

Phil Hill was included in the team at Monza for his Formula 1 Ferrari début, and the other cars were driven by von Trips and Gendebien, Hawthorn eventually reverted to his usual 246 engine to qualify third behind Moss and Brooks, and ahead of Lewis-Evans, while Gendebien, von Trips and Phil Hill were ranged confidently across the second row. At the start Phil came darting through from the second row to lead the opening lap, Hawthorn nearly lost his clutch again at the start as the starter held the grid too long and von Trips had another unfortunate Monza experience, being rammed by Schell's BRM on the opening lap, his Dino cartwheeling into the trees. He emerged with a leg injury, but the car was destroyed.

Hill led until lap five when Hawthorn went by, but then the serious business of the day got under way as Moss became involved at the front with his Vanwall. Hawthorn was quicker than his rivals, but he knew he would have to stop for fresh Engleberts, so he needed a big cushion over the Vanwalls if he was to emerge with victory and the World Championship title. At the end of the day it was a Vanwall victory, however, Brooks saving the day after Moss's gearbox packed up on lap 18. Hawthorn, slowing towards the end with a failing clutch, managed to gesticulate to Phil Hill and persuade the American to slow, staying behind him in third place as he crept round the final few laps to take a crucially important second place. Gendebien was an early retirement with a bent de Dion tube in the Monza 500 special "MI" after being rammed by Brabham, but Phil Hill bagged fastest lap, keeping it out of Moss's grasp.

Five weeks lay between Monza and the final race in the Championship, the Moroccan Grand Prix at Casablanca's Ain-Diab road circuit. Hawthorn used a 256 engine in his Dunlop disc-brake equipped Dino to take pole position from Moss, Lewis-Evans, Behra's BRM, Phil Hill's drum-braked Dino 246 and Gendebien in the Dino "MI" which had now been fitted with Girling disc brakes for the purpose of comparison. Moss needed to win and set fastest lap to take the Championship, but his efforts would be in vain if Mike Hawthorn was to finish second.

Hawthorn decided to play things carefully from the start and settle for second place, so Moss led the race for Vanwall from start to finish, harried for the first three laps by the tenacious Phil Hill before he attempted to pass the English car and, finding his drum brakes no match for the Vanwall discs, slithered up an escape road. Hill recovered, roared back through the field and was waved ahead into second place by the canny Hawthorn. Mike then became embroiled in a battle for third with Brooks's Vanwall, but when Tony retired with engine failure on lap 30, the Ferrari team leader found himself back in a comfortable third place. Moss set fastest lap, but with Phil Hill dutifully conceding second place in the final moments of the contest, Mike Hawthorn emerged as World Champion, the first British driver to achieve this distinction, by a single point.

Sadly, Mike's great day was shrouded by another tragedy. Stuart Lewis-Evans crashed his Vanwall after the engine failed, the car catching fire, and the young Englishman sustained serious burns from which he died a few days later. Vanwall took the Constructors' Championship with little pleasure as a result of this catastrophe.

True to his word, Mike Hawthorn retired from racing after winning his Championship title, much to the disappointment of Enzo Ferrari who'd treated him with more warmth and consideration than he lavished on most of his drivers. A varied and interesting business career beckoned for the 29-year old from Farnham, but on January 22, 1959, he was killed at the wheel of his Jaguar 3.4 saloon in an accident on the Guildford bypass. Cliché or not, Mike Hawthorn's death truly closed a fascinating chapter in post-war international motor racing for good.

Dan Gurney watches as Phil Hill begins a little "illicit" pre-race practice on the Reims-Gueux road circuit prior the the 1959 French Grand Prix. The car is the Dino 246 used in the race by Olivier Gendebien.

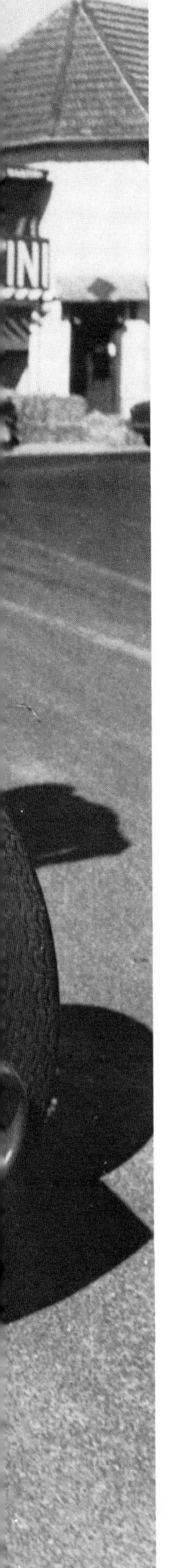

Section III: 2½-litre heyday, 1954-60

Chapter 5
Into the front-engined twilight

Back at Maranello, Ferrari faced the prospect of rebuilding its team round a squad of new drivers after losing Musso, Collins and Hawthorn within a few months of each other. The Dino 246 development continued smoothly under Carlo Chiti's guiding hand and these well-balanced front-engined machines featured several major revisions for the new season. Equipped with not only Dunlop disc brakes but also Dunlop tyres as standard (Hawthorn had "unofficially" tried some Dunlops during practice for the previous year's British Grand Prix and the indications were very positive), the Dinos also sported de Dion rear ends complete with coil springs and distinctive new bodywork from Fantuzzi. The rear mounted fuel and oil tanks were totally enclosed by this new bodywork and a revised exhaust system was fitted with the tail pipes emerging beneath the rear suspension. The cockpit sides were much higher than on the 1958 Dino and the nose section more elegantly styled. The wheelbase was increased by 2.3in to 87.4in and a revised gearbox with five speeds was provided.

On the driver front things were very different. Phil Hill and Olivier Gendebien were still on the team, but von Trips had fallen briefly from favour, so three new drivers were signed up for 1959. One was Jean Behra, the volatile, excitable, talented and extrovert Frenchman; another was down-to-earth British newcomer Cliff Allison, an uncomplicated and straightforward farmer/garage owner from Westmoreland, and the last to join was former Vanwall driver, the supremely able Tony Brooks. Inevitably, with all his accumulated experience and record of success, Brooks was quickly to become regarded as team leader, much to Behra's indignation.

There could hardly be more of a contrast in character between the likes of Hawthorn and Collins and the quiet, formal, yet unstintingly civil former dental student who'd proved himself the equal of Stirling Moss in the Vanwall team through 1957 and '58. Brooks only took the Ferrari drive late in the day because there was nothing left for him in the way of front-line drives after Tony Vandervell effectively quit the Grand Prix scene: 25 years later he recalled the circumstances of his arrival at Ferrari, and the difference between the two autocrats, Tony Vandervell and Enzo Ferrari. . .

"After my stints at Connaught and Vanwall, I'd always thought of myself as waving the Union Jack, which might seem terribly unfashionable today, but I don't apologize for that. So, in actual fact, be it whispered, I went to Ferrari because there was nothing else around! I'd been hanging on for Tony Vandervell to make up his mind, and frankly he was very slow, which I don't blame him for at all, because the death of Stuart Lewis-Evans really upset him . . . by the time he said 'definitely not', Ferrari was the only option.

I'd never, ever approached a team . . . people had always approached me. That's the way I'd always done things. As you've got to appreciate, coming from a professional background, I was as commercially minded as our dog next door! The idea of going out and selling myself, well . . . as I say, I was just a terribly conservative public schoolboy from a professional background. That was quite a handicap in a commercial world. I'd always waited for people to come to me. I can't remember how it happened, but the Ferrari offer came and I thought 'jolly good' so I went over and we quickly came to an agreement." As an afterthought, and in a typically modest piece of understatement, Tony added "I think I was regarded as a good catch."

As far as Vandervell and Ferrari were concerned, Brooks reflected, "I think they had a lot in common in that they were both actually dictators within their teams, but then I don't believe you can gain Grand Prix success without having one guy whose word is absolutely gospel. It's so competitive that somebody must be available to make instant decisions. However, I must say that it was very reassuring when we had Tony Vandervell at the races because it gave him a good insight into what was going on in the field. Staying in the factory, getting reports and watching on TV isn't the same as hearing all the cursing and swearing first-hand. I don't think I actually saw Enzo Ferrari more than two or three times during my whole year with his team . . ."

Over the winter testing continued as usual at Modena, the regular drivers sharing this task with works tester Martino Severi. Cliff Allison recalls an occasion he went down to Italy with Tony Brooks to test both transverse leaf and coil springs on the rear of the Dino 246, an occasion on which they found themselves measured against the "Modena local" who'd got far more practice than they had at the airfield track.

"On first acquaintance that coil sprung Dino felt like an American car it was so soft, but they wouldn't change any of the spring rates until we'd proved that it was quicker than the leaf sprung car. They just said that we had to prove the coil sprung car was faster. We took about three days to prove the point . . . and then they thought about changing the spring rates. As for Severi, he could be a bloody nuisance: he did nothing but go round and round Modena all day and we, the regular drivers, were expected to beat his time immediately we stepped into the car. He was quick at Modena, but nowhere else!"

Brave Jean Behra shows off the sleek, distinctive lines of the Fantuzzi-bodied 1959 Dino 246 as he leads Stirling Moss's Rob Walker Cooper out of Station hairpin during the Monaco Grand Prix. Eventually the Frenchman's enthusiasm proved more than the V6 engine could put up with and it blew to pieces in spectacular fashion!

However one sliced it, the Dinos were in decline in 1959, desperately fighting a rear guard action against the crop of central-engined Cooper and Lotus opposition. Brooks's début with the team was at the non-Championship Aintree 200 on April 18, a worthwhile "warm up" for the British Grand Prix which was to be held on the Liverpool circuit in July. Ranged against BRM and Cooper-Climax opposition, the Ferraris were not the fastest cars on the track, but they were the most reliable and Behra took his 256-engined Dino to an eventual victory, aided by retirements, from Brooks in one of the regular 246s. Before the start of the Grand Prix season the team also contested the BRDC International Trophy at Silverstone, Brooks qualifying on pole but retiring with a misfire, while Phil Hill was fourth in the other 246 entry, a lap behind Jack Brabham's winning Cooper-Climax at the end of the 40 lap contest.

The opening World Championship round at Monaco on May 10 underlined the fact that the more agile central-engined machines would have a significant advantage at all but the fastest circuits. The trio of Dino 246s for Behra, Phil Hill and Brooks were equipped with larger radiators and cut-back nose sections for this tight, hot circuit and Behra did well to qualify second alongside Stirling Moss in the Rob Walker Cooper-Climax. The Frenchman led in the opening phase of the race, shadowed by both Moss and Brabham's works Cooper, and the Ferrari kept ahead until lap 20 when it suddenly slowed and, five laps later, the Dino 246 broke its engine spectacularly, spewing oil and hot metal all over the track at the Gasworks hairpin.

As was so often to be the case in 1959, Moss's Cooper-Climax seemed set for an easy victory, only to fall victim to mechanical problems. On this occasion the

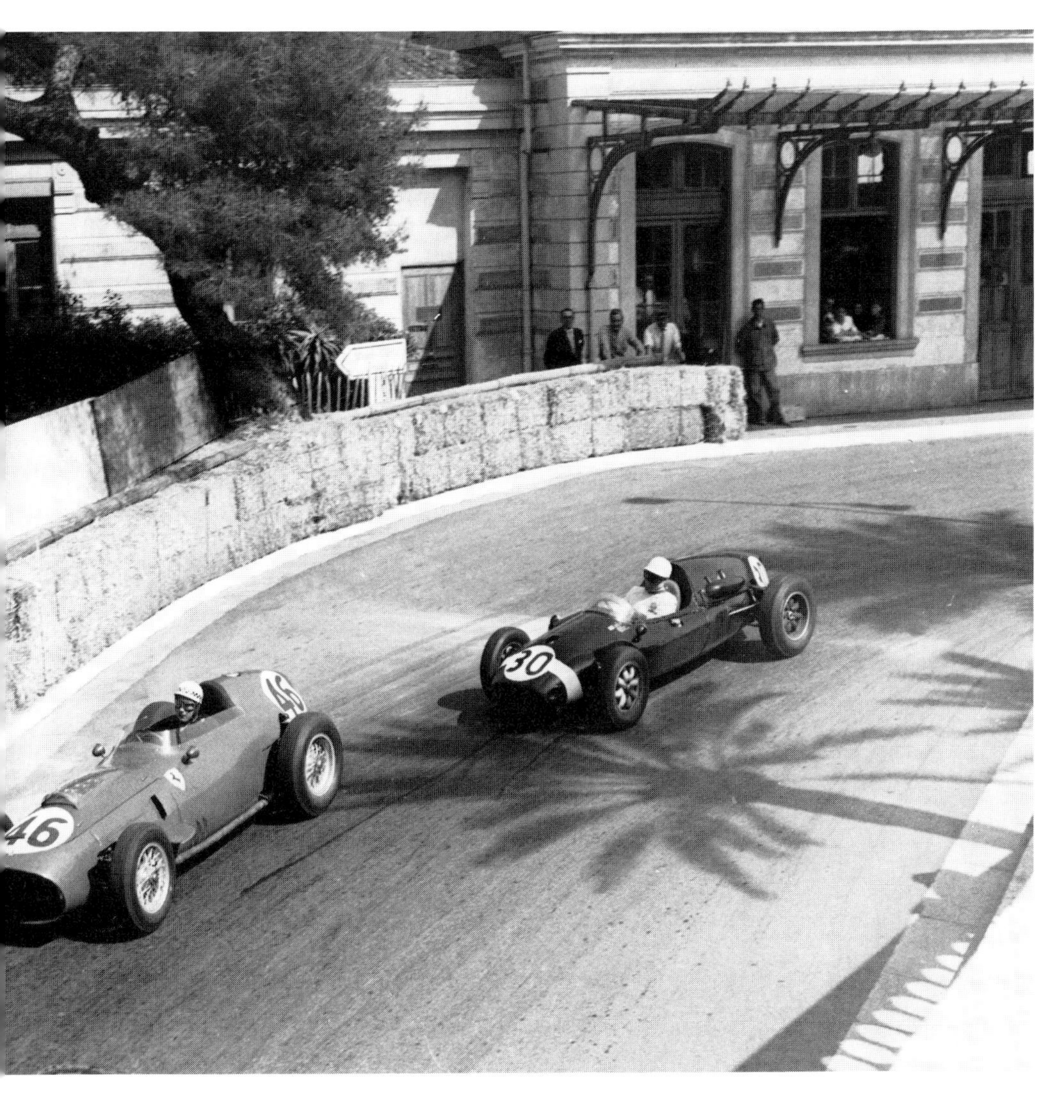

transmission caused trouble in the final stages of the race, leaving Brabham to score a well-judged victory from the hard-trying Brooks, Trintignant's Cooper and Hill in the other Dino, three laps down after a couple of earlier spins had dropped him from what might well have been second.

The Monaco race result gave rise to the only occasion on which the normally placid Brooks was mildly annoyed with the Italian popular press, so often the "bogeyman" for a foreign (i.e. non-Italian) Ferrari driver.

"The exhaust fumes had built up in the cockpit to the point where I was physically sick, but I finished second to Jack. If I hadn't been ill, I'd have been able to give him a better run for his money, even though a front-engined Ferrari versus a well-sorted rear-engined Cooper round Monaco would have been a tall order anyway. Then there were suggestions in the Italian press that I was rather sick and weakly . . . I suppose if I'd retired they'd have said 'well, he did his best' but to carry on in your own vomit to finish the damned race, feeling like nothing on earth with a splitting headache, round that circuit, I thought I did damned well finishing second."

Unfortunately the Belgian Grand Prix was cancelled in 1959, depriving Brooks

Continued on page 130

Alberto Ascari wheels his Lancia D50 into Monaco's Station hairpin during the 1955 Grand Prix: the Italian finished this race in the harbour a matter of seconds before he would have inherited the lead on the retirement of Stirling Moss's Mercedes-Benz. Less than a week later this great Italian champion would be dead, killed practising a sports Ferrari at Monza — and in a matter of months the whole Lancia D50 project passed to Ferrari as the Turin marque withdrew from Grand Prix racing.
Photo: LAT Photographic

Paul Frère shows off the distinctive lines of the type 555 "Super Squalo" as he speeds past the pits at Spa-Francorchamps on his way to fourth place in the 1955 Belgian Grand Prix. Generally, the "Squalos" were unloved by their drivers, but Frère was one of the few who realised that a change in driving style was necessary to get the best out of this difficult machine.
Photo: LAT Photographic

Eugenio Castellotti "inherited" this bruised and battle-scarred Lancia-Ferrari D50 after Fangio had abused it in uncharacteristic fashion during the opening stages of the 1956 Monaco Grand Prix. The Italian driver did well to nurse the battered machine home in fourth place behind Moss's winning Maserati 250F. Fangio (who'd taken over Peter Collin's Lancia-Ferrari) and Jean Behra's Maserati.
Photo: LAT Photographic

Showing off the lines of the 1957 "final derivative" of the Lancia-Ferrari marriage, Luigi Musso swings his 801 through Rouen's Noveau Monde hairpin on his way to second place in the 1957 French Grand Prix behind Fangio's Maserati.
Photo: LAT Photographic

English hero: Peter Collins's Dino 246 speeds through the Silverstone cornfields on its way to a dominant victory in the 1958 British Grand Prix. A couple of weeks later he was to crash fatally racing for the lead at the Nürburgring . . .
Photo: Geoffrey Goddard

This splendid "over the driver's shoulder" shot shows the angled Dino 246 engine and the aero screen, within the wrap-round windscreen, which was so favoured by Mike Hawthorn.
Photo: Graham Gauld

26

DUNLOP DU
20

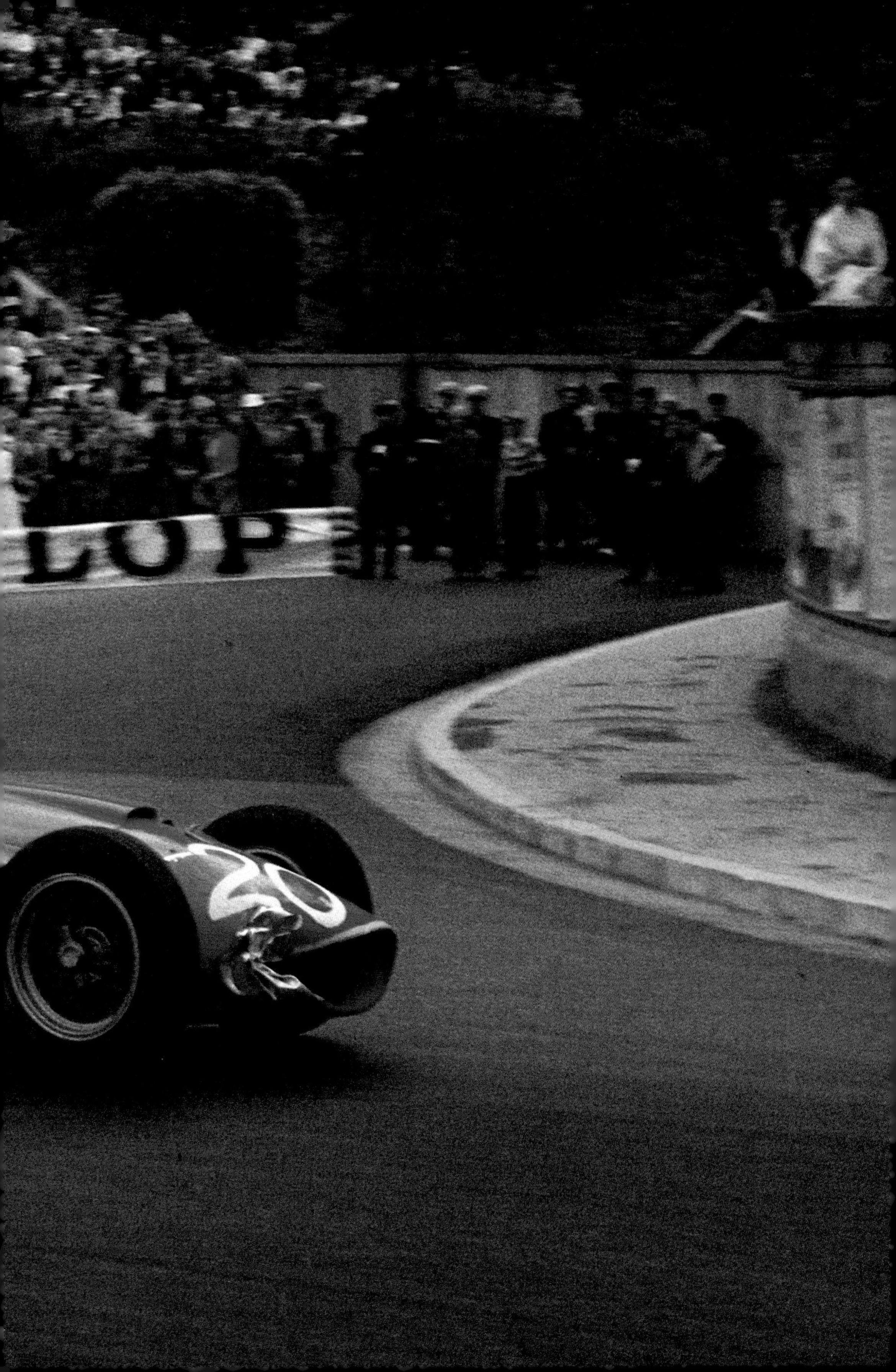
LOP
20

10

INA

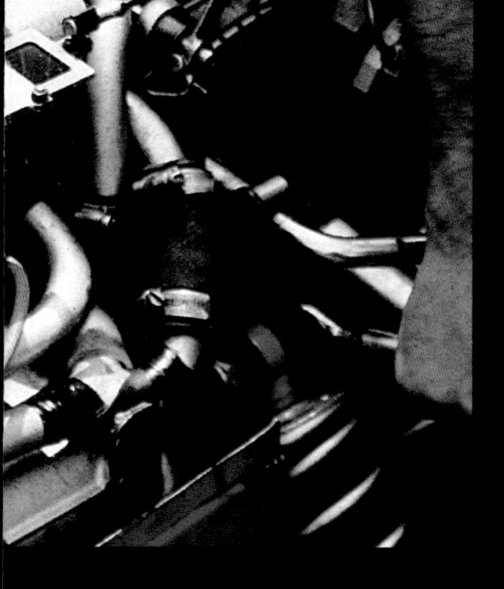

8

6

18

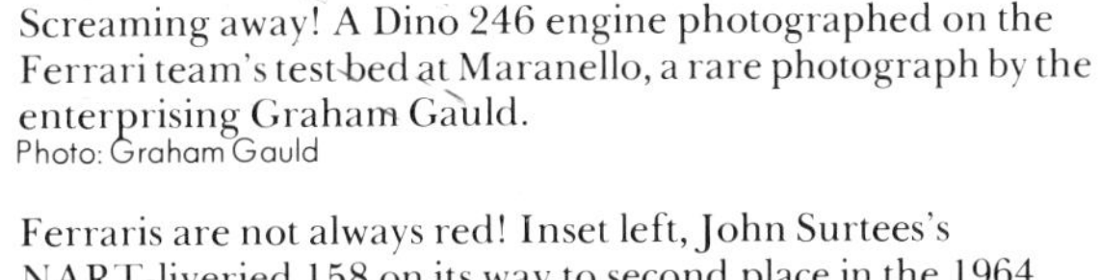

Screaming away! A Dino 246 engine photographed on the Ferrari team's test-bed at Maranello, a rare photograph by the enterprising Graham Gauld.
Photo: Graham Gauld

Ferraris are not always red! Inset left, John Surtees's NART-liveried 158 on its way to second place in the 1964 United States Grand Prix at Watkins Glen. Right, displaying the magnificent canary yellow livery of Equipe Nationale Belge, Olivier Gendebien's 65-degree 156 rounds Spa's La Source hairpin during the 1961 Belgian Grand Prix. He finished fourth.
Photo: Geoffrey Goddard (right), LAT Photographic (inset)

1961 World Champion Phil Hill stands in the cockpit of his 156 as he fastens his helmet prior to the start of that year's British Grand Prix at Aintree. He finished second to team mate Wolfgang von Trips.
Photo: Graham Gauld

This magnificent close study of the 1963 Ferrari 156 shows new recruit John Surtees locking tightly over through *Station Hairpin* at Monaco during his energetic chase to fourth place.
Photo: Geoffrey Goddard

Ferrari's neat little 1½-litre V8 was designed by Angelo Bellei and regarded by many at Maranello as a "stop-gap" between the V6 and Forghieri's neat flat-12. This photograph shows its neat installation, engine cover removed, in the 158 chassis.
Photo: Graham Gauld

Lorenzo Bandini was a stalwart supporter of the Prancing Horse, driving for Ferrari, on and off, from 1962 until his death in 1967. His only Grand Prix was here at the Zeltweg airfield in the summer of 1964 where his 156 held off Richie Ginther's BRM V8 to triumph in the first World Championship Austrian GP.
Photo: Geoffrey Goddard

Ludovico Scarfiotti's win in the 1966 Italian Grand Prix at Monza was one of the few bright spots of the Ferrari team's 1966 season after John Surtees left. Here the Italian sweeps through *Parabolica* at the wheel of his 36-valve 312 on the way to a great victory.
Photo: LAT Photographic

So sad. Lorenzo Bandini shows off the beautiful lines of the 1967 36-valve 312 during the Monaco Grand Prix. The willing Italian was, in the words of Chris Amon "just beginning to emerge from the shadow of John Surtees", but his talent was never to develop any further. Shortly after this photograph was taken, Bandini crashed and sustained injuries which were to prove fatal.
Photo: Phipps Photographic

Sitting low in the Dino 246 cockpit, Behra is seen here at speed during the 1959 French Grand Prix at Reims-Gueux. It was his last Grand Prix for Ferrari, as he thumped team manager Romolo Tavoni after a heated debate when he retired the Dino . . .

of another opportunity to score a win on a circuit which would have suited both the front-engined Ferrari Dino and his meticulous driving style. At Zandvoort for the Dutch Grand Prix, the 256 engine with Weber 50DCN carburetters was installed into the F2 156 frame and Behra decided that he preferred it to his regular car after some juggling round in practice, so he used it in the race. Jo Bonnier took pole position for BRM flanked by the Coopers of Brabham and Moss and Behra on the inside of the second row. But the race itself brought forth little in the way of luck for the Dinos: Brooks and Behra ran third and fourth in the early stages, but Tony retired after 45 laps after an oil union had pumped most of the engine's lubricant over the Dino's rear end and tyres while Behra wound up fifth, one lap down on Bonnier's winning BRM, after a typically erratic drive under pressure. Moss, once again, broke down with transmission problems whilst well in the lead. Phil Hill finished sixth while Cliff Allison, on his Grand Prix début, brought his Dino 246 home ninth.

On the political front, it was clear that Jean Behra felt that he should be regarded as the team's number one driver and a degree of friction was building up within the team as the Commendatore again declined to specify which one of his men was actually team leader. Yet, by the time the French Grand Prix at Reims-Gueux was over, Brooks would have established his position as the fastest, best driver employed by Maranello . . . and Behra would be out of the team!

The temperature recorded at Reims on July 5, 1959 was the hottest for some 86 years and in these parched, sun-scorched conditions, Tony Brooks stamped his utter and complete domination on the French Grand Prix. He started his Dino 246 from pole position, some 5.3s faster than Hawthorn's stupendous race record from the previous year, and drove away from the opposition in the relaxed style that had become his trademark. For this race the Formula 1 cars had revised de Dion rear suspension which improved their handling and, geared for 8800rpm in fifth, Brooks was topping 180mph regularly on the long straight.

Talented trio! Ferrari's English-speaking 1959 driver line-up seen awaiting the start of practice at Avus. Phil Hill, left, would become World Champion for Maranello two years later, but Tony Brooks (right) was to leave at the end of '59 to concentrate on his garage business at home in England. A crew-cut Dan Gurney (centre) left Ferrari for BRM, then Porsche, Brabham and his own Eagle organization . . .

Behra, who'd qualified on the outside of the second row behind Brabham, Phil Hill and Moss's BRP-liveried BRM, stalled on the line but staged a superb recovery which got him up to third at one point before over-shooting a corner and dropping back to fourth. Unfortunately, on lap 29, just after equalling his own lap record set earlier in the afternoon, Jean's engine expired with a melted piston and he coasted into the pits. In his highly-charged emotional state, this was no time to start a debate with the French driver but Tavoni prompted a discussion which quickly got out of hand. Behra lost his temper and, after thumping the Ferrari team manager, his place in the Maranello F1 squad as well.

Brooks recalls the volatile Frenchman: "My status within the team hadn't been sorted out by the start of the Reims weekend and Behra, I was told, had his nose out of joint over the whole business. I must admit I never spoke to him, apart from saying hello, how are you. I always tried to be polite, but he didn't seem a very outgoing guy and didn't speak very good Italian. I did, for an Englishman, but I didn't speak French. I don't think we exchanged more than half a dozen sentences the whole time we were together on the team. It wasn't a case of me trying to be difficult and I don't think he held anything personally against me – his argument, I think, was with Ferrari. Whether they'd told him he was going to be number one, I don't know, but I just joined the team on the understanding that I was going to get a car as good as everybody else. At Ferrari I always got a car which was the equal of my team-mate's – which is more than I can say for the time with Vanwall."

After Behra left the team, Brooks cemented his own status as team leader with a fine victory on the absurdly fast Avus track in Berlin, a section of dual carriageway autobahn linked by a hairpin at one end and a spectacular, brick-surfaced 180-degree banking at the other. Brooks won both of the 60 lap heats for an aggregate victory ahead of team-mates Dan Gurney (who'd made his début at Reims) and Phil Hill. Cliff Allison had actually qualified fastest during practice, but as he was a reserve entry he had to start the first heat from fourth row despite a stunning 2m 5.8s (147mph lap), a tenth of a second quicker than "official" pole man Brooks.

Looking untypically relaxed, "Wild Willy" Mairesse rounds Spa's La Source hairpin on his Dino 246 début in the 1960 Belgian Grand Prix. This was the race in which he was involved in the frightening battle with Chris Bristow's Yeoman Credit Cooper, resulting in a fatal accident to the young Englishman.

Allison, whose Dino 246 retired early in the first heat with clutch trouble, recalls that quick lap round Avus with a mixture of amusement and pride: "I thought my car was exactly the same as the other three, but it just wouldn't pull the same revs. So I thought to myself, I'll go through the kink on to the banking without lifting . . well, I did, and I nearly slid sideways all the way up the banking. I thought, Christ, I'm coming in after this. When I pulled into the pits everybody was cheering because I'd done this record lap. But the engine still wasn't pulling maximum revs. Then they told me that it was an experimental engine and they were worried that it wouldn't last, so they'd fitted the car with a longer top gear . . but they never told me that before!" Sadly Allison's other memory of this race at Avus involved having an uncomfortably close view of former team-mate Jean Behra's fatal accident when the Frenchman crashed his Porsche sports car over the top of the banking.

Prior to the German Grand Prix Ferrari had missed another good opportunity by failing to contest the British Grand Prix at Aintree, another circuit on which Brooks had harboured hopes of doing well in view of the early season result in the Aintree 200.

On August 23 the Portuguese Grand Prix took place at Lisbon's Monsanto Park circuit where Ferrari fielded Dino 246s for Brooks, Hill and Gurney. The bumpy road circuit left the front-engined Italian cars pretty well out of the hunt and Gurney emerged the best-placed survivor, a lap down on Moss's winning Walker

Cooper-Climax in third. Phil Hill collided with namesake Graham's Lotus 16 as he sought to make up time following an early excursion up an escape road, but Tony Brooks was just plain slow, out of contention and placed ninth at the finish. "I just couldn't get it together," he reflected, "we were driving into the sun for half a lap. . . There's a lot in this theory of biorhythms, I think, so perhaps I was just down on that particular day."

If Brooks thought his driving wasn't up to par at Lisbon, then he recalls the 1959 Italian Grand Prix at Monza as "the lowest day in my career." On home ground, in the one remaining race that the Ferrari Dinos could be expected to acquit themselves with certain honour, Tony's car burnt its clutch out on the line as he attempted to accelerate away from his place in the middle of the front row of the grid between the Coopers of Moss and Brabham. This was the race at which he could well have clinched the 1959 World Championship, but he was left to watch from the sidelines as Phil Hill sped to a confident second place behind Moss's winning Cooper. The Ferrari made routine pit stops for fresh tyres, so Stirling knew full-well that he was in good position sitting behind Phil in the opening stages. Just as in Argentina, the Ferrari team was waiting for Moss to come in and change in the closing stages, but the nimble Walker Cooper ran through non-stop to beat Phil quite easily. Brabham wound up third with the Dino 246s of Gurney, Allison and Gendebien blaring home in the next three places.

The World Championship decider didn't take place until December 12, when the United States Grand Prix at Sebring rounded off the Formula 1 season, so the title contenders were left biting their nails for three long months . . if one can honestly imagine either Brabham or Brooks actually biting their nails! For this final fling three of the Dino 246s were reworked with a totally independent rear suspension system comprising double wishbones and co-axial coil spring damper units, while a de Dion F2 chassis was provided for Phil Hill (and painted in American national blue and white livery) powered by a single cam Dino 196S-type sports car-based engine.

Bugged by unpredictable handling, Brooks was the fastest Ferrari qualifier on the inside of the second row, almost six seconds slower than Moss's pole position Cooper. Von Trips, Allison and Hill were also in the team, but on the opening lap the enthusiastic German driver ran into the back of Tony's 246 and the Englishman pulled in at the end of the first lap to check for damage. It might well have cost Brooks his World Championship, but to continue non-stop would have been out of step with Tony's personal creed.

First lap scramble! Round the hairpin at one end of the Avus autobahn circuit goes the pack early during the second heat of the 1959 German Grand Prix. Bonnier's BRM is leading from Phil Hill's Dino (No.5), Bruce McLaren's Cooper, the Dinos of Brooks (No.4) and Gurney (No.6) and the Walker Cooper of Stirling Moss.

"I felt a responsibility to myself to come in and check the car," he explained, "I think that taking an uncalculated risk could lead to what amounts to suicide and I have a religious conviction that such risks are not acceptable. I learnt from my accidents at Le Mans with an Aston Martin and at Silverstone with the BRM that I would never try and compensate for a mechanically deficient car. So I just felt that I was morally bound to stop. . ."

The race was eventually won by Bruce McLaren's Cooper after Moss's transmission failed, Trintignant finishing a close second in Walker's other car. Brabham ran out of fuel on the last lap, leaving Brooks to finish third, but the Australian pushed his Cooper across the line to take fourth place and clinch the World Championship title. Phil Hill retired with clutch trouble after nine laps,

Hawthorn's protégé. Westmoreland farmer/garage owner Cliff Allison grins from his perch atop the fuel tank of his Ferrari Dino 246 in the Buenos Aires pits prior to the 1960 Argentine Grand Prix. Allison reckons that Mike Hawthorn's influence at Maranello helped earn him a place in the team.

Allison drove well to finish second in the 1960 Argentine Grand Prix, an inadvertently incorrect tyre choice perhaps depriving him of the chance of challenging McLaren's winning Cooper.

Allison's 246 suffered a similar fate whilst running third – "I was sick, I really felt I could have caught those two Coopers", recalled Cliff – while von Trips was well placed until the last lap when his engine broke and he wound up sixth at the end.

A close call for Ferrari's last front-engined machine, but as close as the Dino 246 would ever get to winning its second Championship. At the end of the 1959 season Tony Brooks quit to return to England, driving for the uncompetitive Yeoman Credit team the following year in order to be able to concentrate more on his fledgling garage business in Weybridge.

"It was a hard decision," he smiles, "because while I could see them having only a moderate year in 1960, it didn't need a genius to see that the World Champion would be a Ferrari driver in 1961 simply because they were winning Formula 2 races in what amounted to their 1961 F1 car back in 1959. It was a terribly difficult thing to do because I realized that I was probably giving up another chance of the title. There was no number one driver at Ferrari, but my winning two Grands Prix had left me very well placed within the team. But I don't regret it, largely because, you see, the right guy wasn't winning the Championship anyway."

As will be explained in a separate section, the Dino V6's engine development programme was to lead Maranello into a strong position at the start of the 1½-litre Formula 1 which began in 1961. But, on the existing racing front, the 1960 season still had to be tackled – using the ultimate Dino 246 derivative, arguably the most finely-honed front engined Grand Prix car of all. On the driver front Dan Gurney had opted for a switch to BRM, having seen their new central-engined prototype and received a worthwhile financial proposition, but fellow Californian Phil Hill stayed loyal to the Old Man. Partnering Phil in the opening World Championship round at Buenos Aires on February 7, 1960 were Cliff Allison, Wolfgang von Trips and local veteran Froilan Gonzalez, having yet another one-off home outing.

The way in which the chassis layout of the final Dino 246 version was arranged indicated yet again just how willing Ferrari was to retrace his own technical path if the need arose. One could, with some justification, say that this was back to square one, for Carlo Chiti had decided to concentrate as much weight within the wheelbase as possible, Squalo-type pannier fuel tanks being mounted on either side of the cockpit, only retaining a small fuel supply and the oil tank in the tail of the car. The V6 engines were moved back in the chassis some 9.8in as an additional contribution to improved weight distribution and handling characteristics. The engines were now angled the other way across in the frame for the new season, from left front to right rear, and the final drive/gearbox assembly was revised, providing a left-hand gear-change for the drivers with a totally new gate pattern. This was to be Cliff Allison's undoing, by his own admission, during practice at Monaco.

The 1960 four-cam Dino 246 engine was officially quoted as developing 280bhp at 8500rpm, but providing improved torque at lower speeds than the 1959 unit. Hill's car at Buenos Aires had a two-cam Dino engine again, but the other two machines were four-cam machines and it was Cliff Allison who emerged from the 80 lap, 312km event in the best shape with a fine second place to Bruce McLaren's winning Cooper-Climax. Von Trips managed to take fifth place, Phil Hill was a heat-troubled eighth and Gonzalez tenth and last.

It was another "if only" race for the enthusiastic, taciturn driver from rural Westmoreland, spoilt by a mix-up when fitting the Dunlop tyres to his 246 prior to the race. Allison: "Dunlop's Vic Barlow told us that we could either use 5mm tread depth and a light fuel load in order to run fast and then make a pit stop, or we could go through with a full fuel load and 7mm tyres. I said that I'd go through non-stop, but although they topped up my tanks to the brim, a tyre fitting mix-up saw me going to the line with 5mm tread tyres fitted. I was six seconds behind Bruce and decided to give it a run when the marker strips began appearing on my front tyres . . I'm sure I could have won on the 7mm treads!" None the less, Cliff's performance tended to endorse the view of those at Maranello who thought he had quite an F1 future ahead of him.

Prior to starting the European season, Hill and Allison had an abortive outing in the BRDC International Trophy at Silverstone on May 14. Innes Ireland won the race impressively in his central-engined Lotus 18-Climax and the front-engined Ferraris were outclassed. Hill was fifth, Allison eighth: both were lapped.

The Monaco Grand Prix meeting two weeks later saw the début of a most significant Ferrari, the experimental rear-engined Dino 246 which Phil Hill and Martino Severi had briefly tried at Modena the previous week. Built round a multi-tube spaceframe and featuring double wishbone independent suspension in the style of the front-engined Dino 246s, it was powered by a regular four-cam engine with twin coil and distributor ignition and its drive was transmitted by means of a totally new five-speed gearbox in unit with the final drive incorporating an overhung clutch at its rear end. The car was entrusted to new Formula 1 recruit, Californian Richie Ginther.

Practice was marred by a spectacular accident when Cliff Allison clipped the chicane in his Dino 246, the car pirouetting violently, throwing its driver out on to the track from whence he was rushed to hospital with unpleasant head and facial injuries. Cliff had set a promising grid time on the first day of practice only for the time to be scrubbed due to a failure in the circuit timing apparatus: by the time

Ouch! The end of Cliff Allison's Ferrari Grand Prix career as he is pitched out of his Dino 246 after hitting the chicane at Monaco during practice for the 1960 Grand Prix. By his own admission, he'd changed from fifth to second, locking the rear wheels, "and woke up in hospital speaking French . . .which was strange, because I didn't know any French!"

Tavoni communicated this to Cliff, the Englishman was waiting to do a full-tank run on new tyres. . .

"But I decided that I would have to go for a time,' reflected Allison somewhat regretfully, "and going down into the chicane I got caught out by that revised gear shift, went from fifth to second, locked the rear wheels and glanced the barrier. No excuse, it was all my own fault . . ." Sadly, it was also the end of Cliff Allison's Ferrari racing career.

With so many good, competitive central-engined cars around, it was too much to expect Maranello's front-engined "museum pieces" to show particularly well and they all qualified towards the middle of the grid. In the race, however, Phil Hill drove with controlled brilliance, refusing to give up in the face of apparently overwhelming odds, and wound up a splendid third behind Stirling Moss's Walker Lotus 18 and McLaren's Cooper. Ginther was classified sixth in the rear-engined prototype, pushing it across the line after stopping to investigate transmission noises, and von Trips's clutch broke after 62 laps.

The customary Dino 246 débâcle followed at Zandvoort on June 6 where Ginther was included as a member of the "front-engined squad" for the Dutch Grand Prix after the central-engined car appeared briefly in practice. Despite a tremendous start from Hill, who poked his 246 up into fifth place in the opening rush, erratic throttle control gremlins slowed him and he eventually retired after an abortive pit stop. Brabham's new works lowline Cooper-Climax ran out an easy winner with von Trips and Ginther surviving to a lapped fifth and sixth.

On the wide open spaces of Spa-Francorchamps, the Dino 246s could be expected to give a reasonable account of themselves in this twilight season and Phil

A sign of things to come. Works test driver Martino Severi puts the new rear-engined Dino 246 through its paces at Modena prior to Richie Ginther's race début with the car at Monaco.

Long time colleague of Ferrari was veteran engineer Luigi Bazzi, seen here making notes in the Monza pits about the rear-engined 156 used by von Trips in the 1960 Italian Grand Prix.

Hill performed magnificently to get on to the outside of the front row flanked by Brabham's pole-winning Cooper and the Yeoman Credit car of former Dino driver Tony Brooks. Phil hacked round splendidly in the leading bunch, getting his Dino 246 alongside Brabham on the Masta straight early in the race and really revelling in the whole business.

Further back, a horrifyingly spectacular battle between Belgian F1 debutant "Wild Willy" Mairesse (Dino 246) and Yeoman Credit Cooper driver Chris Bristow came to a tragic end when the Englishman got badly off-line as he entered the plunging right-hander at *Burnenville*, slewing off the road into a fence and being killed instantly in an appalling accident. Later in the race Alan Stacey was also killed when he was struck by a bird whilst at speed in his Lotus on the Masta straight and, with Stirling Moss lying hospitalized after a serious practice accident, the 1960 Belgian Grand Prix was truly a race to forget. Willy's Ferrari retired shortly after this tragedy with transmission trouble, and with von Trips out with a broken driveshaft, Hill was left on his own to fight for Maranello's honour. Unfortunately he stopped out on the circuit on lap 29 when a cold petrol leak from a capillary tube to the fuel pressure gauge briefly ignited. Phil extinguished the fire, toured round to the pits for a permanent repair to be effected and continued to finish a lapped fourth.

Phil went on the attack again at Reims-Gueux, venue for the French Grand Prix on July 3, Maranello hoping for another victory, but despite a furious effort from the American – which included him getting close enough to Brabham's winning Cooper that he bumped his 246 nose on one of its rear wheels – the Italian cars were out of luck. Hill lasted until lap 29 when his wheel-to-wheel battle with the Australian World Champion ended in transmission failure. Mairesse and von Trips succumbed to similar failures, so that was that.

Only Hill and von Trips contested the British Grand Prix at Silverstone, predictably a bit of a waste of time. Eclipsed again by the central-engined brigade, Phil and Taffy struggled home sixth and seventh, two laps behind winner Brabham in another race to push to the back of their memories. In the Portuguese Grand Prix at Oporto, Hill sprang into contention from his fourth row grid position and ran third in the early stages behind Surtees's Lotus 18 and Moss's similar Walker car. Unfortunately his Dino's clutch later packed up, he missed a gearchange and understeered off into some straw bales, deranging the steering. Phil tried to get the car running again in order to qualify as a finisher, but the organizers wouldn't allow him to wait at the start/finish line. He tried to get the car started again, but with the clutch unable to disengage, there was no way.

With the German Grand Prix organizers opting for a Formula 2 race in order to give their home team, Porsche, a good chance, there was only one more World Championship Grand Prix left on the calendar: Monza. It was the Italian organizers intention to run the 1960 Italian Grand Prix on a combination of banked and road circuits, perhaps sensing this wouldn't meet with the British constructors' approval. They were right! Perhaps unwilling to risk their "fragile" central-engined creations on the bumpy banked section, the British constructors contacted the Royal Automobile Club on the matter.

At an RAC Competitions Committee meeting on July 13, 1960 it was reported "that the main British constructors had advised the Italian Automobile Club of their unwillingness to participate in the Italian Grand Prix, which this year is the Grand Prix of Europe, as it is to be run over the full circuit of Monza, i.e. the banked track and the road circuit combined. They would be prepared to enter an event on the road circuit only, as has been the case since 1957. So far, no reply has been received."

The Italians couldn't have given a damn about the British teams. They went ahead with their own Grand Prix on their own terms and the sight of Phil Hill, Richie Ginther and Willy Mairesse ranged across the front row, dominant in their Dino 246s, was sufficient to sent the *tifosi* into paroxysms of delight. Despite two stops for fresh Dunlops, the front-engined Dinos came home 1-2-3 in the order Hill, Ginther, Mairesse, only Giulio Cabianca's Cooper-Ferrari 4-cyl. breaking up a grand slam by splitting von Trips' 1½-litre rear-engined V6 156 away from its bigger-engined stable-mates by taking fourth place.

On that ecstatic note, the Formula 1 Grand Prix Dino 246s drove into the history books. You only need Ferrari to keep an Italian crowd happy!

Section IV: Initial advantage dissipated:

The 1½-litre cars, 1961-65

Chapter 1
The higher they fly, the harder they fall . . .

The 120-degree Chiti-designed Dino V6 which necessitated the bowed-out upper chassis rails in the engine bay to façilitate its installation.

Ferrari dominated the first year of the 1½-litre Formula 1 through being, technically, "in the right place at the right time," but it was to be a short-lived renaissance. The lesson that had been drummed out to Maranello in 1959, namely that chassis technology was now just as important as engine power output, continued to be the case. In 1961 Ferrari's V6 engines were to power a distinctly indifferent chassis to victory in the World Championship : in 1962, the advent of multi-cylinder engines from BRM and Coventry-Climax enabled the British constructors to leap-frog back into a position of dominance, far stronger than anything they'd exerted in 1959 or '60. Ferrari, through unfortunate circumstances, simply stagnated on the Formula 1 front in 1962.

The story of the 1961-65 1½-litre Formula 1 really began on October 29, 1958 within the lofty portals of the Royal Automobile Club in London's Pall Mall. The occasion was the presentation of awards to Mike Hawthorn and Tony Vandervell to commemorate their victories in the World Drivers' and Constructors' Championships respectively. But CSI President Auguste Perouse threw an absolute bombshell into the meeting when, following the presentations, he announced that the 1½-litre Formula 1, with a 500kg minimum weight limit, would supersede the current 2½-litre formula at the start of 1961. The proposal came from France, who had nothing in the way of racing cars to contribute to the new formula, and the instigation of the new formula was confirmed by a vote on the CSI Committee which came out in favour of the new regulations by 5-2 : only Britain and Italy voted positively for the continuation of the current 2½-litre formula.

The English constructors were almost apoplectic with rage and the RAC Competitions Committee meeting on the afternoon of Wednesday, November 12, 1958 saw Lord Howe report that, "despite the efforts of the RAC, backed up by technical information offered by leading drivers and manufacturers, a decision had been taken which was most unpopular with British interests . . .The only redeeming feature appeared to be that Great Britain, Italy and the United States had been authorized to propose another formula to suit their mutual interests which for the time being was referred to as an 'inter-continental' formula. A meeting of British interested parties would be held to consider this."

The Inter-Continental category was to flourish briefly on the British domestic scene as a 3-litre "F1/formule libre", but it soon withered as it became clear that the 1½-litre Formula 1 was not only going to get off the ground, but Ferrari, after his initial objections, was well down the road towards preparing a competitive challenge in 1961. As has so frequently been the case over the past twenty years, the British lobby within Formula 1 racing found itself out of step with its

Richie Ginther launched Ferrari's assault on the 1½-litre formula with a stupendous performance in the 1961 Monaco Grand Prix, establishing a new lap record as he chased Stirling Moss's Lotus-Climax home in second place.

European rivals and in a position where it misjudged the intentions of the sport's governing body. By the time Climax and BRM got started on their V8s, it was already mid-way through 1960 and they clearly wouldn't be ready in time for the start of the new formula. The only progress made by the British teams was getting a reduction in the new F1 minimum weight limit to 450kg.

Throughout the last three years of the 2½-litre formula, development had continued on a small-capacity version of the 65-degree V6 engine and, following the début of the central-engined Ferrari 246 at Monaco in 1960, it was quite clear that such a machine would form the basis of Ferrari's long-term plans for 1961. Carlo Chiti had evolved a revised second generation Formula 2 version, replacing the original 70 x 64.5mm V6, which had made its début back at Syracuse in 1957, with a 73 x 58.8mm, 1476.6cc version which, on 38mm Weber carburetters, produced around 180bhp which was quite adequate to deal with the opposition.

Installed in the experimental mid-engined chassis which Ginther had driven at Monaco, the Dino 156 appeared in the *Solituderennen* round the splendid open road circuit near Stuttgart, Wolfgang von Trips dishing out a defeat to Hans Herrmann's four-cylinder Porsche after starting from the middle of the front row, (beaten, it should be mentioned to pole position by the brilliant Jim Clark in a Team Lotus 21). Since Monaco the car had been extensively re-designed with

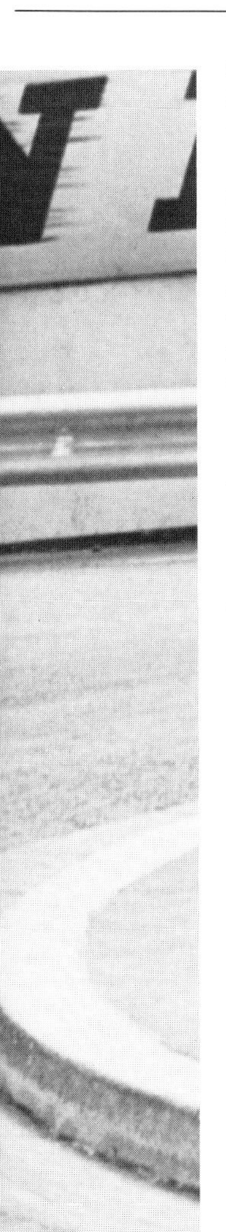

altered suspension, the transmission layout had been tidied up and the car had a more complete look about it thanks to the addition of a smart wrap-round windscreen.

It had originally been planned to run the central-engined car in the Italian Grand Prix equipped with a full 246 engine, but the absence of the British teams allowed the Ferrari team some scope for experimentation, sure in the knowledge that the front-engined Dino 246s could command the event. Thus von Trips was entered in the car with 156 power yet again and was successfully "towed clear" of the opposition by Willy Mairesse's front-engined Grand Prix machine. Only an ill-judged pit stop to check tyre wear dropped the German to fifth behind Cabianca, ruining the symmetry of a Ferrari 1-2-3-4 result.

Von Trips rounded off the "prototype's" first racing season by hurrying to third place at the Modena Grand Prix on October 2, chasing Bonnier's winning Porsche and Ginther's front engined Dino 156 across the line. It was the last outing for the factory front-engined F2 Ferrari, but a promising sign for the 1961 season.

Over the winter Chiti had a long look at the 65-degree engine and decided that he would produce a totally new 120-degree V6 which would suit a central-engined car from the point of view of room for installation and lower centre of gravity. Further, since the original 65-degree unit had been built with capacities of between 1½ and 2½-litres in mind, there was scope for saving some metal (and weight) in the castings for the new, pure 1½-litre unit and there would be ample space within the vee to accommodate any experimental carburettor or fuel injections system that the team might choose to try.

The cylinder heads on the new 120-degree engine were secured by eight studs apiece, as opposed to the 65-degree unit's 12, and the chain driven twin overhead camshafts were retained, the cam drive originating from two half-speed gears on the nose of the crankshaft, the right-hand chain also passing over an extra sprocket, apparently vestigial on the early carburettor engines, but intended in the long-term to drive a fuel injection pump. There were two valves per cylinder and an interesting fundamental difference between the 120-degree engine and its V6 predecessor was that Chiti had arranged the cylinder bank offset with the left-hand bank ahead of the right, rather than vice versa.

Developing a claimed 190bhp at 9500rpm, the 120-degree V6 was installed in a tubular chassis dominated by main upper and lower longerons (of 1½in diameter). Those chassis designated to accept the 120-degree engine had the upper longeron bowed out slightly in order to facilitate installation of the wider engine, while the frames intended for the narrower 65-degree unit had the upper tubes running parallel to the lower. The 65-degree engines were to continue in use as alternative power units for the Ferrari team.

Although, as previously mentioned, a fuel injection system was well to the fore in Chiti's mind, the 120-degree engine started its life fitted with two Weber 401F3C carburettors nestling in the vee. Transmission was handled by developments of the five-speed transaxle seen on the central-engined 1960 prototype, still employing the clutch exposed at the rear of the over-hung gearbox behind the rear axle line. The transaxle casing provided, in effect, a spacer between the engine and final-drive, allowing the V6 engine to be positioned close to the centre of the car in the interests of good weight distribution : it also meant that there would be room to install a larger 87 x 82mm, 2925cc unit which was being made available in the background just in case the Inter-continental formula should get seriously off the ground.

Suspension was by means of unequal length, tubular welded wishbones all round with outboard mounted coil spring/Koni damper units. This essentially rather ungainly chassis, certainly primitive by the delicate tubular standards of Lotus and Cooper, was clothed in distinctively bulbous bodywork, set off by the distinctive twin-nostril "shark's nose" front end treatment and completed by a horizontally-slatted rear aperture at the tail of the bodywork, completely enclosing the engine, gearbox and clutch units. Ferrari also remained the last team in the Grand Prix business to retain centre-lock wire wheels, 15 in. diameter

Phil Hill opened his '61 World Championship season with third place at Monaco, using one of the 65-degree V6 engines in his Dino 156. Here he locks over into Station hairpin, wearing his customary facial expression of great concentration.

Boranni rims being employed for the new 156.

As far as the drivers were concerned, Phil Hill was included in the full-time factory Grand Prix team while von Trips and Richie Ginther were also included. That wiry little Californian Ginther had been a friend of Phil's for several years and was fortunate enough to be "tipped off" by his senior American colleague as to the oft-idiosyncratic ways of Maranello. Richie was thus able to avoid some of the political pitfalls into which Phil had blundered, unknowingly, and certainly enjoyed a fairly relaxed first full season as a Ferrari Grand Prix driver. Hill, by his own admission, was a little irritated by the fact that Ferrari had spent the previous three years building up the "mystique" surrounding Formula 1, and always maintains that the Commendatore could have made more of his skills for longer if he'd let him into the full-time Grand Prix team in 1958. Von Trips, well, he was just von Trips . . .easygoing, uncomplicated and totally unhampered by any sort of technical grasp of the sport. Apocryphal or not, the best tale about "Taffy's" lack of understanding when it came to matters technical, is shown by the alleged occasion he came into the pits and the mechanics told him that a roll-bar was broken. Von Trips glanced up at the Ferrari's *rollover* bar and said, incredulously, "is it?"

In addition to the works cars, a group of Italian racing teams had got together to form the *Federazione Italiana Scuderie Automobilsche* with the intention of promoting a new generation of Italian drivers. They arranged the entry of one of the Ferrari 156s in certain selected events and Giancarlo Baghetti, the 25-year old Milanese driver, eventually gave the 1½-litre Grand Prix Ferrari 156 its race début at Syracuse on April 25. This was a car fitted with a 65-degree engine and, in the absence of Ginther's works 120-degree car, a late withdrawal, the sole Maranello entry present. It was pretty obvious that the new Ferrari was a formidable weapon when the novice Italian qualified second only to Gurney's Porsche, but nobody could have foreseen the impressive outcome of the race, Baghetti eventually working his way to the front and fending off Dan Gurney's Porsche to win comfortably.

Three weeks later the serious business of the World Championship took place at Monaco, an event which turned out to be one of the most exciting and historic events in Grand Prix racing history. The two main protagonists were on the front row: Stirling Moss's pole position Rob Walker Lotus 18, with its outdated four-cylinder Climax engine, and Richie Ginther's 120-degree V6 engined Ferrari 156. Jim Clark's new Team Lotus 21 completed the front row, half a second slower than Moss's pole winning 1m 39.1s, while Phil Hill's 156 was alongside Graham Hill's BRM-Climax on the second row. Phil and von Trips were using 65-degree engines, the sole 120-degree unit (which was still regarded as experimental) being in Richie's machine.

Despite the lack of Monaco experience, Ginther took the initiative at the start although Moss's Lotus and Jo Bonnier's Porsche soon moved through and relegated the American to third place. Hill and von Trips started gently, but Phil eventually battled it out with Bonnier's Porsche and moved through to second place, while Ginther, who'd been chased by von Trips, came back after his team-mates after getting ahead of Bonnier as well. By half distance the order was Moss, Hill and Ginther, with Stirling using the Lotus's agile, nimble handling to extract an overall advantage over the more powerful, but clumsy Ferraris. It was one of Stirling's heroic performances, neat and precise, stamped with the hallmark of a truly brilliant driver. Hill did everything he could to close in on Stirling, getting to within five seconds on lap 55, but by lap 70 Moss's controlled flair was taking him away from the Maranello cars and on lap 72, Ginther took the 120-degree V6 through into second place. Despite the fact that all the Ferraris were hampered by carburettor flooding which frustrated their engine response out of the hairpins, Ginther stood his 156 on its ear and set a new circuit record as he slashed Stirling's advantage to 3.6s at the chequered flag.

Ginther was to win the final race of the 1½-litre formula for Honda at Mexico City in 1965, but none the less rates the 1961 Monaco drive as his greatest race.

Historic moment. Few who watched the 1961 French Grand Prix at Reims-Gueux imagined that Grand Epreuve débutant Giancarlo Baghetti was in with a chance. But as his faster opposition retired, the Italian's FISA-entered 65-degree 156 came to the fore in a battle with the Porsches of Jo Bonnier and Dan Gurney. In a sprint to the line Baghetti, seen here leading

the two silver German cars, outfumbled Gurney to win the first and only Championship Grand Prix of his career.

"My car and my effort were stronger there than they were when I won in the Honda which was just plain *faster* than its oppostion," Richie recalls, "but at Monaco both Stirling and I were three seconds below the pole time in the race - staggering, isn't it? I set the lap record very late (16 laps from the end) but Stirling equalled it next time round. That son of a gun! If you did well against him, then you'd really done something special." And Richie had indeed done something special that Monaco afternoon!

On the same afternoon, Giancarlo Baghetti was busy despatching some make-weight opposition to win the Naples Grand Prix over 60 laps of the Posillipo circuit, setting the fastest race lap in the process, so the future looked promising for this young Italian. Meanwhile the works Grand Prix team was preparing for the Dutch Grand Prix at Zandvoort, scheduled for Whit Monday only eight days after Monaco. Hill, Ginther and von Trips all faced proceedings at Zandvoort armed with 120-degree V6 machines. Phil qualified on pole ahead of von Trips (sharing 1m 35.7s) while Ginther completed the front row. Von Trips led this event from start to finish while Phil, who'd been irritated after the warm-up to find his clutch pedal inoperative, had a troubled time early in the race. A replacement pivot pin was fitted to the clutch pedal to replace the original one which had apparently fallen out, but the pedal movement remained erratic. Jim Clark's Team Lotus 21 forced its way ahead of Hill in the early stages, but the American eventually put the ambitious young Scot in his place and sprinted up on to von Trips' tail to keep him honest for the last few laps to the flag. Clark and Moss finished third and fourth with Ginther, whose car throttle return spring had broken, grappling his way home to fifth.

On June 18 the Ferrari team staged a splendid, not totally unexpected, 1-2-3-4 victory at Spa-Francorchamps, Phil Hill turning the tables on von Trips to win by a close 0.7s after a wheel-to-wheel hotly contested "demonstration run". Ginther's works 120-degree car was third while OlivierGendebien's yellow-painted *Equipe Nationale Belge*-entered 65-degree 156 finished fourth. It was during practice for this event that Dunlop engineer Vic Barlow told Chiti that he was very worried about the amount of negative camber the 156s were using at the rear. He managed to persuade Chiti that it should be wound off slightly because of the way in which the cars were eating the inside edges of their tyre treads — and the handling

seemed to improve!

Of course, there was one familiar aspect of the Ferrari *modus operandi* which hadn't changed and was getting rather concerning. Despite the fact that his team was fielding cars which were generally superior to their oppostion, the Commendatore continually declined to nominate a team leader. This guaranteed that the trio of works entries would continue to involve itself in time-wasting internecine battles which could well have jeopardized the outcome of several races. An example of the way this "keeping everybody on their toes" policy almost went wrong was in the *Grand Prix de l'ACF*, held at Reims-Gueux on July 2.

Baghetti's FISA-entered 65-degree car supplemented the regular factory trio and Phil Hill excelled himself with a 2m 24.9s pole-winning lap, a second and a half faster than von Trips, who was second quickest. This margin unsettled the German driver who began to grumble about his car, his complaints being settled when Phil took out von Trips' machine and turned a lap almost a second quicker than the best managed by the German Count. There was more than a touch of

Typically British summer weather at the start of the 1961 Grand Prix at Aintree with Ginther (No.6) and Phil Hill (No.2) getting the jump on eventual winner von Trips (No.4) as they accelerate away in a shower of spray. Car No.22 is Tony Brooks's BRM-Climax, the Englishman doubtless envying his rivals the Italian V6 cars he gave up the chance of driving, while No.28 (behind Ginther) is Stirling Moss's Rob Walker Lotus-Climax.

gamesmanship involved in this from Phil's point of view because he'd heard there was some oil on the track down at *Thillois*, so he offered to try his team-mate's machine while there was "cover" for a slow time. When Hill found there was no oil to speak of, he went like the wind . . .and then came in to apologize for such a *modest* lap in a matter-of-fact fashion. Von Trips went grey with disappointment . . .

Ginther squeezed his third 156 on to the outside of the front row, but blotted his copybook with a spin at *Muizon* as early as lap four, so Hill and von Trips were left alone in their tussle for the lead. On lap 13 Hill let "Taffy" through, but seven laps later the German's car trickled into the pits to retire with a cooked engine: a stone had punctured the water radiator and all the coolant had vanished. By this time Ginther had worked his way up into second place ahead of Moss's Walker Lotus and when, on lap 38, Hill spun at *Thillois* on melting tar and was then clouted by Moss's Lotus, Phil stalled the engine. This let Ginther into the lead . . .

"But eventually I came into the pits because I knew the engine was going to break. The oil pressure was going. I was leading, and that's a difficult thing to do, but I didn't want to destroy it. They insisted that I went out again, but it blew up before I got to the first hairpin. I would have loved to have thought it would last, but I knew it wouldn't . . ." Ginther's retirement on lap 41, incredibly, allowed Giancarlo Baghetti into the lead, the young Italian being attacked on all sides by the four-cylinder Porsches of Gurney and Bonnier.

It seemed incredible to think that this young novice, driving his first World Championship Grand Prix, could pull it off, but in a perfectly-timed dive out of Gurney's slipstream on the final lap, Giancarlo Baghetti wrote himself a page of motor racing history by becoming the first (and so far only) driver to win a World Championship qualifying round at his first attempt. He had driven three Formula 1 races to date and won them all, but, sadly, it was to be downhill all the way to early oblivion as far as the rest of his racing career was concerned.

Phil Hill finished ninth with fastest lap to his credit at Reims and the Championship battle was simmering nicely as he and von Trips went into the British Grand Prix at Aintree on July 15. The contest began in pouring rain, making Aintree look more depressing than usual, and von Trips emerged from an early charge with a healthy advantage, driving smoothly and precisely to victory on what was a treacherous track surface for much of the afternoon. The wind had been taken out of Hill's sails on lap 10 when he'd got a lurid slide on a huge puddle at Melling Crossing, shaving a solid-looking gate post as the tyres gripped once more, a milli-second from disaster . . .

Moss moved into second place behind von Trips before spinning at the same place and Ginther briefly occupied the second place before Hill retook him as the track began to dry out in the closing stages, the Ferraris scoring a 1-2-3 triumph. Moss's Lotus eventually retired with brake trouble.

Baghetti's Formula 1 honeymoon had come to an end at Aintree when he spun his 156 pretty heavily into the guard rails, so his place in the team for the German Grand Prix on August 5 was taken by "Wild Willy" Mairesse, the Belgian having his first crack at the rear-engined 1½-litre Ferrari Grand Prix car in a race. The Nürburging proved desperately hard on the Ferrari's wet weather, soft rain tyres, which Hill was using in the dry to lap in the 9m 3s bracket but he ended up with a staggering 8m 55.2s for pole position which left him glassy-eyed with surplus adrenalin. That was more than *six seconds* quicker than Jack Brabham's prototype Cooper-Climax V8 which took second place on the grid. As an indication of how much quicker Phil was than his team-mates, von Trips' 156 did a 9m 05.5s for fifth place and Ginther, the slowest of the four, could only manage 9m 16.6s behind Mairesse's 9m 15.9s.

When it came to the race, however, Stirling Moss weaved his Monaco magic yet again. Against Dunlop's counselling, he started his four cylinder Rob Walker Lotus 18/21 on sticky wet-weather rubber and pulled out a substantial advantage in the early stages of 15 lap contest. The tyres on the leading Lotus gradually became more marginal and it seemed likely, with three laps to go, that von Trips and Phil Hill would catch him again. With two laps left, a welcome shower of rain gave Moss the break he needed and the Englishman came home to score another superb victory, the last, as it was to turn out, of his long illustrious career. Von Trips just beat Hill home to second place after they'd both survived lurid slides on the wet surface towards the end of that final lap. Mairesse crashed and Ginther was a lowly, distant eighth.

The World Championship contest was wide open between Hill and von Trips when the Ferrari team arrived for the Italian Grand Prix at Monza on September 10, the penultimate round of the title chase. There were five entries for this race, the three regulars, Baghetti in a 120-degree V6 now entered by the local Scuderia Sant'Ambroseus, and the absurdly brave, highly talented 19-year old Mexican Ricardo Rodriguez. Along with his brother Pedro, this son of a wealthy and politically well-connected Mexican businessman had won a remarkable reputation for himself with some fabulous drives in North America, and Luigi Chinetti tipped off the Commendatore who offered them both "renta drives" at the end of 1961. Business commitments obliged Pedro to decline the offer (how motor racing in the early sixties might have changed if he'd accepted!) but his younger brother was safely installed in the cockpit of a 65-degree engined 156 for the start of Monza qualifying.

By the end of practice, many people could hardly believe the grid order. Von Trips had snatched pole position with a 2m 46.3s lap (the combined banked/road circuit was being used) but Ricardo was alongside him on the front row, one-tenth slower on his Formula 1 début. The race, of course, represented one of the most tragic chapters in post-War motor racing history. In order to conserve their engines during this long hard run, the Ferraris were all fitted with high final-drive ratios which meant that they were tardy getting off the line, allowing Jim Clark's Lotus 21 to get in amongst them on the first lap.

Coming down to *Parabolica* second time round, von Trips was getting into his stride and had just passed Jim Clark before the braking area, but it appears that he moved over on the Lotus before he had completely cleared its left front wheel . . .The two cars interlocked wheels, and the Ferrari cartwheeled up the bank, along the spectator fence, before crashing back on to the grass at the side of the circuit. Clark emerged unhurt, badly shaken, but von Trips had been hurled from his car and lay fatally injured at the track side. Behind the spectator fence, fourteen members of the public had also been killed.

Baghetti, Rodriguez and Ginther all eventually fell by the wayside with engine problems, leaving Phil Hill alone to cross the finishing line victorious, thereby becoming the first American to take the World Championship title. The team's celebrations which followed were understandably muted and calm by the normal standards expected after the Ferrari victory at Monza, and the team subsequently decided that it would be appropriate to give the final round of the Championship, the United States Grand Prix, a miss after this appalling catastrophe.

With Ferrari emotionally down, and battling against a typically relentless wave of hostile criticism from within his own country, Phil Hill responded by agreeing that he would stay loyal and drive for the team again in 1962. It was only after committing himself that the American discovered there had been a major dispute within the higher management echelons at Maranello. It has never been clear what the argument was about, but several luminaries including Tavoni, Chiti and financial expert Ermano Della Casa (who subsequently returned, though, and still deals with Ferrari driver contract fees to this day, amongst other things!) stalked out in high dudgeon. Chiti and Tavoni, of course, were determined to beat Ferrari at his own game and established the catastrophically ill-fated ATS outfit which flickered into brief, uncompetitive life in 1963, soon to dwindle and vanish. Phil Hill reckoned that it would have been nice to know about these changes *before* he had agreed to stay!

Plucky little Richie Ginther decided that he had spent long enough at Maranello and pushed off to join BRM. He wasn't even allowed to go round the factory and say his formal goodbyes. Richie shrugs it off : "Oh, that's true, but it was only Mr.

The track is drying here in this picture of Wolfgang von Trips, his Ferrari set against the backdrop of the Grand National jumps. The German Count drove a fine race at the Liverpool circuit to win the second Grand Prix of his career, putting himself firmly in contention for the World Championship.

Ferrari himself who was annoyed. I saw all the mechanics and technicians I worked with before I left because they came and found me . . ."

Even in the late 1970s senior members of the Ferrari team recalled Richie Ginther's ability as a test and development driver with some pleasure. Richie himself recalls the day after which he was regarded with near-awe by the Ferrari mechanics owing to his apparently "magical" capacity for accurate prediction. "I was supposed to be carrying out a series of tests running on the full banked circuit," Ginther remembers, "and I came into the pits before I was scheduled to stop. The pit crew told me that it wasn't time to come in, so I replied 'wait a minute, this thing is going to blow up. I can feel a vibration'. So they revved it up in the pits and told me it was OK, but I said I didn't want to go out in it because I didn't reckon an engine failure on the banking would be particularly nice. I told them it would blow up after another 12 laps, a figure I'd just mentioned at random. So they put Willy Mairesse in and he had the engine fail on him . . .after 12 laps. From that point on they thought I was magic!"

On the driver side, Phil Hill was to be partnered by Giancarlo Baghetti and

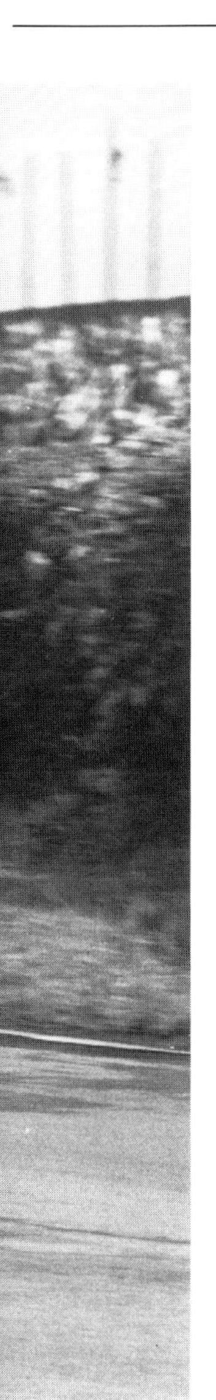

Lorenzo Bandini, with Mairesse taking Ginther's place as occasional number four and chief tester. Ricardo Rodriguez and Olivier Gendebien were also retained as potential Formula 1 competitors.

On the technical front, Chiti's departure resulted in accelerated promotion for two young engineers who were working under Franco Rocchi and Walter Salvarani in the engine department. One was Angelo Bellei, whose career path would lead him, as *Dottore Ingegnere* Angelo Bellei, to the status of Director of Product Design and Development on the road car side at Maranello by the late 1970s. The other was the son of a pre-War Scuderia Ferrari pattern maker who'd worked on the cylinder heads of the original Alfa Romeo 158s. This experienced technician still worked for Ferrari at Maranello in the early 1960s:his name was Reclüs Forghieri, and his son Mauro was destined to become one of the most respected Grand Prix car designers of the next two decades.

Recalling his background, Forghieri (junior) talked to the author with as much demonstrative, excitable enthusiasm as he channelled towards Ferrari Formula 1 fortunes. "My grandfather had to live outside Italy," explains Mauro, "he was a writer, not a reporter, but more a social commentator, something of a poet. He spent most of his time in France, living around the Cote d'Azur, and his socialist political views meant that he had to leave Italy.

"That's why my father has an unusual French name, Reclüs, and when he was allowed back into Italy he was obliged to give an undertaking that he would not be involved in any sort of political activity or make any political comments. That was in the 1930s, but the Fascists still came round and took him down to the police station regularly to ask 'where have you been, what have you been doing . . .', that sort of thing. But he stayed in Italy and worked for Ferrari, only retiring about 15 years ago.

"As far as I was concerned, I never had any real interest in racing cars when I was growing up. My passion was aviation engineering and I wanted to go to the United States to work with Lockheed or Northrop, but my military service intervened just as I left the University of Bologna with a Diploma in Mechanical Engineering at the end of 1958. My father got on well with Mr. Ferrari and he made the suggestion that I should join the company. Well, I'd first been to the Ferrari factory in 1957 to do a University project and I eventually started there full-time at the end of 1959, working in the engine department doing calculations for the 120-degree V6 programme.

"Engines have always been my principle interest and when I went to Ferrari I didn't know anything about chassis design. I suppose over the last twenty years I have become equally interested in chassis, suspension and gearbox work, but engines were my first love . . .I regarded my work on the 1½-litre Ferrari 156 as my schooling period in the art of chassis development!"

Forghieri admits that he closely studied the technical paper presented by Porsche designer Eberan von Eberhorst to Vienna University shortly after the last War and this, allied to his detailed scrutiny of the British opposition in the early 1960s, helped him apply his mind to the fresh challenge of developing the 156 into some semblance of a good-handling car. Even today, he refuses to minimize the problems involved and it's clear that he and Chiti simply didn't have anything in common, on a personal or professional level. "That 156 was a very bad chassis," he says, shaking his head energetically, "it just corkscrewed like a spring through the corners."

Forghieri and Bellei were left to rake through the coals of what Chiti had left behind him. Work had been proceeding on a variety of cylinder heads with differing valve/spark plug arrangements and, for 1962, a four-valves per cylinder, single sparking plug version of the 120-degree V6 was settled on, complete with a revised six speed gearbox mounted between the engine and differential, although retaining the exposed clutch at the tail end. Such a car, which incorporated minor alterations to the rear suspension and which sported a shorter tail section, was shown at Ferrari's Maranello press conference in December 1962. But however optimistic the team might have been about the 1962 prospects, the new cylinder head didn't materialize in action when the season got underway and it only took a handful of races to see that Maranello was getting badly left behind with this outdated machine.

There was another *bête noire* to bother Phil Hill throughout 1962 in the shape of Ferrari's newly appointed team manager Eugenio Dragoni. A wealthy business-man who'd made a fortune out of pharmaceuticals, Dragoni's enthusiasm for motor racing was dominated by a passionate desire to further the interests of Lorenzo Bandini's career, a task which he pursued with a zeal which embarrassed the good-natured Italian driver. Over the previous few years, Hill had got on with Romolo Tavoni pretty well, enjoying the good-humoured ribbing the old team manager had directed towards him, but Dragoni was a totally different proposition. He quickly decided that the team's lack of form in 1962 was a result of Phil's emotional response to the von Trips tragedy, a smug, self-righteous assumption which got right under the American's skin. Morale at the start of 1962 could hardly have been lower "in the ranks" at Maranello because there were also thinly-veiled plans to provide a 156 for the Rob Walker stable to field Stirling Moss, something which didn't exactly amount to an unreserved vote of confidence in the factory drivers!

As far as Ferrari was concerned, the 1962 Formula 1 season started on a fleetingly optimistic note, thereafter plunging into a morass of failure and disappointment. Willy Mairesse was despatched to the Heysel circuit for the Brussels Grand Prix, a three-heat affair at which Ferrari sought to gauge the potential of the British V8 opposition. Mairesse's 156 was equipped with an experimental 67 x 70mm, 1480.73cc, 65-degree V6 for this race, allegedly giving 185bhp at 9500rpm, and the usually wild Belgian driver kept a tight rein on his talents to score a good aggregate win on home soil. Three weeks later, Ricardo Rodriguez (120-deg) and Lorenzo Bandini (65-deg) represented Scuderia Ferrari at Pau for the first time since 1955, Rodriguez emerging from this French non-title F1 thrash second place behind Maurice Trintignant's Rob Walker Lotus 24 while Bandini was fifth.

The pre-Championship season "warm-up" programme continued with Phil Hill and Baghetti contesting the Aintree 200 on April 28, Phil's 120-degree car employing the inboard six-speed gearbox for the first time. He was almost four seconds away from Jim Clark's pole position Lotus 24-Climax V8, though, and despite the fact that he and Baghetti wound up third and fourth, they were miles out of contention.

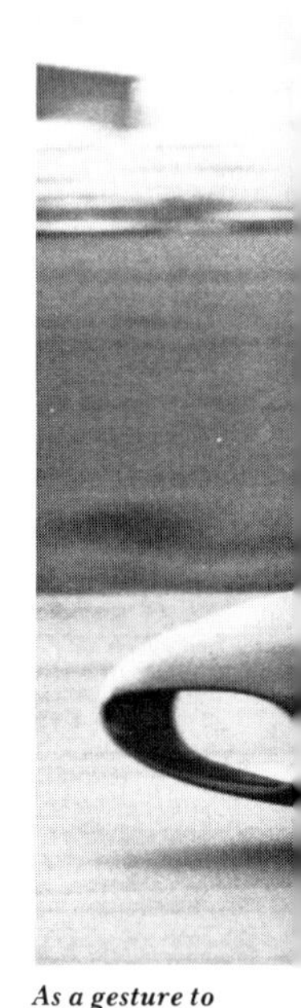

As a gesture to Stirling Moss, and in recognition of Ferrari's plans to supply Rob Walker with a car for the 1962 season, this works 156 was entered in the International Trophy at Silverstone for Innes Ireland to drive a few weeks after Moss's Goodwood accident. Innes liked the "unburstable" engine, but wasn't very impressed with the chassis' behaviour in the wet conditions . . . He finished fourth.

Some of the spice had been taken out of the prospects for 1962 when Stirling Moss had his terrible accident at the wheel of his UDT/Laystall Lotus 18/21 -Climax V8 at Goodwood on Easter Monday, and Ferrari contrived to write a strange, if rather touching postscript to this tragedy. Obviously out of affection for Moss, with whom his relationship had been warming progressively over the past couple of years, the Commendatore made available Baghetti's Aintree 156 for Innes Ireland to handle in the BRDC International Trophy at Silverstone on May 12. With a pale green stripe down its nose (a gesture from Ferrari, not a request from UDT!) Ireland drove steadily to fourth place in the rainy event.

"I was asked to submit a report to Ronnie Hoare at Maranello Concessionaires," remembers Innes, "presumably for onward transmission to the factory. I told them that it wasn't just understeering, but that the wire wheels were flexing . . .everywhere! I suggested that they fit a wider track . . .I tried hurling it through the corners to induce oversteer, but the transition was frighteningly quick when it lurched to oversteer. You could rev. it like hell, though . . ." Innes also recalls, "I later discovered from BP's Dennis Druitt that I was under consideration for the Ferrari Grand Prix team . . .but I was a BP contracted man, and Ferrari ran on Shell!"

The 1962 Grand Prix season was a largely painful experience for the Ferrari V6s, whose drivers had to watch as Jim Clark's Lotus-Climax V8 and Graham Hill's BRM V8 carved up the Championship pickings between them. Hill, using the inboard gearbox configuration and the Ireland-suggested wide track which, to his annoyance, had been adopted by Forghieri, emerged from the Dutch Grand Prix at Zandvoort on May 20 with an apparently respectable third place behind Hill's BRM and Trev Taylor's Team Lotus 24. On the same day, Mairesse cantered home ahead of Bandini to win the non-Championship Naples Grand Prix in the same machine he'd used at Heysel, so perhaps things were not too bad.

Sheer determination and a rare glimpse of his World Championship-winning form combined to help Phil Hill sustain Maranello's brief Indian summer at Monaco, where he duplicated Ginther's 1961 performance as he chased home Bruce McLaren's triumphant Cooper-Climax V8 to take second place. All three race cars for Phil, Bandini and Mairesse sported wide rear tracks for this race, but the inboard gearbox was seen only on the spare 65-degree test car practised (but not raced) by Rodriguez. On the opening sprint to the first corner, Mairesse had made an absurd dog's dinner of the whole business, triggering off a multiple

pile-up which was made worse by the fact that Ginther's BRM had its throttle jam open in the middle of this *mêlée*. Bandini drove smoothly home to third place, while Willy crept round gently at the back after his early pantomime, eventually being classified seventh after stopping ten laps before the end.

Hill, Baghetti, Mairesse and Rodriguez contested the Belgian Grand Prix at Spa, all using 120-degree V6s with overhung rear mounted six speed gearboxes. This race marked the occasion of Jim Clark's first Grand Prix victory, and while Phil and Ricardo squeezed home third and fourth after swapping places for much of the race, Mairesse got himself involved in a massive accident. Embroiled in a ferocious scrap with Trev Taylor's Lotus 24, Mairesse got too close to the Lotus at *Blanchimont* and the two cars collided spectacularly, the Lotus taking down a telegraph pole while the Ferrari turned over and caught fire.

"Willy got too close," smiled Trev Taylor 19 years later, "our Lotus used a ZF gearbox with its selector rod sticking out the back, and he got close enough to nudge me out of gear with the nose of his Ferrari! I immediately snapped sideways, but I've got to thank Mairesse, because his car then pushed me straight again before I hit the telegraph pole *broadside* . . .which wouldn't have done me any good at all . . ." Interestingly, Trev feels that Mairesse was driving quite smoothly and tidily and that the shunt was "just one of those things."

A familiar bout of industrial unrest amongst the Italian metal workers gave Ferrari an excuse for missing the French Grand Prix at Rouen, plus the non-title

Ricardo Rodriguez brakes for Spa's La Source hairpin a few lengths ahead of team-mate Phil Hill during the 1962 Belgian Grand Prix. The Mexican's hair-raising driving style on this super-fast track more than held Phil's attention for much of the race, but the American squeezed ahead to take third place at the flag.

races at both Reims and Solitude. But a single inboard gearbox car was fielded for the reigning World Champion in the British Grand Prix at Aintree on July 21, although they might as well have not bothered. After struggling *up* to a disgraceful ninth place, Phil retired after 47 laps with ignition maladies.

At the Nürburgring, venue for the German Grand Prix on August 5, the first signs of Forghieri's influence in the chassis design department could be seen in the arrival of a new, experimental 156. Built round a small-tube spaceframe, it had a further-inclined driving position to reduce the car's height and cross-sectional area and the steering rack was moved ahead of the front axle line to allow the pedals to be mounted further forward and the front brake calipers were moved to the rear of the discs to make room for the track rods. Cooling water was transmitted from radiator to engine and back through the chassis tubes and lightweight pannier fuel tanks were fitted, their fillers now at the forward end rather than rearward. Suspension was broadly usual 156 in layout, but the rear geometry had been altered to improve the car's weight distribution and the "shark nose" had gone, replaced by a single aperture.

Bandini qualified the car a lowly 18th, the slowest of the four 156s, and spun off the road early in the race, so the most charitable conclusion one could reach about

the new car was to say that its début had been "inconclusive." Hill briefly shone in his inboard gearbox 156, flashing into third place for a short distance in the rain-soaked race's early stages. But he eventually retired, physically as worn out as the car's rear dampers which had played up and made the car undriveable. Ricardo Rodriguez emerged with a fine sixth place in a pure 1961-spec. 65-degree 156 while Baghetti slithered home a demoralized 10th in a "regular" 120-degree V6.

On August 10, Bandini and Baghetti outdistanced ten privateers with ease to win the Mediterranean Grand Prix at the super-fast Enna-Pergusa circuit in Central Sicily, the two Ferrari drivers searching for Italian Championship points at this event, before returning to Monza for what was destined to be the Scuderia's last outing of the season. The 1962 Italian Grand Prix, held on September 16, took place solely on the road course (the banking was destined never to be used again for a Formula 1 Grand Prix) and Maranello fielded five entries for Hill, Baghetti, Bandini, Rodriguez and Mairesse. Phil used his inboard gearbox 120-degree V6 while Baghetti and Rodriguez used regular 120-degree cars, Bandini had an old 65-degree machine and Mairesse was given the Nürburgring experimental car which Bandini had shunted in the German Grand Prix.

"Wild Willy" out-qualified all his Ferrari rivals on his first Formula 1 outing since rolling his 156 into a ball at Spa, and he was the most successful in the race, recovering from a slow start from tenth place on the grid and finishing fourth, close behind McLaren's Cooper. Baghetti was fifth after a spin, Bandini eighth and Phil Hill a morale-crushing 11th after a pit stop for fuel which Dragoni said he couldn't have because it wasn't necessary to top up. Soon after this débâcle Enzo Ferrari wrote to his drivers informing them that, owing to industrial problems, he wouldn't be competing in either the United States or South African Grands Prix, two remaining rounds in the Championship.

By the start of 1963, Hill and Baghetti had unwittingly written *finis* to their Grand Prix careers by signing for the renegade Chiti/Tavoni ATS set-up while Ricardo Rodriguez, tipped to remain on the Maranello books, had been killed practising Rob Walker's Lotus 24 for the non-Championship Mexican Grand Prix in the autumn of 1962. This allowed Mairesse to stay in the team to partner Ferrari's new number one driver, while Bandini went off to drive for "Mimmo" Dei's Scuderia Centro-Sud.

ADE
21

Section IV: The 1½-litre cars, 1961-65

Chapter 2
The new dawn approaching

Having swept the board clean, Maranello took a totally fresh look at Formula 1 in 1963. In the short-term, Forghieri was left to hammer out another interim chassis to accommodate the 120-degree V6, but, long-term, it was quite clear that a new engine would be required. Thus Forghieri and Bellei also began work on a new generation of Grand Prix engines, Mauro concentrating on a four-cam, horizontally opposed 12-cylinder, while Bellei followed Jano's plans for a four-cam V8 which would be built first. However, the Grand Prix test programme was knocked back quite severely by heavy snow in early 1963 allied to the company's work on the central-engined 250P V12-engined sports car. So the 1963 Grand Prix season turned out to be very much a development year, the whole momentum sustained largely by Forghieri's good relationship with the team's new number one driver, John Surtees.

Already a hero in Italy thanks to his World Championship-winning rides on two wheels for the MV-Agusta motorcycle team, the serious-minded Surtees had earlier been offered a Ferrari seat — and declined it.

Recalls John, "I was originally asked out to Maranello at the end of 1960 where I met Chiti and everybody else. I wasn't very happy with the scene with him and I wasn't very happy with all the drivers they seemed to have on their books. And, frankly, I realized that I didn't really know enough about car racing. By this stage I'd only done four GPs, a couple of F2 races and three F/Junior events. So I thought, judging by past experience, it wasn't right to go somewhere new like this as such a novice. I decided not to go into a hornet's nest like that at the time without some sort of knowledge, so I didn't accept the offer.

"I liked many of the things I saw and I love the Italians and many of the things they do. I like their creations, their attitude. After I'd got Yeoman Credit to back the 1962 project with the Lola project I'd learnt more than ever through that season, so when I was asked by Ferrari again, I agreed to join them.

"It had to be the finest time to go to them. They were on the floor, but they also wanted to pick themselves up and have a bit of a go. Forghieri had come in and I got on with him fine. He was a new boy and I think I was able to inject a little of my experience into things, so there was something of a fresh approach. It was all a hotch-potch really, because we had to choose from a great pile of bits and pieces to put something together. We started with this hacked-about tubular chassis car which I thrashed round Modena. That little V6 was a good engine . . ."

The 1963 Ferrari Formula 1 programme made a gentle start, the team missing several early non-title events it usually contested. Eventually Surtees and Mairesse "got on the road" at the BRDC International Trophy on May 11, armed with a pair of new cars equipped with the latest, Bosch fuel-injected version of the 120-degree V6.

***Previous pages:* John Surtees's World Championship career with Ferrari began on a high note at Monaco in 1963. Despite failing oil pressure towards the end of the race, he finished fourth, with fastest lap to his credit, in this Forghieri-revamped 120-degree 156.**

***Unhappy.* Surtees wasn't very impressed with the 156 on the fast Spa-Francorchamps circuit and was an early retirement from the 1963 Belgian Grand Prix.**

9

In the Silverstone pit lane, Surtees looks on thoughtfully as mechanic Giulio Borsari examines the 156 engine bay and the late John Bolster (in deerstalker) also takes a peep, during practice for the 1963 British Grand Prix. The Fantuzzi-bodied 156 was in good shape at this race, finishing a distant second to Jim Clark's Lotus 25.

The new cars were constructed round much lighter, more compact multi-tubular spaceframes incorporating a centre sheet fuel tank below the driver's seat in the current Cooper-Climax style. Double wishbone front suspension with outboard mounted coil spring/damper units were retained, but at the rear Forghieri had taken a leaf out of the Lotus and Lola book by employing a single top link, reversed lower wishbone and twin radius arm arrangement. The tubular single top links were threaded to make for rapid camber adjustments, there were splined sliding joints on the drive shafts and the rear disc brakes were mounted inboard on the side of the transaxle casing. The inboard six-speed gearbox was retained, drive from the steeply raked V6 engine going via a torsional coupling to the primary drive shaft, which took it through the transmission unit as before to the overhung rear-mounted clutch, thence via a concentric drive forward beneath the final drive to the inboard gearbox, now a very short assembly with the six forward gears clustered on three shafts.

Swiss fuel injection specialist Michael May had been recruited as a consultant on a "no cure, no pay" basis to help with the development of the special Bosch high-pressure injection system and he recalls "finding possibly eight to ten bhp!"

Surtees recalls the V6 during that first season, in which it was reputedly developing 200bhp at 10,000rpm "The problem was that it wasn't safe to rev. it where it developed its full power. If you took it to 11,000rpm it was fantastic, but if you went over 10,000rpm you ran into piston and valve troubles, so effectively we were considerably down on power against our rivals. There was no comparison with the Climax or BRM V8s . . .

"On the rough-and-ready circuits, where you needed to manhandle it about, you could get some results, but where sheer power was involved you were at a bit of a loss. It wasn't on. They were talking about that flat-12 for a long time, but in the meantime they built the V8 which I feel they should have never completed. It was never quite as quick as the V6 in its best form, but you could run the V8 more reliably. I think they should have pressed on with the 12 and forgotten the V8 . . ."

Clad in sleek new aluminium Fantuzzi bodywork, the smart 1963 Ferrari 156s came to the line for the International Trophy with Surtees qualifying fifth on the second row, his 1m 36.2s comparing with Innes Ireland's pole time of 1m 34.4s in the UDT/Laystall Lotus-BRM V8. Although Surtees's efforts were thwarted by an oil leak in the race, he was up into second place chasing Clark's Lotus 25 for all he was worth when he stopped, so it was clear that Maranello was back on the road towards competitiveness once again. This realization helped the team accept the fact that Mairesse had backed his brand new machine into an earth bank at Stowe corner . . .

Overleaf: Ludovico Scarfiotti, standing in for the injured Willy Mairesse, took the team's second 156 to a reliable sixth place in the 1963 Dutch Grand Prix at Zandvoort.

At Monaco on May 26 there was a replacement, brand new car for Mairesse to drive, but Surtees was predictably the faster of the two Ferrari runners and qualified a splendid third on 1m 35.2s, 0.9s away from Clark's pole position. The race lead was initially disputed between Clark and Hill, but Big John got through to run third behind Hill's now oil-leaking BRM and finally passed it on lap 57. Unable to see through his oil-streaked goggles without the reassuring shape of the BRM to follow, Surtees stopped for fresh goggles and resumed, only to find his V6's oil pressure fluctuating alarmingly. Towards the end of the race, confident that the 156 would last, Surtees piled on the pressure to set fastest race lap (1m 34.5s) on the final tour in a vain effort to dislodge McLaren's third-placed Cooper. Mairesse's 156 had retired earlier from sixth place with a final drive failure after 37 laps.

The fast open swerves of Spa-Francorchamps left both Surtees and Mairesse less than convinced about the new Ferrari's high-speed handling and braking characteristics and the 156s were seriously off the pace in practice for the Belgian Grand Prix on June 9. Mairesse briefly showed in third place for a few laps before skating up the La Source hairpin escape road and retiring with a misfire, while Surtees consolidated his hold on third place until lap 14 when he pitted with a misfire. He briefly joined the battle, but soon retired for good.

By the time the Dutch Grand Prix came round on June 23, Mairesse was back in hospital, this time suffering from burns when his Ferrari 250P (which he was sharing with Surtees) caught fire whilst leading at Le Mans. Ludovico Scarfiotti was drafted into the team as his replacement, the Italian driving unobtrusively, with the exception of a wild spin, to finish sixth. Surtees wound up third behind Clark's Lotus 25 and Gurney's Brabham. Not bad . . .

Surtees was the only Ferrari driver to come to the line at the start of the French Grand Prix at Reims-Gueux on June 30, Scarfiotti having slid off the rain-soaked road and demolished a telegraph pole during practice, injuring his knee in the process. Surtees qualified fourth and had just battled his way up into second place, way behind the fast-disappearing Jim Clark, when his Ferrari's fuel pump failed and he dropped from contention. Pit treatment failed to rectify the problem, so after trying the car briefly again, he retired for good after 13 laps.

Although Clark's mastery of the World Championship trail seemed complete and unquestionable, Surtees came away from the British Grand Prix at Silverstone on July 20 in a highly optimistic frame of mind. With Mairesse and Scarfiotti both out of action, Surtees had a choice of two cars for his lone entry. The night prior to the race John had stayed up with Forghieri and the mechanics to help fit a three gallon auxiliary fuel tank since the team was worried that fuel capacity might be marginal in this 80 lap, 240 mile contest. It was just as well they did : after racing competively in Clark's wake, Surtees inherited second place on the last lap when Hill's BRM V8 spluttered out of fuel and had to coast across the line. John also established the race's fastest lap third time round, before the circuit became coated with oil.

It was now pretty clear that the Surtees/Ferrari combination would only need a small sliver of good luck running in its direction to race successfully to the winner's rostrum, and that good fortune finally came the team's way on August 4. Having missed the non-Championship Solitude race, Surtees and the engine department had spent several days collaborating closely with Bosch in a successful attempt to

Grappling with understeer, John Surtees drops a wheel on to the grass at East London during the 1963 South African Grand Prix. Two weeks after scoring a 1-2 in the Rand Grand Prix at Kyalami, this was an unhappy outing for the Ferrari V6s with only Bandini surviving to fifth place at the finish.

improve the engine's mid-range torque through adjustments to the fuel metering system. This attended to, Surtees adjusted the 156's suspension settings to near-perfection when the team arrived at the Nürburgring for the German Grand Prix and managed to qualify second to Clark's Lotus 25, his best of 8m 46.7s being a mere 0.9s away from Formula 1's established pacemaker. Mairesse was on the outside of the second row, but Bandini's Centro-Sud BRM V8 made it on to the front row alongside Surtees, bringing a self-satisfied smirk to Dragoni's face.

In the race, Clark got away first, but his Climax V8 began cutting out intermittently and, once Surtees caught up after his tardy getaway, the Scot simply couldn't shake that Ferrari V6 from his tail. On lap four Surtees sailed through into the lead and stayed there to score a convincing victory, establishing a new lap record of 8m 47.0s in the process. Clark's spluttering Lotus was the only other runner remotely in touch with Surtees at the chequered flag. Mairesse, making his return after the Le Mans accident, got off-line as he crested the *Flugplatz* hump and smashed off the road, sending himself back to hospital with a broken arm and

sadly killing a medical attendant in the process. It was the end of his works Ferrari career this time, and the start of an unhappy decline for the enthusiastic Belgian driver, culminating with his suicide in Ostend some six years later.

This morale-boosting victory was just the tonic Ferrari needed and Surtees underlined that things were now going Maranello's way by winning the Mediterranean Grand Prix at Enna-Pergusa on August 18, dominating this non-title event to keep Peter Arundell's Lotus 25 back in second place. Bandini had qualified his Centro-Sud BRM a mere whisker slower than Big John at Enna, sufficient a feat for him to be invited back into the Ferrari team for Monza, where he was to remain for the rest of his career.

The 1963 Italian Grand Prix was intended to see the début of the Bellei-developed four-cam 64 x 57.8mm, 1487.5cc V8 installed in Forghieri's latest semi-monocoque chassis which had been tailor-made to suit the new engine. However, when it came to the event, the new 90-degree V8 wasn't race ready and Forghieri's new chassis was compromised to accept the trusty V6 once again. In

The rather crude cockpit of one of the 156 "Aeros", late 1963. Ferrari standards of welding may have been effective at this time, but they were hardly well-finished!

designing the new car, Forghieri had looked closely at the current BRM and Lotus before putting pen to paper and the end result was a compact, purposeful challenger from Maranello which boded well for the team's future fortunes.

The heart of the new chassis was two parallel tank pontoons which ran from a forward transverse bulkhead to the rear of the cockpit. The fabricated pontoons were riveted over a framework of two tubular longerons, rather than allowing the chassis stresses to be taken by the pontoons alone. There was a stressed floor panel uniting the two pontoons which were riveted at either end to transverse bulkheads while additional stiffening was provided by an instrument panel structure in the middle of the cockpit area. The front bulkhead was "doubled" to sandwich the inboard coil spring/damper units, operated by means of a forged top rocker arm.

The bulkhead behind the cockpit was particularly hefty, because Forghieri had decided to build sufficient crankcase rigidity into both the V8 and the forthcoming flat-12 so that they could be used as fully stressed members, the rear suspension being hung on to the engine/transmission aggregate. This was ambitious design philosophy, going ahead of even Lotus and taking up Jano's example of the semi-stressed Lancia D50 designed some nine years earlier. At the rear, suspension was by means of a single top link, reversed lower wishbone and parallel radius arms. The gearbox was now overhung at the rear with the clutch and flywheel in a conventional bell-housing on the back of the engine. The prototype V8 engine was briefly tested in the new chassis, but although it seemed fast enough, there were question marks over its reliability.

Therefore, the decision was taken to revise the chassis to accept a revised 120-degree V6, not the work of a moment by any stretch of the imagination. A new crankshaft was produced to accept the inboard clutch/flywheel, while the gearbox was now overhung behind the rear axle line. The crankcase casting had to be modified in order that it could be bolted to the bulkhead on the rear of the cockpit, but since the 120-degree V6 had never been designed to be employed as a stressed unit, a secondary supporting tubular sub-frame was fitted beneath the engine to take some of the suspension and chassis loads. This splendidly executed Ferrari Formula 1 hybrid had the same 93.7in wheelbase of the tubular spaceframe '63 chassis, but a narrower track and weighed in at 460kg (1014 lb), about 5kg (11 lb) lighter than its immediate predecessor.

Surtees proved faster in practice over the combined banked/road circuit, but the notorious banking caused some suspension failures for rival teams and led to the race being held on the road circuit only. The hybrid "Aero" V6, as it was dubbed, slammed round to take pole position in 1m 37.3s, a full 1.2s faster than second man Graham Hill's BRM, so it was obvious that Ferrari had initiated another massive leap forward into newly regained competitiveness. In the race John made a slow start but soon recovered to race closely with Clark's Lotus for second place behind Hill's BRM, but this only lasted until lap 17 when the "Aero" smoked into the pit lane with a dropped valve. Bandini's spaceframe machine went out with gearbox failure, so this turned out to be an ignominious defeat for Ferrari on home ground.

Be that as it may, there were none the less some highly promising straws in the wind which prompted Maranello to see the World Championship season right through to its finish. In the United States Grand Prix at Watkins Glen on October 6, Surtees took the spare spaceframe V6 into a battle for the lead with Hill's BRM, eventually establishing a place at the front of the field which evaporated only with John's retirement after 83 of the race's 110 laps were completed. Bandini's older car finished fifth.

There were still three more Formula 1 races on the International calendar after the Glen and Ferrari contested them all. A second "Aero" was flown out to Mexico City's Magdalena Mixhuca park circuit for the first Championship Mexican Grand Prix on October 27, Surtees qualifying his older monocoque car second to Jim Clark's Lotus 25. Unfortunately John was in trouble almost from the word go, tyre-smoking understeer indicating that the front suspension was collapsing and, when the "Aero" wouldn't restart after an investigative pit stop, the attempted push-start was halted by marshals and Surtees retired. Bandini's new car retired with a misfire on lap 36.

Prior to the South African Grand Prix at East London on December 28, the Ferrari duo contested the non-title Rand Grand Prix at Kyalami on December 14, Bandini back in a spaceframe car for this event as the second "Aero" was being held back for the Championship finale. In the two heat Kyalami event, Surtees and Bandini finished first and second in both to take an easy 1-2 triumph on aggregate. Down by the Indian Ocean for the final race, both drivers used their "Aero" V6s but were bugged by lack of low-down torque and Ferrari's 1963 World Championship season fizzled out on rather an uninspiring note, Surtees retiring from an off-the-pace third place with engine failure after 43 laps. Bandini was an unspectacular fifth, lapped by Jim Clark and Dan Gurney who finished first and second.

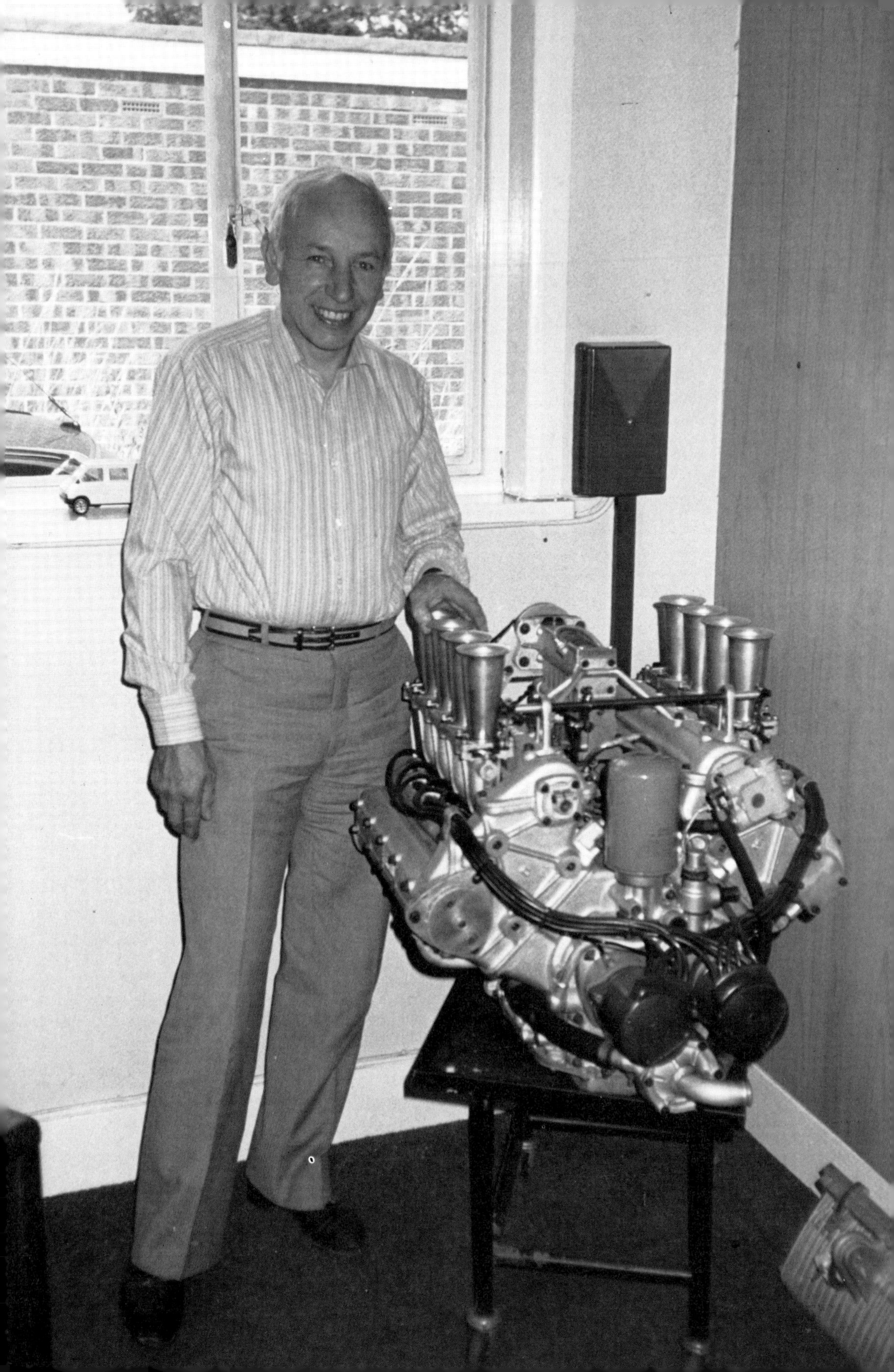

Section IV: The 1½-litre cars, 1961-65

Chapter 3
Another Championship . . . and beyond

Champion driver with his engine! John Surtees, photographed in 1983, with one of the Bellei-developed 158 V8 engines he used to win the World Championship in 1964. This one is mounted on a stand at his Edenbridge business headquarters. Ironically, Surtees reckons Ferrari should have gone straight from a V6 to a flat-12 without bothering about the V8!

After those initial tests prior to the 1963 Italian Grand Prix, Bellei's V8 didn't finally appear in competitive action until the Syracuse Grand Prix on April 12, 1964, by which time the engine with its aluminium alloy crankcase/cylinder blocks, five main bearing crankshaft and gear-driven twin overhead camshafts had been revamped with a bore and stroke of 64 x 57.8mm for a capacity of 1487.54cc. The cylinder head now had the inlet ports entering between the two camshafts, down amongst the twin sparking plugs per cylinder, the exhaust ports being on the outside of the cylinder heads with each set of four pipes merging into a long tail pipe with a slender megaphone on each end. The Bosch high pressure fuel injection unit was mounted within the vee and horizontal slide throttles were employed, pulled rearwards across the inlet pipes by a linkage system coupled to the throttle pedal. Injectors were screwed directly into the block, injecting into the individual cylinders near the top of the piston stroke. Bosch coil ignition was employed and the injection pump was driven by an exposed internally-toothed rubber belt from a pulley on the rear of the inlet camshaft on the right-hand bank.

The power output was claimed to be around 210bhp at 11,000rpm, a figure guaranteed to keep Maranello competitive with both Coventry-Climax and BRM. As far as the chassis was concerned, there were modifications to be seen on both the 90-degree V8 and the 120-degree V6 car entered in this Syracuse season-opener. Instead of attaching the rear suspension and springs to the bell housing, a fabricated bulkhead surrounded the bellhousing/clutch unit and was attached to the bulkhead behind the cockpit by two longerons running beneath the engine, thus giving added torsional stiffness to the rear end of the car.

Surtees qualified the new Ferrari 158 second to team-mate Bandini's older 120-degree V6-engined machine, but after a handful of laps in front, Lorenzo deferred to his team-mate and dropped back to follow respectfully in second position. On lap 27 the Italian's visor was shattered by a flying stone during this rainy race and Bandini hurtled into the pits for a replacement, returning to the fray to win a spectacular, hard-fought battle against Peter Arundell's Lotus 25, successfully snatching second place behind his team-mate. It was certainly an impressive, if not too significant, début for the new V8 and the trusty V6 had underlined that it still had a few good races left in it yet.

It was originally intended that the 180-degree, horizontally opposed 12-cylinder engine would be available to supplement the V8, but Forghieri's latest "baby" wasn't finally to make its competition début until the Italian Grand Prix in September, although development behind the scenes continued throughout the summer prior to that race.

Ferrari had kept away from the domestic British national Formula 1 races at

Snetterton, Goodwood and Aintree and the Italian cars had only faced Team Lotus at Syracuse, so the Italian V8's first real trial of strength came at the 100 lap Monaco Grand Prix on May 10. In beautifully sunny conditions, Clark underlined that he and Team Lotus would sustain their 1963 Championship-winning momentum, the Scot planting his 25D-Climax V8 on pole by a tenth of a second from Jack Brabham's similarly-powered Brabham and pulling out a five second advantage over the first three race laps. Surtees had Maranello's lone V8 for this race, Bandini staying with his Dino 156 while a second such machine was on hand as spare, the experimental Marelli electronic ignition replaced on the second V6 by the normal Bosch coil ignition as employed on the other cars. Surtees qualified the V8 fourth on the outside of the second row, but encountered gearbox problems from the start and they eventually led to his retirement before he could show any sort of form. Bandini succumbed to similar problems with the V6 as Graham Hill and Richie Ginther toured home to their second successive 1-2 in the Principality.

The pattern of the 1964 season was familiar to so many other Ferrari Formula 1 seasons during the sixties. The company's necessary preoccupation with its sports car programme, culminating with Le Mans in June, Maranello's technical show case (particularly now that Ford was flexing its muscles within the endurance racing arena), almost invariably meant that the Grand Prix cars took something of a back seat. So it was in 1964, the V8 getting bogged down with a series of early, often trifling, mechanical failures which contrasted with the promising spurt to Surtees's World Championship in the second half of the year.

On May 24 the Dutch Grand Prix took place over 80 laps of Zandvoort, Ferrari producing a pair of V8s for its two drivers, the defective ball races in the gearbox of Surtees's Monaco machine having been sorted out, but Bandini had to start practising with his 156 as his new V8 wasn't quite ready. For Maranello the result actually looked better than it was: although Surtees managed to come home second, he wasn't in the same league as Clark's winning Lotus 25D despite being the only other competitor to go the full distance. Bandini eventually started his new 158 from the outside of row four, slower even than former *Ferrariste* Phil Hill's Cooper-Climax. Lorenzo's race ended when the V8's fuel injection pump drive broke.

Fuel injection problems during practice at Spa-Francorchamps meant that the Ferrari V8 still wasn't front row material when it came to the Belgian Grand Prix on June 14, Surtees qualifying fifth for the 32 lap, 451.2km thrash, some 4.3s away from Dan Gurney's pole position Brabham. However, John actually squeezed through ahead on lap two and led across the line to begin his third tour only to limp into the pits at the end of that lap with a suspected broken piston. Bandini's V8 was out with a sick engine after 17 laps, leaving Jim Clark to win one of the luckiest victories of his career after Gurney's Brabham, Hill's BRM and McLaren's Cooper all lost their chances of a win through either running out of fuel or suffering fuel pick-up problems.

Surtees at last got the 158 on to the front row of the grid at Rouen-les-Essarts for the *Grand Prix d l'ACF* on June 28, qualifying third alongside Clark's Lotus and Gurney's Brabham. He ran with the leaders before stopping at the end of lap three with a split oil pipe to the fuel injection pump, a problem which delayed him, and he eventually retired with engine trouble. Bandini's V8 came home an uninspiring, off-the-pace eighth, two laps down on Gurney's winning Brabham — the first World Championship victory for that marque. After the fuel injection maladies at Spa, both V8s had been fitted with finned fuel filters mounted on the left-hand side of the engine behind the driver's shoulder, but their effectiveness was difficult to judge as the weather was very much cooler at the French race.

On July 11, Brands Hatch hosted the British Grand Prix for the first time in its history, a race which was highlighted by Graham Hill's epic, dogged, but unsuccessful pursuit of Clark's winning Lotus. Surtees took no part in this particular battle, but at least his V8 was on the same lap in third place at the chequered flag, a reasonable performance, while Bandini, driving a 156 on this occasion in the interests of reliability, lost out in a battle with Jack Brabham and wound up fifth. Still, there were two Ferraris in the points for the first time that season . . .

Le Mans was over by the time of the British Grand Prix, but it wasn't until the German Grand Prix at the Nürburgring on August 2 that Surtees really began to emphasize his World class. The former motorcycle ace had the 158 well cranked up during qualifying, edging Clark's Lotus out to take pole with an 8m 38.4s lap, 0.4s faster than the Lotus 33. Gurney's Brabham (8m 39.3s) and the determined Bandini's 156 (8m 42.6s) made up the front row and Lorenzo actually got the jump on his rivals for the first few hundred yards, getting the V6 into South Curve in the lead, although he was quickly swamped by the V8s.

As they went over the bridge beyond North Curve, Clark was through into first place and away, but Surtees was right on his tail as they completed the first 14 mile lap, cutting ahead into South Curve second time round and then pulling quickly away. Clark's Lotus was in trouble with what turned out to be a dropped valve, eventually causing his retirement. But Surtees wasn't going to have things completely his own way because Dan Gurney's Brabham briefly darted through to take the lead on lap four, but, true to the style of the Californian's appalling luck, his Brabham encountered overheating problems, allowing Surtees to storm home victorious by more than a minute from Graham Hill's misfiring BRM. The worthy Bandini's 156 was a good third ahead of Jo Siffert's private Brabham-BRM V8, these three runners being the only cars on the same lap as the winner at the finish.

On August 23, the Zeltweg military airfield turned its runways over to racing cars as the scene of the first Austrian Grand Prix, a reflection of the commendable enthusiasm from the local club which was eventually to be behind the construction of the splendid Österreichring, a mere couple of kilometres from the airfield. By the mid-1970s, the airfield would be dotted with executive jets at Austrian Grand Prix time, symbolizing the new wealth of the sport's most successful exponents. But in 1963 Formula 1 was a much more hand-to-mouth proposition from a financial point of view and although the 3.2km straw bale-lined perimeter/runway track looked pretty crude even by the fairly tolerant standards of the day, most people present praised the initiative and enthusiasm of the Austrian organizers in having staged a World Championship event at all.

There were two V8 Ferraris on hand for Surtees to choose from, Bandini's trusty V6 backing up the Englishman's challenge. In a practice marred by the rutted, bumpy and precarious state of the track surface, which snapped suspension members like twiglets, Hill's BRM took pole on 1m 9.84s from Surtees's Ferrari 158 (1m 10.12s), Clark (1m 10.21s), Gurney (1m 10.40s) with Bandini on the outside of the second row on 1m 10.63s. Gurney led off the line but Surtees nipped through into the lead on lap two only for the 158 to have its rear suspension collapse as he was braking for the hairpin on the eighth lap, so that was the end of John's race. It then looked as though Gurney would win, particularly when what looked like his only remaining serious challenger, Clark's Lotus, retired after 41 laps with a broken driveshaft. Alas, and as usual, Dan's Brabham lasted only another seven laps before a front radius arm pulled out of the chassis, so Bandini was handed a lucky win . . .lucky for Surtees as well, for Lorenzo was also taking Championship points from John's rivals.

Having originally been shown at the end of 1963, Forghieri's flat-12 made its first public appearance on the second day of practice for the 1964 Italian Grand Prix at Monza. This 56 x 50.4mm, 1489.63cc unit was based round aluminium alloy crankcase/cylinder blocks, had two gear-driven overhead camshafts to each bank and a seven main bearing crankshaft. Vertically disposed inlet ports were fed by long intake tubes in which were fitted the injectors for the Lucas fuel injection system, two belt driven pumps being employed, while the single sparking plug per cylinder set-up was fed by a coil ignition system. The two distributors were camshaft driven and the engine was claimed to develop 220bhp at 11,500rpm using a compression ratio of 9.8:1. The exhaust pipes ran beneath the car, a bunch of six protruding on either side of the chassis and emerging into single tail pipes.

The engine was extremely compact and, since its overall width was no greater than the bulkhead behind the driver to which the V8 unit was attached, it fitted snugly into the existing chassis complete with the same rear suspension arrangement and a gearbox similar to that employed on the 158 was bolted to the rear of the flat-12 crankcase.

At 94.5in(2400mm), the 1512's wheelbase was less than an inch longer than the 158's 93.7in(2380mm) and the car weighed in at 1046lbs(475kg) with no fluids or driver. Bandini only drove the new car in the wet on the second day of practice, setting his qualifying time at the wheel of a 158. Surtees was on splendid form, qualifying on pole position with a 1m 37.4s, 0.8s faster than Gurney's Brabham. Hill's BRM turned a 1m 38.7s for third place on the outside of the front row, Bandini managing a 1m 39.8s to line up in the middle of row three. Right back on the inside of the seventh row was Ludovico Scarfiotti who recorded a 1m 41.6s at the wheel of the faithful old Dino 156 . . .

As the starting signal was given, Hill's BRM lurched forward a few yards and then stopped, its clutch thrust mechanism having seized, and McLaren took full advantage of the resultant confusion to nip through to a briefly-held lead with his Cooper. Gurney and Surtees were through ahead of Bruce by the end of the first lap and after John forced the 158 into the lead on lap two, the battle for supremacy lay between Ferrari and Brabham with Clark's Lotus and McLaren hanging on in the slipstream. Eventually Clark retired with a broken piston, McLaren lost touch with the leading bunch and, finally, Gurney was delayed by a misfire and resultant pit stop, dropping to an eventual 10th, three laps behind. This allowed Surtees to make up for his previous Monza disappointment with a popular victory ahead of Mclaren. Just to add to the joy of the *tifosi*, Bandini outfumbled Ginther's BRM to snatch third place on the run up to the line . . .and further down the field there was more wheel-to-wheel stuff as Baghetti's Centro-Sud BRM got the verdict for eighth place by a similar margin over Scarfiotti's 156. Surtees was cheered to the echo, but, for many of the screaming fans, there was no doubt that Bandini was hero of the day as first Italian driver home!

Before the teams went to North America for the final two Grands Prix of the season at Watkins Glen and Mexico City, Ferrari had a row with the Italian Automobile Federation over the disputed homologation of the 250LM sports car and, in a fury, announced that he was relinquishing his entrants licence and wouldn't be fielding cars in his name on home soil again. As a result, the Formula 1 Ferraris appeared at Watkins Glen for the US Grand Prix on October 4 carrying the blue and white national colours of that country and entered by Luigi Chinetti's North American Racing Team.

Clark took the pole for the 110 lap, 407km race and although his Lotus was moving first, Surtees burst through to lead at the end of the opening lap and began to pull away initially. Clark fought back and repassed him only for the Lotus to encounter fuel injection problems which dropped it from contention: Surtees's chances of victory were then compromised by a time-consuming spin whilst lapping a slower car, so John's 158 had to settle for second place behind Graham Hill's BRM. Bandini retired the flat-12, one bank of exhausts smoking badly, with "electrical trouble".

As Clark, Hill and Surtees went into the Mexican Grand Prix on October 25, any one of them had a good chance of the Championship title. Surtees had a pair of Ferrari 158s to choose from, Bandini had his lone flat-12 and an old 156 was on hand for local hero Pedro Rodriguez to handle. Shorter inlet pipes had been flown from Italy specially for this race, improving the cars' pick-up out of tight corners at this high altitude track. The flat-12 was really beginning to show form now and Bandini beat his regular team-mate to third place on the grid by 0.1s, Clark and Gurney sharing the front row of the two-by-two grid ahead of them.

At the start Jim began motoring off into the distance in typical style, Surtees finding himself badly bogged down in the middle of the pack on the opening lap because his engine seemed reluctant to rev. properly, but it eventually picked up and he began clawing back the lost ground. Hill moved up to third place with his

Surtees's 158 brakes hard for Tabac at Monaco during the 1964 Monaco Grand Prix, running ahead of Richie Ginther's BRM. John retired from this race with gearbox trouble.

BRM, displacing Bandini on lap three, but Lorenzo came back to harry him in determined fashion, running into the back of the English V8 as it exited the hairpin on lap 31, spinning Graham's car lightly into the guard rails. This damaged the BRM exhausts and obliged Hill to stop at the pits for attention. Thus, when Clark's Lotus, which had been gradually losing oil in the closing stages of what looked to most people like a dominant, flag-to-flag World Championship victory run, finally seized its Climax V8 thanks to its lack of lubricant on the last lap, Surtees virtually fell into the World Championship! Gurney went through to win the race for Brabham and Bandini was signalled to concede second place to JS on the final tour, enabling his team-mate to take the drivers' title by a single point and also clinching the Constructors' Championship for Maranello.

It had been a fortunate victory for Ferrari, against the prevailing trend which was clearly continuing in favour of Jim Clark's Lotus-Climax. In the final season of the 1½-litre formula, Ferrari would fail to win a single race, largely because a fully developed version of the next flat-12 engine wasn't available until towards the end of the 1965 programme. Equipped with a 32-valve Coventry-Climax V8, Jim Clark's Lotus 33 swept impressively to the 1965 World Championship, a task he completed by the end of the German Grand Prix such was the level of his dominance. For the first part of the 1965 season Surtees continued to concentrate his efforts on the V8, taking over the flat-12 from Silverstone onwards, the engine eventually appearing at Monza equipped with revised cylinder heads with two sparking plugs per cylinder, reputedly developing 255bhp at this stage.

"As far as the Nürburgring was concerned, the V6, V8 and flat-12 all worked pretty well there," reflects John, "I won in '63 with the V6, '64 with the V8 and I feel I might have done it again with the flat-12 in 1965 if it hadn't suffered gear linkage problems as I accelerated away from the line. The initial flat-12 had a big problem with oil surge and it was a bit temperamental until we got those new heads at Monza, and then it really flew. In its final form it had a decisive advantage over anything else, but I lost out because I had my accident at Mosport with my Lola

Wheel to wheel! John Surtees's 158 keeps a few feet ahead of Dan Gurney's Brabham-Climax during their dice for the lead of the 1964 Italian Grand Prix at Monza. John won the race.

before the North American races took place.

"What really surprised me is that the flat-12 didn't go over and dominate those two races because, as far as I recall the way it was going at Monza, nobody else would have seen it. Prior to Monza it had lacked development time and it was so heavy on fuel that it was touch-and-go whether it would finish, which is one of the reasons why I often drove a V8 in 1965 even though it was slightly slower. The only reason that Lorenzo's flat-12 had been able to finish in Mexico in '64 was that they leaned off the mixture considerably before the race . . ."

For the first race of the season, the South African Grand Prix at East London, although the Ferraris were back in their red livery, they were entered by team manager Dragoni as Enzo Ferrari still hadn't got his entrants' licence back after his 250LM row. The 158 was much as before and Surtees qualified second alongside Clark's Lotus 33B, albeit 0.9s slower. Clark and team-mate Mike Spence ran away initially in 1-2 formation, but Surtees was quickly up to third place which became second when Spence's inexperience led him into a couple of spins which dropped the other Lotus to fourth at the finish.

An abortive outing in the Race of Champions, where the V8 never ran properly, led Surtees back to another confrontation with Clark's Lotus at Syracuse, although in the race on April 4 the pair of them had to fight a fantastic wheel-to-wheel battle with Jo Siffert in Rob Walker's Brabham-BRM V8. The Swiss driver eventually missed a gearchange and ruined his engine, while Surtees's V8 went sick and Clark pulled out almost a full minute over the Ferrari to win the 56 lap event easily. Bandini's third-placed flat-12 was the only other car not to be lapped. Interestingly, one of the Ferrari 158s appeared at this race with English-made glass fibre bodywork for the first time, and Surtees recalls that he introduced the team to this method of bodywork manufacture. "I took Peter Jackson (of Specialised Mouldings) over there and we made up the first glass fibre nose sections which appeared in 1963/64. We were going to set up our own company in the old Colotti gearbox factory, but then Ferrari decided to do the whole thing in a much bigger way with Scaglietti . . ."

On May 15 Surtees had to give best to Jackie Stewart's BRM at the Silverstone International Trophy, John's 158 three seconds adrift after 52 laps of Silverstone but with a new F1 record of 1m 33.0s(182.34kph/113.30mph) in his pocket for his efforts. Two weeks later there was no Gurney or Clark to face at Monaco as they were off contesting the Indianapolis 500, leaving Surtees's V8 and Bandini's flat-12 to match up against Hill, Stewart and Brabham as their principal competitors.

Hill landed pole position with a 1m 32.5s from Brabham on 1m 32.8s, Stewart's BRM(1m 32.9s), Bandini(1m 33.0s) and Surtees(1m 33.2s). Hill and Stewart led from Bandini and Surtees in the opening sprint, but what looked like a BRM demonstration run was ruined when Hill was forced up the chicane escape road to

avoid a slower competitor on lap 25. This handed the advantage to Stewart, but he spun at *Ste. Devote* five laps later, so Bandini tore into the lead with Brabham, who had got ahead of Surtees with little difficulty, chasing the flat-12 for all he was worth. Unfortunately Jack's rev. counter had packed up, so he eventually abused his Climax V8 beyond what it was prepared to accept, so the second half of the race saw Graham Hill coming back at the two Ferraris with a vengeance.

Hill got past Surtees to take second place with little drama, but Bandini battled long and hard to keep the BRM behind him, struggling against overwhelming odds from lap 53 to lap 65, when Hill cut past into the lead once again.

From that point on Bandini cut his Ferrari's rev. limit by 1000rpm in the interests of fuel consumption, so Surtees went through into second place — only for the V8 to run short of fuel on the penultimate lap, allowing Bandini back through into second place behind Hill's victorious BRM. Surtees was eventually classified fourth behind Stewart.

Clark was back from Indianapolis in time for the Belgian Grand Prix at Spa-Francorchamps on June 13, this rain-soaked 32 lap event turning out to be a

Below, looking curiously thoughtful for a man who has just become World Champion, Surtees cruises into the Mexico City pits after his triumphant parade lap. In both photographs the repositioned fuel pump, out in the air stream above the driver's left shoulder, can clearly be seen.

Fleeting promise. Now fitted with revised cylinder heads, the Ferrari 1512 leads the pack at Monza, 1965, in the hands of John Surtees. In this photograph the flat-12 is ahead of Jackie Stewart and Graham Hill (BRMs) and Jim Clark's Lotus 33. It didn't last, however, clutch failure eventually sidelining the 1964 World Champion . . .

race for Maranello to quickly forget. After qualifying on the inside of row three (Surtees's V8) and the outside of row six (Bandini's flat-12), John was out with a broken engine after six laps and his very dejected team-mate trailed home ninth "this not being his idea of racing at all . . ." Clark and Stewart lapped the lot in first and second places.

Another Scottish demonstration run followed in the French Grand Prix at Clermont-Ferrand, Surtees following Clark and Stewart home a distant third with his V8 engine fluttering for much of the race. The engine's rectifier had broken away from its mounting and, after a pit stop to cut it away, Surtees continued with the misfiring getting worse as AC current was pushed into the battery instead of DC. Bandini slid off the road with three laps to go while holding fifth place, glancing a bank, and soon afterwards a wheel came off and his 1512 slithered down the road in a shower of sparks and suspension components.

Surtees used the flat-12 for the first time at Silverstone for the British Grand Prix on July 10, finishing third after a close battle with Mike Spence's Lotus 33, but Bandini blew his V8 up in a shower of steam and smoke on the second lap

following a missed gear change. The team's form plunged even further in the Dutch Grand Prix at Zandvoort, Surtees's car bugged by serious handling problems caused by unevenly-wearing tyres and could only scrape home a lapped seventh with Bandini ninth after a spin.

There was a brand new flat-12 on hand for Surtees at the Nürburgring, but the Englishman spent most of the time at the wheel of his original machine during practice, only to take over the new car for the race and experience those gear selector problems as he accelerated away from his position on the outside of the front row. John was obliged to do a full 14-mile lap before he could reach the pits for attention, so his chances of a German Grand Prix hat trick were finished scarcely before the battle had begun. He eventually got back into the race over two laps behind Clark's fast-disappearing Lotus and made an attempt to topple Jim's lap record before the gearbox went on the blink again and he called it a day. Bandini brought his 158 home sixth after a spin.

Using those long-awaited revised cylinder heads, Surtees managed to qualify the flat-12 on the front row of the grid at Monza alongside Clark's Lotus which took pole position. Originally Ferrari had intended to field an entry of four machines: Surtees, Bandini and Scarfiotti with flat-12s and Nino Vaccarella with a V8, but in the event Scarfiotti didn't race and Vaccarella took his car, leaving a spare flat-12 for *Il Grande John*. As the cars lined up on the starting grid, Surtees's hydraulic clutch control mechanism was beginning to play up, so when the starting signal was given he got away slowly. In that rush of colour, noise and hysterical confusion which marks the end of the opening lap of every Italian Grand Prix, Surtees was down in 14th place, the clutch having gone completely solid, but he quickly caught up the leaders again and actually contested the lead vigorously before the clutch slipped out of business for good on lap 34 and he retired. Bandini came home a smooth, popular and distant fourth behind Stewart, Hill and Gurney, but Vaccarella's V8 also retired, with engine failure.

For the final two races of this somewhat ignominious season for Maranello, Surtees was out of the equation, the Englishman fighting for his life after a serious accident at the wheel of his Lola-Chevrolet T70 Can-Am car at Toronto's Mosport Park shortly after the Monza race. Bandini therefore spearheaded the flat-12 attack in the 110 lap US Grand Prix at Watkins Glen on October 3, while Pedro Rodriguez drove the second 1512 and Bob Bondurant handled the 158, both these latter machines being NART entries. Bandini qualified fifth fastest and finished a lapped fourth, Rodriguez was fifth and Bondurant ninth.

Finally, on October 24 at Mexico City, Bandini and Scarfiotti appeared at the wheel of works flat-12s while Rodriguez drove a third such machine, again in NART colours. This latter arrangement allowed Pedro to try Firestone's latest Firestone semi-slick tyres, free from the constraints of the works team's Dunlop contract, but before he could reach any conclusion on their worth (the data was anxiously required back at Maranello) he crashed heavily, so, unsurprisingly, Scarfiotti had to forfeit his car for the race. Off the pace, Pedro finished seventh while Bandini was the eighth and last finisher in the very last Grand Prix to be held to 1½-litre regulations.

As an interesting tailpiece, when Rodriguez's damaged car was taken back to Maranello it was tucked away in the loft of the racing department and forgotten for several years. Eventually it was spirited out of the factory in 1974 and is now owned by none other than John Surtees, the man who fleetingly demonstrated its tremendous potential during those early laps at Monza in 1965 . . .

Section V:

The 3-litre twelves, 1966-80:

A golden era for Maranello

Chapter 1
The V12s: Defeat snatched from the jaws of victory

It was back in 1963 that the CSI announced technical regulations for the new Formula 1 which was scheduled to start on January 1, 1966. Even by the end of the third season catering for the 1½-litre Formula 1, most people within the professional motor racing business were agreed that a move to more powerful cars would be appropriate at the next change of formula, so it was decided that the new rules would provide for 3-litre normally aspirated cars or 1.5 litres supercharged. The latter provision was originally evolved as a stop-gap measure to help any entrant who wanted to continue in Formula 1 but couldn't get his hands on a 3-litre engine in time for the start of 1966. It was anticipated that some of the teams who had used the 1½-litre Coventry-Climax V8 might arrange to have them supercharged, but when one really analysed the situation the whole concept was pretty unlikely, particularly as Coventry-Climax decided on a complete withdrawal from Grand Prix racing anyway at the end of 1965.

Taken overall, there was significantly less bitching and binding about this change in Formula 1 regulations compared with the stupidities which followed on after the announcement of the 1½-litre formula at the end of 1958. Several British constructors were worried about sources of engine supply, admittedly, but there was no large-scale rebellion or suggestions that an alternative category be established to prolong the use of outdated machinery.

As far as Ferrari was concerned, the 3-litre Formula 1 was just fine by him, but the speed in which he produced his first prototype V12 type 312 may have helped create something of a false impression about potential for Ferrari dominance once the new formula got under way. Whilst Cooper was still working hard on its first prototype V12-engined Maserati-powered machine, whilst BRM's complex new H-16 was still blowing itself apart on the Bourne test beds, and the seeds of the Cosworth-Ford DFV concept were germinating in the mind of Ford's Walter Hayes, the first Ferrari 312 was wheeled out into the factory courtyard to be presented to the press in December, 1965. Unpainted, and wearing Firestone

Delicate touch! In the mist and rain that shrouded the 1968 German Grand Prix at the Nürburgring, Jacky Ickx's pole position 312 heads towards an eventual fourth place, showing off splendidly its "central" aerofoil position. Ickx never got close to Amon in the race, but Chris, typically, failed to finish . . .

Fine win for Surtees. Big John's 312 (No.8) accelerates away from pole position at the start of the 1966 Belgian Grand Prix at Spa-Francorchamps. After a well-judged tussle with Jochen Rindt's Cooper-Maserati (No.19), Surtees scored a worthy win. It wasn't good enough for team manager Dragoni, though, and within weeks John would be partnering Rindt at Cooper.

slicks for the purposes of this unveiling, the new car certainly looked the part. The specialist magazines and the daily press hailed Ferrari's new car as a potential winner, simply, it seems, on the basis that it was ready before most of its rivals. Few bothered to question the nature of its power unit . . . or the fact that the 312 was very big indeed.

The engine was closely related to the 3.3-litre, 4 o.h.c. Le Mans engine, Ferrari's engineering team opting for the expected 60-degree V12 with a bore and stroke of 77 x 53.5mm giving a total capacity of 2989 c.c. Lucas port fuel injection was employed, the engine had coil and distributor ignition, two plugs-per- cylinder – and the factory was claiming a power output of 360bhp! However, it should also be recalled that they were claiming that its weight was 548kg at a time when the minimum weight limit was set at 500kg: the fact that it tipped the scales during scrutineering for its Syracuse début at 604kg may have reflected another example of the Ferrari's occasional, yet charming, tendency towards self-delusion!

The 312 employed a five-speed gearbox in unit with the final drive and the main chassis was constructed from riveted aluminium sheeting overlaying a steel tubular base. The fuel tanks were boxed in on either side of the cockpit and the chassis structure extended rearwards along either side of the engine bay, formed round tubular longerons. This formed a support for the V12 engine to be installed in, the tubes on either side having the engine mountings welded into them, and the extensions ended with a rear bulkhead on which the rear suspension was mounted. This was by means of outboard coil spring/damper units, a single top link, lower wishbone and twin radius rods. Up at the front, the coil spring/damper units were mounted inboard and operated by forged rocker arms. There was also a wide-based lower wishbone.

On the face of things, Ferrari did look in good shape at the start of 1966, but the 312's on-paper promise was only part of the reason. The other major factor in the team's favour was the complete recovery made by former World Champion John Surtees following that dreadful crash at Mosport Park at the wheel of his Lola sports car the previous autumn. Demonstrating a remarkable amount of determination and refusal to accept physical defeat, Surtees had forced the pace of his recovery and was back in a Ferrari, testing at Modena, before the winter was over. It really was a fantastic effort on the part of the Englishman and the fact that he managed to run a full Grand Prix distance during that testing, without any problem, underlined the fact that he had completely regained his stamina.

Surtees himself has nothing but happy memories of Ferrari's reaction to his quick recovery. "The Old Man had rung me up after the accident and said 'John. Which leg is it?' I told him 'the left one' and he replied 'That's OK, if necessary we'll make you an automatic!' What's more, I think it should be said that although I didn't have the accident in a Ferrari car, their insurance covered me. They looked after the hospital and everything else. The same thing happened to Pironi in 1982, though of course he *was* in a Ferrari, but he told me that they'd been fantastic.

"Anyway, when I got back to the factory for the first time all the mechanics were crying. I was on my crutches still, so they got one of those little hoists that they used to move the engines about, and they winched me into the car they'd built for me, the little Tasman Dino 246. The car had stayed at the factory after my accident – in fact, the Old Man had agreed to sell it to me. I used it as a training car to get myself back into the groove again . . ."

Ferrari didn't bother to send any cars to the non-Championship South African Grand Prix in January, holding back the V12's début to the Syracuse race on May 8. By the time Surtees took the trip down to Sicily, however, he was starting to feel a trifle worried about the season's prospects.

"I'd been round and round Modena in that little Tasman 246," he recalls, "then, of course, the V12 was wheeled out . . . and it looked absolutely *enormous*. And everybody was saying 'Ah, 3-litre formula, Ferrari will walk it, foregone conclusion, Surtees has got no problems . . .' So I take this thing out and its *two-and-a-half seconds* slower round Modena than the V6. Flat as a bloody pancake! It transpires that all it is a sports car engine reduced to 3-litres. And everybody's saying 'poor old Jack Brabham has only got 290/300bhp from his Repco engine'. This bloody V12, which weighed God-knows how much, is really only giving about 270bhp . . . I went off to win at Syracuse, but I had to row it along like hell. Luckily Syracuse had some very tricky bits over the back, so I was able to gain a bit of time . . ."

In fact, John's début win with the car looked pretty convincing to most onlookers, the V12 only being headed by Bandini in the Tasman Dino 246 during the first three laps while the bigger engine shrugged off a brief misfire caused by fouled plugs. But Surtees wasn't convinced, and when the new 312 was convincingly outclassed by the new Brabham-Repco V8 in the 35 lap, 165km, 18th Silverstone International Trophy race on May 14, he returned to Maranello and made his feelings felt very firmly indeed.

The spaceframe Brabham with its Repco light-alloy, production-based V8 had been present at Syracuse, but minor technical problems had prevented it from showing its true potential. On the wide open spaces of Silverstone, the Ferrari V12 was confidently expected to have the edge on the Australian's machine, but lightness, agility and excellent handling combined to defeat the somewhat questionable number of Maranello horses propelling Surtees's car that afternoon. Surtees did everything in his power to redress the balance, but Brabham beat him by seven seconds. The crowds filed out of Silverstone that afternoon wondering just what would happen once the World Championship struggle got under way in Europe.

Back at Maranello there was obviously some friction developing between Surtees and one or two other members of the technical staff. Mauro Forghieri dismisses Surtees's allegations that the engine was giving less than 300bhp at the start of the season. "Surtees isn't correct on that one," he told the author, "about 360bhp was the *average* power output over the year taken as a whole. At the start of the season it may have been 20/25bhp less. What Surtees forgets is that the Tasman Dino was at least 100kg lighter than the V12 and we were getting around 280bhp from that – more than 110bhp per litre, which was pretty reasonable. It was smaller, lighter and had a smaller frontal area than the V12. That makes a considerable difference."

Surtees none the less told Forghieri and engine man Franco Rocchi exactly what he thought of the gutless V12 and, according to John, "they went very quiet and said 'well, of course, we can't really afford to build a totally new engine, you know. We've got to streamline things a bit, use interchangeable parts with the sports car programme'. So I made it clear just how hard I had to wind the thing up at Silverstone . . . but the engineers knew full well what the situation was. I mean, I used to go to the bloody engine test house and knew exactly what the engines were giving – even though they were saying all sorts of other things . . ."

Into this little technical disagreement entered the uncompromisingly patriotic, if somewhat unrealistic, Eugenio Dragoni, still banging his nationalistic drum in favour of Lorenzo Bandini. The Ferrari team manager could see a situation developing in which he could capitalize on circumstances to favour Bandini over Surtees: the problem which was really going to come to a head for the Englishman at Le Mans began fermenting seriously as the Formula 1 team prepared for Monaco. And Surtees wasn't one to deal tactfully with such problems, preferring to come out into the open and call a spade a spade, even if it might have been more beneficial for his racing career if he'd laid low for a short while.

Surtees: "We cracked on and started a re-design on the V12's cylinder heads, using revised ports and different valves, rather like the development we'd done on the little 1½-litre flat-12. This took the engine from 270bhp to around 310/315 bhp. But I didn't get to use it until we went to Spa, the second race in the Championship . . .

Meanwhile, Monaco loomed ever-closer on the calendar and Surtees was aching with frustration over his Modena test runs in the 312. "I was still struggling to get within two seconds of my best time with the V6, so I went to the Old Man and said 'look, this is pointless. I want the V6 for Monaco.' And I went along to the race with expectations of driving it. Then Dragoni came out with 'we make 12-cylinder road cars, so we have to race 12-cylinder cars. You are the lead driver, so you will have to race the 12-cylinder' . . ." In retrospect, Dragoni must have known that such a remark would have been like a red rag to a bull as far as JS was concerned. Immediately the Englishman went on to the defensive.

Ferrari's "new" power unit for the 3-litre Formula 1. The fuel-injected V12 was originally shown at the end of 1965 – it may have been the first of the 3-litre power units, but it wasn't to be the most powerful . . .

"But we want to win the race," said Surtees firmly. "Oh, you'll win the race alright," replied Dragoni. That stupidly bland assumption, calculated to annoy Big John, prompted a very accurate prediction from the team's number one driver. "I told him, 'yes, I'll stay in front for a few laps and I'll tell you what will happen. The bloody thing will break its gearbox because I'll be winding it up so hard to stay there . . .'

"And, as you know, I held the lead for a few laps and then it went crunch. Stewart was handed the win on a plate, although I was having to drive pretty hard to stay in front of him. Then the old V6 comes rushing through the field . . . I mean, if I'd used it we would have won the race. It nearly did with Lorenzo. But, as far as that V12 was concerned, even if I hadn't retired, I doubt whether I would have made it to the end because its fuel wouldn't have lasted the distance."

Surtees's view was vindicated quite conclusively in the view of most observers and Bandini's failure to quite get to grips with Stewart's winning 2-litre BRM P261 must have aggravated Dragoni about as much as the Italian had upset Surtees prior to the race. In fact, Surtees had done a fine job during practice at Monaco, grappling with the big V12 to qualify second on 1m 30.1s, a mere 0.2s off Jim Clark's pole with the more nimble 2-litre Lotus 33-Climax V8. Clark was out of the equation from the word go when his gearbox stuck in second as he accelerated off

the line, so Stewart climbed all over Surtees unhindered. On lap 13 John felt the differential beginning to "snatch" and Stewart was through into an unchallenged lead. The tiring, 100 lap thrash through the sunlit streets saw Bandini get to within 12s of Stewart on lap 92, but despite setting the race's fastest lap with ten still to run, Lorenzo conceded defeat and had faded to more than 40s adrift by the time the chequered flag was shown.

On June 13, the Grand Prix circus arrived at Spa-Francorchamps for the Belgian Grand Prix and Surtees capitalized on the interim engine revisions and Firestone's very effective dry-weather rubber to take the 312 round to pole position with ease. Bandini "opted" for the V6 2.4-litre car again after trying a second V12 in practice: at the time it was stated that Lorenzo felt more secure in the "less powerful" car on this very quick circuit, but it may well be that the Italian was no fool and reckoned the 3-litre machine didn't really represent much of an improvement.

Shortly before the start it became obvious that it was going to rain, so Surtees's 312 was fitted with Dunlop wet-weather tyres and, sure enough, as the pack approached *Malmedy* on the opening lap the rain arrived from the opposite direction. In a sequence of unfortunate events that were to virtually condemn Spa-Francorchamps as a Grand Prix circuit in the eyes of most "professional" drivers, there were suddenly cars spinning in all directions on the now-glassy surface. This little drama, which included a big accident to Stewart when his BRM went off on the Masta Straight, left Surtees in command, and although Bandini (who had never demonstrated much form at Spa in the past) briefly poked the V6 ahead of the field, John finally emerged a well-deserved winner of the 28 lap Grand Prix. For much of the race he'd chosen not to set the pace, preferring to follow in the wheel tracks of the spectacular Jochen Rindt's Cooper-Maserati, pressing home his attack to snatch victory in the closing stages. Bandini, lapped, finished third.

None of this, predictably, pleased Dragoni. He criticized Surtees strongly for not having led from the start. Surtees replied, "when you tell me how to drive the race, then that'll be the day. Winning is the only thing that matters." Dragoni replied that the Ferrari was now so superior "with our new three-valve cylinder heads we will be in a position to employ lesser drivers and win anyway . . ." A week later, in a row over driver pairings at Le Mans, Surtees had his final bust-up with Dragoni and stormed out of the Ferrari team for good. He was immediately snapped up by the Cooper-Maserati team, leaving Ferrari's team manager to pursue unhampered his somewhat individualistic theories for the remainder of the season.

Unfortunately, it *was* just a trifle simplistic to think in terms of lesser drivers being competitive thanks to a power surplus: in fact, the whole concept was doubly simplistic in 1966 because Ferrari wound up with the worst of both worlds. Dragoni's blind faith in the ability of the team to field the most competitive cars in the business resulted in the remainder of the season just petering out. It seems that Surtees was the only person within the Scuderia to have read the message written by Brabham at the International Trophy . . .

Surtees's place in the Ferrari Grand Prix team was taken by Michael Parkes, a solid, reliable driver who'd built a firm reputation as a sports car man but had never seriously tried single seaters. He was employed as a development engineer at Maranello and, in Surtees's personal demonology, could be regarded as the Grand Diabolarch. Despite the fact that the two men were English, something which might have brought them closer together working at Ferrari, they each affected a studied disregard for the other. Surtees *knew* he was the better driver, but thought of himself also as something of an engineer: Parkes *knew* he was the only engineer of the two, but mistakenly regarded himself as a top-class Grand Prix driver. It was a case of oil and water . . .

With Surtees out of the picture, Parkes could now spread the wings of his ambition as far as Formula 1 was concerned. He made his Grand Prix début in the French Grand Prix, held in 1966 at the stunningly fast Reims-Gueux circuit, and managed to squeeze his specially lengthened 312 (Parkes was more than six feet tall!) on to the outside of the front row with team leader Bandini on pole and none other than Surtees's Cooper-Maserati between the two of them. It must have been a sweet moment for Big John as the starting flag fell and he beat the two red cars away from the line, but the moment turned bitter as fuel vaporization intervened as he swung into the first corner . . . he was engulfed by the Ferraris and the rest of the pack.

On this super-fast circuit Bandini had the legs of all his rivals. The Italian led comfortably, pulling away from Jack Brabham's Repco-engined machine, only for the 312 to break its throttle cable as he approached *Thillois* on lap 38. The Italian car coasted to a silent halt, and although the willing Lorenzo searched around for some baling wire and made up a splendid jury-jig to work the throttles long enough to return to the pits, he was completely out of the picture when he resumed the contest. Brabham sailed onwards, unchallenged, to an historical victory, while Parkes came home an excellent second. Not too bad, perhaps, for the Prancing Horse without Surtees?

From that point onwards, however, the sun really began to go behind the clouds as far as Maranello's Grand Prix effort was concerned. On July 24 the Dutch Grand Prix took place at Zandvoort, a circuit on which it wouldn't have been unreasonable to expect a decent performance from a *really* powerful Formula 1 car, but the 312s were quite simply out of the picture. They'd missed the British Grand Prix at Brands Hatch (officially due to "strikes" in Italy) and their form at the Dutch seaside circuit was such as to indicate they'd have been a laughing stock if they'd turned up at the Kent circuit. Neither Parkes nor Bandini could get anywhere near the well-balanced, good-handling Brabham-Repco V8s and whilst Mike managed to squeeze on to the second row, Lorenzo couldn't improve beyond row four. The race was a disaster, Parkes spinning off early on and crashing his 312 into Rindt's parked Cooper-Maserati, while Bandini staggered home sixth, three laps behind Brabham's winning machine, after a spin.

A telling demonstration of the 2.4-Litre Dino V6 car's potential came once again at the Nürburgring during practice for the German Grand Prix on August 4. Ludovico Scarfiotti was drafted into the team to drive the neat little machine and managed to qualify on the outside of the front row: Bandini and Parkes could only make row two with the "more powerful" V12s. Further, if one assumes that Scarfiotti genuinely ranked as number three in terms of driving ability when considering the team's drivers at that time, the way in which Ferrari seemed hell-bent on squandering its resources in 1966 seems to slip even more clearly into focus. The race was another one for Maranello to forget: while Brabham's Brabham battled with Surtees's Cooper-Maserati on a rain-soaked *Nordschleife*, all three Ferraris were totally outclassed. Bandini limped home a sodden sixth, by which time Parkes had spun off the road and Scarfiotti's V6 had succumbed to electrical problems. Brabham notched up his fourth win of the season.

And so to Monza, where Ferrari just *had* to pull something out of the bag. After a season experimenting with various valve configurations, Forghieri and his colleagues came up with the new three-valve cylinder head (two inlet, one exhaust) which, they claimed, boosted the power output to between 370 and 380bhp. This, by obvious implication, cast retrospective doubt on the power figures that had been stated earlier in the year (if they were only producing 370-ish bhp at Monza, how could Forghieri claim that the *average* for the season was 360bhp?). However, they were obviously quite an improvement on the two-valve V12s, a fact which Surtees confirms by his observations from the cockpit of his Cooper-Maserati. "By Monza, they had a distinct power advantage," he insists, adding, "but my Cooper-Maserati was a better handling car . . ."

On the wide open spaces at Monza, Ferrari gave the *tifosi* precisely what they wanted. Mike Parkes qualified on pole position with a 1m 31.3s best while Scarfiotti's V12 was next up (1m 31.6s) and Jim Clark's complex H16 BRM-engined Lotus 43 completed the front row. Row two contained former team-mates Surtees (1m 31.9s) and Bandini (1m 32.0s). At the start Scarfiotti was away first, but Bandini led at the end of the opening lap and this seemed a heaven-sent opportunity for Lorenzo to score the most crucially important victory of his career. Sadly, the long-awaited home victory for the crowd's hero was never to be. On lap two Lorenzo was in the pits with a broken fuel line and that delayed him very badly, leaving his two team-mates to fight it out at the front for the glory of Italy. Parkes managed to hold on, at or near the front, until Scarfiotti came through on lap 13 and held his advantage to the finish. Parkes was left with the task of fending off the tenacious Denny Hulme's Brabham-Repco, the two cars becoming embroiled in a truly frantic dice which continued right up until the chequered flag where Parkes just managed to keep his 312 ahead by a matter of yards to round off a Ferrari 1–2 on home soil. Bandini rejoined and lapped in close company with the leaders for a long time before finally retiring on lap 34. The little Tasman Dino 246 made another guest appearance in this race, handled by Giancarlo Baghetti under the Parnell Racing banner after the Italian had run into problems with the team's Lotus-BRM. The 1961 Reims winner got up to fifth place in the closing stages only for gearbox problems to drop him to 10th at the end.

To round off the season, Ferrari sent a single three-valve V12 to Watkins Glen for the United States Grand Prix on October 2. Lorenzo qualified third, taking the lead on the opening lap. Brabham squeezed ahead on lap 10, but the Italian fought back and was in the lead once more by the time the V12 suffered an internal breakage, probably caused by a broken sparking plug, and came into the pits for good with 34 laps completed. After this ignominious performance, Ferrari failed to participate in the Mexican Grand Prix, final round of the Championship, and returned home to prepare for 1967.

Ferrari's challenge for the new season centred round evolutionary versions of the 312 chassis fitted with further improved V12 engines. The unit retained its three valves-per-cylinder configuration, but the camshafts were reversed so that while the inlet ports were still down between the camshafts, the exhaust ports were also inside which called for a complex and distinctive exhaust system in the middle of the vee. The factory records claim a power output of 390bhp at 10,000 rpm, but there was the usual scepticism amongst the drivers as to whether this was an accurate figure. The '67 specification chassis, in order to accommodate the central exhaust engines, were built with higher side pontoons alongside the engine bay, this also providing more space for the fuel load.

On the driver front, Lorenzo Bandini started out as a team leader, partnered by Ludovico Scarfiotti and newcomer Chris Amon, but with Mike Parkes also on the books; it was a somewhat confusing situation for Amon who didn't quite understand how the whole thing would work out. As in 1966, the team declined to compete in the South African Grand Prix, even though it was a Championship qualifying round this year, and an entry of three cars was made for the Daily Mail Race of Champions at Brands Hatch. Amon and Scarfiotti were entered with a pair of '66 specification V12s while Bandini handled a brand new chassis with its revamped engine. In the event, Amon got himself involved in a minor road accident whilst driving to Brands Hatch at the wheel of his Sunbeam Tiger the Friday prior to practice. No bones were broken, but Chris was quite badly bruised and, after a handful of practice laps, he decided to withdraw rather than risk making a fool of himself and destroy his Ferrari Grand Prix career almost before it had started.

The Race of Champions format included two 10 lap heats leading up to a 40 lap final round the twisting, 2.65-mile circuit. Dan Gurney's new Eagle-Weslake V12 emerged triumphant in all three "events", but while a misfire kept Bandini down in 10th place during both heats, the latest Ferrari V12 was superbly on song when it came to the final and he rocketed through the field to finish a close second, a mere 0.4s behind the winning American. Scarfiotti wound up fifth in the " '66 spec." car.

There was one more non-Championship race to be held before the all-important Monaco Grand Prix, and Ferrari sent a single 312 to the BRDC's International Trophy meeting at Silverstone on April 29. Mike Parkes was entrusted again with his specially lengthened chassis (with "inside" exhaust engine) and won the 52-lap event quite comfortably from Jack's Brabham-Repco after an early challenge from Jackie Stewart's BRM H-16 had evaporated. Prospects looked good for Ferrari: they'd obviously made progress with their car and had accumulated more than enough drivers to see them through the year. Within a matter of weeks, however, that situation was going to alter dramatically, landing the entire responsibility for Ferrari fortunes firmly on Chris Amon's shoulders . . .

Prior to joining the Italian team, Amon's career had been patchy and showed all the hallmarks of a talent which had peaked too soon. A protégé of Reg Parnell, he was a pudgy-faced 19-year old when he stepped off a plane at London Airport and rushed to Goodwood for his Formula 1 début in the 1963 Easter International, handling one of Parnell's private Lola-Climax V8s. The only child of a wealthy New Zealand sheep farmer, Chris had initially attracted Reg's attention with some outstanding drives at the wheel of an outmoded Maserati 250F during the '62 Tasman Series, and he continued to drive for Parnell Racing throughout 1963 and '64. But after Reg sadly died in the winter of '63/'64, Amon lost a mentor whom he badly needed. At the end of '64 he lost his seat with the team, and although he was invited back for a few drives the following year when regular driver Dickie Attwood injured himself, it looked as though his career had petered out.

During this low period in his racing fortunes, the youthful Amon earned himself a reputation as something of a hell-raiser. A seemingly never-ending succession of parties, plenty of drinking and a less-than-serious approach to life put a large question mark over Chris's potential in the eyes of many influential racing people. But there was one man who knew that Chris had what it takes: fellow Kiwi Bruce McLaren. Bruce recruited Amon into his Can-Am sports car team and, under his compatriot's sympathetic tutelage, Chris began to reassemble his reputation. During this period Amon also became involved in a considerable amount of Firestone tyre testing, developing talents as a test driver which were to be of considerable use when he finally landed that drive with Ferrari.

"My first contact with Ferrari came through Shell's Keith Ballisat," Amon recalls. "He approached me at one of the North American races and said 'you should come and talk to Ferrari'. Now, I wasn't really very certain what 'talking to Ferrari' meant, but I flew over to Maranello between a couple of the Can-Am races. At the interview I found myself desperately wanting to ask him whether in fact I would be driving Formula 1, but all he would say was 'I know what you want to do . . .'. Anyway, I signed a contract on the spot and flew back to America where I told Bruce. I don't think relations between Bruce and I were ever quite the same again because he'd been making long-term plans to run the V12 BRM engines in his cars for 1967 and I was intended to be part of those plans. I don't think he was exactly pleased to hear that I was leaving." As an indication of how things have changed in the Grand Prix world, the terms of Amon's Ferrari contract are particularly interesting: "In '67 he paid me nothing – just a percentage of the prize money, which was fine by me . . ." Chris was on his way.

The 1967 Monaco Grand Prix took place, as usual, over 100 laps of the famous Mediterranean street circuit on May 7. Ferrari brought along two entries for Bandini and Amon, both drivers provided with the latest central exhaust 36-valve engines and the 312s appeared particularly purposeful, equipped as they were with revised nose cowlings, faired-in mirrors and big brake cooling scoops. During practice Lorenzo's enthusiasm to impress caused him to slam on the power a bit early coming out of the Mirabeau turn, his Ferrari glancing the wall and breaking a steering arm. But with the practical enthusiasm that endeared him so strongly to all his team colleagues, Bandini assembled another splendid jury-rig, just as he'd done at Reims the previous summer when the throttle cable broke, and managed to get the car back to the pits as a result. At the end of qualifying Lorenzo had managed to take second place on the front row, his 1m 28.3s best comparing with the 1m 27.6s pole position time established by Jack Brabham. Feeling his way carefully, Amon started the race way back in 14th position with a fastest lap of 1m 30.7s.

After his previous year's trouncing at the hands of Stewart's BRM, Bandini was in a determined mood and, to the ecstatic delight of the thousands of Italian fans who lined the circuit, pushed his 312 into an immediate lead as the pack hurtled down towards *Ste. Devote* on the opening lap. In his wake Brabham's Repco V8 blew up spectacularly going down to the old Station hairpin, a connecting rod coming out through the side of the V8's alloy block, and Jack limped back to the pits dropping oil everywhere in the process. Thus, although Lorenzo was hanging on in the lead at the end of lap one, Denny Hulme and Jackie Stewart quickly displaced him on the slippery surface. For the first 15 laps it seemed as though Stewart, again handling one of the agile 2-litre BRM P261 V8s, was going to enact a repeat performance of his previous year's success, but the crownwheel and pinion packed up, allowing Hulme's Brabham-Repco through into the lead.

From this point onwards there was never any serious doubt as to the outcome of the race. The craggy, strong Hulme, driving his superb-handling Brabham-Repco was more than a match for Bandini's Ferrari. Lorenzo put everything he'd got into that dramatic chase during that sunny afternoon, but Hulme wasn't to be denied his first Grand Prix triumph. The previous year Lorenzo's second place

OTEL
KENT

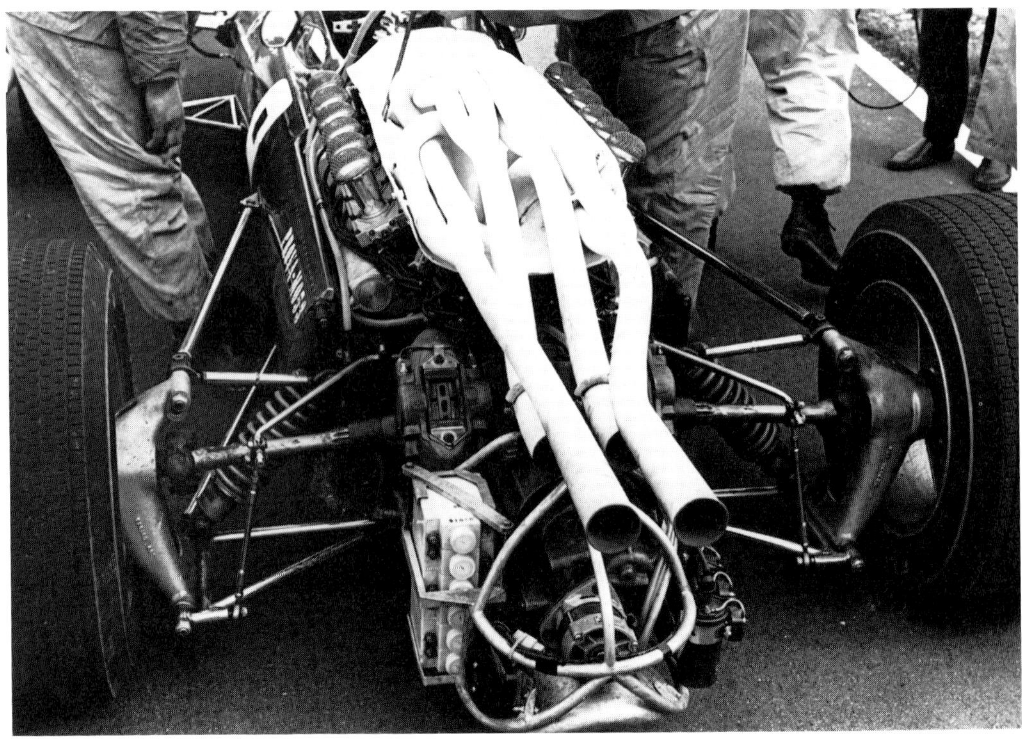

Chris Amon, carrying number one here although he was never World Champion, shows off the graceful lines of the 1967 Ferrari 312 as he rounds Spa's La Source hairpin (a popular photographic point!) on his way to third place in the Belgian Grand Prix. Armed with the central-exhaust 36-valve V12, (below), Amon shouldered most of the responsibility for Maranello's Formula 1 reputation throughout 1967. He told Forghieri and Mr. Ferrari that the car handled well, but that the engine was no match for its rivals. It wasn't a message which was well received!

must have seemed an honourable defeat for Ferrari's number two driver (irrespective of Dragoni's feelings!) but in 1967 it was different. Bandini was team leader and shouldered a tremendous responsibility. Whether he tried too hard, or was simply tiring thanks to the effort of hauling the heavy Ferrari V12 through the Monaco streets, we will never know . . .

On lap 82, as Bandini took the chicane on to the harbour front, his 312 clipped the inside wall with its right-hand wheels. It ran wide to the left, climbing up the straw bales, a wheel came off, the car turned over on to the track – and erupted into a horrifying pillar of flame. By the time Bandini was extricated from the Ferrari's smouldering remains, he was dreadfully burnt and, despite fighting for his life for three more excruciating days, eventually succumbed to his injuries. One can only begin to imagine what a trauma it was for Chris Amon, passing the scene of his team-mate's accident again and again for the remainder of the race. The second Ferrari was briefly delayed with a pit stop to change a deflated Firestone, punctured on some of the accident debris, but Chris did well to come home third behind Hulme and Graham Hill's 2-litre Lotus-BRM V8.

Amon recalls Bandini with affection: "I have to confess that I was a little wary about him when I first joined the team. I suppose his reputation had rather gone before him from the occasion when he knocked Graham Hill off in Mexico back at the end of 1964, so I suppose I thought he might turn out to be a little aggressive towards me. But he was utterly charming. He was *so* pleasant and really helpful when it came to sorting out problems with the car. He really was one of the nicest guys I ever came across, and the greatest tragedy of the whole affair is that he was just beginning to emerge from behind the shadow of John Surtees . . . he really was maturing into a first-class number one in his own right."

As the Italian motor racing fraternity steeled itself to recover from this body-blow, Ferrari sent a pair of V12s down to Syracuse for the non-title race there on May 21. Parkes, using a '67 spec. engine, and Scarfiotti, using one of the previous season's V12s, dead-heated in a morale-boosting demonstration run against makeweight opposition before the serious business of the World Championship continued at Zandvoort on June 4.

The 1967 Dutch Grand Prix, of course, was an historic occasion, marking as it did the sensational winning début of the Cosworth-Ford DFV engine and the Lotus 49. At a stroke, Colin Chapman and Keith Duckworth between them re-wrote the parameters of Grand Prix car performance, Jim Clark winning the race with contemptuous ease in a car which had barely been tested before appearing at the circuit. The Ferrari 312s were quite simply off the pace during practice and the race; Parkes' long-chassis car was the fastest Maranello contender on the outside of the fourth row in 1m 27.0s – a startling 2.4s away from Graham Hill's Lotus 49 pole. Behind Clark at the end of the 90 lap race, the also-rans came breathlessly across the line in the order Brabham, Hulme and Amon (the only runners to go the full distance), while Parkes and Scarfiotti completed the top six with the other two Ferraris entered. There was some satisfaction to be gained from the fact that all three 312s came home in the points, but there was clearly an enormous amount of work to be done before Maranello's V12 could be expected to get anywhere near Northampton's four-valves-per-cylinder V8 newcomer.

At Spa-Francorchamps a fortnight later Amon really got to grips with his Ferrari superbly, setting a 3m 34.3s best to take fifth place on the Belgian Grand Prix starting grid. He was comfortably over two seconds faster than Parkes (3m 36.6s) and four seconds ahead of Scarfiotti (3m 37.7s) – but he was over six seconds away from Jim Clark's Lotus 49 pole position! Down the Masta Straight on the opening lap Jimmy was already getting away from the rest of the pack with Rindt's Cooper-Maserati, Stewart's BRM H-16 "oil bowser", Parkes and Amon leading the pursuit. As they started the long haul back towards the pits from *Stavelot*, Parkes was close behind Stewart, looking for a way past, but the H-16 was spraying a fair amount of lubricant from its oil breathers and on the fast left-hander at *Blanchimont*, Mike overdid things. Both he and Chris reckoned that the BRM's oil was the cause, but the possibility that the ensuing accident wasn't of

Forghieri's fad! Bespectacled Ferrari chief engineer Mauro Forghieri adjusts the Ferrari 312's rear aerofoil in the pits at Spa, 1968. Mounted over the rear wheels, Amon reckoned it was "fantastic", but when Forghieri subsequently moved it forward to the centre of the car, the New Zealander told him it wasn't as good . . .

his own making did nothing to minimize the appalling leg injuries Parkes sustained as his 312 first went broadside, then flipped sideways down the track, hurling him out . . . right in front of a horrified Amon's gaze. The accident finished the Englishman's Formula 1 career and so depressed Scarfiotti that the Italian virtually gave up and cruised gently round for the remainder of the race. At the end of the day Chris emerged third after an energetic battle with Pedro Rodriguez's Cooper-Maserati, behind Gurney's winning Eagle and Stewart's BRM.

For much of the remainder of the season, Chris was thus left to shoulder responsibility for Ferrari's Grand Prix challenge completely alone. And it was during this spell that he really made his Formula 1 reputation with a succession of determined battles at the wheel of a car which never looked *quite* up to par. He had an unlucky outing at the French Grand Prix, held in 1967 on the uninspiring Bugatti "car park" circuit at Le Mans, retiring with throttle control problems, but he followed this up with two tremendous battles against the Brabham-Repco V8s at Silverstone and the Nürburgring. It's fair to record that the Cosworth-Ford DFV-engined Lotus 49s were completely in a class of their own for the remainder of the 1967 season, so anybody else could only struggle to try and win the "second division" contest: and in that league, the Brabham-Repco V8s and Ferrari V12 were probably the most consistently promising runners.

Chris was over a second away from Clark's pole at Silverstone, even on a circuit where the Ferrari handled superbly. For much of that 80 lap contest he sat a few feet from Brabham's gearbox working out just how to out-flank the wily Australian: Chris finally slipped ahead going into *Woodcote* with five laps left to run, but there wasn't sufficient time left to catch Hulme's similar machine for second place. At the Nürburgring, Amon found himself banked up behind Brabham again in third place as Hulme raced on to win his second Grand Prix of the season: this time Chris really couldn't find a gap and, once more, had to be satisfied with third.

Amon reported back to Maranello that their V12 didn't have sufficient steam, echoing the words of John Surtees more than 12 months earlier. "There was no question about it," Chris remembered, "that chassis was an absolute dream to drive, but they'd got an oil scavenging problem which prevented them from realizing the engine's full potential. The Old Man got really quite annoyed when I insisted that it wasn't as quick as the Repco V8, telling me that we'd got more power . . . but I'd sat behind them at Silverstone and the' Ring and I told him that I knew otherwise. Forghieri touched on the problem briefly and we went testing at Modena that summer with me under instructions to cut the engine and drop the clutch at high revs before coasting into the pits. Then they took off the sump to see how much oil was round the bottom of the engine; something which I felt was a little on the crude side because I was never sure they were very confident about how much oil they should be *expecting* to find anyway!" There is probably rather less to this than meets the eye!

Between the German and Italian Grands Prix, the Formula 1 circus crossed the Atlantic to attend the inaugural World Championship Canadian Grand Prix at Mosport Park near Toronto. Held in diabolical rain-soaked conditions, Chris qualified fourth on the inside of row two before blotting his copybook with an early spin on the treacherous surface. By the end he'd pulled back into a reasonable sixth behind Brabham, Hulme, Gurney's Eagle-Weslake, Hill's Lotus 49 and Mike Spence's BRM H-16.

In an attempt to make up some power, Forghieri came up with a 48-valve cylinder head which was totally new in time for the Italian Grand Prix at Monza. The exhaust valves and inlet valves were positioned at a slight angle to each other, giving a slight radial effect, the camshafts on each bank were very close together and there was only room in this compact package for a single sparking plug per cylinder. The inlet tracts were now on the outside of the vee once again, but the exhaust pipes remained in their distinctive position on the inside, nestling between the two cylinder banks. Detailed "tidying up" of the whole package had allegedly reduced the weight of the 312 to around 1200lb and, according to Forghieri, the engine was developed almost 390bhp at 10,800 rpm. Amon admitted that he was pretty impressed: on this circuit where sheer power was the most important asset, he qualified third on the inside of row two only 0.8s slower than Clark's pole-winning 1m 28.5s in the Lotus 49. Unfortunately, this was the year when the starting procedure lapsed into chaos as the cars moved forward to take up their proper grid positions, Jack Brabham anticipating the signal and taking off like a dragster almost before the official with the Italian flag had completed his upswing. Clark hesitated slightly before chasing off after the Brabham-Repco, causing Amon, who was right behind, to dip the clutch of his Ferrari violently to avoid running into the back of the Lotus. The V12's revs shot sky-high, taking the edge off the engine before the race had even begun!

That race turned out to be one of the most exciting and dramatic Italian Grands Prix ever: Jim Clark made up a complete lap on the leaders after an early stop to change a deflating tyre, only to encounter fuel pick-up problems on the last lap which robbed him of victory. Thus the way was left open for John Surtees, now driving the raucous Honda V12, to dive inside Brabham at *Parabolica* on the final lap to score a split-second victory in front of a delighted crowd who, whilst wishing he was still behind the wheel of a Ferrari, loved him none the less. Clark spluttered home third . . . while poor Amon was four laps down in a distant seventh place in the lone Ferrari.

However, undeniably, that four-valves-per-cylinder V12 *was* a considerable improvement and Chris got in amongst the two Lotus 49s in the penultimate Grand Prix at Watkins Glen on October 1. Amon's V12 blew up 12 laps from the end of his 108 lap thrash, but Chris admits "this was one of the few occasions when we'd got a Ferrari V12 which was *really* on a par with the DFV. That's one of the famous races I feel I would have won if the engine had lasted: Clark completed the last couple of laps at a crawl with broken rear suspension, so I'd have caught him, no problem." As an interesting aside. Chris also comments about Clark in 1967: "there was no question about it, he was fantastic . . . but I never had a really good go at him until that 1967 season with Ferrari and, by then, I had the feeling he was marginally past his best. I mean *marginally*, of course, because he was still better than the rest of us, but from my observations it was 1963-65 that saw him at his absolute peak. By '67, of course, he'd got the DFV on his side . . ."

Chris's supreme achievement of 1967 came in the final race of the season at Mexico City where he qualified alongside Clark in second place on the two-by-two grid, less than half a second away from the Lotus 49. After some early place-changing, Amon settled down to consolidate a secure second place, but the V12 ran short of fuel in the closing stages and Chris was just about to abandon it for good at the side of the circuit when he heard the fuel pumps ticking madly . . . so he climbed back in. Unfortunately his last lap took more than twice the time of the winner's fastest lap, so he wasn't credited with it: instead of winding up fifth, he was classified ninth, one place behind the second entry driven by diminutive Englishman Jonathan Williams. "Jonathino", as he'd become known during his F3 and sports car career in Italy, had been partnering Chris in the Ferrari Can-Am team that autumn when Forghieri suddenly told him he was going to drive the second Grand Prix car in Mexico. He finished an outclassed eighth, as singularly unimpressed with his down-on-power machine as Ferrari appeared to be with his driving. Williams, who now flies executive jets from the South of France, remembers the whole thing "as a bit of a waste of time".

That marked the end of Ferrari's 1967 season, apart from a relatively unsuccessful foray for "new boy" Andrea de Adamich in the non-title Spanish Grand Prix "warm-up" for the new Jarama circuit near Madrid. De Adamich was to be included in the 1968 Ferrari line-up as third driver alongside Amon and new recruit Jacky Ickx, the Belgian newcomer who'd won the 1967 European Formula 2 Championship at the wheel of a Tyrrell team Matra-Cosworth FVA MS7 and had made a tolerably impressive Grand Prix début at Monza where he'd finished sixth in a works Cooper-Maserati V12.

At this time, Amon had been pressing to get Jackie Stewart included in the new season's Ferrari Grand Prix team. They'd shared a 4-litre 330P4 sports car at the BOAC 1000kms held at Brands Hatch the previous summer, finishing an excellent second to the Chaparral of Phil Hill/Mike Spence. "I suppose I was a bit on the lazy side," reflects Amon, "and he could have taken some of the testing off my shoulders. And I also figured that if Jackie told them their V12s were short on power they might have believed him . . ." Stewart went to talk with the Old Man but eventually opted to drive for Ken Tyrrell's fledgling team. Five years, 27 Grand Prix victories and three World Championships later, one could hardly avoid reaching the conclusion that Jackie made the right decision!

Amon admits that he would also have liked Jackie in the team "to give me something to measure myself against", but as things turned out it was Ickx against whom he would have to measure himself. Chris never felt particularly relaxed in his relationship with the rather aloof Belgian, feeling that he ought to have become more involved in test and development work: one senses that Amon really didn't appreciate being given the task of "running in" Ickx's cars at Modena prior to the races. His coolness towards Ickx wasn't improved when he heard that "the Old Man was trying it on with me, wanting to pay me nothing again in 1968 when I found out that he gave Ickx a pretty reasonable retainer. So I went to see him and said 'hey, what's all this about . . .' So he paid up! I suppose it was partly my fault

Sympathetic partnership. Chris Amon (left), Mauro Forghieri and Enzo Ferrari formed a good working relationship in the period 1967-69, although the expression on Chris's face in this photograph might convey a different impression!

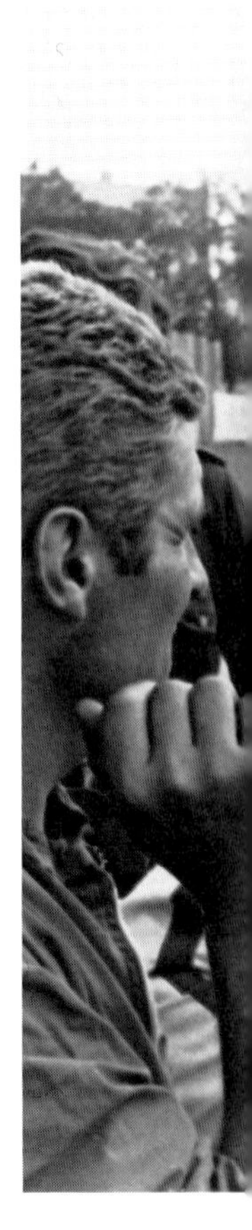

for not pushing these things a little harder . . ."

At the start of the 1968 season Ferrari visited Kyalami for the first time, arriving at the South African Grand Prix meeting with a trio of 48-valve V12s for Amon, Ickx and de Adamich. The chassis had been subtly up-dated over the winter, but they were essentially the same cars that the team had been racing the previous season, although the engines were now rated at 410bhp at 10,800rpm. On paper that was pretty well the same output as the Cosworth DFV, but the English V8 had quite a wide power band compared with the Italian V12 which really had to be kept revving over 9800 if the power wasn't to drop away quite dramatically.

In practice for this first race of the season Jim Clark predictably took pole with his Lotus 49, setting a 1m 21.6s best lap for his rivals to aim at. Rather surprisingly it was de Adamich who emerged quickest Ferrari man with a 1m 23.6s to take seventh place in the line-up, squeezing in ahead of Chris who managed a 1m 23.8s. Ickx was well back with a quickest lap of 1m 24.9s. Amon hung on grimly in the race, but there was no way he could get on terms with either the Cosworths or the old twin-cam Repco powering Jochen Rindt's works Brabham BT24. He eventually wound up fourth, and lapped, behind Jim Clark, Graham Hill and Rindt. De Adamich humbled himself by spinning into the guard rail at Clubhouse Corner quite hard and Ickx's first Ferrari drive ended with a leaking oil pipe and consequent retirement.

At the non-title Race of Champions 50 lapper at Brands Hatch on March 17, McLaren joined the Cosworth-Ford ranks with the new M7As, a fact which must have given Chris something to ponder on as Bruce sped round to secure pole

position on the car's début outing. Amon rather eclipsed Ickx again on this occasion, managing to stay on the same lap as McLaren's winning machine to take fourth place behind his former patron, Pedro Rodriguez's BRM P126 V12 and Denny Hulme in the other McLaren (which might well have been Chris's had he stayed on the team!). By the time the Formula 1 field assembled for that other traditional pre-European season "taster", the BRDC's International Trophy at Silverstone, the Grand Prix world had been rocked to the core by the death of Jim Clark after an accident in a minor Formula 2 race at Hockenheim. The fact that the world's acknowledged greatest driver was no longer present to exert his dominance on the Grand Prix circuits hit Chris particularly hard, but the manner of his going, in this trivial little event, seemed doubly ironic. It was as if Sir Edmund Hilary had been killed hiking in the Peak District . . .

In years that followed Amon's eventual departure from Ferrari, Mauro Forghieri continued to espouse the theory that the New Zealander was one of the most gifted drivers he'd ever worked with, a theory which cut across the opinions of others in the Grand Prix business who saw Chris as some sort of "lesser Brabham". But Forghieri's opinions, formed mainly in 1967 and '68, put Chris on a pedestal as far as the drivers the Italian had encountered. "In my view Chris was the very best test driver I have ever worked with," Forghieri would insist. "He would come back into the pits and tell me precisely what I wanted to know, avoiding secondary things . . ." Mauro would then put on his most demonstratively emotive expression and continue, "Ickx may have won more races on paper, so he's more successful. My opinions are unimportant. The victories remain down the years . . . but in *my* opinion – *my* opinion – Chris was a man as good as Jimmy . . ."

Others would come to similar conclusions during '68 and '69, but with the great Scottish driver gone, Amon had to measure himself against other standards. At that '68 International Trophy he got his 312 going very well indeed, mixing it with the McLaren-Cosworths yet again before "my goggle strap broke, would you believe? I had another pair round my neck, but they caught up the back of my bloody helmet . . . and do you think I could get them up? I was just about to get past Bruce at the time, but the race result – me third behind Denny and McLaren – gave us some encouragement at Ferrari. And it was the only time that we ever managed to stage a New Zealand 1-2-3."

On May 12 the Spanish Grand Prix opened the European World Championship season with a 90 lap event round the tortuous, twisting Jarama circuit which had hosted that "warm up" event the previous autumn. By this time Andrea de Adamich no longer figured in Ferrari's Formula 1 equation: he'd crashed his 312 into a marshals' post at Paddock Bend during practice for the Race of Champions, sustaining injuries that put him on the racing sidelines until the end of the season.

Although the Ferrari V12 wasn't strong on torque, the chassis was quickly developing into one of the best-handling machines in the business and Amon took pole position with a 1m 27.9s lap ahead of Rodriguez's BRM V12, the McLarens of Hulme and McLaren, and Jean-Pierre Beltoise at the wheel of Ken Tyrrell's Matra-Cosworth V8. The Frenchman was standing in for Jackie Stewart who was recovering from a wrist injury.

Amon: "After the first day's practice I wound up fourth, but I sensed that I was really going to get it together round Jarama. And I did, it was my very first Grand Prix pole position. I made a dreadful start as usual and, after Pedro led for a short time, Beltoise went through into the lead. Pedro held me up for a while, but just as I got by him Beltoise stopped as well . . . it was all fairly plain sailing until I ground to a halt with fuel pump failure. It was a sickening feeling when the car stopped because I was on the verge of winning a Grand Prix. Not many laps to go, 25 seconds in the lead. No warning, just gone . . .

"But I suppose it gave us another pretty good boost, although I felt Ferrari failed to capitalize on it. He made the decision to miss Monaco, possibly because of Bandini's accident the previous year, although I never fully understood why. It was a great shame because I'm certain that the 312 would have been very competitive that year, but I was left to go as a spectator. I stayed on a boat with Charles Lucas, got into a lot of trouble, got pissed and fell into the harbour. Ken Tyrrell offered me the Matra, but Ferrari said no." (The car was subsequently handled by Servoz-Gavin, who led in the opening stages before breaking a driveshaft after glancing a guard rail).

These circumstances all helped Graham Hill towards bagging victories at both Jarama and Monaco for Lotus, helping to lift the British team's spirits after the loss of Jim Clark. But Ferrari was back in force for the 28 lap Belgian Grand Prix at Spa-Francorchamps on June 9 and it goes down in the history books that the Italian team was the first to appear with aerofoils fitted to its machines. Both 312s for Amon and Ickx appeared with fixed aerofoils mounted above the gearbox, and although Brabham hastily followed suit on the second day of practice, Forghieri's aerofoils were the first in Formula 1.

Forghieri: "People reckoned that I'd copied the Chaparral concept, but that wasn't really the case. I got my inspiration from the ideas tried by Swiss engineer Michael May who'd tried an aerofoil on a Porsche sports car more than 10 years earlier. May had worked informally as a fuel-injection consultant to Ferrari for some years, so there was already a line of communication . . ."

Amon used the aerofoil on his 312 when he set his pole position lap round the daunting Belgian circuit in 3m 28.6s, sharing the front row with Jackie Stewart's Matra and team-mate Ickx in the second Ferrari. Chris recalls that with the aerofoil positioned over the rear end, the 312 handled like never before, although by the following race Forghieri had moved it up adjacent to the roll-over bar, his theory being that this would offer equal downforce over the entire area of the car. Chris never reckoned it was as good.

Amon: "Ever since the advent of the British specialist chassis manufacturers in Formula 1 at the start of the sixties, I think most people accepted that Ferrari always tended to lag behind somewhat in chassis development. But I honestly think that in 1968 things were the other way round. To a degree, Ferrari became the innovators. I think we surprised quite a few people when we turned up with that aerofoil at Spa . . .

"I was four seconds faster than anyone else, a feat I often wanted subsequently to emulate! I think in terms of driving pleasure a really fast lap at Spa was a fantastic sensation. And in '68 the 312 was really working well there. On the lap I set my quickest time I came down the Masta straight after the kink and pulled up to Brian Redman's Cooper-BRM as we approached *Stavelot* . . . I can remember going by him into the corner, with my foot buried right in it, as he was braking and changing down. The thing felt tremendous . . .

"There's absolutely no way I shouldn't have won that race, I got a bloody good start and must have been 150 yards ahead at the end of the opening lap. I thought that I was going to pull away quite easily, but on the second lap, I found Jo Bonnier limping back to the pits, right on the fast line, as I came out of the Masta kink. I had to back right off and Surtees slipstreamed past me in that Honda. I knew full-well that once he was in front, the Honda was quick enough in a straight line to give me hell's own job to get by again. If I tried pulling out of his slipstream, I just slowed down. I was really furious.

"Then, suddenly, I nearly lost it on the Masta kink, a horrific bloody experience. The Honda kicked up a stone through my oil radiator and the reason I lost it was oil spraying on a rear tyre! I felt a bit sick about that one, coming so quickly after Spain, but little did I know what was to come. That Honda was a bloody nuisance, actually, both in 1967 and '68. It was very quick in a straight line, but always got in the way on the corners. Anyway, after Spa, we were absolutely convinced that the Ferrari would win a race. So we went to Zandvoort . . ."

Amon bagged his third pole position of the season at the Dutch seaside track, turning a 1m 23.54s to beat Jochen Rindt's four-cam Brabham-Repco V8, Graham Hill's Lotus, Brabham's Brabham and Jackie Stewart's Matra after a wet, patchy dry, somewhat turbulent official practice. Chris got slightly bogged down at the start in the streaming wet conditions that prevailed on race day and, for the rest of the afternoon, the Ferrari V12's narrow rev. band made it more of a handful than cars powered by the more torquey Cosworth V8s. It also has to be said that Dunlop's wet weather rubber was vastly superior in 1968 to anything produced by either Firestone or Goodyear, Stewart using it to good effect to triumph convincingly in the Dutch race. Like so many things in motor racing, all is not always quite what it appears to be on the surface and, just as he would enjoy using these Dunlops at the Nürburgring later that same summer, it has to be said that Stewart had a major equipment advantage in both these races. He also fully capitalized on that advantage . . .

The point of this is to emphasize, on the other side of the coin, that Chris Amon was to earn a totally unjustified reputation as being a deficient wet weather driver during 1968. The full circumstances will become apparent in the next few paragraphs, but, meanwhile, we should record that Chris wound up sixth after starting from pole at Zandvoort – although he did make a stop to change on to fresh rubber.

Jochen Rindt put his four-cam Brabham-Repco on pole for the 60 lap French Grand Prix at Rouen, a race at which Amon had been dogged by practice problems, but Ickx performed superbly to qualify third behind Stewart's Matra. Unfortunately as the field moved forward from the dummy grid to the main grid proper, heavy rain began falling, much to the consternation of most team managers. Ickx, however, was the only competitor running on full wet-weather tyres and, apart from a brief spell when Rodriguez dauntlessly slithered his BRM through into the lead, the young Belgian driver dominated the event in superbly confident style to win Maranello its first Grand Prix victory since Scarfiotti at Monza two years earlier. As for Amon, he crawled home a dejected and outclassed 10th after a pit stop, ". . . another bloody fiasco. I never got with it at all."

Happily, Chris had something rather better with which to celebrate his 25th birthday on July 20. After a splendid performance in the 80 lap British Grand Prix at Brands Hatch, he brought his 312 home a good second only 4.4s behind Jo Siffert's Rob Walker Lotus 49. During practice he'd landed the third front row position alongside the factory Lotuses of Graham Hill and Jack Oliver, lapping only 0.6s away from pole, and as the two 49Bs pulled imperiously away from the start, Chris became enmeshed in a ferocious battle with Siffert. He briefly got ahead of the Swiss driver, although this was before Oliver's 49B had joined its team-mate in retirement, so Chris never actually led the race. He hung on tenaciously, though, and was still in close touch at the end.

One of Amon's finest races at the wheel of a Ferrari 312 was the 1969 Spanish Grand Prix at Barcelona's spectacular Montjuich Park circuit. He led superbly, only to suffer engine failure late in the race and hand victory to Jackie Stewart's Tyrrell Matra.

"We were being blown off by the Cosworths out of the slow corners," he recalls, "but I still think if we'd had a bigger wing on the *back* of the car we would have won. I drove absolutely balls-out for the entire race, but I was running short of rubber towards the end . . . I think the Ferrari people were slightly annoyed that I didn't win that one, but when they saw the rear tyres after the race they were slightly more understanding . . ." Ickx rounded off a good result with third place at Brands, lapped by Siffert and Amon.

On August 4, 1968, Jackie Stewart achieved one of the most remarkable feats of his distinguished driving career, totally dominating the 14-lap German Grand Prix held over the Nürburgring's *Nordschleife* in the most unimaginable conditions of pouring rain and thick fog. Jacky Ickx grabbed pole position with his Ferrari 312 on the first day of practice before this diabolical weather set in for the rest of the weekend, managing a 9m 04.0s best, and although Amon squeezed in alongside the Belgian in second place, he was 10s slower round the 14-mile circuit. Rindt and Hill were next up with Vic Elford's works Cooper-BRM on the outside of row two, an indication that this wasn't a representative grid by any means. Stewart's Matra was way back, but once the race began, it was in a class of its own in the wet, murky conditions.

Amon's reflections on that particular event betray just a tinge of bitterness: "We went to the 'Ring with high hopes because we had gone really well in testing there, but I was really dreading the race when I woke up on Sunday and found the rain still pouring down and the fog as thick as ever. Down in the garage area Franco

Gozzi and Forghieri told me to get the best start I could and hold the others up while Ickx got away . . . they'd completely lost faith in my wet weather driving, I guess simply because of Rouen. Well, I didn't say anything at the time, but at the start we all got on with it and Ickx never got within half a mile of me in the race!

"I just never saw anything for the whole race. I sat behind Graham in a cloud of spray, but I really felt switched on . . . I was holding some tremendous bloody slides, just sitting there watching my hands working away in front of me. Eventually I pulled out to try and pass Graham coming past the pits and the thing got very sideways, then it gave a big twitch coming out of *South Curve*. It felt very strange all the way up behind the back of the pits and, as I went into *North Curve*, it just swapped ends. I think the differential had packed up. Graham spun about three miles later, so perhaps my retirement was a good thing as I would have probably plunged straight into him.

"Stewart disappeared, of course, and everybody hailed it as the driving feat of the century although I don't believe he went any quicker than Graham or I, comparatively, it was just that he had vastly superior tyres. I remember going down the hill to Adenau on the opening lap with Graham leading and me second – Stewart just drove round the inside of me as if the track was dry. I couldn't believe it . . . he had *so much* more grip that our Firestones." Ickx came home a distant fourth after Chris's retirement, behind Stewart, Hill and Rindt.

On August 17 Chris emerged the sole survivor of a trio of 312s contesting the non-Championship, 40 lap Oulton Park Gold Cup, coming home second only 4.6s behind Stewart's Matra. Ickx retired with an electrical fault, whilst team débutant

The magnificent 312B1 flat-12 3-litre engine – arguably the best Grand Prix power unit ever to emerge from Maranello.

Derek Bell put in a good, controlled performance before retiring with an internal engine breakage.

Throughout the 1968 season the development of movable aerofoils had continued apace in the wake of Ferrari's début with them in Belgium. Forghieri wasn't to be left behind in this area and, in time for the Italian Grand Prix at Monza, had equipped the 312s with a very sophisticated system activated by engine oil pressure and braking effort. The principle was that the wing angle was up in first, second and third gears, when the driver went on to the brakes in fourth and fifth, but it "feathered" in fourth and fifth when the driver was on the throttle. There was also a manual override control in the cockpit which Amon preferred, but Ickx felt happier with the fully "automated" system and had the override control removed from the cockpit of his 312 by the time it appeared in practice for the Canadian Grand Prix.

Derek Bell was also included in the team for the Monza race and the three V12s performed well in practice to take positions on the first (Amon), second (Ickx) and third (Bell) rows of the starting grid. Chris kept in amongst the leading bunch, which included Bruce McLaren's McLaren and Surtees's pole-winning Honda RA301, until lap eight when an oil leak on to the left rear tyre (or a hydraulic fluid leak from the aerofoil control system) caused him to lose control dramatically on the 140mph double right-hander at *Lesmo*. In one of the most spectacular, yet least-publicized Formula 1 accidents ever, the Ferrari vaulted the barrier and flew, upside down, into the trees. Chris found himself hanging from his seat harness, the car wedged amongst the branches of some densely-packed trees, his legs having come up out of the cockpit without any injury, something he fails to understand to this day. He hung there for a short while, listening to the gentle cracking of the branches, before an obliging marshal shinned up the tree with a large knife – not to put Amon out of his misery, but to cut the straps before the Ferrari fell out of the tree on top of its driver!

Surtees's Honda was also eliminated, Big John glancing the guard rail as he sought, successfully, to avoid the Ferrari's crazy flight, and at the end of the afternoon Denny Hulme's McLaren stroked home to an easy victory. After a late-race pit visit to investigate apparent fuel vaporization problems, caused by the intense heat, Ickx rejoined in time to be beaten into third place on the run up from the last corner by Johnny Servoz-Gavin's Matra-Cosworth. The crowds were cheering Ickx into second place almost before they realized that the French car had surged ahead on the line – it was that close! Bell retired early with fuel-feed problems.

Despite the various problems suffered by the Ferrari team throughout the season thus far, Ickx still retained a mathematical chance of winning the World Championship when the teams crossed the Atlantic to take part in the Canadian Grand Prix at the beautiful Ste. Jovite circuit north of Montreal. Unfortunately the Belgian's title aspirations came to an end during practice when Jacky crashed heavily as he grappled with a slightly sticking throttle, wrecking his 312 and breaking a leg below the knee. Amon started from the middle of the front row, having equalled Rindt's pole position time in the Brabham, and pulled away in magnificent style from the fall of the starter's flag. Since the Canadian race was extra long at 90 laps (238 miles) the Ferrari was fitted with additional fuel tanks on the chassis sponsons on either side of the V12 engine bay, but this added weight gave Chris little problem: despite the fact that Siffert's Walker Lotus 49B chased hard in the opening stages, and the Ferrari's clutch went solid after 12 laps, forcing Amon to change gear without it, he dominated that race in a fashion he'd never matched before in his career. Alas, with only 17 laps left to go, the final drive pinion would put up with no more clutchless changes and Chris was out . . . handing Hulme's McLaren another win on the proverbial plate.

The final two races of the 1968 season served to underline just how patchy Ferrari form could be. At Watkins Glen, where Bell and a fresh 312 replaced Ickx and his damaged machine, Chris simply wasn't in contention and although he qualified fourth he retired after 60 laps with the car's cooling system pressurizing and blowing out all its water. Finally, at Mexico City, Chris lined up second alongside Siffert's pole-winning Lotus 49B only to retire after 17 laps with transmission problems. Ickx, his injured leg pinned and wearing an external brace, gallantly returned to the fray, but mercifully for the Belgian, his discomfort was brief as his 312 packed up with ignition failure on the fourth lap!

By the start of the 1969 season, Ferrari finances were getting pretty slim and it was getting very expensive to finance Formula 1, Formula 2, sports car, Can-Am and hillclimb programmes on a budget entirely culled from traditional motor industry sources. Firestone and Shell were putting a lot of money into the Italian team, but this wasn't in the same league as that which would soon be provided by the tobacco barons: in any case, Ferrari was involved in a far more ambitious overall racing programme than any rival team in the business and it was quite clear that, at the start of the 1969 season, the Old Man's company had its back to the financial wall. The company's long-term financial salvation and security was only finally achieved on June 18, 1969 when Enzo Ferrari forged the famous deal with Fiat's Gianni Agnelli to guarantee the marque's future. The racing cars were to remain under Ferrari's personal guidance and influence for the rest of his life, but the road cars would fall much more directly under the influence of Fiat, a fact which can be seen as nothing but a good thing in the light of subsequent developments through the 1970s and early 1980s.

However, by the time Enzo Ferrari saved his company, his team's Formula 1 fortunes had sunk to a frighteningly low level. At the start of the 1969 season Ickx had left the team to drive for Brabham simply because Black Jack's team ran on the same Gulf fuel and Goodyear rubber as the JW/Gulf long-distance team for whom Jacky also wanted to drive, while Mauro Forghieri had been "banished" (in Amon's words!) and the technical direction of the team became the responsibility of Stefano Jacoponi, the man who'd previously worked on the 212E flat-six cylinder hillclimb car development.

Amon stayed on for another season grappling with the V12s, but by no stretch of the imagination did he enjoy such a sympathetic relationship with Jacoponi as he'd done with Mauro. "In fact I gave him a really hard time," recalls Amon, "particularly when we went testing in the '69 V12 and I was absolutely convinced that the thing was slower than the '68 car. In fact we'd had around 405bhp with the '68 car at its best and they were now trying to tell me that we'd got 435bhp with the latest V12 – even though it was a second slower round Monza during a back-to-back test with the old car."

When the 1969 World Championship season got under way at Kyalami on March 1, Ferrari fielded just a single 312 for Amon to drive. The chassis looked rather different, but in fact only the moulded-in aerofoils on either side of the nose sections altered the outward appearance of what was essentially a '68 chassis updated for the new season. The V12 engine's gas flow had been reversed yet again, the inlets now on the inside of the vee and the exhausts returning to the outside, but claims for that magical 435bhp still didn't put Amon on a par with the Cosworths. He qualified fifth and retired in the race after the engine suffered a bearing failure.

The team missed the Race of Champions and then put on a disgracefully inadequate display in the International Trophy at Silverstone, the Firestone-shod Ferraris floundering about in the rain to finish 9th (Bell) and 10th (Amon) in a race the team would rather forget. But for the 90 lap Spanish Grand Prix, held over Barcelona's magnificent Montjuich Park road circuit, Ferrari put together a couple of very special V12s for Chris to use. They'd got revised camshafts and titanium connecting rods, but there was a big "hole" in the power curve between 9800 and 10,400rpm and Amon recalls having a lot of trouble gearing the 312 correctly.

After both works Lotus 49Bs crashed when their aerofoils collapsed, Chris was left in a commanding lead over Stewart's Matra MS80. On lap 56 the V12 blew up as Amon crossed the start/finish line, so that was the end of Chris's last Grand Prix which he would ever lead in one of the red cars from Maranello. From that point

Trying to be convinced. Chris Amon accelerates the prototype flat-12 engined 312B1 out on to the track at Modena, late summer 1969. A spate of major engine failures convinced him that he should abandon his Ferrari career in favour of the new March organization.

onwards the Ferrari V12's Grand Prix career was doomed, although Chris managed to claw his way on to the front row at Monaco and hung on in second place behind Stewart's fast-disappearing Matra until the differential packed up on lap 17.

At Zandvoort "miraculously", in Chris's words, he enjoyed a great dice to finish third behind Stewart and Siffert, but that was his last race finish behind the wheel of a Ferrari. In the French Grand Prix at Clermont-Ferrand, "I was screaming the guts out of it when a piston blew" and in the British Grand Prix at Silverstone, where Pedro Rodriguez was included in the team as his number two, "the engine was bloody awful and the damn' thing kept jumping out of gear, so I chucked it in."

Meanwhile, of course, Mauro Forghieri was working away back at Maranello: he'd only been banished in the sense that he was putting all his efforts into new projects. With extra finance behind the company thanks to the Fiat deal, Forghieri had two major programmes in the pipeline. One of them, a 4WD Ferrari Formula 1 chassis, was stillborn, although all the components were completed. The other was a new car, a car which would lay the foundations of Ferrari's Formula 1 competitiveness for the next ten years: the 312B1, powered by the sensational 180-degree 12 cylinder horizontally opposed engine.

This new machine was, in the view of many people, probably the most visually attractive Formula 1 car to be built under the current technical rules. There was nothing about the 312B1 which could be regarded as breaking any fresh technical ground, but the way in which the whole package was so neatly executed and so tidily presented made favourable impressions on most rival team designers. Drawing on his experience with the little 1½-litre flat-12 back in 1965, Forghieri and his team produced a compact 78.5 x 51.5mm, 2991.01cc engine which was slung under a rearward extension of the car's chassis which also contained extra fuel tankage apart from that built into the main monocoque structure.

Forghieri had opted for this engine configuration for two reasons: there would be a slight weight saving as compared with a V12 and the centre of gravity would be lower with a 180-degree twelve than with any other arrangement. This not only enabled Ferrari to install it neatly into the chassis, but it also aided a smooth air flow over the upper surface of the 312B1, particularly over the rear wing. The engine employed four main bearings (shell bearings for the two centre mains and roller bearings at either end of the crankshaft which itself was machined from a special alloy billet imported from the USA) while the four chain-driven overhead camshafts ran on needle rollers. To get round the early spate of crankshaft breakages during testing in the late summer of 1969, a specially developed coupling was evolved by Pirelli for insertion between the crankshaft and the flywheel, the purpose of which was to transfer flexing stresses evenly along the length of the crankshaft. The inlet trumpets for the Lucas fuel-injection were mounted on the upper surface of the engine with the exhaust ports below, the exhaust piping threading its way neatly in amongst the rear suspension before ending on either side of the Ferrari five-speed gearbox which was mounted longitudinally behind the rear axle line.

The 312B1 chassis design followed Ferrari's long-established format with a base of small-diameter tubing panelled in aluminium sheeting. In the suspension department there was really nothing much new; at the front the rocker arm arrangement operating the inboard mounted coil spring/dampers could still be seen, while the outboard spring/dampers were retained at the rear together with single top links, lower wishbones and twin tubular radius rods. The water radiator was situated at the front, but the oil coolers were neatly mounted at the rear, standing on either side of the gearbox, and fed by smart ducts facing forwards over the rear bodywork of the car.

Ferrari's new Grand Prix contender had a quoted official power output of around 460bhp at between 11,500 and 11,700 rpm; that would turn out to be more than sufficient to deal with most Cosworth DFV-engined challengers in 1970. However, initial tests during the summer of 1969 were plagued with major mechanical breakages and they really depressed Chris Amon who by now was considering other possible teams for 1970.

Following the débâcle of the British Grand Prix at Silverstone, Ferrari didn't bother sending any V12 cars to the German Grand Prix at the Nürburgring, Amon concentrating his efforts on more test runs at Modena in preparation for the 312B1's hoped-for début in the Italian Grand Prix. Chris was convinced that the new flat-12 was a tremendously powerful proposition and made it abundantly clear to Ferrari that unless he ran the new car at Monza, then he wasn't desperately interested in trailing around in one of the outclassed V12s. But, as Amon recalls all too vividly, "every time I drove that flat-12 the thing flew to pieces. It's not as if they were minor failures either . . . it was either blowing pistons or breaking its crankshaft. I thought to myself, God, I can't stand any more of this."

At the end of the day another major crankshaft breakage prevented the 312B1 from making an appearance at Monza, so a single V12 was sent along to Ferrari's home race. In the interest of reliability on home ground, the 312 appeared with one of the outdated, central-exhaust 1968 engines installed and it was given initially to F2 graduate Ernesto "Tino" Brambilla, a not-too-young Italian who had earned himself a reputation for fearless handling of the Dino 166 F2 Ferraris. Unfortunately Brambilla was out of his depth making his Formula 1 début on this dauntingly quick circuit and, after managing a 1m 34.10s best on the first day, he was replaced by Pedro Rodriguez for the rest of practice and for the race itself. The Mexican qualified on the sixth row of the grid and, in a sensational race which saw Jackie Stewart clinch his first World Championship title in a photo-finish from Jochen Rindt, Rodriguez drove steadily home to finish sixth, two laps behind the winning Matra-Cosworth.

As far as the factory was officially concerned, that outing represented Ferrari's last "official" foray on the Grand Prix scene for 1969. However, that old V12 was "loaned" to the North American Racing Team and was entered for Rodriguez to handle in the Canadian, United States and Mexican Grands Prix. He retired with low oil pressure in the first of these races, but finished a distant fifth at Watkins Glen and rounded off the season with a seventh place on home ground. Thus ended the racing career of Ferrari's most recent V12 Grand Prix engine, a career which had promised much four years earlier but whose full potential had never quite been realized. Quite who was to blame for that failure depends on whether the critic examining this period of history is a Ferrari fan or not.

Shell
Shell
Firestone

Section V: The 3-litre twelves, 1966-80

Chapter 2
The start of a long road

Lost Italian talent. Mauro Forghieri has said that Ignazio Giunti could "possibly have been Italy's next World Champion", but the talented Roman only enjoyed a brief flirtation with Formula 1 in 1970. Here he is seen in discussion with Enzo Ferrari during practice for the Italian Grand Prix at Monza. Giunti was killed at the start of 1971 when his Ferrari 312PB crashed during the Buenos Aires 1000kms sports car race.

Chris Amon finally made up his mind that he would not be staying with Ferrari for a fourth season. He accepted an offer from the fledgling March team to drive a car identical to that which Jackie Stewart would be handling for Ken Tyrrell: almost irrationally tantalized by the prospect of taking on Stewart on even terms, the New Zealander confidently changed camps. Back into the Maranello ranks came Jacky Ickx after his one-year "sabbatical" with Brabham and, after an initial test run behind the 312B1's wheel at Vallelunga in October 1969, the Belgian could hardly conceal his delight. Coming straight from the cockpit of a Cosworth-engined car, Ickx knew full-well that here was a Ferrari engine quite capable of taking on the best in a straight fight. "It felt strong, smooth, torquey . . . and very powerful," smiled Ickx at the time.

With Ickx back on the team as number one driver, it was Ferrari's intention to try a couple of young newcomers in the second car as the season wore on. But the Belgian had a pair of the new flat-12 machines to himself when the 1970 World Championship season opened at Kyalami on March 7. For the observer watching from the sidelines it was a little difficult to get things into perspective when Amon and Stewart, driving their new and technically unremarkable March 701s, tied for fastest practice time at this first event of the year. Ickx qualified fifth on 1m 20.0s, 0.7s slower than the joint-fastest March duo, and although he poked the 312B1 briefly into second place behind Stewart in the opening sprint, he gradually fell back to fourth place from which he eventually retired after 61 laps having cracked an oil pipe when he rode over one of the bevelled kerbs, the resultant loss of lubricant ruining the engine.

Jack Brabham won that first race of the season in his Brabham-Cosworth BT33, but it didn't take long for a pattern to emerge in the struggle for World Championship honours. Put simply, the battle was to be between the dramatic chassis innovation represented by Colin Chapman's striking, chisel-nosed Lotus 72, and the extremely powerful, yet conventionally laid-out, Ferrari 312B1. Chapman reckoned that his new machine, handled by the mercurial Jochen Rindt, could use a 435bhp Cosworth DFV more effectively that Ferrari's new 460bhp flat-12. By the end of the year both cars would have won four Grands Prix apiece, but Rindt would be World Champion driver, albeit posthumously.

However, it is fair to say that both cars took some time to get working really effectively, allowing a few races in which their technically less sophisticated rivals could enjoy a brief field day. Ickx's World Championship aspirations almost came to a premature end in the 90 lap Spanish Grand Prix at Jarama on April 19 when, after qualifying a lowly seventh after a hard struggle in practice, the Belgian's Ferrari was "T-boned" by Jack Oliver's out-of-control BRM P153 on the opening lap. The English car broke a front stub-axle under hard braking as it went into a tight downhill left-hander and Oliver was a passenger as his car hurtled across the infield and struck Ickx's machine in the side. The Ferrari's heavily-laden fuel tanks almost immediately erupted into a bright orange pillar of flame which quickly engulfed the two cars: Oliver escaped unhurt, but Ickx emerged from the conflagration with his overalls ablaze and suffered, fortunately minor, burns which caused him some discomfort and irritation for much of the season. Both cars were totally destroyed.

Back in the cockpit for Monaco, Ickx was an early retirement with a broken inner universal joint on the right-hand driveshaft and was forced to retire after only 12 laps, long before Jochen Rindt's stupendous last-corner victory at the wheel of an outdated Lotus 49C – achieved when Jack Brabham slid, flustered, straight on into the straw bales. At the next race, the Belgian Grand Prix at Spa, Ferrari decided to enter a second 312B1 – driven by an Italian.

Ignazio Giunti's Ferrari Grand Prix career was unfortunately brief, encompassing as it did only four races during the 1970 season, but the 28-year-old Roman quickly marked himself out as having outstanding talent. He had learned his craft at the wheel of various Autodelta Alfa Romeos, showing sufficient promise to be given a test in one of the works Ferrari 512S sports cars in 1969. Ferrari signed him up officially for the 1970 season and it was eventually decided that he would "alternate" in the second 312B1 with Swiss Clay Regazzoni. Giunti drove in the Belgian, French, Austrian and Italian Grands Prix; at the start of the following season he was retained to handle the flat-12 engined 312PB 3-litre sports prototype which Ferrari was entering in all World Championship sports car events. Leading the opening round of this series, the Buenos Aires 1000kms, Giunti's Ferrari collided with Beltoise's near-stationary Matra and the Italian was killed in the ensuing accident.

On his Grand Prix début at Spa, Giunti lapped a mere two seconds slower than Ickx round the 8.7-mile circuit in the Ardennes, lap speeds which had been slightly reduced thanks to the inclusion of a chicane at *Malmedy* just before the start of the Masta Straight. Despite briefly and erroneously being black-flagged for dropping oil, Giunti came home an excellent fourth behind Rodriguez's winning BRM P153, Amon's works March and Beltoise's wailing Matra V12. Ickx, who had qualified fourth, also held fourth place for much of the race before a cockpit fuel leak drenched his overalls and he stopped to change into a fresh set: the petrol obviously irritated his partially-healed burns, but Jacky bravely resumed to finish eighth.

The Dutch Grand Prix at Zandvoort seriously marked the start of the Ickx/Rindt rivalry which was to continue through to Jochen's tragic fatal accident during practice for the Italian race at Monza. After a disappointing début at Jarama, the Lotus 72's torsion bar suspension system had been redesigned to remove its anti-dive and anti-squat characteristics and Rindt rewarded the effort of Chapman's lads by planting it convincingly on pole at Zandvoort. Stewart's March and Ickx's B1 shared the front row with the Austrian and Jacky made a fabulous start to take the lead at the first corner. The Ferrari B1 was a little on the unstable side full-up with fuel, so Rindt had no problems at all when he outbraked Ickx going into *Tarzan*, running right round the outside of the Italian car to take a lead from which he was never dislodged. At the end of the race Jochen was half a minute ahead of Stewart's March with Ickx, who'd been delayed with a pit stop to change a deflated tyre, third ahead of the impressive débutant Clay Regazzoni. The Swiss driver, who'd previously been branded with a reputation as a somewhat wild and unpredictable performer, hadn't put a wheel wrong on his Ferrari début and matched Giunti's fourth place at Spa with the same result at Zandvoort.

It looked as though Ickx was going to pay Rindt back for his Dutch defeat when it came to the next two races: at Clermont-Ferrand he put the B1 on pole position only for his prospects to virtually evaporate before he took his place on the starting grid. As the car was being warmed-up prior to the start, an unwelcome mechanical harshness indicated that a valve seat was cracked: there wasn't sufficient time available to install a fresh engine, so the valve was rotated slightly and Ickx was able to lead the race for 16 laps. He then briefly dropped behind Beltoise as the flat-12 suddenly lost power, stopping for good after 18 laps with a major valve breakage. At Brands Hatch he qualified third, behind Rindt and Brabham, but shot into an immediate lead again at the start, only for differential failure to scotch his chances as he swept imperiously into his seventh lap.

Regazzoni finished fourth again at Brands Hatch after an aggressively controlled performance which earned him another outing in the B1 at Hockenheim, venue for the German Grand Prix in 1970 whilst the Nürburgring's "face lift" was being completed. On the long fast straights of this circuit near Heidelberg, the superior aerodynamics and handling of the Lotus 72 seemed perfectly matched against the extra power of the Ferrari B1s. Ickx managed to take pole position with a lap in 1m 59.5s while Rindt grabbed second place on the two-by-two Hockenheim starting grid, with Regazzoni a magnificent third inside Siffert's March 701 on the second row. The race developed into a spectacular four car battle for supremacy between the two Ferraris, Rindt's Lotus and Chris Amon's March, although the New Zealander remembers that he was very much the odd man out in this tussle, "hanging on for dear life in the slipstream" and

Giunti in his 312B1 rounds La Source (again!) on his way to fourth place in the Belgian Grand Prix at Spa-Francorchamps.

Up shoots Jacky Ickx's arm as his Ferrari 312B1 pulls to a halt with driveshaft failure during the 1970 Monaco Grand Prix.

unable to force his way to the front of the group.

Although the main issue was fought out between Ickx and Rindt, Regazzoni surged to the fore on laps 22 and 23 to lead a World Championship Grand Prix for the first time in his career. Unfortunately his retirement from the race followed shortly afterwards when his gearbox began to seize up and he spun off as a result. Amon retired with a burst engine which hadn't been able to stand the strain of all this flat-out, high-revs running, so the capacity crowd in the huge grandstands which line the Hockenheim stadium waited with anticipation as Ickx and Rindt started the final lap in that order. It really did look as though the Ferrari B1 was about to score its first Grand Prix triumph, but Rindt knew precisely what he was doing and nipped past quite confidently on that final lap to give the crowds the victory they so dearly wanted. Jochen, not renowned for his modesty at the best of times, was so impressed with the easy ride his Lotus 72 had given him that he refused to take the credit for the win. "Anybody could have won this race in this car," he said generously, a remark which must have been some consolation to Ickx who'd battled long and hard in his Ferrari all afternoon.

Not only was this Rindt's last Grand Prix victory, it was also his last finish in a World Championship race. At the Österreichring where the Austrian Grand Prix was being held for the first time, Jochen put his Lotus 72 on pole position in the face of a challenge from a trio of Ferrari 312B1s, but Regazzoni led on the opening lap before dropping back to sit dutifully behind Ickx all the way to the chequered flag. Rindt was chasing the two Ferraris hard in third place when his engine failed spectacularly, leaving Ickx and Regazzoni to cruise home

comfortably to score an impressive 1-2 for the new Ferrari flat-12. In fact, the Scuderia was unlucky not to score a 1-2-3 finish because Giunti was keeping up in fourth place very confidently during the early stages of the race, only dropping back to finish seventh after a section of tyre tread lifted from one of his front Firestones and he was obliged to call at the pits for a replacement.

For Ferrari, the 1970 Italian Grand Prix was an occasion of joy and relief, Clay Regazzoni surviving to win one of those classic "slipstream specials" at the pre-chicane Monza circuit at an average speed which topped 143mph. The trio of 312B1s driven by Ickx, Giunti and Regazzoni were right in contention from the outset of the weekend's activities, the power of their engines reflected by the fact that Ickx was able to secure pole position quite comfortably with a lap in 1m 24.36s – even though his car retained rear wings and nose fins through the two days of practice. Most Cosworth-engined cars cast aside their aerodynamic appendages in an attempt to obtain every ounce of straight line speed and such an experiment may have been at least partially responsible for Jochen Rindt's fatal accident in the Saturday afternoon session.

The Austrian's Lotus 72 started weaving violently under hard braking for the Parabolica corner as Jochen fought to get on terms with the Ferraris: just as it looked as though Rindt had got his car under control, it suddenly speared off to the left, impacting very violently against one of the uprights supporting the guard rail, before spinning to a standstill with its front end ripped right off. Practice was halted and the stupefying news eventually trickled back to the paddock that the man who had the World Championship title seemingly in his pocket had succumbed to appalling leg and chest injuries in the sordid confines of an Italian ambulance.

In hard motor racing terms, the elimination of Rindt from the Monza equation virtually handed the Italian Grand Prix to Ferrari on a plate – assuming at least one of their 312B1s survived intact. And so it proved on race day: fighting off desperate, but vain, challenges from BRM, Matra and Tyrrell March, Clay Regazzoni eventually broke away from the main leading bunch and triumphed over Stewart's March by slightly less than six seconds. Ickx's B1 succumbed to clutch failure, while Giunti's sister car retired with a persistent misfire: but Clay had survived, defeated the strong opposition and more than justified his position within the team by scoring a very emotional and significant victory. It was a success that guaranteed him a full-time place in the Grand Prix term for 1971.

With three races remaining on the Championship calendar there was now an outside chance of Ickx winning the drivers' title and Ferrari taking the Constructor's crown, although it was clearly going to mean winning all three events. That wasn't quite as unlikely a prospect as one might have imagined, and when Ickx and Regazzoni cruised home to another 1-2 result in the Canadian Grand Prix at Ste. Jovite, such a possibility looked as though it was on the cards. Admittedly, Jackie Stewart's new Tyrrell-Cosworth was a factor which now had to be taken into account and when the Scot led at both Ste. Jovite and Watkins Glen, where the United States Grand Prix took place two weeks after the Canadian event, the Ferrari team took very careful note for 1971. The Tyrrell finished neither race, however, but although Stewart's failure at Ste. Jovite had deposited another race win into Ickx's lap, Jacky was in trouble with a leaking fuel line at the Glen. He recovered magnificently from 12th to fourth place at the finish, but Rindt's posthumous World Championship title was now secure along with the Team Lotus's Constructor's crown.

Ferrari rounded off the season with yet another Ickx/Regazzoni 1-2 formation finish at Mexico City, the Belgian driver emerging from the 1970 season only five points behind the late Jochen Rindt's total in the Championship standings. As far as the Constructors' Championship was concerned, if only the team had fielded two cars from the outset, it might have mounted a more effective challenge, although, in fairness, it has to be said that, up until his death, only Rindt scored Championship points for Lotus. Emerson Fittipaldi and Reine Wisell, Chapman's two new boys, surprised everybody by coming home first and third at Watkins

TOTAL TOTAL

Overleaf: Getting down to it! A sight calculated to stir the hearts of any enthusiasts as the Italian Grand Prix, 1970 edition, gets underway with Jacky Ickx's Ferrari 312B1 sprinting into an early lead. Chasing hard are Pedro Rodriguez's BRM P153, Jackie Stewart's Tyrrell March 701, Clay Regazzoni's 312B1 (No.4), Jack Oliver's BRM P153 and Giunti's 312B1 (No.6). Regazzoni saved the day for Maranello . . .

Glen, without which unexpected success Ferrari would have certainly taken the Constructor's title.

By the end of the 1970 season the new Ferrari engine was regarded as the most formidable unit in Grand Prix racing. It had taken 12 months for the engine to be refined into a reliable and competitive proposition, and although it should be remembered that some of its outstanding success was partly due to the opposition suffering a whole sequence of mechanical problems with the 10-series Cosworth DFV engines, to score three 1-2 victories in a first season racing is a quite outstanding record for any car. With Ickx and Regazzoni staying on the driving strength, it was really rather difficult to see how 1971 could be anything less than another Ferrari *tour-de-force*.

Mauro Forghieri was never a man to stand still when technical development was concerned, so he pressed ahead with his new chassis design for the 1971 season as well as initiating some improvements to the flat-12 engine specification. Clearly influenced by the "wedge" profile of the Lotus 72, his interpretation of this aerodynamic theme manifested itself in the Ferrari 312B2 which made its public début during pre-race testing prior to the South African Grand Prix. The 12-cylinder engine was still slung beneath a rear pontoon chassis extension, but the frontal area was slightly smaller and the tubular chassis frame was clad in 16-gauge aluminium alloy skin in accordance with the requirements of the latest Formula 1 constructional regulations.

Whilst the B2's front suspension was basically unchanged from the original 1970 car, Forghieri decided on an inboard arrangement at the rear end. The wide, flat engine meant that there was no room to mount the coil spring/damper units vertically, so they were positioned at an angle across the rear of the engine and were actuated by a bell-crank top wishbone and single upper radius rod and a wide, non-reversed lower wishbone. A revised oil tank was also incorporated, as were different gearbox side plates in order to facilitate the installation of inboard rear disc brakes.

In order to improve the flat-12 engine's breathing even further, Forghieri revamped its dimensions to 80mm x 49.6mm in the interests of improved combustion, this now giving a total swept area of 2991.8cc. Full roller-bearing bottom ends were employed and the maximum rev. limit was raised to 12,800rpm at which point the 12-cylinder unit now produced 485bhp. Minor detail changes included the repositioning of the fuel metering unit on the top of the engine instead of its hitherto somewhat inaccessible location low down on the left-hand side of the engine's front end. There were minor changes to the block casting as well which meant that the 1972 units would only fit into B2 chassis and that made life just a little bit complicated when the team was fielding both B1 and B2 chassis during the course of the season.

It had never seriously been intended to race the 312B2 at Kyalami and Regazzoni confirmed that decision when he crashed the new car heavily during testing, ripping off a front wheel and badly rippling the outer monocoque skin. None the less, for the first few races of the 1971 season it seemed as though Ferrari couldn't put a foot wrong. Despite the fact that there was now tremendous opposition from Jackie Stewart in his well-sorted Goodyear-shod Tyrrell-Cosworth to contend with, Ferrari's flat-12s emerged victorious from the first three races of the season.

At Kyalami Mario Andretti, an occasional "third string" member of the team, was handed a lucky victory in the closing stages of the 79 lap event when Denny Hulme's dominant McLaren M19 slowed dramatically as a radius rod began to work loose. Mario's 312B1 never missed a beat all afternoon and a couple of weekends later Regazzoni's B2 won the Race of Champions at Brands Hatch, surging his slick-shod machine into the lead in the second half of the race as a typically damp winter track surface dried out and forced Stewart's Tyrrell, shod with Goodyear "intermediates", to drop back to a distant second place. Hardly had the dust settled from that little confrontation than Andretti was back in the winner's circle again a week later, his 312B1 taking both 32-lap heats of the

F1/F5000 Questor Grand Prix at California Ontario Motor Speedway. Mario had to fight hard, even on this very fast circuit, though, to keep ahead of Stewart's Tyrrell-Cosworth: the Scot was runner-up in both heats and Ferrari returned to Europe fully aware that Jackie would be the man to beat for the rest of the season.

So it proved. Ickx, Regazzoni and Andretti were all on hand to contest the Spanish Grand Prix at Montjuich Park, and although a single B2 was available as a spare, all three drivers raced the older chassis. The team was now being managed by the pleasant Swiss Peter Schetty, whose family owned a Basle textile business, and who had won the 1969 European Hillclimb Championship at the wheel of the flat-6 engined Ferrari 212E which had, obliquely, spawned the 3-litre flat-12.

Barcelona proved to be a good race for the Ferrari team: one of the few they were destined to enjoy for the remainder of the season. At the start, Ickx shot into an immediate lead from his position on the outside of the front row and, for the first few laps, it seemed as though the B1 was going to have the legs of the field. But Stewart was leading the pursuit and the Tyrrell driver attacked strongly, knowing that he had to get the better of the Ferrari whilst its fuel load was still heavy. The blue Tyrrell gradually hauled in the Italian car, slipped by and began to pull away, easing out an advantage of almost 10s at one point. As the Ferrari's fuel load was consumed in the second half of the race, Ickx found his B1 handling better with every lap that passed and launched a furious counter-attack against his adversary: with three laps to go he set a new lap record and was only 3.4s behind Stewart at the chequered flag. Both his team-mates retired.

As the season progressed, Ferrari fortunes waned. The problem was that the B2 wasn't a very predictable and progressive machine to drive close to the limit and Forghieri's efforts to sort out its handling were not helped by continual complaints from the drivers in addition to enormous and increasing problems with Firestone's tyres. There was far too much "back-tracking" to the B1 throughout the summer, and it became increasingly difficult to pin-point whether the B2's handling traumas were really due to an inherent design defect in its rear suspension set-up or simply stemmed from the continual tyre imbalance and vibration problems which reached a head in the middle of the season.

Largely in response to his drivers' complaints about the B2's erratic handling on rough surfaces, Forghieri added extra horizontal dampers to the rear suspension layout, but this didn't really improve matters significantly. It was no consolation, either, that most Firestone teams were also suffering tyre vibration problems: the new Ferraris seemed to suffer worse than all the others!

Firestone personnel recall having more complaints from Forghieri on this subject than from all the other teams put together, but at least Peter Schetty was regarded as sufficiently competent a driver to try the B2 and confirm that, in his view at least, his drivers' complaints were entirely justified. "Honestly, those vibrations were really frightening," recalled Schetty, "when you were hard on the throttle coming out of a corner they developed into such high-frequency vibrations that every muscle in your body seemed to ache and the instruments just started to blur in front of your eyes."

Firestone was in the process of developing tyres with an increasingly low aspect ratio in 1971 and the vibrations became more serious as the sidewalls became more shallow. In effect, the tread was trying to lift from the track surface in an attempt to run over itself, causing the sidewalls to distort. On the face of it the only thing to do was go back to tyres with a taller, stiffer carcass, but no amount of experimentation with constructions seemed to rectify the problem. Of course, all these problems were being tackled in the height of the racing season and Stewart was reeling off a succession of Grand Prix victories in his Tyrrell whilst Ferrari floundered about.

Ickx, after making a rather conservative choice of tyre compound, came through to finish third at Monaco behind Stewart and Ronnie Peterson's March 711, took an easy win against lightweight opposition with a B1 in the Jochen Rindt Memorial Race at Hockenheim, and then displayed all his driving brilliance in streaming wet conditions (where Firestone had a distinct advantage) to take a B2

Jacky Ickx's Ferrari 312B1 leads the 1970 Mexican Grand Prix ahead of team-mate Regazzoni who has Jackie Stewart's new Tyrrell alongside him. Crowd control was non-existent at this event which, happily is recalled for its Ferrari 1-2 outcome, not the terrible tragedy which so easily could have arisen.

to victory in the Dutch Grand Prix. All three drivers were allotted B2s to drive in this latter event, but Andretti ended up having to race one of the older cars after one of the new wide rear tyres he was trying pulled off the wheel rim and he crashed heavily going into *Tarzan*. Mario wasn't too bothered about being obliged to drive the B1 because he reckoned it was a much nicer chassis to drive than the later car; "you knew where you were with the B1. It was nice and progressive and very responsive to any alterations you might make to it. You were never very sure what the B2 was going to do next . . ."

Despite all their theoretical power surplus, the Ferraris were comprehensively defeated by Stewart's Tyrrell on the wide open spaces of Paul Ricard, new venue for the French Grand Prix in 1971, and that embarrassment continued at Silverstone despite Regazzoni earning pole position after a remarkably brave performance in his B2. Ickx's ultimate disappointment occurred at the Nürburgring, where he felt his reputation was *really* at stake: fighting gamely to stay with Stewart, he spun off the road on the second lap of the German Grand Prix and slid very firmly into a guard rail.

The addition of oil-filled harmonic inertia dampers on the B2 rear suspension uprights had done nothing to minimize the tyre vibration problem, and another disastrous day out at the Austrian Grand Prix meant that the atmosphere at Maranello was gloomy in the extreme prior to the Italian Grand Prix. Enzo Ferrari

even began indicating to his technical staff that unless there was a dramatic improvement, it might be just as well to give Monza a miss. Forghieri and his colleagues responded with some revised cylinder heads which were intended to provide slightly more torque without any loss of top-end power (not that torque was exactly one of the pre-requisites for Monza!) and the organizers made suitably sympathetic clucking noises to woo the Old Man into sending his entries along to the race as usual!

Ickx put his foot down very firmly, both on and off the circuit, insisting that he be allowed to race a B1 in the Italian Grand Prix. He got his way, qualifying on the front row of the grid alongside Amon's Matra: the Belgian even tried a set of Goodyear G24 tyres at Ferrari's personal request, a move which sent shudders of indignation through the Firestone camp! Despite all these efforts, the race was a fiasco. Ickx retired after 16 laps with serious rear-end vibrations while Regazzoni, who had used a B2 and blatantly jumped the start from his fourth row position, lasted only two laps longer before his engine broke.

After another squalid performance in the rain during the Canadian Grand Prix at Mosport Park, where the B2s qualified 12th, 13th and 18th in practice, Ickx insisted on using a B1 again in the United States Grand Prix at Watkins Glen – despite the fact that Forghieri had produced a further-revised B2 with wider track rear suspension. Electrical problems intervened to cause Jacky's retirement in this final race of the year, but he was closing in on Francois Cevert's winning Tyrrell at the time. Thus ended a season which had promised a great deal, and delivered very little.

The 1972 Grand Prix season was to be characterized by Team Lotus's racing renaissance and Emerson Fittipaldi's impressive progress towards winning his first World Championship title. Tyrrell's new car was late on the scene and this, combined with the fact that Jackie Stewart was having medical problems with a stomach ulcer for part of the season, gave Lotus a much easier time that one might otherwise have expected. However, Ferrari wasn't in a position to do significantly better than in 1971: despite the advent of the team's new, tailor-made test track at Fiorano, adjacent to the Maranello factory, with its computers and video cameras to monitor all aspects of car performance, the technical recipe proved to be much as before. Although Forghieri had some ambitious plans for a totally new chassis, one with its weight concentrated as much as possible in the middle of the car in order to minimize the changes in handling as the fuel load was consumed, this design was not completed until the end of 1971. There was clearly little prospect of the finished car seeing the light of day much before the end of the following

Revamped, but not better? The 312B2 at its formal unveiling at Maranello. Several drivers reckoned the old B1 was better – except Regazzoni, who would race anything anywhere with considerable gusto and delight!

racing season.

Thus the 312B2 continued to spearhead Ferrari's Grand Prix challenge, although Ickx was relieved to see the complicated inboard rear suspension system replaced by a more conventional arrangement with an outboard mounted coil spring/damper unit and the uprights located by top links, lower wishbones and twin parallel radius rods. A wider front and rear track was also finalized and Ickx started the season in a reasonably confident vein, again backed up by Regazzoni and Andretti. The Argentine Grand Prix opened the season at Buenos Aires, this event making a return to the international calendar after an absence of 12 years, but with Stewart's Tyrrell dominating proceedings it didn't look as though things were really destined to be much different than throughout the previous year. Ickx and Regazzoni came home a distant third and fourth. Perhaps thinking that part of the Tyrrell's success was due to its full-width nose cowling, the B2s appeared similarly equipped at Kyalami for the South African Grand Prix, but the flat-12s refused to rev. properly and Andretti was the sole Maranello runner to finish in

Second in a B1. Jacky Ickx chasing Jackie Stewart's Tyrrell round Montjuich Park during the 1971 Spanish Grand Prix. Although he led in the early stages, the Belgian's flat-12 was defeated by the Cosworth-propelled Scot.

the points, an uncompetitive fourth.

Test and development work continued on a somewhat piecemeal basis for the next couple of months as various minor alterations were tried in an attempt to improve the 312B2 handling. There didn't seem to be a great deal of rhyme or reason behind some of the changes, much of the progress being made as much through "trial and error" as through any logical and pre-planned programme. In time for the Spanish Grand Prix at Jarama the Ferrari B2s had been fitted with bigger rear wings and the engine oil coolers had been repositioned down on either side of the gearbox. The wings were mounted further forward than previously and the three drivers reported that the cars felt much more controllable on this tight circuit than they had before. Ickx justified his comments by qualifying on pole position and, despite making an appalling start, briefly challenged Emerson Fittipaldi's Lotus 72 during a mid-race rain shower: at the end of the day, however, the Belgian was no match for the cool young Brazilian driver and Ickx had to settle for second place.

Second in a B2. Ickx splashes round Massenet into Casino Square during the rain-soaked 1972 Monaco Grand Prix. Despite being racing's acknowledged wet-weather expert at the time, Ickx had to give best to the Marlboro BRM P160 driven by Jean-Pierre Beltoise. "There was nothing I could do to catch him," conceded Jacky afterwards.

The one place where Ickx could reasonably be expected to waltz away from the opposition was at a rain-soaked Monaco two weeks later. The Belgian's wet weather ability had been emphasized at Zandvoort the previous year, but suddenly he was obliged to play second-fiddle to another Firestone runner. Jean-Pierre Beltoise's Marlboro BRM P160 got the jump on Ickx at the start of the race and there was simply no way that Jacky could stay with him. The Ferrari engines had been fitted with special camshafts to offer more torque on this tight street circuit, and whilst that might have given Ickx and Regazzoni an advantage in the dry, it was of no consequence at all in the torrential conditions.

Regazzoni slid into the barriers at the hairpin before the pits and this unfortunate streak was sustained by the determined Swiss driver when he tripped over Nanni Galli's flat-12 Tecno during his Belgian Grand Prix chase of Emerson Fittipaldi's Lotus at the bleak Nivelles-Baulers autodrome near Brussels. In the month prior to the French Grand Prix at Clermont-Ferrand, Forghieri presided over an exhaustive tyre testing programme at the Nürburgring and further revised the B2 rear suspension with a single upper radius rod, revised uprights and a new triangulated lower wishbone. Ickx wasn't impressed by these alterations when he began practising at Clermont-Ferrand, but he still managed to qualify second alongside Chris Amon's Matra MS120B. Even less impressed was Regazzoni: he'd broken a bone in his wrist whilst horsing around with the mechanics in the paddock at the Österreichring the previous weekend during the Austrian 1000kms sports car meeting. His place in the team was taken by the man who'd heaved him off the road at Nivelles, Nanni Galli! Happily for Clay, Galli proved to be hopelessly uncompetitive and his "stand-in" place for the British Grand Prix was taken by the wiry, diminutive Arturo Merzario – who sat so low in the cockpit that many people felt the main reason he went as quickly as he did was the fact that he couldn't properly see where he was going.

Sweeping memories of a disappointing French Grand Prix under the table, Ickx

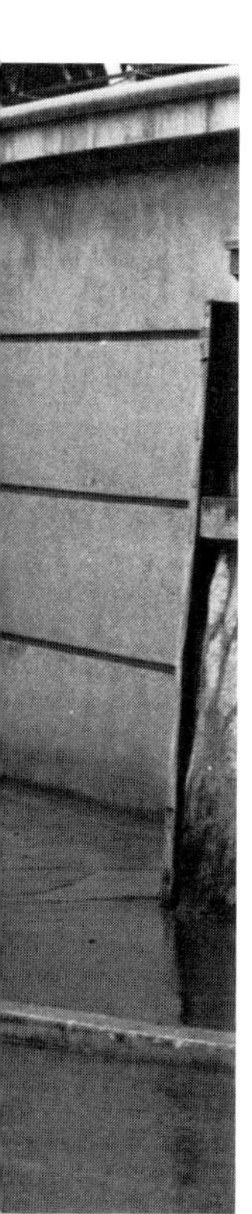

had the legs of everybody at Brands Hatch, keeping ahead of Stewart's Tyrrell and Fittipaldi's Lotus with no trouble until a leaking oil union, a cloud of expensive blue smoke and loss of pressure heralded the end of his race. As some compensation for Ickx's retirement when victory was virtually within his grasp, Merzario's Grand Prix débût was rewarded with a fine sixth place.

On July 30 1972, Jacky Ickx scored what was to be the last Grand Prix victory of his illustrious career, but from the manner in which he achieved this triumph, one would never have guessed that the Belgian would never again stand in the number one spot on the GP winner's podium. Determined to avenge his defeat in the 1971 German Grand Prix, Jacky out-qualified Stewart's Tyrrell by 1.7s at the Nürburgring. He led the 14 lap event from start to finish in faultless style and team-mate Regazzoni backed him up with a splendid second place: the Swiss also turfed Stewart into the barrier as the Tyrrell driver attempted to pass him in the Hatzenbach forest on the last lap. Jackie was livid, but Clay simply shrugged his shoulders. "He was off line . . ." he grinned sheepishly.

As the 312B2s staggered through to the end of another patchy season, their unpredictable form continued. Right off the pace at the Österreichring, with all the drivers complaining about fuel vaporization misfires, Ickx and Regazzoni were bang on form yet again at Monza for the Italian Grand Prix. Ickx took the lead from the start only for Clay to go pounding through on lap 14 – and then trip over Carlos Pace's Williams March 711, eliminating both cars in a shower of sparks and broken suspension. That allowed Ickx to pull comfortably ahead once again, but an electrical short-circuit only ten laps from the chequered flag caused the Ferrari's engine to cut out suddenly and the race was a gift for Fittipaldi's Lotus, thereby clinching the Championship title for the Brazilian driver. Andretti, back in the team again, clipped a chicane kerb and was forced to stop for a new wheel to be fitted: he wound up seventh.

Andretti missed the Canadian Grand Prix owing to a USAC commitment at Trenton, New Jersey, so there were only two cars at Mosport Park and Regazzoni made the best of a bad job by finishing fifth. Mario was back behind the wheel of his regular B2 for his home Grand Prix at Watkins Glen where he managed to take a single Championship point for sixth place. Ickx was fifth, Regazzoni eighth. Ten years would pass before Mario would again handle a Grand Prix Ferrari: the next occasion would see him plant a 126C2 on pole position for the 1982 Italian Grand Prix at Monza!

Back at Maranello, the atmosphere was appalling. The short-term, non-productive witch hunts which always seem to be typical of a Ferrari rout, were in full swing, Forghieri had completed his first prototype 312B3, with its short wheelbase, central weight bias and square-cut appearance. The new car conformed with the 1973 regulations as far as deformable structures were concerned, but it quickly stood condemned on the basis of some initial tests with Ickx and Merzario. One is bound to say that, unattractive as the prototype B3 certainly was, it wasn't given a fair trial. Forghieri himself was on the receiving end of much criticism for the relative failure of the B2 chassis during 1972 and there were elements within the Ferrari organization who were now only too happy to sustain that criticism when it came to the prototype B3. The end result of all this bickering was that Forghieri was taken off the Formula 1 team at the start of the 1973 season, just as he had been in 1969 when he was developing the flat-12 car in the first place. The result of this move was the virtual total collapse of Ferrari as an effective Grand Prix force: only when Forghieri was finally instructed to revamp the "English-built" 312B3 (which followed on once his prototype had been shelved) did Maranello start on the long road back to competitive respectability. But there was one aspect of supreme irony here: if Forghieri had been allowed to pursue his original B3 line of development, Ferrari might have saved themselves a season in the wilderness. For when Forghieri's successful '74-specification B3 took to the circuits, it bore all the hallmarks of the original prototype: central weight bias with side radiators fed by ducts in the side pods, low polar moment of inertia . . . In fact, the whole episode was a parallel of the Lancia D50 saga in which

most drivers disliked the car despite its high level of cornering ability, because of the suddenness with which it ultimately lost adhesion. But Forghieri survived the storm.

The end of the 1972 season also marked Clay Regazzoni's departure from the Ferrari team, albeit briefly. Enzo Ferrari had made it clear to the easygoing Swiss that it looked as though there would be only sufficient finance available in 1973 to run a single entry from Maranello. "He told me that I was free to do a deal with another team," recalls Clay, "but he also hinted that there might be a chance of my returning at some time in the future." Regazzoni went off to drive for the Marlboro BRM team, but clearly decided that this partnership was taking his career nowhere fast and, by the following summer's British Grand Prix, had virtually agreed terms for a 1974 return to Ferrari!

Throughout the early part of the 1973 Grand Prix season, Ferrari Formula 1 design and development was under the control of former Innocenti engineer

The John Thompson-built monocoque Ferrari 312B3 is pushed out for practice at Barcelona, 1973. The car wasn't a great success, the tempo of the team's development programme slowing drastically that season, but it provided Mauro Forghieri with the bones of his successful 1974 development.

Sandro Colombo. Following the dramas with Firestone in 1972, Ferrari signed to run on Goodyears for '73, but this certainly proved to be no instant palliative for their continuing ills. The first three races of the season saw Ickx and Merzario (the money for a second car seemed miraculously forthcoming after all) struggling round at the wheel of out-dated B2s. Ickx survived to take fourth place in the Argentine Grand Prix at Buenos Aires, during practice for which the entire Ferrari team got a nasty fright when Regazzoni secured pole position in his Firestone-shod BRM P160. Reliability rather than competitiveness earned Ickx and Merzario fourth and fifth places in the Brazilian Grand Prix at Sao Paulo's spectacular Interlagos circuit a couple of weeks later: both these South American events were won by Fittipaldi's Lotus 72, incidentally. The B2 finally had its last Grand Prix outing in the South African race at Kyalami on March 3 where Ickx found himself involved on the fringe of that fiery accident which oh-so-nearly cost Clay Regazzoni his life. But for the quick, and very brave, reactions of Mike

Hailwood (who was awarded the George Medal for his conduct) the Swiss might well have been badly burnt in the accident: as it was he survived with only a few minor scorches. Merzario finished fourth, miles behind the leaders.

The second-generation Ferrari 312B3 made its race début in the 1973 Spanish Grand Prix at Montjuich Park on April 29. Drawn at the Maranello factory under Colombo's watchful eye, the first three monocoques for this design were actually constructed in England. There was so much industrial strife in Italy at the time that Ferrari was worried that its supply of sub-contracted components could not be guaranteed. It was thus decided to commission an English specialist company, TC Prototypes of Weedon, near Northampton, to produce these monocoques.

John Thompson, boss of TC Prototypes, recalls the almost casual way in which Ferrari made its approach to his company. It was around the time of the 1972 London Motor Show "when I got a telephone message to say that a Mr. Colombo would be arriving at the factory the following day. He arrived, presented me with the Ferrari drawings and simply asked how much I would charge to produce three of them. We agreed the deal on the spot. I produced the three bare monocoques, not piped or wired in any way, and they were duly airfreighted out to Italy. I still remember just how impressed we all were over the high standard of the detailed drawings they provided me to work from. They were of a quality far superior to anything I'd seen before in the Formula 1 business . . ."

At this time there was also a suggestion mooted that Chris Amon, whose career hadn't exactly prospered during his two-year post-March stint with Matra, should run a non-works Ferrari B3 with backing from Marlboro. The deal didn't come together for a variety of reasons, but the fact that it was seriously kicked around indicates just how desperate things had become in 1973.

At first glance, the "Thompson B3s" (as they were to become informally dubbed) looked very big racing cars indeed by the standards of the day. Squat, flat and low, they could hardly be described as attractive: nor were they to prove particularly effective. The detail design was nicely executed, however, and Ferrari had used magnesium alloy quite extensively in the car's design. The front suspension was quite straightforward with inboard coil spring/dampers actuated by top rocker arms (fabricated now, rather than forged) and a wide-based lower wishbone located the bottom of the uprights. At the rear, however, the "pontoon" suspending the engine was now gone and the flat-12 was installed as a stressed-member mounted on a cast-magnesium sandwich plate which also provided the mounting point for the rollover bar. Across the rear of the engine was a large cast alloy "bridge piece" which carried the conventional rear suspension and the alternator was now mounted atop the engine along with the fuel metering unit. From the point of view of accessibility, this 312B3 was a much more convenient proposition.

Ickx had tried one of these cars in side-radiator form at Fiorano a few days prior to the Spanish race and it quickly became clear that this cooling arrangement wasn't adequate. The second car was thus hurriedly converted to front-radiator specification in time for the Barcelona event where only Ickx was entered following these last-moment overheating dramas. He briefly tried the one side-radiator B3 during practice (carrying the race number of Merzario's cancelled second entry) before switching permanently to the front-rad car. The B3 qualified sixth in the Belgian's hands and ran sixth in the race before making a precautionary stop to have the brakes bled. He eventually finished 12th.

Ickx's home race, the Belgian Grand Prix, took place at Zolder for the first time in 1973 against the backcloth of a threatened drivers' strike over the deplorable condition of the track surface. Jacky by this time had resigned from the Grand Prix Drivers' Association and wouldn't have anything to do with this planned boycott, least of all at his home race, so for some of practice his was the only car out on the circuit. The Ferrari team was pretty encouraged when he qualified the new B3 in fourth place, but their optimism was cruelly dashed on race morning when it was found, shortly before the start, that the oil pump had been jammed by a tiny needle roller. Since only the camshafts ran on these tiny bearings, there was clearly something very wrong inside the Ferrari's engine, and six laps into the race the B3 expired in a cloud of oil smoke as the problem cropped up again.

For Ferrari enthusiasts it is painful to recall the balance of the 1973 Grand Prix season. Not since 1969 had Maranello experienced a season devoid of victories, but this time there was not even the promise of running at the front of the field before the cars broke down. Lethargy seemed to reign, with neither Ickx nor Merzario apparently able to shake the team out of its irritating rut. Both retired at Monaco and the fact that they managed to finish fourth and seventh in the French Grand Prix at Paul Ricard simply reflected the high rate of retirements. Finally Ickx finished eighth in the British Grand Prix at Silverstone and Ferrari's Formula 1 effort drew to a virtual standstill.

The team failed to contest the Dutch or German Grands Prix. Ickx was highly dissatisfied with the whole affair, Mr. Ferrari himself wasn't very well and Forghieri's attentions were obviously not focussed on the F1 problems. At this point Fiat decided to take a hand in the affairs of the Ferrari team. After all, since 1969 they had been effectively under-writing Ferrari's financial security and the Grand Prix team was a prestigious and important aspect of their decision to become involved with the company in the first place.

As a result of Fiat pressure, Forghieri was ordered back from the Special Projects department to reassume his authority over the technical side of the Formula 1 programme. From the time he was "reappointed" he had just 20 days to prepare a revamped 312B3 for the Austrian Grand Prix, a task he successfully completed. The car was driven by Arturo Merzario since Ickx had virtually agreed by now to sever his links with the Ferrari team and go his own way. This revamped B3 represented a turning point on Ferrari Grand Prix design which would influence the team's cars for the next three seasons. Forghieri had won another political battle within Maranello's portals and was now free to pursue his "low polar moment" philosophy unchallenged.

The revised B3 was based round one of the Thompson monocoques, but was visually transformed. The front radiators had been replaced by long thin radiators laid at a shallow angle along the sides of the monocoque, the air ducted in beneath them and out through the top. The oil tank was now positioned to the right of the engine, immediately behind the rear cockpit bulkhead and the oil radiator was situated in a corresponding position on the opposite side of the car. As much weight as possible was concentrated within the car's wheelbase and the suspension geometry had been appropriately revised to deal with these weight revisions. The most visually distinctive feature of the car was its full-width front aerofoil and its cold air box which fed both banks of the flat-12 engine.

Merzario qualified sixth and finished seventh in Austria, prompting sufficient renewed interest from Ickx to entice the Belgian back into a Ferrari cockpit for the Italian Grand Prix at Monza. He finished eighth in that race, but never drove a Ferrari Formula 1 car again. Merzario drove the last two races of the season in Canada and the USA, but even before 1973 was over, the remnants of that unsuccessful season were already being swept under the carpet as far as Maranello was concerned. 1974 would see a new dawn for the Prancing Horse, opening an era of unprecedented success for Ferrari's Formula 1 team.

NIKI
LAUDA
GOODYEAR
Marlboro
Niki Lauda
arexons
CHAMPION
FERODO
FERRARI IMPORTADOR
TAYRE

Section V: The 3-litre twelves, 1966-80

Chapter 3
Lauda's sustained success

Niki's first win. Lauda's 312B3 heads Ronnie Peterson's Lotus 76 in the opening, rain-soaked stages of the 1974 Spanish Grand Prix at Jarama, the first of many Lauda victories for the Prancing Horse.

Three key personalities were responsible for Ferrari's renaissance in 1974: Forghieri, Niki Lauda and Luca di Montezemolo. From this point onwards, until he left the team in 1984, Forghieri enjoyed virtually unfettered control over the technical side of the team's Grand Prix cars. Niki Lauda, the talented, intelligent and very promising Austrian who'd made a name for himself with BRM, joined the team alongside old hand Regazzoni. Finally, Montezemolo, a member of the Agnelli dynasty, was appointed as Ferrari's liaison man at the circuits, following in the footsteps of such legendary figures as Ugolini, Tavoni and Dragoni. But Montezemolo's prime function was to safeguard Fiat's interests and he fulfilled a crucial role, communicating the Formula 1 team's fortunes to Mr. Ferrari in a totally impartial and accurate fashion. Luca neutralized some of the absurd political intrigue and he did so from a position of strength and influence: he stayed in this role throughout 1974 and '75, but the ripple-effect of his influence helped sustain the team's momentum throughout 1976 and '77 as well.

Lauda was a gifted opportunist who'd first come to Enzo Ferrari's attention when he kept his Marlboro BRM P160 ahead of Ickx's 312B3 at Monaco during the 1973 race. He had secured himself a place within the BRM team by dint of signing a long-term contract: but that didn't prevent him from leaving to join Ferrari when the opportunity presented itself. Rightly, Lauda reasoned, there wouldn't be too many breaks like this! After some legal wrangling his BRM

contract was eventually formally settled without ever getting as far as the court room: Niki paid them some nominal damages and the matter was forgotten along, one may add, with the BRM team as an entity!

Throughout the winter of 1973/74 the Ferrari team worked absolutely flat-out on test and development work at Fiorano. The Scuderia had withdrawn from endurance racing with its flat-12-engined 312PBs and thrown all its resources behind the Grand Prix programme. The cars stayed on Goodyear rubber but acquired a new fuel sponsor. After years of profitability problems, Shell Italiana withdrew not only from the Ferrari team but also from petrol marketing in Italy: Agip took their place and remain Ferrari fuel sponsors to this day.

By the time the 312B3s appeared in practice for the Argentine Grand Prix at Buenos Aires on January 13, 1974 Forghieri's concept had been further revised with almost 30 additional modifications. The most striking alteration was the moving of the cockpit and fuel cells some five inches forward within the wheelbase, considerably improving the car's balance, and some exhaustive work on the flat-12 engines resulted in revised cylinder heads which helped boost the power to 495bhp at 12,600 rpm as well as conferring considerably improved torque characteristics. The revised B3s finished second and third in this race, underlining their promise, and a fortnight later Regazzoni finished second to Fittipaldi's Marlboro McLaren M23 in the 40 lap Brazilian Grand Prix at Interlagos, briefly pushing his way to the top of the Drivers' Championship points table as a result.

Throughout 1974 Lauda and Regazzoni earned a reputation as reliable and consistent competitors. Niki's inexperience cost him a shot at the World Championship, for he crashed on the opening lap of the German Grand Prix at the Nürburgring and also slid off the road at Mosport Park where he had apparently got the Canadian Grand Prix in his pocket. On the other side of the coin, the young Austrian drove magnificently at Jarama and Zandvoort, winning the Spanish and Dutch Grands Prix in superb style, and only a puncture robbed him of a similarly dominant victory in the British Grand Prix at Brands Hatch. Regazzoni won the German Grand Prix, but at the end of the day Fittipaldi's canny approach to the business of points-gathering won the Brazilian his second World Championship title.

Echoing the reaction of so many others on their first visit to Ferrari, Lauda recalls "when you see all the facilities at the team's disposal it's a little difficult, at first glance, to understand why they don't win every race without any difficulty. It was quite clear to me that the only reason they had failed in the past was politics and Montezemolo made a tremendous contribution to our 1974 fortunes in that respect. He got everybody working in the same direction with a tremendous sense of purpose and he kept the Old Man in touch with what was going on, reporting to him in a totally objective manner. In the past those lines of communication obviously hadn't been totally impartial!"

The Ferrari flat-12 engine proved to be outstandingly reliable throughout 1974, although major failures at the Österreichring and Monza, in particular, proved particularly disappointing. The 312B3 chassis remained substantially unaltered throughout the year, apart from minor bodywork revisions to improve its aerodynamic penetration, but Forghieri was still not satisfied that he had realized all the potential available. No matter how one adjusted the B3 chassis set-up, the car always tended towards slight understeer, and by the end of the 1974 European season the first of the team's 1975 cars had been completed at Maranello. Although the new car was officially unveiled to the press after the 1974 North American Grands Prix it wasn't destined to make its race début until the 1975 South African Grand Prix on March 1. By the time that race came round it was regarded as the most eagerly awaited Formula 1 car since the Lotus 72 five years earlier.

The most interesting aspect of the new 312T (for *trasversale*) was the adoption of a neatly executed transverse-mounted five-speed gearbox, positioned ahead of the rear axle line in accordance with Forghieri's continuing quest for the lowest possible polar moment . . . The shafts in the gearbox obviously lay at right angles to the car's centre-line and the power was transmitted by means of bevel gears on the input side of the box, the final drive being by a system of spur gears. The 312T chassis was very much narrower at the front end than the B3 it superseded and the rocker arm front suspension had undergone a major re-design. Tiny coil spring/damper units were now mounted on a small magnesium platform fitted to the front bulkhead and these were actuated by long, fabricated top rocker arms with wide based lower wishbones. The rear coil spring/dampers were mounted outboard with single top links, upper radius arms and lower wishbones. The disc brakes were outboard at the front, inboard at the rear.

Lauda conceded that he was rather lukewarm about the 312T project when Forghieri first showed him the drawings, the Austrian admitting that he frankly didn't appreciate what a major step forward the new car would represent. However, it was largely due to Niki's perceptive ability as a test and development driver, and his willingness to adapt his driving style to accommodate the new car's characteristics, that the 312T enjoyed the instant success that awaited it during the 1975 season. After the B3, the new Ferrari was quite a "nervous" machine to drive close to the limit, but those limits were extremely high when compared to most of the opposition, and when it came to sudden changes of direction the 312T was notably agile and responsive. Its basic handling was absolutely neutral and Lauda's increasing ability to drive close to the limit for long periods, whilst seldom over-stepping them, will be recalled with pleasure by those who watched his "on rails" driving style throughout the 1975 season.

For the first two races of the 1975 season Lauda and Regazzoni stayed with the out-classed B3s which were reduced to the role of also-rans in both Argentina and Brazil. They were fourth and sixth in Buenos Aires, fourth and fifth at Interlagos, with Clay heading Niki home on both occasions. Then came the début of the 312T at Kyalami, but even that was something of an initial disappointment. Niki had a nasty fright in practice when Fittipaldi's McLaren blew its engine up spectacularly right in front of him and the new Ferrari went skating into the catch fencing on the ensuing oil slick. It was repaired for the race, but Regazzoni and Lauda could only trail round in fifth and sixth positions: Clay's car had been set up with too much understeer for this fast circuit and Niki couldn't get past him because his car's engine felt badly down on power. Not one usually to make excuses for a poor performance, Niki was subsequently relieved to be told that the metering unit drive belt had lost some teeth and was slipping badly as a result: when the engine was put back on the test bed at Maranello in this condition it was found to be producing only around 440bhp.

After some morale-boosting back-to-back tests at Fiorano, which proved quite conclusively that the 312T was quicker than the old B3, Lauda celebrated the new car's first victory at Silverstone in the non-title Silverstone International Trophy race. After James Hunt's Hesketh 308 retired whilst leading, Niki held off a last-corner challenge from World Champion Fittipaldi's Marlboro McLaren M23 to take the chequered flag first. Two weeks later, at the strife-torn Spanish Grand Prix where the drivers very nearly boycotted the Montjuich Park circuit, Niki and Clay started from alongside each other on the front row . . . only to collide at the first corner. Niki was out on the spot, but Regazzoni resumed only to eliminate his 312T later in the race through violent contact with another unyielding guard rail. This particular race will be sadly recalled for the terrible accident which befell Rolf Stommelen's Hill-Cosworth: after its rear aerofoil support broke as he led the race up over the brow beyond the pits, Rolf's car cartwheeled into a restricted area, killing four onlookers as a result. The Montjuich Park circuit was never used for a World Championship Grand Prix again.

For Ferrari, all this early disappointment evaporated at Monaco when Lauda led the 1975 Grand Prix almost from start to finish. The event started in heavy rain, but the circuit gradually dried out towards the finish and Lauda eased back, in characteristically cautious style, to let Fittipaldi close to within a few seconds at the chequered flag. Two weeks later at Zolder, on May 25, Niki repeated the dose

McLaren sandwich, with the 312B3s of Regazzoni and Lauda providing the bread as the two Italian cars fight vainly to keep control of Emerson Fittipaldi's M23 in the 1974 Belgian Grand Prix at Nivelles-Baulers. The Brazilian got ahead, however, and beat Lauda to the line, and victory, by a couple of lengths.

after dispatching a challenge from Carlos Pace's Brabham BT44B in the early stages of the race, the Austrian winning from Jody Scheckter's Tyrrell 007, Carlos Reutemann's Brabham BT44B, Patrick Depailler's Tyrrell 007 and Regazzoni. To the uninformed and often superficial minority amongst the international press corps, Lauda's dominant progress was simply a reflection of the Ferrari engine's "enormous" power surplus, but on June 8 Niki silenced his detractors by winning a hard-fought battle for victory in the Swedish Grand Prix at Anderstorp. This was no demonstration run for the Austrian who had to work desperately hard to haul in Reutemann's Brabham BT44B with only ten laps left to run. Regazzoni did a good supporting job to finish third, but Niki's victory will be recalled as probably his most impressive performance of 1975.

Throughout the summer of 1975 Niki Lauda's World Championship challenge progressively strengthened, although apart from a routine victory in the French Grand Prix at Paul Ricard he would have to wait until Watkins Glen before securing his fifth win of the season. In unpredictable wet/dry conditions at Zandvoort, Lauda had to give best to James Hunt, the Englishman driving his Hesketh 308 with magnificant flair to score his first Grand Prix victory, while his luck was out again when it came to the British Grand Prix, this year held at Silverstone in capricious wet/dry/wet weather conditions so typical of an English summer! Lauda and Regazzoni were beaten to places on the front row of the two-by-two starting grid by Tom Pryce's Shadow DN5 and Pace's Brabham BT44B, and although Clay managed to lead between laps 13 and 19, he then spun off at Club, damaging his 312T's rear aerofoil as a result. The circuit was shortly afterwards deluged beneath a tremendous thunder storm which sent most of the field slithering off the circuit on their slick tyres. By the time the race was prematurely finished after 56 laps, Fittipaldi was an easy winner and Lauda wound up eighth after a chaotic pit stop which saw one of his Ferrari's rear wheels come off as he accelerated down the pit lane to rejoin the race after changing on to wet weather rubber. It was a fiasco for Ferrari to forget!

On August 3 Lauda turned in a splendid 6m 58.6s lap round the Nürburgring to qualify on pole for the German Grand Prix which he then led in splendid style to fend off a strong challenge from Depailler's Tyrrell for the first eight laps. The Frenchman's car suffered a suspension breakage at this point, apparently presenting the Ferrari with an unassailable advantage. Unfortunately Lauda's car suffered a front tyre deflation and the shredded Goodyear virtually destroyed the Ferrari's front aerofoil as Niki hurried back to the pits for repairs. This drama dropped him to third at the chequered flag, behind Reutemann's Brabham BT44B and Jacques Laffite's reliable, plodding Williams FW04.

Despite qualifying on pole for his home Grand Prix at the Österreichring, Lauda fell victim to another torrential thunder storm and could only trail home sixth in the Austrian round of the World Championship. Vittorio Brambilla's March speed-boated its way to a highly unexpected success and the race was stopped at half-distance, thus only counting for half points in the Championship. Thereafter Regazzoni had some recompense for his largely disappointing season to date: he won the non-Championship Swiss Grand Prix at Dijon-Prenois on August 24, two weeks before taking his second Italian Grand Prix victory at Monza. Clay led from the first lap, aided somewhat by Lauda adopting a prudent approach to this event in which he knew he could clinch the Championship. The Austrian stroked his 312T home third behind Fittipaldi's McLaren M23, thus becoming the first Ferrari-mounted World Champion driver since John Surtees eleven years before.

Just to round off his tremendously successful season, Lauda utterly dominated the final round of the Championship at Watkins Glen. Starting the United States Grand Prix from pole position he led all the way to the chequered flag, chased vainly by Fittipaldi's McLaren once again. Unfortunately Regazzoni's undisciplined antics during this event were a matter of some regret for the Ferrari team: his well-intentioned, but absurdly excessive efforts to help Lauda saw him block Fittipaldi for lap after lap. The Swiss was eventually black-flagged out of the race, a move which resulted in Montezemolo almost coming to blows with SCCA director Burdette Martin. An unfortunate way in which to celebrate the team's splendid finale to a successful season!

A change in the Formula 1 technical regulations for 1976 precluded the use of those distinctive, high-mounted cold air boxes which had been such a part of the Grand Prix scene during the two previous seasons. Although the new regulations didn't come into force until the Spanish Grand Prix, leaving the team free to use the existing 312Ts in the Brazilian, South African and Long Beach Grands Prix, Ferrari unveiled the revised 312T prior to Christmas 1975.

The most obvious alteration on the 312T2 was the distinctive body top incorporating ducting running along either side of the cockpit, channelling cold air into each cylinder bank of the engine. The car's wheelbase was slightly longer (2.2in) and it was claimed that something over 20 pounds had been saved through various detail improvements throughout the chassis. More interestingly, when the 312T2 was first shown to the press at Ferrari's annual conference, which included a visit to Fiorano, the car sported a de Dion rear end: locating the two hub carriers was a tubular "bridge" structure extending across the back of the chassis, held sideways at the top by means of a telescopic shock absorber lying horizontally and attached by a lug to the top of the transmission unit at one end. From the lowest point on the hub carrier, transverse tubular links extended inwards to another short pivoted link, providing a Watts linkage in the horizontal plane. Tubular radius rods were provided as usual to locate the hub carriers in a fore-and-aft plane.

Lauda spent a considerable amount of time testing the de Dion rear suspension, both at Fiorano and at Kyalami, but he was never convinced that it was any better than a conventional suspension set-up. Consequently, once the helter-skelter of the 1976 racing season got under way, the system was shelved. Another feature of the T2's original specification was the provision of aerodynamic deflectors ahead of the front wheels, moulded as one with the brake cooling scoops, which turned in company with the front wheels. At the French Grand Prix meeting the CSI formally decreed that they were outside the regulations as they amounted to movable aerodynamic devices. They were taken off the cars and never seen again.

The cancellation of the Argentine Grand Prix meant that the Brazilian Grand Prix at Interlagos started the '76 season and Lauda opened his innings as reigning World Champion by taking the '75-spec. 312T to a comfortable victory over Patrick Depailler's Tyrrell 007. It wasn't quite the clear-cut victory it appeared on paper, however, for Regazzoni's sister car got the jump on everybody at the start and held the pace of the race down for the first nine laps so that not only Niki, but also James Hunt's pole position McLaren M23 and Jean-Pierre Jarier's Shadow DN5, were banked up in a tight queue behind him. Niki made his break on lap nine "because I'd realized Jarier would be the man to beat after seeing his times in the warm-up session, and I wanted to be well clear of him by the time I started lapping slower cars." Hunt followed Lauda through, but Jarier and Regazzoni had a brief coming-together which delayed the Swiss with a deflated front tyre. Lauda got away comfortably, but Jarier was coming back hard at the Ferrari with six laps to go when he slid off on oil deposited by James Hunt's crippled McLaren, its oil coolers fractured after a spin into the catch fencing caused by a throttle malfunction. Lauda had it easy for the last few miles to the flag.

Again using the 312T, Niki walked the South African Grand Prix at Kyalami, although his regular sparring partner Hunt again out-qualified him for pole. There was a flurry of excitement in the closing stages as the leading Ferrari began to show signs of fading with a soft rear tyre, but by that time the Austrian could afford to ease off slightly and still had 1.3s in hand over James at the flag.

The 312T2's race début took place in the Brands Hatch Race of Champions on March 14, but a leaking brake pipe obliged Lauda to retire after 17 of the 40 laps had been completed. He'd qualified an encouraging second. Scuderia Everest had borrowed a '75 spec. 312T from the factory for this race and for the forthcoming Silverstone International Trophy, the car being handled on both occasions by new boy Giancarlo Martini. He crashed on the warming-up lap at Brands, finished tenth at Silverstone . . . not a happy or particularly worthwhile experience!

The 312T's swansong came at Long Beach on March 27 where Clay Regazzoni led the United States Grand Prix West from start to finish from pole position. Lauda seemed unable all weekend to match his team-mate's pace, and in the closing stages of the race was slowed by gearbox problems. So far so good: three Grands Prix, three victories.

However, from those modest and undramatic beginnings, the 1976 World Championship Grand Prix season would grow into a dramatic sporting battle which focussed media attention on the motor racing world in a manner seldom previously seen. Since Emerson Fittipaldi's sudden defection from McLaren to consolidate the fortunes of his family Grand Prix team, James Hunt had taken over as team leader and his rivalry with Niki Lauda became one of the sport's talking points. And at the Spanish Grand Prix, held at Jarama on May 2, *everything* seemed to happen!

Lauda arrived for this race in considerable pain: he'd sustained two cracked ribs when the tractor he was driving rolled over on top of him whilst he was working in the garden of his Austrian lakeside home. Displaying all the determination that would be seen to characterize his whole approach towards life later in the season,

Niki forced himself to practise the T2 and qualified second alongside Hunt's McLaren. Lauda led the race initially, but Hunt eventually passed the Ferrari and went on to win – only to have his McLaren disqualified in a post-race scrutineering drama when it was found that the M23's rear track was a minuscule 1.8cm too wide. So Niki was the winner – for a while! On appeal from the McLaren team to the CSI, Hunt's victory was subsequently restored and a nominal 3000 dollar fine imposed in its place.

It seemed as though Jarama was but a momentary hiccup in the path of a familiar, inevitable Ferrari steamroller. Lauda was back on form at Zolder for the Belgian Grand Prix on May 16 and the Monaco Grand Prix on May 30. He dominated both races from pole position until the fall of the chequered flag. At Anderstorp he had to give best to the Tyrrell P34 six-wheelers which finished first and second in the hands of Jody Scheckter and Patrick Depailler to wrap up the Swedish Grand Prix. But third place wasn't too bad and Niki considered he'd done a pretty reasonable job.

The dominance which the Ferrari team had exerted throughout 1975 and the early part of 1976 was the logical product of endless methodical testing, a fact understood and appreciated by Niki Lauda probably more than anybody else in the team. At the start of the 1976 season Luca di Montezemolo left his position with Ferrari and his place was taken by former Lancia rally team chief Daniele

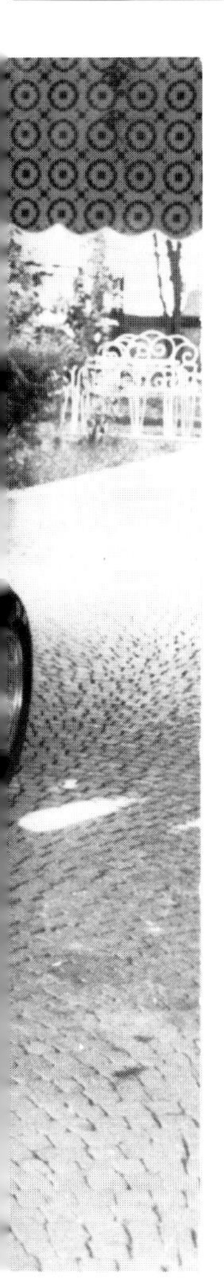

Audetto. The relationship between Lauda and Audetto frequently seemed rather tense: Niki didn't seem to be able to communicate to his new colleague that the crucial tempo of test and development work was doubly important when the team was on top. Slowly, almost imperceptibly, one could see the Ferrari team being lulled into a false sense of security: they were about to be duped again by that time-consuming old myth "*anybody* can win in a Ferrari . . ."

The French Grand Prix at Paul Ricard on July 4 brought with it a drama of unusual proportions. The one thing the Ferrari team had learnt to count on over the previous couple of seasons had been the splendid reliability record of its flat-12 engine. Now, suddenly, it was faced with a series of major failures. Lauda's engine broke during practice at Paul Ricard, and the replacement seized up as the World Champion was building up towards maximum speed on the circuit's long back straight during the early stages of the race. Niki had been walking away with the event, in familiar style, but when Regazzoni's T2 succumbed to precisely the same problem, actually spinning off as the rear wheels locked, Forghieri and his technical colleagues were horrified. The problem, on subsequent detailed examination back at Maranello, turned out to be that the flange pressed into the end of the crankshaft, taking the drive to the ignition and other ancillary equipment, was incorrectly machined. Tiny cracks were thus able to form, gradually enlarging until the engine failed under full throttle loadings.

As if all that wasn't enough, Lauda and Regazzoni staged a repeat of the 1975 Barcelona first corner collision as they accelerated away from the grid at Brands Hatch, venue for the British Grand Prix. Lauda chopped across in front of his team-mate, triggering off a multiple shunt as Regazzoni spun across the pursuing pack. The race was red-flagged and subsequently restarted in a welter of criticism, bad feeling, acrimony and allegation. At the centre of most of this trouble was a dispute over whether Britain's favourite, James Hunt, would be allowed to join the grid for the restart at the wheel of his McLaren M23. Hunt had been involved amidst that first corner carnage and was cruising back to the pits with damaged steering when the race was stopped; eventually he and Lauda lined up on the front row together in their original formation.

Lauda led away, but Hunt fought back to pass him and the McLaren beat the Ferrari to the flag quite comfortably. Unfortunately Hunt was later to be deprived of his victory when an FIA Court of Appeal, convened to consider a protest from the Ferrari team, concluded that Hunt hadn't in fact been running when the red flag was shown at Brands Hatch, shouldn't have been permitted to re-start and, accordingly, was disqualified from the results. That gave Lauda another win,

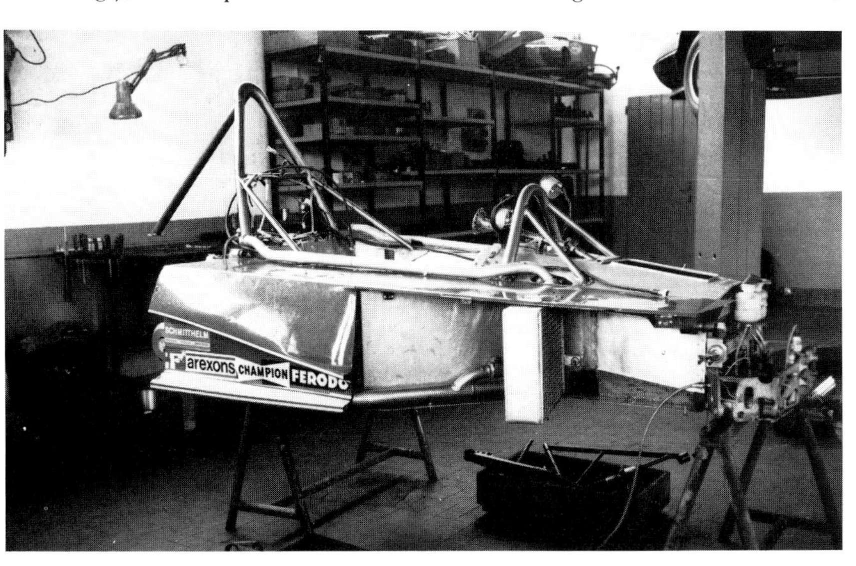

Start and finish of a Ferrari racing career. Above, the un-numbered first 312 *trasversale* ***at its Modena press launch at the end of 1974. Below, one of the later 312T2s is renovated for a private collector at the premises of Sport Auto in Modena; specialists who pride themselves in this sort of Ferrari-approved renovation work.***

YEAR GOODYEAR
GOODYEAR
Niki Lauda

12
GOOD YEAR

***Overleaf:* Niki Lauda showed tremendous speed and determination in the 1975 German Grand Prix at the Nürburgring, climbing back to third place after sustaining damage to the front aerofoil which was caused when a front tyre deflated after this photograph of his 312T aviating at Pflanzgarten was taken. In the author's opinion, he was to be unjustly pilloried for the abandonment of the Nürburgring as a racing venue: he was far from its sole critic and his "apprehension" about the place played no part in his terrible accident the following year.**

although by the time it had been confirmed most people in the business had forgotten the entire episode.

Within another fortnight the whole complexion of the World Championship struggle was to change dramatically and Niki Lauda was set to become one of international sport's great celebrities, although the manner in which he would achieve that status would almost cost him his life. The Nürburgring had, over the previous decade, frequently attracted concern from the Formula 1 racing fraternity and its "tidying up" between 1969 and '71 had only gone a limited way to allay the worries of those drivers who raced round it. The problem wasn't that it was unduly *dangerous* from the point of view of its configuration, although it was supremely *difficult*, but the organizational problems that went hand-in-hand with administering a circuit more than 14-miles long were foremost in the minds of the complainants. The length of time that it might take rescue services to reach an accident was a matter of some concern to those who quite naturally, if rather unrealistically, expected the same number of marshals at the same intervals as on short circuits like Brands Hatch and Silverstone. Niki Lauda was one of those who made his reservations about the Nürburgring very public and, because he was reigning World Champion, they carried more weight than most. Although Niki had broken a wrist when his BRM P160 crashed during practice for the 1973, this incident hadn't prejudiced him unduly against the track, as many of his critics suggested. They were all too quick to forget that he'd been on pole position for the 1975 race and, in 1976, managed a 7m 07.4s best to line up a mere 0.9s slower than James Hunt's pole position McLaren M23.

Race day at the Nürburgring in 1976 turned out to be depressingly overcast and wet. On the starting grid 23 drivers opted for wet weather tyres, but McLaren number two Jochen Mass, tipped off that the track surface was gradually drying at the other end of the circuit, chose to start on slicks. Regazzoni burst through to lead from the start, although a mighty spin mid-way round the opening lap dropped him way back and it was Ronnie Peterson's March 761 that led at the end of the first 14-mile thrash, with most of the leading competitors pulling off into the pits to change on to slicks. On the second lap Mass was way out in the lead on the damp, but drying surface . . . and then the race was stopped.

Lauda rejoined the race near the back of the field after his pit stop for slicks and was beginning to move up through the ranks of the slower cars as he crossed Adenau bridge and began the gentle climb up towards *Karussell*. But his Ferrari 312T2 never even got as far as the tight right-hander at *Bergwerk*: in an accident witnessed by only a few, and recorded briefly by an amateur film cameraman, Lauda's car went violently out of control on a fast left-hand bend. The most interesting aspect of the accident, and one which tends to absolve Lauda of any responsibility for a driving error, is the fact that the car spun with its tail out to the *left*: on a left-hander, the tail would naturally swing out to the right if the driver was simply losing control. The Ferrari shot through the catch fencing on the outside of the bend, smashed into a rock face, burst into flames and then careered back into the middle of the road where it was hit by Brett Lunger's Surtees TS16. Lauda's helmet was wrenched off in the impact and, before he was extricated from the wreckage thanks to the brave efforts of Arturo Merzario, Guy Edwards, Lunger and a track marshal, the Austrian had inhaled toxic fumes from the wrecked car's glass fibre bodywork. Lauda was removed quickly to hospital and the German Grand Prix restarted: Hunt won the new race with ease from Scheckter and Mass, and Regazzoni's surviving Ferrari T2 ninth after a pit stop.

Lauda hung between life and death for a few days, after which his tremendous will-power quickened the pace of his physical recovery. Once he'd recovered from the effects of the inhalation of those fumes, Niki's other problem was dealing with the unsightly burns that slightly disfigured the upper part of his head and face. In typically casual style, he shrugged them off . . . as late as 1983 he told the writer, "Some people are born ugly. I'm lucky, at least I've now got an excuse for being ugly!" What's more, as history has related time and time again, this remarkable man would be back in the cockpit of a Formula 1 Ferrari less than six weeks after a

Roman Catholic priest administered the last rites to him as he lay in a hospital bed.

Immediately after the German Grand Prix some people came publicly to the conclusion that the Ferrari must have broken its suspension for Lauda to have got involved in such an unlikely accident, and of course such "outrageous" allegations sent Mr. Ferrari into a huff and he declined to send an entry to the Austrian Grand Prix on August 15. A fortnight later he had changed his mind somewhat and Clay Regazzoni turned up at Zandvoort for the Dutch Grand Prix with a lone 312T2: he finished a close second to Hunt's McLaren and an equal distance ahead of Mario Andretti's Lotus 77, but that wasn't deemed a sufficiently impressive result for those behind the scenes at Maranello. Little did the easygoing Swiss know, but by then the decision to replace him for 1977 had long ago been made. The fact that the Ferrari management kept Clay messing about until just before the Japanese Grand Prix before formally releasing him – by which time potentially good alternative drives at McLaren and Brabham had been filled – was symptomatic of that curious, enduring blind spot that the company seemed to sustain towards its drivers. A year later, when Lauda trumped Enzo at his own game, walking out before the end of the season after clinching his second Ferrari World Championship, the Commendatore squealed like a stuck pig. But to keep Regazzoni in suspense for three months saw the boot on the other foot: and that seemed to be quite acceptable behaviour!

After the Dutch Grand Prix at Zandvoort, Carlos Reutemann, disillusioned with his disappointing season behind the wheel of the Brabham-Alfa Romeo BT45, bought his way out of his contract with Bernie Ecclestone and signed up with Ferrari for 1977. As a result, Ferrari found himself having to field three cars in the Italian Grand Prix at Monza, for Lauda, against all the odds, turned up and announced that he was ready to drive again. And drive again he did, magnificently. Twice towards the end of the Grand Prix he set fastest lap, but eventually winner Ronnie Peterson topped his efforts with the March 761. None the less, whilst Regazzoni hammered home second between Peterson and Jacques Laffite's Ligier-Matra JS5, Niki brought the crowds to their feet in typically passionate Latin applause by finishing fourth. Reutemann, troubled by cramp in a cockpit which was far too small for him to fit comfortably, struggled home ninth, already impressed with the Ferrari engine and gearbox after his experiences with the Alfa Romeo.

"I drove the T2 for the first time ever on the Thursday prior to the Italian Grand Prix. I tried it at Fiorano and then it was rushed up to Monza for me to practise the following morning," recalls Carlos, "the engine had an incredible feeling of strength about it, plenty of torque and a superb gearchange . . ." After his Italian Grand Prix outing, Reutemann concentrated on testing at Fiorano for the rest of the season, leaving Lauda and Regazzoni to race together in North America and Japan.

Although Lauda had clearly quickly recovered his ability behind the wheel, the tempo of Ferrari's test and development programme had clearly slowed significantly, even in the six weeks during which he had been absent. Goodyear's rubber had been progressively tailored to suit the McLaren M23, now clearly the car to beat, and at Mosport Park Niki had a difficult time over the bumps to qualify a lowly sixth with Hunt on pole. James won the race in splendidly confident style, fighting off a challenge from Depailler's Tyrrell P34, but a broken rear suspension top link caused Lauda to slow significantly and he finished eighth. Regazzoni squeezed home sixth, but only by dint of pushing Carlos Pace's Brabham-Alfa into the pit wall as the Brazilian made an attempt to overtake!

At Watkins Glen on October 10, the issue in the United States Grand Prix was clear-cut between Hunt's McLaren and Scheckter's Tyrrell, the two swapping places before finishing in that order, and Lauda's Ferrari T2 was an off-the-pace third. Revised front suspension geometry offering more camber change and, consequently, a better chance of warming up the Goodyears, offered Lauda more optimism during practice for the final race of the season, the Japanese Grand Prix, at the Mount Fuji circuit which is within sight of the famous volcanic peak

Continued on page 258

Masterly! Jacky Ickx drove superbly in conditions of streaming rain to win the French Grand Prix at Rouen-les-Essarts in the 1968 312.
Photo: Phipps Photographic

High-winged twilight. Chris Amon's Ferrari 312 is caught during early morning practice for the 1969 Monaco Grand Prix against the backdrop of the Hotel de Paris as he crests the hump out of Casino Square. The following day, the CSI banned the controversial high wings and they were never seen again.
Photo: Nigel Roebuck

One of Chris Amon's greatest races for Ferrari was the 1968 British Grand Prix at Brands Hatch. He finished a splendid second, chasing Jo Siffert's Rob Walker Lotus for all he was worth . . .
Photo: Nigel Roebuck

The controversial prototype Ferrari 312B3 which never raced, seen in a rural Surrey drive on its way to a Japanese collector. The "snowplough" almost finished Forghieri's career, but he survived the storm to prosper again.
Photo: Geoffrey Goddard

The magnificent Ferrari 312B engine installed in one of the 1974 312B3s, photographed at the Nürburgring during the German Grand Prix weekend.
Photo: Geoffrey Goddard

Hurry up! At the start of the 1974 Monaco Grand Prix, Clay Regazzoni jumped into an early lead and rather held up team-mate Niki Lauda for the first part of the race. Here the pair of 312B3s brake for Tabac pursued by Ronnie Peterson's Lotus 72 (the eventual winner) and the Shadow DN3 of Jean-Pierre Jarier.
Photo: Geoffrey Goddard

T2 début: the 1976 312T2 makes its public début at Ferrari's Fiorano test track: the aerodynamic deflectors ahead of the front wheels were subsequently deemed illegal by the CSI and removed.
Photo: Franco Lini

Great drive! Clay Regazzoni neatly turned the tables on Niki Lauda at Long Beach in 1976, winning the United States Grand Prix West in splendid style with this 312T.
Photo: Geoffrey Goddard

TOTAL

Shell
5
C. AMON

GOODYEAR

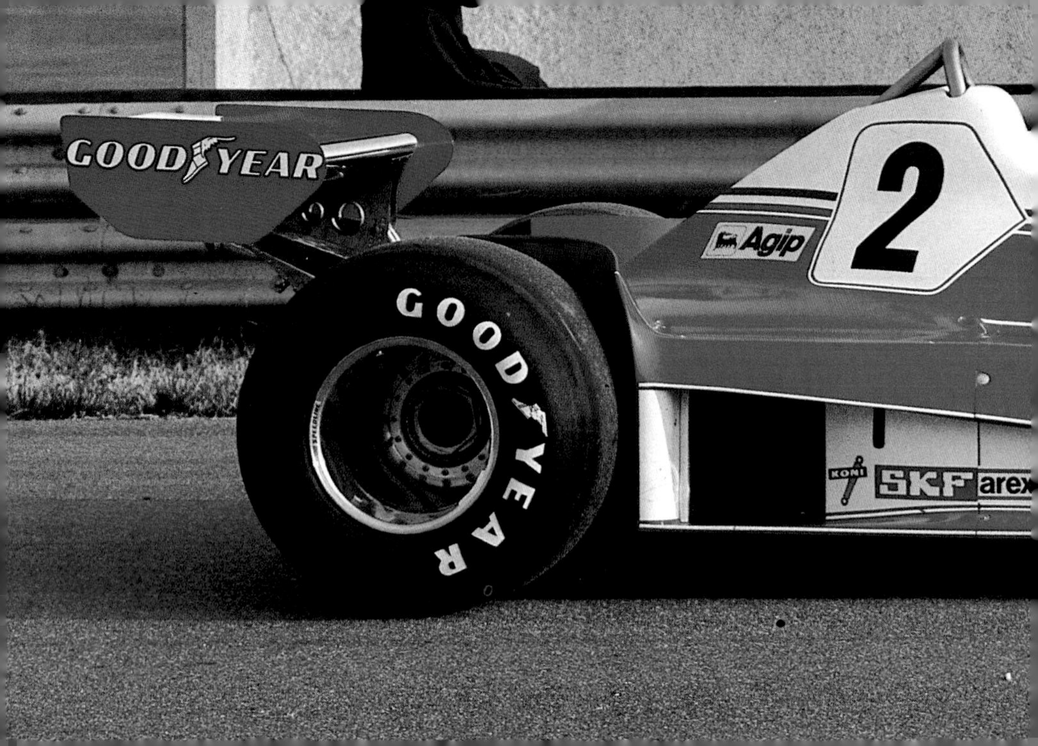
GOODYEAR
2
Agip
GOODYEAR
KONI
SKF
arex

MAGNETI MARELLI
SCHMITTHELM
FERODO
GOODYEAR

2
GOOD YEAR

MICHELIN
11
HEUER
Agip MICHELIN Agip
12

MICHELIN
MICHELIN
BROOKLYN
Agip
11
11
HEUER
MICHELIN
Agip

MICHELIN
Didier Pironi
Agip
Marlboro
CANDY
HARIBO
olivetti LONGINES

TALBOT
28

Shell Oils
Shell
Lucas
FIAT
28
FIAT
27

Shell Oils
EPL International
RENAULT
RENAULT
elf
parmalat
HONDA

GOODYEAR

Marlboro
Agip

EniChe

GOODYEAR

GOODYEAR

SIMPSON

Carlos Reutemann didn't like the Ferrari 312T3 very much, but that didn't prevent him from winning three fine victories with it during 1978. Here he rounds Druids hairpin at Brands Hatch on his way to winning the British Grand Prix.
Photo: LAT Photographic

Gilles Villeneuve shows a clean pair of heels to Jacques Laffite and Jody Scheckter as his 312T4 races away to victory in the 1979 United States Grand Prix West at Long Beach.
Photo: LAT Photographic

Turning the tables: Jody Scheckter on his way to a timely victory in the 1979 Monaco Grand Prix in the Ferrari T4.
Photo: Nigel Snowdon

Didier Pironi tries the Brown Boveri Comprex equipped 126 during practice for the 1982 United States Grand Prix West at Long Beach. Both cars used KKK turbo chargers for the race, however.
Photo: Nigel Snowdon

Mario Andretti made an emotional return to Ferrari at the end of 1982 and delighted the *tifosi* by putting this C2 on pole position for the Italian Grand Prix at Monza. He finished third in the race behind Arnoux's Renault and Tambay in the other Ferrari.
Photo: LAT Photographic

Sweeping through Copse at the start of the 1983 British Grand Prix at Silverstone, the brand new 126C3s of Patrick Tambay and René Arnoux are side by side at the head of the pack. They eventually faded to third and fifth at the finish — the penalty of running with those small centre pillar rear wings perhaps?
Photo: Nigel Snowdon

Ferrari led the final race of the turbo era: in the 1988 Australian Grand Prix at Adelaide, Gerhard Berger abandoned all fuel consumption constraints, elbowing past Prost's McLaren-Honda to run at the front of the field until his F1/87/88C was eliminated in a collision with the Ligier of former *Ferrariste* René Arnoux.
Photo: Nigel Snowdon

Waiting for the off . . . the late lamented Gilles Villeneuve in his C2, Rio de Janeiro, 1982. If ever there was a typical Ferrari driver . . .
Photo: Nigel Snowdon

from which the track gets its name.

Certain elements of the Italian press were now making rather partisan observations in public, effectively "blaming" the Austrian driver for Ferrari's sudden downswing in performance since they felt that Lauda wasn't fully recovered from his injuries. This was arrant nonsense, of course, but it didn't prevent at least a small degree of that scepticism from rubbing off on some Ferrari team members. Hunt qualified on pole at Fuji with Mario Andretti's much-improving Lotus 77 separating the Englishman from his Austrian rival . . . the rest is history. The race took place in quite horrifying conditions of streaming rain, the circuit awash with enormous puddles in many places. Lauda, having survived a heart-stopping slide as he went into the first corner, pulled in and retired at the end of the second lap. Objective to a fault, Lauda reckoned that the conditions were too dangerous: he might also, inwardly, have reckoned the mathematical chances of Hunt finishing the race were a hundred-to-one against. Niki went into that race still holding a three point lead in the World Championship and, although he has denied to the writer on several occasions that any sort of mathematical gamble lay behind his decision to stop, I nevertheless feel that it was perhaps an unconscious factor which prompted his actions.

Of course, Hunt, despite a late-race pit stop to change a deflating Goodyear

which had succumbed to the pressure of hard use on a drying track, slipped home third behind Andretti's Lotus and Depailler's six-wheeled Tyrrell P34. It was sufficient to win him the Drivers' Championship by a single point, but Ferrari's consistency took the Constructors' title back to Maranello for the second successive year.

Lauda stuck to his decision in characteristic style. A year after that Fuji disappointment, when he was World Champion again and on the eve of leaving Maranello to drive for Bernie Ecclestone's Brabham team, he told the author in an *Autocourse* interview:

"Look, at the time I reckon I was right. I still do. You know very well that you thought we were all mad during those first few laps. All right, so everything dried and James was World Champion. But people forget how the conditions were. All right, nothing happened. Hunt was Champion and Lauda the idiot pulled out. But think for a moment. If something had happened. If something had gone wrong with James's pit stop and he would have lost a few more seconds. If, say, somebody had been killed. If I had been champion. Then they would have all been dancing round saying 'Lauda, he's a genius, he's fantastic, what a tactician . . .' But this would have been nonsense because I'm not: it's just not reality to think like that."

Hunt, then Lauda, then Hunt . . . In this picture Lauda leads Hunt in the 1976 Spanish Grand Prix. Hunt won the race with Lauda second, but was temporarily disqualified when his McLaren M23 was discovered to be 1.8 cm too wide. Later, however, controversy led to a Court of Appeal decision to reinstate Hunt.

But within the influential corridors of power at Maranello, Lauda knew that he would be damned . . . until he overturned the prejudice against his decision in Japan by scoring some hard results again. He faced the 1977 season partnered with Reutemann and, even taking Lauda's ability to live with any situation into account, he could well do without the Argentinian on a personal level. The most cutting remark ever credited to Niki involved his South American team-mate. Asked whether he considered Reutemann a team-mate or a rival, the Austrian replied, "Neither."

It was unusual for Lauda to become irritated by individual personalities, but it

Domination, Lauda-style. Niki's 312T2 heads the pack into the first corner of the 1976 Belgian Grand Prix at Zolder, pursued by James Hunt's McLaren M23 and Clay Regazzoni's 312T2.

may be that Reutemann epitomized everything within the Ferrari organization at the start of 1977 which had been stacked against him. By the end of the season, of course, Niki would emerge on top of the situation.

During the winter of '76/'77 Lauda found himself almost pointedly left out of the team's test programme and the 312T2s appeared at Buenos Aires in virtually the same trim as that which they had completed the previous season. The engine department claimed 12bhp more from the flat-12 engine, but otherwise there were no obvious changes. Carrying Fiat identification on their cockpit sides for the first time the T2s qualified quite respectably with Lauda fourth, albeit more than a full second slower than Hunt's pole position Marlboro McLaren M23, and Reutemann seventh. In the race Niki briefly held third place before dropping away and eventually retiring with a fuel metering unit malfunction, leaving his team-mate, who had survived an early spin and a stop to change a blistered front tyre, to finish third behind Jody Scheckter's Wolf WR1 and Carlos Pace's Brabham BT45-Alfa.

Hunt set the pace at Interlagos a couple of weeks later, but Reutemann joined him on the front row with his T2 after a late spurt in the final few minutes of practice. However, Carlos's performance was not an accurate reflection of the Ferrari team's general level of competitiveness and for much of practice both drivers had complained of appalling handling, lack of grip and shortage of speed on the straights. The use of a "demon" rear wing to haul Reutemann on to the front row really put Lauda's back up and he is adamant that he was never offered the use of it: Forghieri contradicts this view, saying that the wing had been sitting in the garage for three days. Either way, Carlos was lucky to get away with it, for a post-practice check revealed the wing to be 4cm too high: nobody worried though!

Reutemann was in with the leading bunch from the start, and as his rivals dropped away with various problems, he assumed a confident and secure lead to the end. Hunt, after a stop for fresh tyres, wound up second while Lauda was third, although he achieved that result by simply existing mid-field as the quicker cars ahead of him dropped out. He was seething with annoyance by the end of the race.

At this point Lauda went straight back to Maranello and abruptly snapped the team out of its somewhat soporific mood. He made Forghieri bring every 312T2 chassis out to Fiorano for exhaustive tests and then continued the programme at Kyalami for a week prior to the South African Grand Prix. By the time official practice started, Lauda's T2 sported revised rear suspension pick-up points, altered bodywork, re-positioned water radiators and a completely new rear wing.

Although Hunt scored his third successive pole position of the season, Lauda quickly picked him off and cantered away to a well-earned victory. Sadly, the race was marred by the bizarre fatal accident to Welshman Tom Pryce, killed at the wheel of his Shadow DN8 when it collided with a young marshal crossing the circuit carrying a fire extinguisher. Debris from the accident was scattered on the start/finish straight and Lauda's Ferrari ran over part of the wrecked Shadow's rollover bar, puncturing its water and oil radiators. With the oil pressure warning light blinking ominously for the last few laps, Lauda eased off slightly and came across the finishing line with most of the car's coolant and lubricant leaked away. It wasn't a day to celebrate, but Niki's performance had proved that he was back in business in a big way. Reutemann finished eighth after a minor collision with Andretti's Lotus 78, but he was never in the same class as his team-mate.

The 1977 season would see Lauda regaining his World Championship crown, although this time he wouldn't exert the same dominance that he had demonstrated with the 312T two years earlier. Colin Chapman was in the process of rewriting the parameters of Formula 1 chassis development with his ground-effect concept, and the Lotus 78 driven by Mario Andretti would undoubtedly have taken the title but for a succession of engine problems, some stemming from the striking new Lotus's marginal cooling system. It's also fair, in retrospect, to say that some designers severely under-estimated the potential advantages that a ground- effect chassis could exert over a conventional car: in 1978 Lotus would therefore catch many of its rivals off their guard when Chapman unveiled the sensational type 79.

Lauda won two more Grands Prix in 1977, well-judged rather than inspired victories at both Hockenheim and Zandvoort. In each case faster cars in front of the Ferrari wilted, but the flat-12's mechanical stamina meant that the Austrian was right there to capitalize on their misfortune. Niki also distinguished himself with a splendid pole position at Long Beach, although he had to give best to Andretti's Lotus 78 in their race-long battle for the lead of the United States Grand Prix West, and there were also fine second places at Monaco, Zolder,

Silverstone and Monza to add to the impressive tally.

However, there were problems looming on the horizon. To start with, it was clear that Goodyear's efforts were being directed towards building tyres with tremendously stiff sidewalls to deal with the down-force developed by the Lotus 78s. This meant that Ferrari gradually found that its 312T2s were experiencing increasing difficulty warming up their rubber to the correct working temperature. Ferrari's relationship with Akron thus became rather strained and it surprised few people when a deal with Michelin for 1978 was forged. On the non-technical front, Lauda's relationship with the Ferrari team, despite his success, was quickly falling apart.

Lauda told *Autocourse*: "One morning I just found myself not feeling about Ferrari as I had felt in the past. Like painters, we drivers have an artistic inclination and are individualists. Our task is to have a free head, come to the race and do more than normal people can manage. But it became like being married to a bad woman. If you're in that situation then you haven't got a clear head, you can't give of your best. I worked there for four years, some good, some bad. But suddenly I realised that I hadn't got the same feeling towards the team as a whole that I had in the past.

"I expect other people around me to try and attain the same high standards that I set for myself. I worked hard this year with the team. I had always been prepared to give 110 per cent to Ferrari, but to do that you have got to be in a very happy situation. You might work all night, for example, for an employer whom you like and get on with well. If you do a normal job, without this special relationship, you simply take the attitude 'well, it's five past five, time to go home'. You need so much to have a good relationship with the person you're driving for in this business.

"As far as Enzo Ferrari was concerned, things began to change this year. Political problems, aggravation, Italian press . . . In the past I'd have done anything he wanted me to do. Suddenly my freedom had gone and I felt I didn't want to do more than normal. But only to do that would mean not to win: I knew that I *had* to work hard to be successful. I realized that if we didn't do what we did in the past, then we wouldn't be successful . . ."

In the middle of the summer, Lauda arranged to drive for Ecclestone's team in 1978 and from that moment onwards it seemed that he was racing against time to win the Championship: if his rivals didn't beat him to it, then the deteriorating atmosphere within the Ferrari camp might scotch his chances anyway. At the end of the day a well-judged drive in streaming rain at Watkins Glen clinched the issue with fourth place in the United States Grand Prix. He then abruptly told Ferrari that he wasn't very well and wouldn't be available to drive for the team in Canada and Japan – a decision fuelled, at least in part, by Ferrari's disgraceful decision to fire Niki's chief mechanic, Ermanno Cuoghi, the night before the Watkins Glen race simply because he indicated that he would be following his driver to Brabham at the end of the season.

Section V: The 3-litre twelves, 1966-80

Chapter 4
A fighting finish for the flat-12

Lauda's departure from the team at least allowed Carlos Reutemann the opportunity to consolidate his reputation in 1978, now partnered by the brilliant young French Canadian Formula Atlantic graduate, Gilles Villeneuve. James Hunt must be given a great deal of the credit for launching Villeneuve on to the Formula 1 scene: at the end of 1976 the Englishman had been invited to drive in the Canadian F/Atlantic race on the *Trois Rivieres* road circuit in Quebec. He returned home enthusing about the speed of this local who had convincingly trounced both him and Alan Jones. As a result of this, Villeneuve was given the opportunity for a sensational début in the British Grand Prix at Silverstone in 1977, but McLaren boss Teddy Mayer, displaying a remarkable lack of perspicacity, did not snap up his services. Ferrari did, and he made his début at the wheel of a 312T2 in the '77 Canadian Grand Prix at Mosport Park.

By this time, the T2 was proving singularly unable to warm its Goodyears up to anywhere near the correct temperature, a task not helped by the bitterly cold weather in North America that autumn. Villeneuve recalled the T2 as feeling "unbelievably bad" as he slipped and slid his way through qualifying in front of his home crowd, crashing the car lightly as he did so. In the race, both he and Reutemann retired, and Carlos's distant second place in the season's finale in Japan did little to hide the Ferrari team's disappointment and dismay when its new recruit drove over the back of Ronnie Peterson's Tyrrell and was launched into a horrifying series of cartwheels which cost the lives of two onlookers who were standing in a prohibited area. As he would so frequently in the future, Gilles walked away unhurt . . .

For the 1978 season, Mauro Forghieri had a brand new chassis design in the

Gilles Villeneuve rounds Brands Hatch's Druids hairpin on his way to victory in the 1979 Race of Champions.

course of completion in which the flat-12 engine would continue into its ninth year of competition. The car wasn't ready for its race début until the South African Grand Prix at Kyalami, third round of the Championship, so Reutemann and Villeneuve relied on Michelin radial-shod 312T2s for the first two races in Argentina and Brazil. At Buenos Aires the T2s sported a slightly wider front and rear track, but they were obviously working on the French radial tyres far more effectively than on Goodyear's cross-ply rubber during the second half of the previous season.

Reutemann, seemingly fated never to get a good result in his home Grand Prix, qualified second alongside Andretti's Lotus 78 and stayed with the American in the opening phase of the race until it became clear that the Ferrari choice of tyre compound had been too conservative. Carlos subsequently became involved in a collision with Jacques Laffite's Ligier-Matra, made a pit stop for fresh, much softer tyres, and then staged a sensational come-back. Demonstrating the sheer undiluted brilliance of which he was so obviously capable, yet so seldom displayed, he slashed through the field from 16th to seventh place at the chequered flag. Villeneuve finished eighth after a smooth and undramatic performance which indicated that the French Canadian had the self-control to keep his brilliant talent under tight rein when necessary.

The 1978 Brazilian Grand Prix departed with tradition, foregoing the Interlagos circuit at Sao Paulo for the flat, uninspiring, but insufferably hot Autodromo Riocentro on the fringes of Rio de Janeiro. On this occasion, Reutemann simply drove the opposition into the ground. Fourth on the grid, headed by the Lotus 78s of Peterson and Andretti, plus Hunt's McLaren M26, the dusky Argentinian streaked into the lead at the start and drove away into the distance with consummate ease. It wasn't simply a case of Michelin tyre superiority, although there's no doubt that the Goodyears were outclassed in the sub-tropical temperatures: at the end of the race Reutemann stepped from the car without a trace of sweat or over-exertion. Bred in a broiling South American climate, for Carlos, the Brazilian Grand Prix had simply been a pleasant demonstration run on an autumn afternoon!

Villeneuve got involved in a collision with Ronnie Peterson (again) before spinning into the catch fencing at the end of the long back straight, thus giving his critics more welcome ammunition.

Built round a brand new monocoque, the Ferrari 312T3 made its début at Kyalami and enjoyed a less-than-auspicious race. Designed by Forghieri to cater for the specific characteristics of Michelin radial tyres, it was very different to the car which it succeeded. The T2 front suspension, with its tiny coil springs operated by long fabricated rocker arms, was gone for good. In its place Forghieri had opted for tubular front rocker arms actuated much bigger coil spring/damper units which were now mounted on a bracket outside the monocoque footwell wall. At the rear the suspension was unremarkable, a transverse top link with radius arms and outboard mounted spring/damper units. The water and oil radiators were still mounted within the side pods, but the upper body aerodynamics provided a contrast: the T2's rounded, flowing lines gave way to a square-cut, predominantly flat body top and engine cover, maximizing the air flow both over and under the centre pillar rear wing.

The Ferrari T3s displayed very promising form during pre-race testing at Kyalami but encountered serious tyre troubles in the race, preventing either driver from demonstrating the car's true potential. Reutemann, in any case, was not convinced that the new car represented any significant improvement over the T2 and the Argentinian's attitude was destined to cause bad feeling with Forghieri as the season progressed. By the time Ronnie Peterson was forcing his Lotus 78 ahead of Patrick Depailler's Tyrrell 008 during a last-lap cliffhanger, Reutemann had slid into the catch fencing at Crowthorne corner – ironically, on an oil slick dropped by his team-mate.

The team didn't have long to wait before exacting its revenge. At Long Beach on April 2, Reutemann and Villeneuve had got on top of the tyre compound selection

HELIN
Agip

The 1979 Ferrari 312T4 had a single, central fuel cell and as narrow a monocoque as the flat-12 engine would allow in order to generate as much ground-effect as possible. Below, the T4 engine installation is seen at Monza by which time the brakes had been moved to an outboard position and this car was used by Jody Scheckter to win the race, clinching his Championship title.

problem. Carlos grabbed pole position for the United States Grand Prix West and his vastly less experienced team-mate lined up alongside him in second place: but the run down to the first corner, between unyielding concrete barriers, saw the positions reversed a matter of seconds after the race began.

John Watson made an ambitious, perhaps precarious, run up the inside of the Ferraris as they went into that tight hairpin – and nearly lost control of his Brabham BT46-Alfa in the process. Lauda's Brabham and Reutemann's Ferrari were both forced out on to a wide line, allowing Villeneuve to nip round on the inside line into the lead. For the next 39 laps the Grand Prix fraternity was obliged to sit up and take notice as the confident little French Canadian held off every challenge thrown at him by his more exalted and experienced colleagues. Both Brabham-Alfas retired with niggling, minor problems, and despite a challenge from Alan Jones's impressive Cosworth-engined Saudia Williams FW06, it didn't look as though anything would stand between Gilles and his first Grand Prix triumph. Then, after a momentary misjudgement, the race was handed as a gift into Reutemann's hands. Lapping Regazzoni's slow Shadow DN8, Gilles miscalculated things a fraction, vaulted over the backmarker's left rear wheel, and slammed his Ferrari into a tyre barrier on the outside of a slow corner. But Gilles Villeneuve had made his mark . . .

A spate of tyre problems, allied to the fact that they were pitched up against the sensational Lotus 79 in the battle for Championship honours, compromised the Ferrari team's efforts for the remainder of the season. None the less, both Reutemann and Villeneuve drove magnificently. Monaco was a disaster, with Reutemann's pole position T3 getting nudged at the first corner by Lauda's Brabham, thus puncturing a tyre and dropping the Argentinian from contention. Later in the race Villeneuve suffered a tyre deflation in the tunnel, emerging into the daylight on three wheels before slithering to a standstill at the chicane.

The remainder of the season was patchy, fortunes varying dramatically depending on the suitability of Michelin's rubber. Villeneuve consolidated his reputation with a splendid chase of Andretti's superior-handling Lotus 79 in the Belgian Grand Prix at Zolder, although a tyre deflation obliged him to pit for fresh rubber and he finished up fourth behind Mario, Peterson and Reutemann. At Jarama, Anderstorp and Paul Ricard the car/tyre combinations were quite simply hopeless: Reutemann made five pit stops for fresh rubber in the French Grand Prix and, having almost run out of tyres and ideas, the Ferrari team fitted a set of super-soft qualifiers at that final stop, at least enabling their driver to salvage fastest lap from this débâcle!

Yet at Brands Hatch, venue for the British Grand Prix, Reutemann and Ferrari produced one of their most impressive performances of the season. Although not in the same league as the Lotus 79s (nobody was!) Carlos moved into contention behind Niki Lauda's Brabham BT46. When the two cars lapped Bruno Giacomelli's Marlboro McLaren M26 at Clearways, going on to the start/finish straight, Lauda momentarily hesitated . . . and went for the outside line. Reutemann put the two right-hand wheels of his T3 on the grass and opted for the inside, and correct, line. He was through into the lead and, despite shattering the lap record in the closing stages, Lauda was unable to get back on terms with the Ferrari.

Despite his success in chalking up his third Grand Prix victory of the season, Reutemann's criticism of the T3 had made him *persona non grata* with Forghieri and the next thing Carlos knew were rumours as to how he was being replaced for 1979.

"I honestly never felt the T3 was as good a car as the T2," Reutemann reflected with a degree of candour that was to aid his downfall, "and that's why my victory in the British Grand Prix was so satisfying. It didn't seem to me that any adjustments to the chassis made any difference. The car just understeered and that's all there was to it: and when we fitted it with skirts, it just understeered all the more. I disagreed with Forghieri a lot of the time because I told him that I felt it would never be a proper ground- effect car and that was the end of the matter. And I

MICHELIN

Team discipline. Gilles Villeneuve followed team orders scrupulously at Monaco in 1979.

don't think he was too pleased when my choice of hard compound Michelins for Brands Hatch turned out to be the correct one. He wanted me to run soft compounds, but I stuck to my opinion and eventually got my way. The first I knew that I might be replaced in 1979 was when Jody Scheckter rang up and began discussing things about the new season. Nobody at Maranello had even mentioned anything about it at that time . . ."

By the end of the European season Reutemann had come to understand that he wasn't going to be included in Ferrari's 1979 scheme of things. Although the team fared badly at Hockenheim, Villeneuve managed to come through to a fine third place in the wet Austrian Grand Prix at the Österreichring, but Carlos was disqualified for receiving assistance from a marshal following a spin on the wet track. Villeneuve continued to underline his brilliant potential by battling long and hard for the lead of the Italian Grand Prix at Monza, but Mario Andretti's Lotus 79 eventually defeated him in a straight battle. Sadly, the two men were penalized for jumping the start and eventually found themselves rewarded with sixth and seventh places at the end of the day. What's more, it was a day to forget: the Monza race was marred by that tragic multi-car pile-up in the opening few seconds after the start which resulted in the death of everybody's favourite driver, Ronnie Peterson. The event was prematurely stopped and then restarted: it was then, in those stress-laden and tense moments after this tragedy, that Mario and Gilles inadvertently went a fraction before the starter's signal.

In North America, the last two races of the year were Ferrari showpiece demonstrations. At Watkins Glen, Carlos Reutemann sought to indicate to those in power at Maranello that they were making a big mistake getting rid of him. He defeated Mario Andretti on home ground to score a fine win in the United States Grand Prix, although the World Champion elect was using his team-mate's car after his regular chassis broke a stub-axle and shed a wheel during the pre-race warm-up session. Villeneuve was following in his team-mate's wheel tracks for 23 laps before his flat-12 suffered a piston failure.

Seven days later, on Montreal's Ile Notre Dame circuit which was being used to host the Canadian Grand Prix for the first time, Villeneuve gave his excited countrymen precisely what they wanted. Although unable to keep up with Jean-Pierre Jarier's Lotus 79 in the opening stages (the Frenchman had been recruited to take Ronnie Peterson's place in the team), Gilles kept in touch in second place and surged through to score an historic victory when the faster Lotus stopped with a terminal oil leak. Villeneuve had arrived: following him dutifully home was his new team-mate Scheckter, having his last drive for Wolf, and his outgoing partner Reutemann in the other 312T3. What better rewards could 1979 possibly hold in store?

On reflection, one could only sit back and praise the achievements of the Scuderia in 1979. Using the ultimate flat-12 engined machine, the 312T4, the World Driver's Championship fell to Jody Scheckter, the South African driver thus defeating the predictions of his many critics who felt that the combination of Ferrari's collective Latin temperament and Scheckter's sometimes abrasive South African frankness would be a recipe for disaster.

Jody had joined Ferrari after a two year spell driving for Walter Wolf's impressive independent team, during which time he had been privileged to try the Wolf WR1 at the Fiorano test facility: whether that was due to Wolf's personal good relationship with Ferrari, or an opportunity to "size up" the South African disguised as a gesture of generosity, we'll never really know. Jody knew full-well that life might be difficult at Ferrari, particularly when he was paired with an obvious new star like Villeneuve, but he reckoned he had made the correct decision; even when the striking new 312T4 wasn't ready for the opening races of the season, and the two men were obliged to rely on the old T3s.

Scheckter's début for Ferrari didn't really bode well for the future. In a first corner pile-up which resulted in the Argentine Grand Prix at Buenos Aires being stopped and restarted, Jody hurt his wrist when his "skirted" T3 made violent contact with John Watson's Marlboro McLaren M28. After being examined by the

Villeneuve dutifully followed Scheckter home at Monza, knowing full-well that all he had to do to be Champion was to overtake his team-mate. That he didn't, demonstrated that Gilles was a man of honour .

circuit doctor, Scheckter wasn't permitted to take part in the "fresh" Grand Prix. With Villeneuve eventually retiring his T3 with engine failure after a spin and a stop for fresh rubber, the opening race of the season had proved to be a pretty comprehensive catastrophe for Maranello.

The outcome was improved, but not very much, when the team assembled for the Brazilian Grand Prix at Interlagos. In the race both T3s wore out their Michelins quite dramatically and were obliged to stop for fresh rubber to be fitted: Gilles eventually led Jody across the line in fifth and sixth places, one full lap down on Jacques Laffite's winning Ligier-Cosworth JS11/15.

Let off the leash! Gilles Villeneuve's 312T4 battling bravely with Alan Jones's more ground-effective Williams FW07 in the 1979 Canadian Grand Prix at Montreal. Jones got through to win, but Villeneuve kept him on his toes all the way to the flag!

Although it had been seen at an official press conference in Italy earlier in the year, Forghieri's new 312T4 didn't make a competitive appearance until Kyalami. The finished products reflected the enormous amount of work which had been carried out in the Pininfarina wind tunnel as the Ferrari design team worked feverishly to produce as effective a ground-effect machine as possible within the constraints imposed by the wide flat-12 cylinder engine.

The finished article was nearly 10in longer overall than the car it replaced but its wheelbase was less than 6in longer at 106.4in to the T3's 100.8in. The cockpit was positioned virtually centrally within the wheelbase and the fuel load was right behind the cockpit in a single cell. The T4's sculpted under-side curved downwards from each outer extremity to meet in the centre at what looked like a central backbone or keel. The T4 followed its predecessor's style inasmuch as the upper body panelling was notably flat, but visually it was still a distinctively different machine. The water radiator found its home in the left-hand side pod while the oil cooler was in a corresponding position on the right-hand side.

The inboard mounted front suspension was broadly similar to that employed on the T3, although the T4's footwell was narrower and the spring/damper units were tucked in as close as possible to the monocoque's outer wall in order to minimize the disturbance to the air flow beneath the car. At the rear, the coil spring/damper units were also mounted inboard, running in their own channels within the casting behind the rear axle line, and were operated by tubular rocker arms similar to those employed at the front.

Most people admired the 312T4 as a functional and effective machine, but it certainly wasn't terribly attractive. Scheckter and Villeneuve, however, working on the basis of Denny Hulme's old adage "if she wins the race, she'll be the most beautiful bloody car in the world!" might have felt differently. Jody qualified his T4 in second place to Jean-Pierre Jabouille's Renault Elf turbo on the front row of the grid, with Gilles tucked inside on the second row in third place. The race started as a bit of a fiasco with everybody on slicks when a blanket of torrential rain doused the circuit as the field completed its first lap: the red flag was immediately shown at the end of lap three and the whole affair came to a premature end.

At the restart tyre choice was crucial, Villeneuve romping into an immediate lead when the green light was shown, building up an impressive lead on wet-weather rubber until lap 15 when he made a quick stop for slicks. Jody, who had started on slicks, assumed a half minute advantage when his team-mate stopped, but towards the end of the race his tyres were in bad shape as he fought to fend off Villeneuve's counter-attack. Consequently, a quick stop for fresh Michelins dropped him to second place and he was 4s behind Gilles when the chequered flag came out.

To Scheckter's tremendous and enduring credit, he never voiced the slightest complaint that Villeneuve hadn't let him through again, and he behaved with similar dignity when his team-mate dished out another defeat for him in the United States Grand Prix at Long Beach. For this event the 312T4s were fitted with street circuit rear wings mounted ahead of the rear axle line, their end plates fixed to the outer extremities of the car's bodywork. It was difficult to see precisely how Villeneuve could do anything wrong this year, particularly as he added the non-title 40-lap Race of Champions to his tally at Brands Hatch shortly afterwards, winning at the wheel of the skirted "T3½" against an admittedly less than representative field.

However, Scheckter retained all his confidence as he was to tell *Autocourse* in his World Champion interview at the end of the season!

"I'd made the decision to join Ferrari and that was that. Now it may sound funny, but I don't care whether a car is good or bad once I've signed a contract. If it is bad, then I just consider that I'm unlucky and I've made a bad decision. But I've got to live with that. The time to worry is when you're negotiating contracts at the start of the season. Meanwhile, you've just got to do the best you can.

"But Ferrari has been good. I thought things would be difficult but I didn't find it anywhere near as difficult as I'd been told. I've enjoyed myself this year, even though I felt, if I hadn't been enjoying things, I'd have still got myself into one of the best cars with the best teams in the business. But as it's turned out, I have enjoyed myself.

"As far as Gilles is concerned, I'd have probably won the Championship earlier if I hadn't had such a fast team-mate. But he has made some mistakes, mistakes which have probably cost him a chance of the Championship. I just wanted to do things my way. Do what I had to do and try my best. And it all worked out alright. I didn't get flustered under pressure and try too hard and start crashing, which, on the face of it, I might have done with Gilles going down so quickly. Here I was, the

Gilles Villeneuve at the wheel of the unloved 312T5 during the 1980 Brazilian Grand Prix at Interlagos. Although quicker than the Championship-winning T4, Ferrari was left far behind in the ground-effect technology race and the flat-12 era consequently ended on a low note.

established driver, apparently getting blown off by Gilles . . .

"Gilles is good, very good, but I see things in his driving that I used to do when I was younger. He regularly drops wheels in the dirt, but I try to keep the car off the kerbs. Sure, he kept up the pressure, but I was always confident."

Michelin's staying power in really hot weather was proving somewhat questionable, so Scheckter was fortunate to emerge from the Spanish Grand Prix at Jarama with fourth place. But he won a somewhat fortunate victory in the Belgian Grand Prix at Zolder, a race which might have gone Villeneuve's way had he not tangled with Clay Regazzoni's Saudia Williams FW07 on the opening lap and damaged the Ferrari's nose section badly enough to require a pit stop for attention. As Jody took the chequered flag, Gilles seemed on course for a fine fourth place after a magnificent climb back through the field, but his hard driving took its toll on the T4's fuel consumption and Villeneuve ran out on the last lap!

From pole position, Scheckter then moved ahead to completely dominate the Monaco Grand Prix, Villeneuve moving up to sit on his tail before transmission problems ended his protective presence behind the South African. Towards the end of the race Clay Regazzoni's Williams counter-attacked superbly, but Scheckter knew precisely what the situation was and kept control to win by half a second.

Probably Gilles's most memorable drive of all came at Dijon-Prenois in the closing stages of the French Grand Prix where, despite badly worn Michelins, he broke up a potential Renault Elf 1-2 by defeating René Arnoux in a hectic, wheel-banging final two laps which had everybody in the place on their feet

BROO
LYN
CHEWIM
G GUM
Agip
CHAMPION
Lockheed

Desolation! A stunned Jody Scheckter stands in the Montreal pit lane alongside his unloved 312T5 seconds after being told that he has failed to qualify for the 1980 Canadian Grand Prix, penultimate race of his career.

cheering madly. For the next few races the T4s demonstrated consistency and reliability rather than any great flair: they were not true ground-effect cars by the standards of some of their Cosworth-engined rivals, but they did have tremendously powerful, torquey engines which put them in a competitive situation on circuits with tight corners. Scheckter was fifth at Silverstone, fourth in Austria and a magnificent second at Zandvoort where an overheating clutch had dropped him to the tail of the field on the opening lap. By this stage in the season the Williams FW07 was very much proving itself to be *the* car of the season, but Ferrari's early success meant Scheckter was able to clinch his World Championship title at Monza. In front of delighted locals, Jody and Gilles fought off challenges from Arnoux's Renault and Laffite's Ligier to come home first and second, Villeneuve dutifully playing the number two role to his team-mate just as Jody had been forced to do at Kyalami and Long Beach. This time, however, things were slightly different, because Gilles was right behind the South African for much of the way, knowing that all he had to do to be World Champion was to pass him . . . The fact that he didn't, just as Ronnie Peterson had been content to defer to Mario Andretti at Lotus during the 1978 season, marked out Gilles Villeneuve as a man of integrity as well as a brilliant racing driver. That sort of integrity wasn't shared by others he was to encounter, as Gilles would later find out.

Jody had employed a revised T4B at Monza, incorporating revised rear suspension, new exhausts, outboard-mounted rear brakes and twin calipers all round. It proved ideal for the task in hand and, once Jody's Championship was secure, Villeneuve was free to "go for broke" without any constraints on his performance. Starting from second place on the starting grid at the Canadian Grand Prix, Gilles shot into the lead from the beginning of this race round the Ile Notre Dame circuit and seemed determined to repeat his previous year's success at the wheel of the T3. But eventually Alan Jones forced his Saudia Williams FW07 through into the lead as they went into the tight 180-degree corner before the pits. Once through, Jones found it absolutely impossible to shake the Ferrari from his tail and the two cars finished first and second with only a few lengths between them. A week later Villeneuve got his own back at Watkins Glen where he splashed to a splendid triumph in the pouring rain, Jones's prospects ruined by a fumbled tyre change in the pits which saw the Williams shed a rear wheel half a lap after rejoining the fray . . .

It was the end of a golden year for Ferrari, but by now Forghieri and his colleagues were hard at work on the 120-degree V6 1½-litre turbocharged engine which would eventually take over as the team's spearhead at the start of 1981. That meant that the normally aspirated flat-12 engines would have to last the team throughout 1980 and the net result turned out to be nothing short of a disaster. It seemed impossible to believe that a heavily-revamped version of the T4 could be a total disaster, but that's how racing history will record the 312T5.

Thanks to a combination of mechanical unreliability and Michelin tyre troubles, the famous Ferrari flat-12 engine went out with a miserable whimper rather than a spectacular bang. For the 1980 season the team dismantled three T4s and rebuilt them to T5 specification. This included much slimmer front ends to the monocoques, new bodywork, suspension geometry and aerofoils. There were also some early experiments with new cylinder heads incorporating valves positioned at a very wide angle to save width on the engine as a whole in order that every possible square inch could be squeezed out of the under body sections in the interests of ground-effect. Unfortunately these revised heads caused so much mechanical unreliability that they were abandoned by Monaco and never seen again.

Alan Jones's Williams dominated the opening Argentine Grand Prix at Buenos Aires, both T5s retiring. Scheckter's suffered engine failure, while the irrepressible Villeneuve was tramping on hard in second place when a steering arm breakage hurled him off the circuit into the catch fencing. At the Brazilian Grand Prix, Gilles made a stupendous effort to lead the first five-mile lap of

Interlagos, but fell back through the field as his tyres deteriorated: eventually he was obliged to stop for fresh rubber and finally quit with a throttle malfunction that threw him into a nasty spin. Scheckter? Another broken engine . . .

Cosmetic changes were made to the T5s throughout the season, but nothing could mask their basic lack of competitiveness – nor their inability to get the best out of Michelin's rubber which was now, understandably, being tailored to suit the increasingly competitive Renault turbos. An integral component in every race turned out to be Ferrari pit stops for new tyres, so it should be recorded that Villeneuve's sixth places at Zolder and Hockenheim were achieved *despite* his "routine" stop, a quite remarkable reflection of his ability and refusal to accept any prospect of defeat.

Scheckter, on the other hand, simply couldn't motivate himself properly to race for 10th place with the same gusto and commitment that he used to put into battles for victory. By his own frank admission, the "pure pleasure" aspect of race driving had long dimmed in his own mind, so this dismal season with the 312T5 prompted him to announce that he would retire from the sport at the end of the 1980 season. This decision had finally been sealed when his T5 qualified last-but-one on the grid for the British Grand Prix at Brands Hatch and confirmed as correct in his own mind when he failed to qualify at Montreal in bitterly cold weather conditions.

Villeneuve dauntlessly fought a "rear guard" action on Ferrari's behalf, getting up to fourth place at Imola (venue for that year's Italian Grand Prix) in the opening stages before a massive accident, caused by tyre failure, finished his race and destroyed his car. "When I opened my eyes after the impact, I couldn't see anything," he remember later, "but I could hear cars rushing past . . . I was sure worried, I can tell you!" His performance on home ground, when he finished fifth at Montreal in the T5 after another classic climb through the field, was probably as good a drive as any other during his entire career.

In the final race of the season, at Watkins Glen, Gilles damaged his T5 when he clipped a kerb and was forced to retire, while Scheckter rounded off his Formula 1 season with a smooth, undramatic race into 11th place – the final finisher in the event. That was the end of the South African's final appearance as a professional racing driver – and the flat-12 engine's last outing in a motor race.

Eleven seasons had passed since Ickx's 312B1 made its first promising début in the sunshine at Kyalami, and those racing years had seen the most sustained period of success for Ferrari's Grand Prix cars. Out of 169 World Championship races, the flat-12 engined cars had won a staggering 37 victories – not to mention four World Constructors' Championship titles. But at the end of the day, whilst the engine had proved to be the marque's strongest point throughout this era, the chassis had ended up proving its weakest aspect.

However, a new era was beckoning – one which would place increased emphasis on engine technology and thus, in theory at least, would suit Maranello down to the ground.

Section VI: Into the turbocharged future: The 126 V6s, 1980-84

Chapter 1
A new V6 for the eighties

Beyond question, Forghieri's 3-litre 180-degree 12-cylinder engine was the most remarkably effective of all Ferrari Formula 1 power units. It had won its first Grand Prix at the Österreichring in 1970 in the hands of Jacky Ickx and scored its final triumph at Watkins Glen in 1979 thanks to the efforts of Gilles Villeneuve. But although it was still probably the most powerful normally aspirated Grand Prix engine around in 1980, the failure of the 312T4 chassis to match up to the rival ground-effect products from British constructors, meant that the flat-12 entered a depressing twilight zone. The prevailing technical trend with Formula 1 was clearly going to be the development of turbocharged 1½-litre engines, notwithstanding the bitching and binding from many British teams, and Ferrari attacked the task of building a completely new unit with some relish.

It was during the summer of 1980 that Ferrari first showed his 1½-litre turbocharged car and Gilles Villeneuve delighted the crowds at Imola, venue for that year's Italian Grand Prix, by appearing at the wheel of the second-such car during second practice on Saturday September 13. Villeneuve and Scheckter were still concentrating their racing efforts on the old T5s, but it was quite clear that Gilles couldn't wait to get his hands on the new car. To say that the first 126C (for *Competizione*, not *Compressore*, according to the Commendatore at the time) was something in the nature of a travelling test bed would be something of an understatement. The chassis construction followed typical Maranello lines with a multi-tubular spaceframe overlaid with stressed alloy sheeting: the suspension was by means of rocker arms operating inboard coil spring/dampers all round, but the whole affair looked a bit crude and makeshift.

Not so the 120-degree, 81 x 48.4mm, 1496.43cc engine which was being fussed over by the team's technicians with all the affection of a mother for a new baby. This four-cam unit had its inlet camshafts on the outside and exhaust camshafts on the inside of the vee, enabling short exhaust pipes from each bank to feed into the turbines and compressors mounted just behind the large central fuel cell. The outlets from the turbines ran rearwards into turbocharger boost pressure relief valves and there were short tail pipes just ahead of the final drive unit.

Air intakes for the compressors were mounted on each side of the fuel tank and the compressed air fed out into intercoolers mounted in the side pods: from there the inlet manifolds ran rearwards with individual inlet pipes running upwards under the cylinder head. A transverse gearbox was employed and the car was officially quoted at the time as having the same 106.3in (2700mm) wheelbase as the 312T5: the engine itself weighed in at 375 pounds (175kg) (as compared with the flat-12's 353lb/160kg) and had a claimed power output of 540bhp at between 11,500 and 12,000rpm.

Marlboro
WORLD CHAMPIONSHIP TEAM
Ferrari

The Brown-Boveri Comprex pressure wave super-charging system was tested by Ferrari exhaustively over the winter of 1980/81, but never saw race action. As this photograph shows, the Comprex sat high in the 126 engine bay and Maranello's engineers quickly decided that the KKK turbocharged route would reap bigger dividends in the long term.

Although the handling of the first 126C wasn't terribly impressive round Imola, Villeneuve revelled in the power available to him and recorded a 1m 35.751s during qualifying which was 0.6s faster than he managed in the T5, although he raced the flat-12 engined car in the race. This time compared with the 1m 33.988s managed by René Arnoux's pole position Renault Elf RE25, but although the new Ferrari clearly wasn't in the same league as the much more experienced French turbo team on this occasion, the 126C *was* quicker than many Cosworth engined machines "straight out of the box" which was something for Maranello to feel encouraged about.

Over the winter of 1980/81 the new Ferrari took part in a large number of development test sessions, apart from the work carried out back in the competition department of the Maranello factory. Not only was more work carried out with turbocharged versions of the V6, using turbochargers from Kuhnle, Kopp and Kausch, the specialist company based at Eperspach in Germany, but Forghieri and his colleagues took the opportunity to examine the potential of a new system of forced induction developed by the Swiss Brown-Boveri organization.

Brown-Broveri, whose work in the marine and railway gas turbine world has been well-known and respected for many years, had developed their "pressure wave supercharging" system primarily for an application in commercial diesel

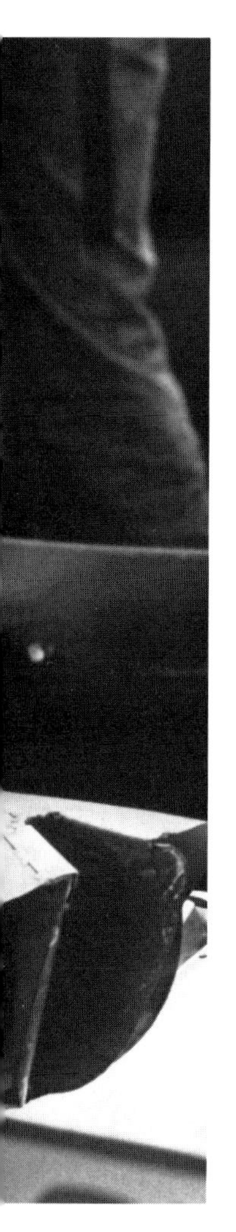

engines. Their "Comprex" system is a directly driven supercharger, the exhaust gases providing the pressure waves to compress the incoming air as it enters the inlet manifold. Unlike the exhaust-driven turbocharger KKK system, the Comprex had no lag while the turbine/compressor unit gains speed when the throttles are opened and the exhaust gases begin their work.

Winter tests with the Comprex indicated that there might be some long-term potential to be realized from the system and Ferrari concluded a deal with Brown-Boveri for the exclusive racing application of the system until the end of 1981. Both Gilles Villeneuve and his new French team-mate Didier Pironi, who replaced Jody Scheckter on his retirement at the end of 1980, reported to Forghieri that they were impressed with the immediate throttle response when they tried this new system at both Paul Ricard and Ferrari's own Fiorano test facility over the winter, so the team arrived at the opening 1981 race, Long Beach, with both forced induction systems on hand.

One unfortunate problem with the Comprex turned out to be related to its installation in a racing chassis and, as it turned out, its *lack* of development potential. The heavy supercharger sat high in the vee of the Ferrari engine, upsetting the 126's weight distribution, a pressurized rotating drum accepting fresh air at one end and exhaust gases into the other. The pressure waves of the exhaust gases compressed the fresh air as it passed into the drum and out again at the same end, while the spent exhaust gases also exited at the same end as they entered. The drum was driven by a toothed belt from an exposed jack shaft running along the top of the engine from the camshaft drive at the rear. The exhaust ports of the engine were on the inside of the vee, as with the turbocharged machine, feeding straight up into the supercharger. Pressurized air was fed forwards into the primary intercooler from where it was channelled into secondary intercoolers on either side of the car, thence into the inlet manifolds on the outside of the vee. Those spent exhaust gases exited by means of a large megaphone with an internal baffle and those lucky enough to be at Long Beach (or at any of the winter test sessions) recall with pleasure the shrill, crisp shriek of the Comprex Ferrari V6. Unfortunately, despite a great deal of assistance from Brown-Boveri, who sent technicians to the races and test outings, Ferrari quickly came to the conclusion that the KKK turbocharged system had more potential so the Comprex was never raced. From the response the author has received on the subject, it seems clear that Brown-Boveri would prefer to forget the whole episode!

The 126CK (as the turbo Ferrari was dubbed) still had considerable shortcomings in the chassis department and its throttle response problems made it a difficult proposition for its two drivers. Such theoretical handicaps didn't prevent Villeneuve in particular from driving right on, and often just over, his very high limits and it can be recorded that the Ferrari turbo actually led its first race. From his starting position on the inside of the third row at Long Beach, the ebullient Gilles hurtled into the lead down the outside going into the first hairpin: he was going far too quickly to make the corner with his advantage intact, though, and ran wide into the escape road, allowing several other cars to go by. Gilles eventually retired with transmission failure while Pironi, who was racing expertly with Mario Andretti's Alfa Romeo V12, lasted some while longer than his team-mate before succumbing to engine failure.

From sunny California, the World Championship field journeyed on to Brazil and Argentina where both cars were badly off the pace, the drivers wrestling gamely with chassis that were quite simply not up to the job. Villeneuve retired in Brazil with a broken turbocharger wastegate and was sidelined with a broken drive shaft in Buenos Aires: Pironi spun off the circuit at Rio, collecting Alain Prost's Renault in the process, and suffered engine failure only three laps into the Argentine race.

By the time the team appeared on home soil for the first San Marino Grand Prix at Imola, fourth round in the Championship and first race in Europe, the 126CKs had undergone plenty of subtle chassis alterations. Villeneuve's race chassis had

Gilles Villeneuve's performances in 1981 helped sustain the Ferrari team's morale at a time when the new 126CK was experiencing a troubled development period.

revised front suspension pick-up points and a longer wheelbase, but the French Canadian found that he really preferred the team's shorter wheelbase spare. And it was this machine which he employed, much to the crowd's delight, to snatch pole position from Reutemann's Williams FW07C, turning a 1m 34.523s to the Argentinian's 1m 35.229s. It was only Ferrari's fifth "turbo race" . . .

The race started in wet conditions with Villeneuve and Pironi going straight into first and second places. Gilles led for 14 laps before deciding that the track was drying out sufficiently to warrant a change to slicks: he dived straight in for them, only to emerge on dry tyres as the rain started again. Immediately, without any hesitation, he stopped again for wet tyres and then began the long hard grind back up into contention. Pironi drove splendidly: grappling with deteriorating tyres, a broken side skirt (these were the days of ground-effect, remember!), he held station until lap 47 when he had to give best to Nelson Piquet's infinitely more agile Brabham BT49C. By the finish, Didier had also dropped back behind Riccardo Patrese's Arrows A3 and Carlos Reutemann's Williams: Villeneuve, meanwhile, had been opposite-locking his way back through the field to finish a crowd-pleasing seventh. Few people left Imola without getting the message. Ferrari's new turbocharged engine was now running reliably – in its fourth race.

As far as many teams were concerned, the 1981 season will be recalled as a time of strife and irritation as their designers spent most of their time trying to circumvent the absurd 6cm ground clearance rule which had been introduced by the FISA in an attempt to control the spiralling lap speeds generated by ground-effect cars. For Ferrari, of course, chassis and engine development went hand-in-hand, and Maranello derived more satisfaction from making its superb V6 engine function reliably than any "rule dodging" its rivals might find themselves embroiled in.

Of course, the Ferrari 126CK chassis was never really a particularly efficient ground-effect proposition and its two most memorable outings came as the result of Gilles Villeneuve's dauntless enthusiasm, flair and determination. The Belgian Grand Prix at Zolder was nothing special for Maranello, although fourth for Villeneuve and eighth for Pironi underlined the car's reliability. Then came Monaco and Jarama, the two unforgettable jewels in Gilles Villeneuve's crown.

For Monaco the 126CKs had been fitted with revised camshafts to improve the engine torque characteristics, but no matter how one sliced it, there was no way that these relatively heavy cars with their thirsty turbocharged engines and less-than-instantaneous throttle response should have been on a par with the Brabham BT49C employed by Nelson Piquet. There had also been changes to the hydro-pneumatic "cheat" suspension systems to deal with the continuing 6cm ground clearance fiasco, but it was Villeneuve's brilliant driving which won the day. He qualified a remarkable second on 1m 25.788s, a whisker behind Nelson Piquet's BT49C (1m 25.710s) and he heaved the 126CK round Monaco initially in second place behind the Brazilian, then third as Alan Jones's Williams FW07C came racing up through the field to do battle with his Brabham arch-rival.

Under pressure from Jones, Piquet made a slight error and slid into the guard rails and it looked virtually certain that the rugged Australian would now win with no trouble. But the first signs of an engine misfire prompted Jones to make an understandable, but incorrect, decision: he came into the pits to take on a few gallons of fuel, assuming his was a fuel system problem. His advantage over Villeneuve had been slashed from 30 to six seconds as a result of this stop, but still the engine misfired . . .

At the end of lap 72, Villeneuve aimed his 126CK up the inside of the white and green Williams as the two cars screamed past the pits: there was barely the width of a cigarette paper between the two rivals, but Gilles never wavered and was through into the lead with four laps to run. The crowd cheered him to the echo all the way to possibly his most memorable triumph of all. *Possibly!*

Even Gilles was exhausted. "I tell you, my car was very hard to drive . . . suspension so stiff it was like a go-kart. I bumped my head all the time on the rollover bar and now I ache all over. It was one of the most tiring races of my life.

Marlboro
Labatt
27
27
olivetti
MICHELIN

Dauntlessly enthusiastic as ever, Gilles Villeneuve's somewhat frayed Ferrari 126CK heads for third place in the 1981 Canadian Grand Prix at Montreal's Ile Notre Dame circuit. Eventually the tattered remnants of the front aerofoil flew off completely, but Gilles just pressed on . . .

My brakes were finished, and when they started to go, I had to be very brutal with my gearbox, but it lasted OK . . . I'm very lucky!" Lapped, Didier Pironi, finished a distant fourth in the other 126CK.

I say *possibly* his finest drive . . . Three weeks after winning on what was, in effect, his doorstep (his home was only a few hundred yards from Casino Square!) Gilles did it again at Jarama, venue for the 1981 Spanish Grand Prix. This time he hoped the 126CK would last ten laps or so . . . but he still spurted into an initial second place behind the fast-disappearing Alan Jones's Williams FW07C. Suddenly, most uncharacteristically, Jones slid off the road and lost his commanding lead, resuming well down the field. Now Villeneuve's Ferrari was in command, chased hard by Jacques Laffite's pole-winning Ligier-Matra, John Watson's McLaren MP4, Carlos Reutemann's Williams FW07C and Elio de Angelis's Lotus 87.

Villeneuve knew his pursuers were quicker than him – if they could get past, they would pull away. *If* they could get past. The French Canadian simply settled down to drive for the rest of the afternoon without making a single solitary mistake: Brabham designer Gordon Murray, walking the circuit infield throughout the event, later remarked "I don't think I've ever seen a driver put in a performance like that. Not one wheel out of place all afternoon." Well, not *quite* true really, for Gilles rode the kerbs like a good 'un all the way to the chequered flag. Lap after lap one would watch the downhill right-hander before the pits *knowing* that Ferrari number 27 just couldn't be ahead *again* – yet, lap after lap, it was! At the chequered flag a mere two seconds covered the first five cars home –

Gilles Villeneuve was the winner again. As it turned out, for the last time . . .

For the rest of the season, Villeneuve and, to a lesser extent, Pironi fought against the prevailing tide with an impressive level of commitment. Gilles was quicker, but his flat-out-all-the-way philosophy left him no margin for error in the unwieldy 126CK. At Silverstone he clipped the kerb coming out of the Woodcote chicane, spinning wildly in a cloud of tyre smoke as he careered into the catch fencing. Jones and the McLaren of Andrea de Cesaris were also eliminated as a result. Pironi retired with engine trouble.

Hockenheim; a frustrated 10th, hampered by a misfire. Austria; a brilliant first lap in the lead after catapulting through from the second row, but then a trip into the guard rail forcing an unwilling car to do more than it possibly could. Zandvoort; a spin into the sand on the run down to the first corner. Monza; turbo failure after six laps. This was the summer of '81 for Gilles Villeneuve. Pironi could be said to be steadier, more reliable. He was also less spectacular, and significantly slower.

Montreal, Gilles's home circuit, had always seen the plucky little French Canadian driver give of his best and 1981 was to be no exception. The 126CK's consistently bad handling meant that Villeneuve had to start the Canadian Grand Prix from a depressing 11th place on the grid, only managing a 1m 31.115s as compared with Piquet's Brabham pole time of 1m 29.211s. But the race took place in streaming rain, ideal conditions for Gilles to demonstrate his virtuoso brilliance to the full.

By lap 15 Jacques Laffite was punching his Michelin-shod Ligier-Matra through into the lead, but Villeneuve was splashing, slipping and sliding along a brilliant second. On the opening lap he and Pironi had inadvertently performed a "pincer" movement on Arnoux's Renault, heaving the French machine off the circuit, and Gilles later glanced the rear of Elio de Angelis's Lotus 87. This incident knocked the full-width Ferrari nose wing askew and it progressively deformed from that point onwards until it was standing vertically up ahead of the cockpit . . . before flying off completely. How did Gilles see? "Oh, I just looked to the right of the front wheel and made sure I never got off the dry line on to the wet . . .", he grinned disarmingly. Of course, why didn't we lesser mortals think of it? By the chequered flag, his car misfiring badly, Gilles had dropped to third place behind Watson's smoothly-driven McLaren. By this time Pironi was long gone with engine trouble.

The absurd chase round the car park at Caesars Palace in Las Vegas rounded off the 1981 Championship challenge, but for Villeneuve the race proved to be a fiasco. He qualified superbly in third place behind the Williams FW07Cs of Carlos Reutemann and Alan Jones, catapulting into second place behind the Australian on the rush down to the first corner. As Jones sprinted clear of the field, Gilles weaved wonders as usual, keeping the unwieldly Ferrari ahead of the rest of the runners until an engine problem intervened and his 126CK stopped out on the circuit. By that time, however, the organizers had decided to disqualify Villeneuve for failing to take up his correct position on the starting grid, within the box painted on the track surface. Pironi finished ninth, two laps down on Jones's winning Williams.

GOOD YEAR
GOOD YEAR
27
MAGNETI MARELLI
Agip

Section VI: The 126 V6s, 1980-84

Chapter 2
A fresh approach to chassis design: the 126C2 and C3

Gilles Villeneuve and Didier Pironi started the 1982 season as probably the strongest driver pairing in the Formula 1 business. But their relationship hit rock-bottom when Pironi, seen chasing Villeneuve in the controversial San Marino Grand Prix at Imola, won this race against team instructions. Villeneuve, infuriated, never spoke to his team-mate again: thirteen days later the French Canadian was killed in practice for the Belgian Grand Prix at Zolder. Later that summer, Pironi's racing career finished when his legs were badly smashed in a practice accident at Hockenheim . . .

For all Villeneuve's brilliance, and notwithstanding his two wins at Monaco and Jarama, 1981 had been a largely disappointing year for the Scuderia Ferrari. But behind the scenes, major changes had been taking place back at Maranello. Enzo Ferrari had every confidence in his engine department to produce a fully competitive turbocharged unit, but his team was lagging behind badly when it came to chassis technology. Therefore, in the middle of 1981 he recruited former Hesketh, Wolf and Fittipaldi designer Harvey Postlethwaite giving the Englishman *carte blanche* to develop a totally new chassis for the 126, drawing on all his considerable experience from the "English school" of Formula 1 design.

Postlethwaite arrived at Maranello in the summer of 1981 and immediately assessed the prevailing situation. By his own admission, he would have liked to build a carbon fibre composite chassis for 1982, but "although I felt I had the necessary experience and knowledge, the team was a long way behind and I told Mr. Ferrari that if we were going to tackle that sort of construction, then we ought to be in a position to do it ourselves. We didn't want to find outselves in a position where we subcontracted the work out. So, whilst we got ourselves organized on this front, I opted to build a honeycomb chassis on the basis that I knew how to put one together and it wouldn't fall apart."

Using bonded Nomex honeycomb sheet, manufactured by the Belgian-based Hexcel company since Ferrari had no resin bonding facilities, the Ferrari 126C2 chassis closely resembled the last Wolf WR7 which Postlethwaite had designed. The honeycomb sheet was "folded" round carbon fibre composite bulkheads and glued together, making a very light and strong structure. The 120-degree V6 engine remained the same, running exclusivély now with KKK turbocharging since the Comprex system had been completely abandoned, the transverse gearbox layout remained pretty well the same and the suspension layout was broadly similar with rocker arms operating inboard mounted coil spring/damper units front and rear.

Other "behind the scenes" developments throughout 1981 had centred round the task of improving throttle response from the turbocharged engine and Ferrari had tackled this problem by causing combustion to take place in the turbine when the throttle was closed, thus preventing the turbines from slowing down too much before the driver opened the throttle once more. Once back on the throttle, the exhaust gases flowed through the turbines again and the combustion within the turbines then ceased. This proved to be a highly effective system, but it exacted a high toll in terms of wear on turbine blades and bearings, so the system was revised during 1982. Changes involves alteration of the turbine to compressor size ratio in conjunction with a bigger turbo boost control valve and detail work on porting,

valve lift, size and spring control of the boost controlling unit.

The Ferrari 126C2's race début was in the 1982 South African Grand Prix at Kyalami where Villeneuve and Pironi ran third and fourth behind the works Renault RE30s during the early stages of the contest. Gilles retired early with turbocharger bearing failure, but Pironi struggled on to be classified 18th, despite the fact that for the second half of the event he was grappling with a serious fuel system misfire.

In Brazil, Villeneuve qualified second behind Prost's Renault and catapulted into an immediate lead once the starting signal was given. Despite pressure from Nelson Piquet's Brabham BT49D and Keke Rosberg's Williams FW07C, Gilles stayed ahead for 29 of the race's 63 laps before getting a wheel on the dirt as he fought to keep Piquet behind, spinning across the Brabham's bows and slamming into a guard rail. Unhurt, he strolled back to the pits. Pironi, bruised and battered following a horrifying Ricard testing accident a couple of weeks earlier which had destroyed one of the latest Ferraris, struggled home eighth after an early spin.

The much-publicized FOCA/FISA wars erupted in the wake of Brazilian Grand Prix post-race scrutineering. In order to enable them to compete with the more powerful, yet heavier, turbocharged cars, the British "Cosworth brigade" had fitted water tanks for their water-cooled braking systems which they then sought

to replenish after the race, in much the same manner as oil catch tanks had been topped up traditionally over the years in order that the cars conform with minimum weight regulations at post-race scrutineering. Renault protested this "disposable ballast" concept and an Appeal Tribunal was eventually destined to uphold this protest after the race stewards had rejected it. Piquet and Rosberg were thus disqualified from first and second places a matter of days prior to the San Marino Grand Prix at Imola.

All this mattered little to Ferrari, particularly over the weekend of the United States Grand Prix at Long Beach on April 2-4. During practice for this event, Mauro Forghieri decided to "take the mickey" out of his British rivals by producing a "staggered" double rear aerofoil, the effect of which was to enable the 126C2 to run an extra-wide rear wing. Forghieri's contention was that this amounted to a pair of 110cm width, legal, rear aerofoils mounted one behind the other – there was nothing in the rules, he said, to prevent them being offset from each other. Villeneuve ran splendidly to third place using this system and later found that the stewards disagreed with Mauro's contention: the French Canadian was disqualified on the protest of a rival competitor! Pironi's C2 was eliminated when he glanced one of the unyielding concrete barriers and damaged his car's suspension.

Back in Europe, the *Gran Premio di San Marino*, held at Imola's emotionally-titled *Autodromo Dino Ferrari*, proved to be a highly memorable affair on two counts. Firstly, smarting under Appeal Court's decision on the subject of "disposable ballast," the event was boycotted by the predominantly British, FOCA-aligned teams. Secondly, it was the day on which Gilles Villeneuve was deprived out of a deserved victory by his team-mate Didier Pironi.

The story of the race is straightforward. The adoring Ferrari fans couldn't have cared less about the absence of the British teams. As long as Gilles and Didier were present with the Ferrari C2s, all was well with the world. In the event, the opening phase of the race turned out to be a titanic battle between the two red cars from Maranello and René Arnoux's Renault RE30, the three cars swapping places all round the circuit. On lap 44, Arnoux retired with a major engine failure, leaving Villeneuve and Pironi, running in that order, at the head of the field.

It has been confirmed to the author by Piero Lardi Ferrari that team

Neat job. The twin KKK turbochargers nestle neatly within the V6 engine's 120-degree vee as this shot of the 1982 Ferrari 126C2 in the pit lane at Kyalami indicates. This was Harvey Postlethwaite's first Ferrari chassis design and the English engineer opted for the alloy/Nomex "honeycomb" route in preference to the more ambitious carbon fibre composite design which was to follow in 1983.

It was generally regarded that Mauro Forghieri was "taking the mickey" out of the "protest-orientated" British teams when he produced this staggered rear aerofoil seen here on Didier Pironi's 126C2. during practice for the 1982 Long Beach race. The British teams had the last laugh, however, because it was used on Gilles Villeneuve's C2 which finished third in the race. The aerofoil was then protested and the Ferrari disqualified!

instructions in such circumstances have always been for the two cars to hold station in the order they assume first and second positions. This is indicated by a "slow" sign from the pits and that was shown to the two Ferrari drivers when Gilles was in front. This didn't prevent Pironi repassing Villeneuve, however, but Gilles wasn't unduly worried. He thought Didier was anxious to put on a show to the crowd and trusted him to play fair when it came to the last lap. The Ferrari drivers both knew that their turbocharged cars would be marginal on fuel consumption, so when Gilles was ahead, he was slowing the pace to around 1m 38s a lap. When Didier was in front, he was running hell-for-leather at around 1m 35s . . .

Gilles was leading into the last lap, but Pironi towed through as they went down to *Tosa*, and by the time Villeneuve realized what was happening there was no way he could get back ahead before they reached the chequered flag. Pironi-Villeneuve. You only had to look at Gilles's expression on the winner's rostrum. He felt cheated, flushed with indignation. His annoyance was heightened when team manager Marco Piccinini was quoted as saying, no, there were no team orders. But there were – and even Enzo Ferrari felt moved to make a comment indicating his sympathy with the French Canadian driver a few days after the event.

Sadly, the damage was done. Villeneuve would never speak to Pironi again. Thirteen days later, during final qualifying for the Belgian Grand Prix at Zolder, Villeneuve went out on to the circuit in an aggressive frame of mind. Pironi had done a 1m 16.501s to Gilles's 1m 16.616s. That was just too much for Villeneuve.

Determined to put the Frenchman firmly in his place, he went out for a final try at grasping pole position. Mid-way round his second flying lap he came upon Jochen Mass's March 821 . . . Gilles didn't lift and, in a split-second misjudgement, the Ferrari went catapulting over the slower car's right rear wheel. As the C2 came down nose-first in the sand at the side of the circuit, Villeneuve was killed instantly by the decceleration, his neck broken. The fact that he was then flung from the Ferrari cockpit as the monocoque disintegrated had no bearing on any of his injuries.

It was a body blow for the Ferrari team which immediately withdrew Pironi's car from the meeting. Back at base, the tragedy numbed the entire factory and clearly hit Harvey Postlethwaite particularly hard. It was the first time that anybody had been killed in a car he had designed and the post-race criticism from rival constructors about the way in which the Ferrari monocoque broke up, particularly irritated him. Subsequently, Ferrari carried out tests on static rigs with both an original 126CK and one of the latest 126C2s, completely destroying both cars. The results satisfied them about the constructional integrity of the cars – and the fact that few people understood the forces involved in such high speed accidents.

Postlethwaite recalls Gilles Villeneuve with great affection and enthusiasm: "He was great. Given the choice between being in the lead and destroying his tyres, and going carefully and finishing third, Gilles would always choose the former. Jody would always choose the latter and he was World Champion, Gilles wasn't. It wasn't that Gilles *couldn't* have done it – he could have done it as well as any man – but there was something in him that wouldn't *allow* him to do it.

"At Zandvoort in '81 Mauro almost went down on his knees and said 'Gilles, *please* take it easy in this race. We've got new turbos and we *must* see how they'll go over a race distance. You haven't got a chance of winning, or even finishing in the points, so *please* don't shunt it . . .' He went off at *Tarzan* on the first lap, over the top of everybody! That's the way he was!

"Did you ever go with Gilles in a road car? *Horrendous!* I mean, I recall one day about a month after I'd joined Ferrari, we went out to eat in a village near Maranello and were hurtling back in Gilles's 308, running down the outside of a traffic stream in the dark, when an old man on a motor scooter without lights turned left across us, I just thought 'oh no, it's going to be in all the papers how we killed this man' – and Gilles avoided him. He didn't just swerve, he was cadence braking, he had the thing sideways . . . I wasn't really scared, because I was sitting alongside probably the best driver in the world. I don't think the old boy on the scooter ever even saw the car.

"Gilles would go down the outside of a traffic queue with a lorry coming the other way just to get warmed up . . . I mean, he had blind faith in his own ability to get through. That's what he was doing running round Mass at Zolder – a total faith in his own ability that he would find the gap. On a personal level, he was the most disarmingly honest, totally non-political guy with absolutely no hang-ups . . . and the Commendatore loved him for this whole approach."

In the wake of Villeneuve's tragic death, the team was totally stunned and it was decided to leave the question of whether or not to participate at Monaco to Didier Pironi. Unsurprisingly, the Frenchman asked if he could compete and Ferrari provided him with a pair of C2s to choose from. Didier went well in this rather chaotic and confused event, finishing second after his car died in the tunnel due to a battery malfunction on the final lap.

The team continued with a single car entry for Pironi at both Detroit and Montreal, one of the chassis fitted with pull-rod front suspension in conjunction with double wishbones to replace the rocker arm system. It wasn't used in the Detroit race, Didier finishing third in his regular car, and since he managed to qualify the older specification C2 for pole position in Montreal the following week, there wasn't much incentive to try the pull-rod car in that race either. However, the pull-rod suspension proved much better in the long term, resulting in significantly reduced front tyre wear and improved response when turning into the corners. Heavy and bulky, the superseded rocker arms had been acting like an

Tragic partnership Gilles Villeneuve and Didier Pironi.

undamped transverse leaf spring, something which had been realized by many of Ferrari's rival teams much earlier.

Sadly, Pironi was to find himself on the periphery of another tragedy at the start of the Canadian Grand Prix. As he tried to prevent his Ferrari from creeping slightly as he waited for the green light, the luckless Frenchman stalled its engine and the C2 was rammed from behind by Riccardo Paletti's Osella. Pironi's Ferrari was badly damaged, but poor Paletti was killed in the impact which resulted in the race being stopped at the end of its first lap. For the restart, Pironi was obliged to use the revised car with its pull-rod front suspension, but it wasn't fully sorted and, after making several pit stops to sort out fuel injection and ignition settings, he was left with the fastest race lap as his sole consolation at the end of a disastrous weekend.

Unbelievably, Pironi was involved in another major testing accident at Paul Ricard before the next round of the World Championship, the C2 he was driving again being destroyed. On this occasion a broken suspension wishbone was cited as the cause of the accident and Pironi was fortunate to escape unhurt. Strengthened wishbones were therefore fitted to the cars by the time they appeared for the Dutch Grand Prix at Zandvoort, the occasion of Patrick Tambay's début as Pironi's new partner.

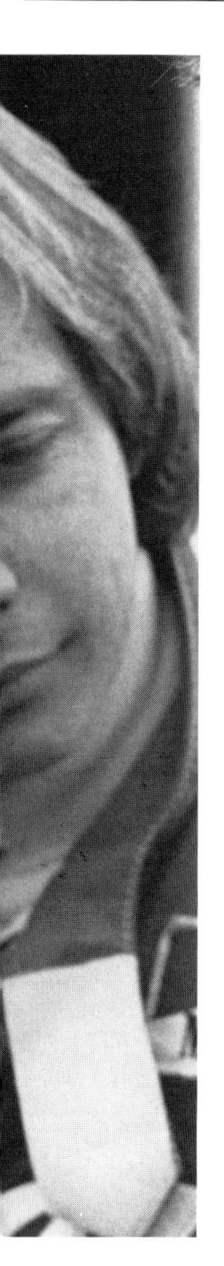

Other modifications being carried out at Maranello at this time included the development of a longitudinal gearbox, in the interests of maximum ground effect, revised rear suspension and a secret water-injection system which was being developed in conjunction with Agip, the team's longtime fuel sponsor.

This system was similar in principal to that used to cool jet engines, the Agip technicians having developed a means whereby a globule of water could be encapsulated within a globule of petrol, this process lowering the temperature of the petrol entering the combustion chambers. Upon combustion, the globule of water turned to steam and "exploded" the surrounding petrol, giving increased atomization and improved mixture control within the combustion chamber. Not surprisingly, Agip remained very tight-lipped about the precise details of the way in which the water was mixed with the fuel, but the development was clearly reaping benefits in terms of sustained power output and engine reliability.

Pironi drove splendidly to win the Dutch Grand Prix at Zandvoort, but Tambay dropped back to a distant eighth, troubled by a frustrating misfire which may have been connected with the new water-injection system. Pironi and Tambay finished second and third in the British Grand Prix at Brands Hatch, then third and fourth in the French Grand Prix at Paul Ricard, totally outclassed on this occasion by the Renault RE30s.

In practice for the German Grand Prix at Hockenheim, Didier Pironi was absolutely *determined* that he should score another victory, and a dominant one at that, to nail the increasing criticism from certain sections of the Italian press that his approach to the World Championship was that of a "points gathering accountant". These accusations really needled the Frenchman who was in a very hyped-up mental state: on Saturday morning, in the pouring rain, he was still barrelling round flat-out in untimed practice, irrespective of the fact he'd taken pole position the previous afternoon, when he ran slap into the back of Alain Prost's Renault RE30 on one of the German circuit's long straights.

In its destructive ferocity, Pironi's accident was the equal of Villeneuve's, but with one crucial difference: Didier's C2 landed on its tail after its crazy flight over Prost's right rear wheel. But by the time it had glanced off the guard rail and shuddered to a halt on the grass at the side of the circuit, the front of the monocoque had been destroyed and Pironi lay in the rain-soaked wreckage with two broken legs. It was the end of his World Championship aspirations. Back at Maranello, on hearing the news, Enzo Ferrari simply remarked "*adieu Mondiale.*"

Just over a day later, the 84-year-old Commendatore was shedding tears of delight. Patrick Tambay had shouldered the burden of sole responsibility for the team's fortunes in admirable style and won the German Grand Prix – a timely morale-booster for both Scuderia Ferrari and the pleasant Frenchman whose "in and out" Formula 1 career to date hadn't produced the hard results his obvious talents so clearly justified. Tambay followed up his Hockenheim triumph with a splendid chase through the field at the Österreichring to finish fourth after an early delay to change a punctured tyre. Sadly, he was then obliged to withdraw from the Swiss Grand Prix at Dijon-Prenois before the race suffering badly with pains in his neck and right arm, an unfortunate by-product of the firm ride produced by the stiffly sprung ground-effect cars of 1982.

For the final two races of the season, the Italian Grand Prix at Monza and the round-the-car-park chase at Las Vegas, one of Maranello's prodigal sons rejoined the Ferrari line-up. Thanks to the generosity of his CART entrant Pat Patrick, Mario Andretti was installed behind the wheel of the second C2 entry and delighted his fans by qualifying brilliantly on pole at Monza. "Beaten . . . beaten by the Old Man," grinned Tambay generously, but it was Patrick who came through to take second place in the race to René Arnoux's Renault with Andretti third. It wasn't quite the overwhelming success that Ferrari was hoping for on home soil, but it was sufficient to clinch the Constructors' Championship title.

Another bout of that arm and shoulder trouble forced Tambay to miss Las Vegas and Mario's C2 suffered an untypical rear suspension failure which caused him to spin off on the dusty infield. It was Andretti's last outing for the team,

Ornament! Most other teams would dearly like to get their hands on a Ferrari 126C2 – but this superseded model now adorns the foyer of Ferrari's road car factory at Maranello. Once replaced by a new machine, there's no place for the old in the racing department!

because although he was delighted to be back in the Formula 1 business, there was no way in which he could enter into a contract for the 1983 season as his commitments in the United States were so wide-ranging and numerous.

In any case, by this stage in the season the 1983 Ferrari line-up had been finalized with René Arnoux joining Tambay – although Enzo Ferrari gave his undertaking that he would be prepared to provide a third car for Didier Pironi, if and when he ever recovered from his injuries. In fact, Pironi's recovery would take far longer than the original optimistic predictions suggested. He never raced a Grand Prix car again and turned his hand to the equally spectacular business of powerboat racing, only to die in an accident off the Isle of Wight in the summer of 1987.

For the 1983 season the FISA decided to grasp an increasingly irritating Formula 1 nettle at its root and took a unilateral decision to ban "ground-effect" by insisting on a flat under-body within their wheelbase for all Grand Prix cars . Ferrari immediately adapted the C2 to conform with the new rules and while Harvey Postlethwaite sat down and designed a brand new car, the 1983 season began with Tambay and Arnoux relying on the C2Bs for the first half of the year.

Many observers had expected Arnoux to be much quicker than his team-mate, but the lack of ground-effect called for a more sensitive approach to tyre conservation and Tambay seemed to have mastered this much better in the early races. From the Brazilian Grand Prix onwards, the C2Bs appeared fitted with enormous rear aerofoils, the sides of which reached forward to mountings on the rear of the side pods housing the water radiators and turbocharger intercoolers. Rival teams quickly developed a renewed respect for the Ferrari engine department on the basis of the power they must have been developing to drag these large aerodynamic appendages through the air.

At Rio, the opening Grand Prix of the season, Tambay managed to struggle home fifth with Arnoux a highly disappointed tenth. At Long Beach, Patrick's fluid and polished style once more saw him eclipse his team-mate, accelerating into an immediate lead which he maintained splendidly until Keke Rosberg's Williams savaged his C2B from behind, spinning it violently out of the contest. At the end of the day Arnoux survived to finish third behind the McLarens of John Watson and Niki Lauda, although the Frenchman had worn his way through three sets of Goodyears during the course of the race.

Prior to the San Marino Grand Prix at Imola, Arnoux contested the non-title Brands Hatch Race of Champions to little effect, wearing out his tyres before

Englishman at Maranello. Harvey Postlethwaite photographed by the large Prancing Horse emblem which is attached to the wall at the entrance to Ferrari's Competition department on Maranello's Via. Alberto Ascari.

retiring with engine problems. But during practice for this event his C2B was fitted with a revised rear suspension system which would eventually feature on the C3. Replacing the rocker arm system employed from the start of the C2 development, the new system had a very wide-base lower wishbone operated by a pull-rod working on a swinging link: This proved to be an instant success and significantly improved the car's handling and tyre consumption characteristics for the last few races of its career.

Tambay became the first Ferrari driver to score a victory in 1983 when he came home winner of the San Marino race after Riccardo Patrese's Brabham BT52 slid off into a barrier a few laps from the finish. Arnoux, after a spin, finished third. Tambay sustained his advantage over Arnoux at Monaco where he breezed

Agip
GOODYEAR
MAGNETI MARELLI
27
KONI
olivetti
Agip
CHAMPION
brembo
SKF

Patrick Tambay, the Prince Charming of Formula 1, scored an emotionally draining victory in the 1983 San Marino Grand Prix at Imola in this 126C2. Carrying the racing number of his great friend Gilles Villeneuve, it was a day for Patrick to remember for a long time.

through the field to finish fourth after bungled team management resulted in his being delayed in his decision to change from "wet" to "dry" rubber. The team manager kept Patrick out on the circuit while the mechanics tried vainly to resuscitate Arnoux's C2B after its driver had slid into a guard rail early during the race, staggering round to the pits with the rear suspension damaged beyond repair.

By the time the Belgian Grand Prix had finished at Spa-Francorchamps, with Arnoux retiring whilst Tambay drove smoothly to second place behind Prost, there were all sorts of rumours about the Ferrari line-up for 1984. With one Grand Prix victory already under his belt, it seemed as though Tambay's consistently impressive form would guarantee him continued employment within Maranello's ranks. What's more, he was showing himself to be a more intelligent and perceptive test and development driver than his team-mate, something which was appreciated by Mauro Forghieri and his fellow engineers. Not only that, as Harvey Postlethwaite pointed out, "Patrick was bloody quick. People tend to forget that . . ."

By the middle of the 1983 season, experienced "Ferrari watchers" knew full-well that one or other of the French drivers would be out of a job at the end of the year. The Commendatore had made it clear that, after a long period of not employing Italian drivers, he would offer a contract to Michele Alboreto when he became available. And with the young Italian's three-year deal with Tyrrell ending after the final race of the '83 season, it was clear that he would be joining the Scuderia Ferrari. But which driver would leave? By the middle of the year Arnoux was almost definitely out. Patrick had been invited to dinner by the Old Man and most people felt the deal had been done.

Unfortunately for Tambay, he'd enjoyed his run of really good results too early in the season. After his San Marino success he would find himself bogged down with a number of trifling mechanical failures. Compounding this, Arnoux "came good" in the second part of the year and it ended up with Tambay as the one who had to leave Maranello.

In time for the British Grand Prix at Silverstone, Harvey Postlethwaite's new 126C3 was ready for action, a Ferrari-built carbon fibre composite monocoque which had been completely constructed at Maranello, for which purpose a giant oven had been installed to "cure" the chassis within the competition department. The C3's monocoque tub was a single structure incorporating the nose cone, cockpit surround and fuel cell as one unit. The 120-degree V6 engine was still the heart of the car, the C2-derived pull-rod suspension was employed all round and the C3's visual similarity to its predecessor was enhanced by the fact that Forghieri adopted C2-type side pods after initial tests with a revised pod layout revealed the

Agitated discussion: Ferrari chief engineer Mauro Forghieri briefs Patrick Tambay in the pit lane at the Österreichring prior to the Frenchman's successful attempt at securing pole position for the 1983 Austrian Grand Prix.

René Arnoux won the Ferrari 126C3's first Grand Prix victory at Hockenheim in the summer of 1983. Here the new carbon fibre composite Ferrari wheels its way through the infield section of the German circuit, showing off to good effect the pull-rod front suspension it inherited from the 126C2.

cooling capability to be marginal, particularly in hot weather.

Arnoux had finally "broken his duck" by taking the C2B to a fine victory in the Canadian Grand Prix and he underlined his revitalized form by planting the new C3 on pole position for its début in the British race. Tambay was alongside him on the front row and beat his team-mate through the first corner, and for the first few laps of the British Grand Prix we had the impressive sight of these two brand new Ferraris running imperiously round in 1-2 formation. However, Forghieri had taken the decision to run smaller, centre pillar rear aerofoils for this race, abandoning the larger aerofoils which had been *de rigeur* up to that point. Tambay counselled against this decision and, in the event, his feelings proved to be correct: the C3s would have done with the extra downforce imparted by the bigger aerofoil and, with reduced grip, they slid around too much and blistered their rear Goodyears. At the end of the afternoon Tambay and Arnoux had faded to third and fifth . . .

At the end of the British Grand Prix the Ferrari team found itself on the receiving end of a protest from Ken Tyrrell on the basis that its water-injection system constituted a "power boosting additive" which contravened the Formula 1 technical regulations. This gave rise to a long and tedious legal battle which was somewhat inconclusive, but which was eventually resolved in Ferrari's favour.

For the balance of the 1983 season the 126C3 was employed exclusively and Arnoux easily won the German Grand Prix at Hockenheim after Tambay's newly-installed engine failed early in the race. In the opening phase of the race, Arnoux completely ignored established team discipline and pushed ahead of Tambay: in the event, Arnoux's indiscipline didn't matter very much because

Agip
27
GOULD
Agip
SKF
arexons

LONGINES

Patrick retired, but Piero Lardi Ferrari told the author at the end of the season that Arnoux was under firm instructions to finish behind Patrick. If Tambay had run the distance, may be René would have conceded. Maybe, maybe not . . .

By this stage in the season the Ferrari team was matching its rivals in the newly-revived art of pit stops for fuel and tyres, a practice made fashionable by the Brabham-BMW team the previous summer after their designer Gordon Murray had worked out that the time lost in the pit lane would be more than saved by lapping quicker on softer tyres and a light fuel load while the cars were out on the circuit. Ferrari's mechanics demonstrated all the concerted discipline required to perform these speedy pit stops with great efficiency and there was seldom a race at which they failed to service their drivers with admirable aplomb.

***Overleaf:* Ferrari's 1984 recruit Michele Alboreto tests one of the new 126C4s at Paul Ricard prior to the first Grand Prix of the new season. The smaller, cut-down fuel cell to cater for the new 220-litre maximum fuel capacity regulations is the most obvious change from the 126C3. The small Marlboro decals refer to that company's payment of the Ferrari driver fees.**

Following on after his Hockenheim disappointment, Tambay was dominating the Austrian Grand Prix at the Österreichring, running confidently and smoothly in front of Arnoux at the head of the field. Once again, René didn't exactly play fair, boxing in Patrick behind Jean-Pierre Jarier's disgracefully obstructive Ligier JS21 as they came up to lap the French car, pushing through into the lead after "wiping him off" against the slower competitor. Tambay was furious, but again it was to no avail because his engine let him down with valve failure and Arnoux finished second. Finally, René clinched his position in the Ferrari team for 1984 by winning the Dutch Grand Prix at Zandvoort, a splendid performance from tenth place on the grid at the wheel of a spare car. Tambay, who had qualified second to Nelson Piquet's Brabham BT52B on the front row, faded at the start with clutch slip and then caught up to finish second behind his team-mate.

Monza saw the season continue in Arnoux's favour, René taking a strong second place to Piquet, with Tambay fourth, and although René lost his World Championship chances with a stupid spin at Brands Hatch during the *Grand Prix D'Europe*, Patrick slid off the road in the closing stages of the race. Within another 24-hours his replacement in the team by Alboreto was confirmed by Enzo Ferrari,

A carbon fibre composite monocoque 126C3 stands in front of the large "Autoclave" oven in the competitions department, specially built and installed for the purposes of "baking" the new cars' chassis. Manufactured by a specialist local Maranello company, Panini, whose premises are "just down the road", its size was dictated by Enzo Ferrari himself. When Harvey Postlethwaite asked "how big should it be?", the Commendatore, always with an eye to the future, replied "make it big enough to hold a 400i!"

a decision which didn't find unanimous approval amongst those Mr. Ferrari employs within his own team. Those dissenters, appreciating "he who pays the piper calls the tune", kept their opinions pretty much to themselves, but there was no concealing the joy within the team when Tambay planted his C3 on pole position for the final race of the season at Kyalami. Sadly, neither car finished the 1983 South African Grand Prix, but the combined efforts of the two French drivers had won Ferrari its second successive World Championship for Constructors.

By this stage work on the car which René Arnoux and Michele Alboreto would campaign in 1984 was well advanced, Harvey Postlethwaite further refining the carbon fibre composite concept. It was intended that the new 126C4 should be equipped with the latest Marelli/Weber electronic engine management system which had been under development during the off-season, in order to ensure that the 120-degree V6 would have no difficulty completing a Grand Prix distance on the newly specified 220-litre maximum permitted fuel capacity.

Although the 126 engine retained the same dimensions, it had been subject to extensive internal modifications and was installed lower in the chassis; up to 660bhp was quoted at the time as its output, dependent on boost pressure. However, Ferrari was to have an unpleasant surprise when the new season got underway, as a rival organization was preparing dramatically to raise the Formula 1 stakes to a level at which Maranello – or indeed anybody else – would find it difficult to compete.

False dawn. Michele Alboreto's Goodyear-shod 126C4 leads the opening lap of the 1984 Belgian Grand Prix at Zolder ahead of Derek Warwick's Renault RE50 (running on Michelin tyres), Arnoux's 126C4 and Manfred Winkelhock's ATS D6-BMW.

Section VI: The 126 V6s, 1980-84

Chapter 3
A disappointing sequel

The most visually obvious difference between the C3 and the C4 was the 1984 machine's cut-down fuel cell conforming to the new regulations which reduced the maximum permitted fuel load from 250 to 220 litres. This gave the new car a much more sleek and purposeful look than its immediate predecessor. In fact, the bottom half of the tub was exactly the same as that of the C3, but its bonding to the modified upper section was revised, the end product being slightly stiffer. Following the success in the 1983 Constructors' Championship battle, many people at Maranello were expecting Alboreto and Arnoux to be able to sustain the team's impetus, but there were several major factors which eventually conspired against them.

While Ferrari testing over the winter produced reasonably promising, if not outstanding, results, once the 1984 season got under way at the end of March, McLaren International's new car instantly proved to be the package to beat. Designer John Barnard had waited as late as he dared before finalizing the definitive configuration of the TAG/Porsche-engined MP4/2, and the fact that it was only tested briefly before being flown out to Brazil caught many of the team's rivals off-guard. McLaren, Porsche and Bosch had done a splendid job working in partnership to produce a fine-handling car which had no problems sustaining a competitive power output throughout a race distance, with no worries about the 220-litre fuel limit.

Meanwhile, the Ferrari team went to Rio with the Marelli/Weber electronic injection system fitted to Michele Alboreto's C4, while René Arnoux's machine started the season equipped with the Lucas mechanical injection which had been standard kit throughout 1983. The team's two race cars were also fitted with large water tanks within the drivers' seats for the purpose of topping up the water injection reservoirs during "routine" pit stops.

Funnily enough, in view of the troubles which were to come, Alboreto's C4 ran trouble-free throughout qualifying and the Italian started his first race for the Prancing Horse from the outside of the front row, second only to Elio de Angelis's Lotus 95T. Arnoux suffered an irritating succession of minor fuel-feed problems, which were later blamed on a sticking valve somewhere deep in the system; as a result, he found himself in tenth place.

With two Goodyear runners on the front row of the grid, it looked as though the Akron supplier's persistence in developing its new range of radial rubber during intensive off-season test sessions was about to pay off, and this view was strengthened when Alboreto accelerated into an immediate lead at the start of this first race of the season. However, all was not as straightforward as it seemed. Driving with unruffled precision, Michele looked as though he might dominate the race but, coming up to complete its 12th lap, the Ferrari suddenly spun violently under braking for the hairpin before the pits. Initially it looked like a simple driving error but, after Alboreto had gathered it all up only to spin again at the next corner, it became clear that something was badly amiss.

Michele cruised gently round to the pits and, after one more gentle exploratory lap, retired for good. Close examination of the right front brake caliper revealed that one of the bolts holding the two halves of that component together had sheared, allowing the brake fluid to leak away, the resultant heat build-up causing the caliper to seize momentarily. Arnoux got up to fourth before an electrical short-circuit shut off the power and he rolled to a standstill out on the circuit, flames licking round the rear end of his C4. On balance, it looked like a moderately promising start for Maranello, but close scrutiny of the lap times revealed that Niki Lauda's McLaren MP4/2 had been gobbling up Alboreto's advantage while the Ferrari was at the head of the field. Clearly, the Michelin tyres used by the English team offered a considerable advantage over the latest Goodyear radials.

Two weeks later the sun went behind a cloud for Maranello in a big way when the C4s arrived to do battle in the South African Grand Prix at Kyalami. It seemed incredible to recall that, some six months earlier, Patrick Tambay's C3 had been on pole for the final race of the 1983 season at the same circuit. From the start of practice, Arnoux and Alboreto complained of unpredictable handling, a lack of grip and a shortage of speed on the straight. It was the classic Kyalami dilemma: if they screwed on sufficient downforce to produce a semblance of reasonable handling on the twisty sections of the track, they paid for this luxury in a lack of speed on the spectacularly long start/finish straight.

Alboreto's qualifying time was a whisker quicker than Tambay's previous pole winner, yet only sufficient to earn the Italian tenth place on the grid, while René – who simply had no suggestions as to how they might improve the C4's behaviour – languished down among the also-rans in an abysmal 15th place.

The race was a similarly undistinguished affair. Michele made a choice of hard rubber for the start, determined to run through non-stop without a tyre change. Largely through the misfortunes of others, he found himself a steady, if unspectacular, fourth when the C4 ran out of fuel with five of the race's 75 laps left to run. Fuel vaporization gremlins had earlier caused Arnoux's retirement and neither car had ever looked even remotely like a front-runner. The team was very depressed indeed as it headed back to Europe after this second race of the season, for the McLaren-TAGs appeared irresistible having won in both Brazil and South Africa.

Recollections of the Villeneuve tragedy make Zolder a circuit which brings unhappy memories, particularly for Ferrari fans, and many of the drivers at the 1984 race must have found it a little depressing to have to drive past a somewhat tasteless, garish monument to the French Canadian driver which had been erected in the pit lane just at the start of the garage area. But the sinuous north Belgian track was as kind to Ferrari in 1984 as it had been cruel two years earlier.

There was a brand new C4 – the fourth – on hand for Alboreto's use, this fitted with a complex new exhaust feeding into the turbines. Previously, the V6 engines had used siamesed pipes from each cylinder, but the new system ran separate pipes to the turbine inlet, so that the junction where the six small pipes from each

Arnoux hurrying towards second place behind Prost's McLaren in the 1984 San Marino Grand Prix at Imola, the former Renault team-mates finishing a lap ahead of their rivals.

Inspired performance. After being obliged to start from the back of the grid, Arnoux dodged the unyielding concrete walls with consummate skill to finish second at Dallas in 1984, headed only by Keke Rosberg's Williams-Honda at the chequered flag.

bank of cylinders came together was something of a miracle of intricate welding work. This new system had been adopted in the interests of improved turbine performance, and the cross-over layout was retained along with the valve-controlled connection between the exhaust and the compressor outlet manifolding.

Whether as a result of Goodyear and Ferrari happening to come up with the ideal tyre choice for the abrasive Zolder track surface or of the team managing to "dial in" the 126C4s to perfection, Alboreto and Arnoux buttoned up the front row of the grid. Michele was the only competitor to break the 1m 15s barrier, claiming pole with a fine 1m 14.846s, while Arnoux recorded a 1m 15.398s to line up alongside him.

When the starting light turned green, Alboreto was gone in a flash. The cool Italian led from start to finish in splendid style, his only minor error being a slide onto the outfield at the tight left-hander beyond the pits when his first set of Goodyears began wearing thin. He held his advantage through a routine pit stop for fresh rubber and cruised home comfortably, over half a minute ahead of Derek Warwick's Renault RE50. Arnoux had a more eventful race, recovering from a spin in the closing stages and finishing third with fastest lap to his credit. There seemed to be no question that this had been an impressive demonstration of the C4's potential. The performance brought grins to the faces of Harvey Postlethwaite and Mauro Forghieri in the pit lane, but the new Ferraris had flattered only to deceive. It would be a long time before Harvey and Mauro smiled again with such spontaneity.

Alboreto: "After the first three rounds of the Championship I really began to believe that I might win five or six races by the end of the season. Although I'd got my nose hard up against a problem in South Africa, where I suddenly realized we hadn't got enough power, when I qualified on pole and led from start to finish at Zolder, I thought Kyalami might have been a one-race problem. I thought, 'Right, from now on it's going to be easy.' And from that moment onwards, I hardly finished another race."

When the action moved to Imola for the San Marino Grand Prix, a succession of problems during rain-spoilt practice saw Arnoux qualify sixth, with Alboreto a lowly 13th. Both plagued by a consistent shortage of grip, they never posed even a remote threat to the pace-setting McLaren-TAGs or Brabham-BMWs. A loss of turbo boost pressure from a fractured exhaust eliminated the Zolder winner after 24 laps, but little René at least managed to raise a few cheers from the otherwise-unimpressed crowd by bringing his C4 home second. Arnoux was the only other runner on the same lap as Prost's winning McLaren, but Alain was only cruising towards the end and there was never any real prospect of the Ferrari catching him.

By this stage of the season, some people close to Maranello could be heard remarking that Ferrari were now paying the penalty for dismissing Patrick Tambay, as astute and worthwhile a test and development driver as one is ever likely to acquire. Arnoux's reputation in this area – hardly his forte during that stint with Renault – had not significantly improved, and Alboreto conceded he was somewhat confused by the handling problems that seemed to bug the C4's progress.

The trend continued at Dijon-Prenois, venue for the French Grand Prix. The twin-turbo 126C engine was clearly producing adequate horsepower as, with minimal downforce, the C4s were among the quickest contenders through the speed trap on the main straight. But tension was building up within the team as the two drivers came no nearer to sorting out their cars' handling and the key to their Zolder success seemed more elusive than ever. Michele and René qualified 10-11, two seconds off Tambay's pole-winning Renault RE50, and although Arnoux survived to finish fourth the result was the product of staying-power rather than competitiveness. Alboreto was eliminated on lap 34 by engine failure.

Before the Monaco Grand Prix the team took the chance to go testing at Imola with a revised version of the Marelli/Weber electronic injection system, but there were still problems with this new development and the Lucas systems were retained on the race cars for the next round of the Championship. Spins and minor contact with the unyielding guard rails in the streets of the Principality punctuated the Ferrari duo's progress during practice, but Arnoux and Alboreto manhandled their way round to take third and fourth places on the grid with 1m 22.935s and 1m 22.937s respectively. This was pretty close to Alain Prost's pole position time with the McLaren-TAG MP4/2, so perhaps things were looking up.

However, the race was run in streaming wet conditions admirably suited to Prost's delicate touch. He was declared the winner when, with daylight deteriorating by the minute, the contest was brought to a premature end by a torrential downpour which almost flooded the track. The decision caused a great deal of controversy and heated debate at the time, for Toleman's rising star Ayrton Senna was on the verge of catching the McLaren when former Ferrari ace Jacky Ickx, Clerk of the Course on this occasion, called a halt to the precarious proceedings. Ferrari were not to be involved in this dispute, however. Hampered by an electrical misfire from his waterlogged engine, Arnoux struggled home a plucky fourth, while Michele wasted a lot of time with a spin up an escape road, emerging, lapped and disappointed, to take seventh place.

Alboreto would probably wish to forget the next two races, held, a week apart, in North America at the end of June – particularly the Canadian Grand Prix at Montreal where he found himself embroiled in a brief, but ugly, pit lane dispute with Italian journalist Eugenio Zigliotto. It appears that Michele took violent exception to something Zigliotto had written and the whole debate got badly out of hand, leaving a thoughtful Michele nursing a swollen lip after a firm punch from the trenchant scribe!

Nelson Piquet's Brabham BT53-BMW set the pace during practice, taking pole position with a time of 1m 25.422s, while Arnoux just beat his team-mate for fifth, the C4s recording 1m 26.549s and 1m 26.764s respectively. Michele's race was brief, the Italian pulling off onto the grass with fuel pump drive failure on lap 11, while Arnoux came home in a distant fifth place, two laps down on the victorious Piquet after an eventful race. Riccardo Patrese finished the day in a pretty vexed frame of mind, claiming that Arnoux had side-swiped his Alfa 184T so hard that the impact broke a steering arm and sent him straight off the circuit. Half-apologetically, Arnoux shrugged, "I didn't see you. I didn't know you were there." Patrese was hardly placated. "That's all very well," he responded tersely, "but I was there, and you put me off the track."

René was also hampered by a slight loss of boost pressure, caused by a cracked exhaust pipe, and only just managed to scramble past Nigel Mansell's Lotus 95T on the last lap to grab his helping of two Championship points. A week later in Detroit, the Marelli/Weber electronic injection made a reappearance on both race cars, along with inlet tracts of varying length, and Michele seemed confident after qualifying fourth on 1m 42.246s, 1.3s away from Piquet's pole time.

Unfortunately, the 1984 Detroit Grand Prix was halted as soon as it had started. As the grid moved off, Mansell attempted to force his Lotus through a gap which really wasn't there between front-row men Piquet and Prost, triggering a multi-car pile-up. As Nelson's stricken Brabham was spun into the right-hand concrete retaining wall, it collected Michele's C4 in the process, the Ferrari ricocheting out the other side with its water radiator fractured and its wheels pointing in different directions.

The race was promptly stopped at the end of the opening lap but, although this gave everybody another chance, Michele was furious that his race car had been damaged beyond immediate repair. He was thus obliged to take the restart in the team's Lucas-injected spare and, although the high rate of mechanical carnage among the other runners allowed him to climb as high as third, on lap 49 his engine expired in an expensive cloud of smoke and steam. Subsequent examination revealed that a stone had pierced the turbo intercooler, which produced a dramatic rise in the inlet temperature, the engine failing as the sensors caused the fuel injection to adjust the fuel/air mixture to an impossibly lean level. "I wound down the boost as soon as it started misfiring," explained Michele ruefully, "but I knew it wouldn't last the distance."

Arnoux's amazing inconsistency, taken over a season, was emphasized by his performances in Detroit and, two weeks later, in Dallas. In the former race he spun and damaged the front suspension as early as lap three, limping into the pits to retire, but the inaugural race in the sweltering Texas city was unquestionably his best of the year.

With all the C4s on hand running Marelli/Weber injection, Arnoux qualified fourth but was late getting away on the parade lap after fuel vaporization in the sweltering temperatures had made his engine reluctant to start. By the time it had been successfully fired up, the entire grid was on its way and, mindful of the rule that forbids a competitor to resume his original grid position if he loses it during the course of the parade lap, a furious Arnoux started from the back of the grid. He tore through the field in brilliantly aggressive style, never easing up a fraction on the deteriorating track surface, and emerged at the finish in second place behind Keke Rosberg's Williams FW09-Honda. If he had started from his originally allotted place, there is little doubt he would have won. His team-mate fell foul of the concrete barriers lining this tight little track, Michele rolling to an ignominious halt on three wheels after wiping off a corner on lap 55.

Visco 2000
BP
28
26
Agip
GOODYEAR

Visco 2000
BP
NGK
26
28
LIGIER
Agip
GOODYEAR

BP
NGK
LIGIER
LOTO
26
antar
GOODYEAR
LONGINES
Agip
MAGNETI MARELLI
WEBER
28
GOULD

Arnoux displays his less predictable side as he barges inside Andrea de Cesaris's Ligier JS23 at the Druids hairpin during the 1984 British Grand Prix at Brands Hatch. The two cars slid onto the grass, but emerged unscathed to resume the chase. René finished sixth, immediately behind Alboreto, who managed to displace the obstructive Andrea with less melodrama!

The Goodyear radials might well have given Ferrari a chance on the street circuits, but back on the smooth, tailor-made European tracks Michelin surged ahead once again. For the British Grand Prix at Brands Hatch the team brought along four cars, two to the "North American" specification and two with repositioned water radiators and intercoolers fitted inside larger side pods with top venting, the intention being to reduce the heat build-up around the electronic injection system, since it had become clear that the discharge of hot air from the radiators against the monocoque was causing the fuel to boil.

Although the Ferraris were badly off the pace again, both men opted to use the latest-specification C4s. Much of the race saw the drivers battling with the absurdly obstructive Andrea de Cesaris's Ligier JS23, the former McLaren and Alfa driver determined that he was not going to concede an inch to the Ferraris. Alboreto squeezed through after a bout of wheel-banging at Druids on lap 34, but it was another 18 laps before Arnoux could nip through, and the two cars briefly slid, wheels interlocked, onto the grass on the outside of the hairpin before he did so. Michele and René finished fifth and sixth, miles behind Lauda's winning McLaren, and flushed with indignation over de Cesaris's behaviour. "They lapped the best part of two seconds quicker after they passed him," mused Forghieri, "so I feel like asking them why they didn't pass him sooner."

The quest for a significant improvement in the C4's handling took another direction at Hockenheim when a new push-rod rear suspension and revised rear diffuser panels were fitted to two cars, leaving two equipped with the earlier pull-rod set-up. But still neither driver could tell Forghieri which he considered the better arrangement and the whole weekend degenerated into another unproductive fiasco. Michele was out of the German Grand Prix as early as lap 14 with electrical failure, leaving Arnoux to soldier on to finish a lapped sixth. Prost and Lauda scored a 1-2 for McLaren and Michelin.

The gloom continued in Austria, where every permutation of multi-pipe-exhaust engine, rear suspension configuration and wheelbase was sampled. Michele used a car with a 13cm (5.1in) longer wheelbase – dubbed C4/M for *Modificato* – to qualify 12th on 1m 29.694s, and Arnoux, complaining that his car lacked speed on the straight as well as having no balance in the corners, was out of sight in 15th slot. Alboreto survived to finish a lucky third, leaving René seventh after a somewhat pointless pit stop for fresh rubber.

After the Dutch Grand Prix at Zandvoort, where another new rear suspension arrangement featuring tubular wishbones and revised geometry was tried in conjunction with the long wheelbase, Enzo Ferrari came under strong criticism at his pre-Monza press conference. The Dutch event was best forgotten, Alboreto's C4 suffering engine failure after only eight laps and Arnoux succumbing to electrical problems late in the race. René had earlier made a routine pit stop for new tyres, backing off so suddenly before darting into the pit entry that Thierry Boutsen's Arrows A7 ran straight over the back of the Ferrari, very nearly having the biggest accident of the season as a result. "Were you trying to kill me?" inquired Boutsen with as much restraint as he could muster. "You were asleep," replied Arnoux abruptly. End of exchange!

By this time the Italian press was in full flow. Who, they asked, was responsible for this dreadful season? What was the future for Forghieri? For Postlethwaite? What was to be done? Patiently, shrewdly, 86-year-old Enzo Ferrari let it be known that he retained complete faith in his technical staff and would not be replacing any key personnel.

None the less, Forghieri decided to stay away from the Italian Grand Prix at Monza – an almost unheard-of development – while Harvey opted for a timely holiday in England. He had no intention of embarrassing his fellow engineer by turning up alone in that pressure-cooker of gossip. Moreover, notwithstanding Ferrari's apparent assertion of confidence, Forghieri was to be moved sideways by the end of the season into the *Reparto URSA – Ufficio Ricerche Studi Avanzati* – which dealt with long-term engineering projects for the whole group, leaving Postlethwaite in overall charge of the Grand Prix programme. Forghieri's fall from grace was caused by his insistence that a four-cylinder turbocharged engine was required following BMW's success with such a configuration during 1983. Spurred on by hints from FISA that the maximum engine capacity would be reduced from 1500 to 1200cc in 1988, Forghieri embarked on this project with enormous enthusiasm during 1984. The Ferrari four-cylinder turbo proved to be a total disaster, however, blowing apart regularly on the test bed. In fact, it never ran long enough to achieve a single power curve and Enzo – always an engine man, first and foremost – never quite forgave Forghieri for the abortive project.

The Monza race required another change of configuration, and the waisted rear body treatment pioneered by John Barnard on the McLarens in 1983 and widely copied was adopted for the 126C4 "M2" models which appeared for the Italian Grand Prix. Practice produced so much in the way of technical trouble that neither driver could reach a worthwhile conclusion about the M2's merits, and the spare, Zandvoort-spec. C4s were used for the race after ignition problems arose on both the revamped machines. It turned out that they had both suffered minor electrical short-circuits during the race morning warm-up session, the type of fault which could be rectified in a few minutes in the (relative) calm of a Monday morning back at the factory, but which took longer to pinpoint in the frantic atmosphere of a pit lane on Grand Prix day.

Alboreto raised cheers from the crowd with a lucky second place behind Lauda's McLaren in the "old" C4, the thousands of hysterical fans allowing themselves some small sliver of consolation as a disastrous season for Maranello drew to a close. The fact that Arnoux retired early on with a broken gearbox mattered little to them, as did the fact that Michele gained his runner-up status only after half a dozen faster cars had retired in front of him. A Ferrari in second place was better than nothing, but hardly a cause for wild celebration at Maranello as the seasonal post-mortem got under way even with two races left on the 1984 calendar.

The penultimate round of the Championship was the *Grosser Preis von Europa*, staged at the sanitized "new Nürburgring" where Alboreto and Arnoux qualified fifth and sixth in "M2"-specification C4s. Michele reported that the chassis felt more progressive, particularly in the wet, although the new circuit's ultra-smooth surface may have contributed to the comfortable ride.

While Prost went ahead to score another commanding victory, Alboreto became embroiled in a late-race battle with Nelson Piquet's Brabham BT53 for second place. Coming into the final corner on the last lap, it looked as though the Brazilian would make it, but his BMW stuttered, almost out of fuel, and Michele surged by onto the home straight. Then the Ferrari, its tanks also virtually bone dry, hesitated and Piquet, weaving furiously to ensure that his engine picked up the last few dregs of fuel, surged back towards it. But Michele just held on to second place. Arnoux was fifth behind Niki Lauda's McLaren, which had been delayed by a spin.

The final race of the year took place at Estoril, where a second-place finish for Niki Lauda was sufficient to clinch the Championship by half a point over race-winner Prost. The C4 "M2s" qualified eighth (Alboreto) and 17th (Arnoux), the latter losing time with a split oil cooler.

In the race Alboreto spun trying to get on terms with Ayrton Senna's Toleman TG184, but recovered strongly to finish fourth, the first Goodyear runner past the flag. Arnoux rounded off the year a distant eighth, confessing that he had performed "miserably" throughout. Michele was placed fourth in the Championship on 30.5 points, behind Lauda, Prost and Elio de Angelis, while Arnoux was sixth with 27 points. It had been a bitterly disappointing season for the Maranello brigade, particularly after winning the Constructors' Championship in each of the previous two years.

Section VII: The uphill struggle, 1985-88: Battling against TAG/Porsche and Honda

Chapter 1 Start of a steady decline

Maranello swansong. Arnoux struggles round to the Rio pits after being savaged by de Cesaris's Ligier in the 1985 Brazilian Grand Prix. He barnstormed his way back to fourth at the finish, but it was to be his last race for the Prancing Horse.

Matching the TAG turbo's combination of usable power and fuel economy was the number one priority for Ferrari in 1985, a task which the engine department under Ildo Renzetti applied itself to over the winter. Meanwhile, Postlethwaite penned a new moulded carbon fibre composite monocoque for the team's latest GP contender which, rather illogically, was given the type number 156/85, rather than the obvious sequential designation 126C5.

The cars began the year fitted with SEP carbon brake discs, employing new Brembo calipers and pads, and, from the outset, it seemed as though Alboreto was in with a chance of the Championship. At Rio he planted the 156/85 on pole ahead of Keke Rosberg's Williams FW10-Honda, the Lotus 97Ts of Elio de Angelis and Ayrton Senna, Mansell's Williams and Alain Prost's McLaren-TAG, with Arnoux in seventh place.

Honda's F1 star was now very much in the ascendant and the fiery Rosberg burst into the lead at the start, with Mansell, on his maiden outing for Williams, hurtling down the outside on the run to the first corner before chopping across abruptly and hitting a startled Alboreto's left front wheel. The Englishman pirouetted to a temporary halt on the outside of the corner, leaving the Italian to run second behind Rosberg for the first nine laps before taking the lead.

LONGINES
PIRELLI
GOODYEAR
28
GOODYEAR

Murky début. Stefan Johansson, left front aerofoil in tatters, heads for the pits at Estoril after a coming-together with Riccardo Patrese's Alfa during his maiden outing for the team in the 1985 Portuguese Grand Prix.

However, Prost's McLaren was clearly going to be a tough nut to crack, particularly as the impact with Mansell had rearranged Alboreto's steering geometry and he was grappling with excessive understeer as a consequence. On lap 18 Prost sailed imperiously by into the lead and Michele could do nothing but chase him home to the chequered flag.

Arnoux had been sixth from the start, but on lap 27 de Cesaris's Ligier drove into the back of him, deflating one of the Ferrari's rear tyres. René was obliged to crawl slowly round to the pits for a replacement but, having resumed in 19th position, he climbed back to a fine fourth place at the finish.

Behind the scenes, Arnoux was causing some concern at Maranello. His two seasons with Ferrari had been characterized by worryingly inconsistent on-track performances and this problem seemed to have been heightened in 1984. This erratic record was a symptom of certain personal difficulties René had suffered and, following a lengthy and candid interview with Enzo Ferrari, it was decided that the Frenchman should leave the team prior to the Portuguese Grand Prix, the second round of the Championship.

Arnoux's replacement was to be the popular Swede Stefan Johansson, whose F1 aspirations seemed to have been beached by the failure of the Toleman team to secure a tyre supply contract for 1985. Thanks to the Toleman Group's generosity of spirit, Johansson was released from his commitment immediately the Ferrari offer was made, and he journeyed to Maranello to meet the Boss. Mr. Ferrari simply asked Stefan, "Are you a fighter?" to which the Swede replied, "I've had to fight for everything I've ever had," and the deal was done.

The bumpy surface at Estoril made life something of a trial for both Ferrari drivers, Alboreto qualifying fifth on 1m 22.577s, over a second away from Senna's Lotus pole time (1m 21.007s). Johansson found the 156's over-firm ride slightly alarming, but Michele confirmed this had not been a problem in Rio. "It's unbelievably nervous," Stefan reported, "and I've had quite a job getting the qualifying rubber up to a decent working temperature." He qualified a disappointing 11th on 1m 23.652s.

The race was run in monsoon conditions, Senna scarcely putting a wheel out of place as he splashed to the first Grand Prix victory of his career. Alboreto ran fourth from the start, but moved through to second after Prost spun into retirement on the start/finish straight and de Angelis ran wide. Johansson, having been pitched into a spin by Patrese's Alfa, recovered to take eighth place at the finish.

On home ground at Imola Alboreto qualified fifth for the San Marino Grand Prix, a mere half-second away from Senna, who was now becoming the man to beat as far as pole-position laps were concerned. Stefan ended practice back in 15th place after a series of niggling little problems including the rear undertray working loose, while Nelson Piquet, Thierry Boutsen and Derek Warwick all spun in front of him at various times.

Alboreto held third from the start, briefly moving into second place – again behind Senna – until an electrical problem forced him to pit on lap 24. He resumed on a fresh set of tyres and set fastest lap before retiring for good with a recurrence of the problem. Johansson, meanwhile, brought the crowds to their feet with an attacking performance which saw him climb from 15th place through to third after Michele had quit the stage.

On lap 54 he grasped second place from Prost's McLaren and was only 10 seconds behind Senna, surging through into the lead when the Lotus's tanks ran dry in this traditionally fuel-marginal race. A Ferrari ahead at Imola – it seemed too good to be true, and the crowds had barely emptied their lungs for the first time in vocal support when Stefan, too, fell victim to a lack of *benzina*. With just over a lap to run, he rolled to a halt out on the circuit, allowing Prost through to be first past the chequered flag – only for the Frenchman to be disqualified when his McLaren failed the post-race weight check, victory being handed to de Angelis's Lotus. It was a disappointing day for Maranello, but Johansson had given the fans plenty to get excited about, the Old Man remarking, with characteristic emotion, "We lost the race – but I have found the driver."

However, when the action moved to Monaco, it was Alboreto who was to challenge strongly for the lead, matching Prost move for move in what must be regarded as one of the Italian driver's best-ever races at the wheel of a Ferrari. With the benefit of slightly modified rear suspension, featuring lower mounting points for the top wishbones, and an engine fitted with smaller turbos for improved response at low revs, Michele qualified third on 1m 20.653s, barely a tenth of a second behind Senna and Mansell who made up the front row.

Qualifying through the streets of the Principality had been a fairly fraught business, with Senna upsetting many of his rivals by cruising round slowly, on the racing line, once he had set his fastest time. It was one of the few occasions on which Niki Lauda had been seen really to lose his temper, while Alboreto was simply grey with fury, even forcing Ayrton's Lotus up the escape road at the *Rascasse* hairpin in an attempt to teach the future World Champion a short, sharp lesson.

Come the race, Michele was well stoked up, nipping past Prost on the second lap to hold a strong second place and diving into the lead when Senna's engine expired on lap 14. Prost elbowed his way past to lead laps 18 to 22, but Michele came back at him and reasserted his Ferrari at the head of the field until lap 31, when a punctured tyre sent him scuttling into the pits. The Italian fought back heroically to second place, but there was no way of catching Prost before the finish. "I was in good shape there, and so was the car," recalls Michele. "It was easy for me to be the quickest car on the track, and that allowed me to make up a lot of time after my tyre stop."

Johansson, meanwhile, ended a miserable weekend by being eliminated virtually at the start. He had qualified a distant 15th after a hectic practice during which he brushed the guard rail following a nasty moment while trying carbon fibre brake discs, and was then inadvertently wiped into the wall opposite the pits when Teo Fabi's Toleman moved over on him. In the race Stefan was hit from behind by Tambay's Renault as he veered left in an attempt to avoid Gerhard Berger's Arrows, which almost stalled at the start. The impact broke a damper rod in one of the Ferrari's rear shock absorbers, forcing the Swede into retirement at the end of the second lap.

Front suspension geometry revisions were on hand for the 156s at Spa, but a crumbling track surface saw the Belgian Grand Prix postponed until September, so the next race on the 1985 schedule was at Montreal's *Circuit Gilles Villeneuve* where Alboreto reckoned the latest car "handled like a Rolls-Royce" compared with the previous year's C4.

Michele was fastest in Friday's first qualifying, dropping to third the following day behind de Angelis and Senna in the Lotus 97Ts. Johansson lined up alongside him in fourth place, so things certainly looked promising for the race, and so it proved. Alboreto tailed de Angelis for 16 laps, then went by to lead to the finish, while Stefan worked his way through onto his team-mate's tail, despite grappling with a slight misfire. Towards the end he closed aggressively on Alboreto, but a touch of additional boost pressure from the leader sent Johansson a message he fully understood and the two cars crossed the line separated by less than two seconds. With this success, Alboreto took the World Championship points lead from de Angelis and would not relinquish it until the Dutch Grand Prix at Zandvoort over two months later.

A week after their Canadian success, Alboreto and Johansson swapped the smooth surface of Montreal for the ripples of Detroit, where the 156s reverted to previous form, continuing their acute dislike of bumpy circuits. Senna was on pole yet again on 1m 42.051s, with Alboreto third (1m 43.748s) and Johansson ninth, his times restricted by excessive understeer – the last thing he needed at a track lined by concrete retaining walls. In the race Alboreto was never in contention, grappling with fading brakes almost from the start, but Johansson chased Rosberg's winning Williams with great verve, finishing a storming second despite a front brake disc disintegrating with three laps to go. Some inspired car control, aided by switching as much brake balance bias as possible to the rear wheels, kept the Swede away from the walls, and the Ferraris came hobbling home in 2-3 formation.

The 1985 Monaco Grand Prix was arguably the finest drive of Michele Alboreto's career. He contested the lead with Prost's McLaren-TAG only to have a possible winning effort thwarted by a punctured tyre.

Alboreto: "It was an easy race for us, really, because the car was good and we had no problems with fuel consumption."

By the time the Championship battle returned to Europe, Maranello had built up a couple of new chassis with lower mounting points for the front shock absorbers, and these were available, along with two regular-specification cars, for the French Grand Prix at Paul Ricard. After trying the revamped 156s in Friday qualifying, both drivers reverted to their original machines the following day, Alboreto running half a second quicker to take third place on the grid with 1m 33.267s.

Johansson, meanwhile, was battling against the debilitating effects of chickenpox and proved almost three seconds slower down in 15th, but while Alboreto's engine blew up on lap five Stefan soldiered on doggedly, lunging round the outside of de Angelis's Lotus going into the daunting *Signes* right-hander to take fourth place on the very last lap of the race.

The British Grand Prix at Silverstone followed, with experiments with slightly repositioned water radiators in order to improve airflow to the intercoolers. Both Alboreto and Johansson reported excessive oversteer, so larger rear wings were fitted which, inevitably, cost the 156s dear in terms of straightline speed. Rosberg blitzed the opposition with a 1m 5.591s pole winner – an average speed of just on 150mph – while the best Alboreto could achieve was a sixth fastest 1m 6.793s, Stefan trailing in 11th place, over a further second slower.

Johansson had another close encounter with Tambay at the first corner, the Renault T-boning the Ferrari as it speared onto the grass. The Swede ground slowly round with a split oil radiator spewing lubricant all over the place, the V6 eventually seizing solid as he reached the pit lane. The main issue for the lead was fought out between Prost and Senna, the McLaren winning commandingly after the Lotus ran short of fuel; Alboreto could only play a supporting role, but at least survived to finish second.

There were more intercooler experiments to be seen when the team returned to the new Nürburgring for the F1 fraternity's second visit in nine months, this time for the German Grand Prix proper. Unpredictable wet/dry conditions in qualifying saw Teo Fabi's Toleman-Hart bag a freak pole position, but Johansson lined up alongside with Michele half a second behind in eighth place. On a smooth-surfaced, medium-speed track the Ferraris were back on the pace, but sheer bad luck wiped out Stefan's challenge almost before the event got under way.

As the green light came on, Fabi got bogged down and Johansson was moving first. "But the engine was hesitating every time I changed up through the gears," he reported and, as Rosberg dived through to take an early lead, Michele came from nowhere on a tight inside line from his starting position on the fourth row – and made contact with Stefan.

In fact, Alboreto's left front nose wing end plate sliced into the sister Ferrari's right rear Goodyear, putting Stefan on course for the pits at the end of the opening lap. "I'm so sorry," said Michele afterwards, with feeling. "I thought, 'Oh no, not Stefan, anybody but Stefan'."

With replacement rubber fitted, Johansson put on an impressive demonstration of what might have been as he accelerated back onto the circuit just ahead of the leading bunch, but almost a lap behind, and initially pulled away from his pursuers. Embroiled in the early stages with de Angelis and Prost in a battle for second, Alboreto eventually found himself fighting the McLaren driver for victory. On this occasion the Italian came out on top, despite his car trailing a slight oil haze in right-handers.

Michele found this a particularly satisfying victory. "Prost had a better car than me that day, so it was good to be able to stay in front," he asserted. Johansson ended up a philosophical ninth.

Even though he had two wins under his belt and was leading the points table, Alboreto remained only guardedly confident about fending off Prost for the Championship. The Ferraris were worryingly unpredictable in their performance from circuit to circuit and the super-fast Österreichring confirmed his worst fears a fortnight later. It was the old, old problem – bad handling over the bumps – and the best Michele could manage in practice for the Austrian Grand Prix was a ninth fastest 1m 27.516s – 2.3s slower than Prost, who would start from pole. At least mechanical reliability was on their side, though, and Alboreto led Johansson home for a 3-4 finish behind Prost's McLaren and Senna's Lotus.

If the Österreichring was bad, then Zandvoort was the team's nadir that season. "The car simply did not work," says the Italian firmly, and the two 156s lined up 16-17, again over two seconds away from the pole time, set on this occasion by Nelson Piquet's Brabham BT53. Again, reliability helped, with Alboreto a solid fourth, aggressively bumping Senna's third-place Lotus a couple of times on the last lap as he sought vainly to gain another position. But the Championship was slipping away now, for Prost had finished second, feet behind team-mate Lauda, thereby grabbing a points lead he was never to lose.

Monza produced the usual big effort, the 156s sporting revised suspension, relocated water radiators, bigger intercoolers, repositioned turbo wastegates, short engine covers and new underbody diffuser panels. It still didn't bring them up to pace, however. Senna took pole on 1m 25.084s, while Alboreto (1m 26.468s) and Johansson (1m 27.473s) were seventh and tenth respectively. Michele never ran higher than sixth in the race before stopping with engine failure, and Stefan was placed fifth, a lap down on winner Prost, after running out of fuel. The McLaren-TAGs had raised the performance stakes and Ferrari were powerless – literally – to compete.

Alboreto never finished again after Zandvoort, Ferrari's challenge toppling like a house of cards after their home outing at Monza. The re-run Belgian Grand Prix proved calamitous: although Michele qualified fourth, he was the first retirement with clutch failure after three laps, while Johansson ended his race straddling a kerb, having spun as a result of a blown engine, only four laps later.

The Brands Hatch bumps pushed both cars right out of the equation at the Grand Prix of Europe, the occasion of Nigel Mansell's maiden victory at the wheel of the Williams FW10-Honda, and Prost's fourth place was sufficient to clinch his first World Championship. Alboreto qualified 15th, two places behind Stefan, the two drivers complaining of a dire lack of grip. Johansson succumbed to electrical trouble.

That was virtually the end of the road. Two "long-haul" races remained to complete the calendar, in South Africa and Australia. At Kyalami the Ferraris qualified 15-16, Michele ahead, but the Italian's engine let him down. Johansson was fourth, lapped by Mansell's winning Williams. Finally, in the inaugural Adelaide event, Alboreto at least managed to qualify fifth, albeit 2.5s slower than Senna's pole-position Lotus. He was out early, however, with a deranged gear linkage, leaving Johansson to round off a bitterly disappointing season with a lapped fifth place.

One of the significant factors responsible for the team's failure to maintain its early-season momentum during 1985 was the lack of an in-house wind tunnel at Maranello. Not until the autumn of 1986 would such a facility be available within the extended premises of the competition department on the Via Alberto Ascari, but its benefits became apparent during the 1987 season, when the Ferrari F1/87s began to present a serious challenge at several circuits.

Yet, three years later, as Alboreto reflected on 1984 and '85, the Italian pinpointed a lack of engine power as the overwhelming problem, together with the Italian media's habit of arousing dissatisfaction at Maranello with the efforts of the team's drivers.

"The media in Italy are capable of convincing the Ferrari management about any aspect of the car's performance," he said wryly. "And they, in turn, are prepared to believe the media far more than the drivers. Throughout those two seasons we kept saying we hadn't got enough power, but then some newspaper would come up with a statistic that we had fastest speed in a straight line at some circuit or another. Then we would have to try explaining that the reason we were quick on the straight was because we were running no wing, and the drivability of the engine is poor because there is no power at the bottom end of the rev range."

Meanwhile, for 1986, Postlethwaite produced another new car which, following a further change to Ferrari's type numbering system, was given the designation F1/86. Its carbon fibre monocoque was manufactured in two pieces, a floor section being bonded to the upper part of the tub. Although the new machine's sloping engine cover, which fully enclosed the rollover bar, gave the impression that it was higher than the car it superseded, it was in fact 16cm lower than the 156/85. The F1/86 also featured new horizontally mounted front dampers, digital instrumentation, a revised gearbox casing to accept new rear shock absorber mountings, new brake calipers manufactured by Ferrari with Brembo components, and a centre-pillar rear wing.

The new car was an improvement, but the opposition – notably the Williams FW11-Honda and Lotus 98T-Renault – were improving faster. At Rio the F1/86s were quick in a straight line, but Alboreto found himself frustrated by a series of fuel pump failures which obliged him to use the spare 156/85 to set his sixth fastest time of 1m 27.485s. He also tangled heavily with Tambay's Haas Lola-Hart, badly damaging his F1/86, which needed a total rear-end rebuild as a result. Another fuel pump drive failure claimed Michele in the race, while Johansson, who qualified eighth, slid into a sand trap after his machine ran out of brakes.

In the interval between Rio and the second round of the Championship at Jerez, Enzo Ferrari had permitted the Minardi team to use Fiorano for testing purposes, only for Andrea de Cesaris to turn some embarrassingly quick times in the Motori-Moderni-engined machine from Faenza, albeit using high boost and soft rubber. Mr. Ferrari made it clear he wanted a decent run from his team in the Spanish Grand Prix, but his hopes were to be dashed again.

Practice saw the team experimenting with Marzocchi gas-filled shock absorbers and stronger fixing plates for the brake discs, but understeer under power and a wearyingly lively ride over the bumps were the abiding problems. Both cars were way off the pace, Stefan lining up 11th on 1m 25.466s – almost four seconds slower than Senna's pole-winning lap – and Alboreto 13th on 1m 26.094s. Both men agreed they needed more downforce. Come the race, the Swede had a massive shunt on lap 11 when his brakes packed up again while he was running eighth. The pedal flopped to the bulkhead and the F1/86 plunged headlong into a tyre-faced barrier, bouncing off it with a shuddering impact, but happily leaving its driver only shaken and bruised. Alboreto sensed a "peculiar feeling" from the front end, pitting to find a wheel bearing had started to break up.

An intensive test session at Imola prior to the San Marino Grand Prix improved the drivers' mood and they reported that the chassis balance was much better. Yet the brakes still failed to imbue them with a great deal of confidence, and the *Autodromo Dino Ferrari* is certainly not a circuit on which to have any worries from that particular standpoint. The F1/86s were also fitted with a complicated new fuel system after a pipe leading to the injectors had leaked, causing a brief engine fire, during practice in Spain.

In the race Prost judged his fuel consumption perfectly to score his first win of the season, taking the chequered flag ahead of the rest in Ferrari's heartland for the third successive year. Piquet's Williams FW11 and Gerhard Berger's Benetton B186-BMW were second and third, leaving Johansson a lapped fourth. Michele had been holding that position with four laps to go when a turbo failed, dropping him to 10th in the final classification.

For Monaco, smaller turbos were tried in conjunction with a butterfly assembly in the throttle mechanism, the aim being to improve engine response. Brembo brake calipers were now fitted all round and in high-downforce configuration Alboreto managed an encouraging fourth on the grid with 1m 23.904s – compared with Prost's pole time of 1m 22.627s. It had been a *banzai* effort on the part of the Italian, who completed that single lap a full second quicker than any of his other times – and had four bent wheel rims to show for it!

Johansson, meanwhile, failed to get a single clear lap and found himself down in 15th place. He was also involved in an unfortunate pit lane accident, bowling over former Renault team manager Jean Sage with one of the Ferrari's rear wheels. Under the circumstances, the Frenchman was fortunate to survive with only minor concussion and a broken shoulder, but Stefan was understandably upset. The incident set the tone for the race, Michele succumbing to turbo trouble for the second successive GP, leaving Johansson to struggle home tenth with a broken gear lever.

The Belgian Grand Prix at Spa at least saw a return to some semblance of mechanical reliability, a switch to Garrett turbos for the race giving Alboreto his first finish of the season. In qualifying, his was the fastest car through the speed trap approaching *Les Combes* at 199.667mph. Not that the Italian was totally satisfied with his fourth place: after a non-stop run on relatively hard rubber, he felt he should have taken the third place on the rostrum, but Johansson, ignoring pit signals, had breezed by to take that helping of four Championship points.

In fact Stefan, who ran softer rubber from the start, briefly led the race before coming in for fresh tyres. Asked if he had been worried about his F1/86 being marginal on fuel, he replied: "I don't take much notice of the fuel computer – it's never been right in the past." This jocular observation went down like a lead balloon at Maranello.

A trip across the Atlantic proved that Ferrari's turbo problems were not yet behind them. In practice at Montreal the team had no fewer than five Garrett turbo malfunctions, although this was put down to quality control problems producing a build-up in back pressure which caused the turbine thrust bearings to fail. The cars also featured a new exhaust configuration and revised underbody diffuser panels, but Alboreto's 11th fastest 1m 24.795s was over three seconds slower than Mansell's pole time in the Williams.

The team had a simply terrible Canadian Grand Prix. Stefan, running seventh, found Johnny Dumfries's Lotus emerging from the pit lane in front of him right on the racing line. Exiting the fast esses after the pits, the Ferrari driver moved right – just as Dumfries did the same – and Johansson ran straight into the back of the slower car, eliminating them both on the spot.

Alboreto, right behind, had to spin wildly in avoidance, banging his knees painfully on the steering rack in the process. Later he lost a couple of gears and faded to an eventual eighth, still badly shaken by his earlier fright.

A new lubrication system helped solve the turbo problems in time for Detroit, while modifications were also made to the braking system, the brake fluid being circulated to cool it, with additional pipes running from twin pumps to the calipers. Stefan qualified an heroic fifth, only to retire with electrical problems in the race, leaving the still-bruised Alboreto to creep home a distant fourth.

Worried expressions. Designer Harvey Postlethwaite and Michele Alboreto have plenty on their minds; Hockenheim, 1986.

CAMPARI
East
28
LOTO
olivetti
canon
canon

For the rest of the season, the Ferrari team experimented, almost on a race-to-race basis, with different combinations of wheelbase and suspension geometry in an attempt to improve the F1/86's level of competitiveness. A 45mm longer wheelbase was tried at Paul Ricard in conjunction with a new push-rod rear suspension set-up and, while all three cars were prepared to this specification for the British Grand Prix at Brands Hatch, by the time they got to Hockenheim the *muletta* featured a reduced wheelbase (down from 2762 to 2632mm), achieved by removing the bellhousing and repositioning the oil tank on top of the gearbox.

There wasn't much in the way of results, either. Having collided with Prost in practice for the French Grand Prix, Alboreto stalled on the grid and spent the entire race hauling back to eighth. Stefan's turbo failed. They both retired with engine problems at Brands, where Stefan was left speechless with rage during practice when he found himself ordered out of the spare car's cockpit to make way for Alboreto after both their race cars had expired!

At Hockenheim Alboreto was just getting into his stride when the transmission broke on lap seven. Meanwhile, sprinting for the first corner, Johansson had been pitched into Fabi's Benetton by Alliot's Ligier, mangling the Ferrari's nose section in the ensuing mêlée. He trailed round for it to be fixed, but eventually stopped four laps from the finish with a loose wing end plate.

Things got worse. Practising at the Hungaroring, venue for the newly inaugurated Hungarian Grand Prix, Alboreto lost a wheel and only qualified 15th. "It's difficult enough driving it on four wheels, never mind three," he was heard to muse. Modifications to the turbos in the interests of reliability produced simply savage throttle response, but Johansson barnstormed his way to a brilliant third place, Michele being eliminated with a deranged nose section after a tangle with Derek Warwick's Brabham BT55.

The inability of the team to repair this accident damage led to the introduction of a new one-piece nose cone assembly for the following weekend's Austrian Grand Prix, Alboreto and Johansson benefiting from mechanical reliability to finish second and third, albeit a lap behind Prost's McLaren, as many faster rivals faded. For Johansson it was a particularly heroic weekend, an apparently innocuous spin across the grass during Friday's untimed practice session ending with his F1/86 "impaled" on a steel pole supporting an advertising hoarding. "The pole came through the bottom of the monocoque and hit the bulkhead behind the seat," he winced. "It was like being hit with a hammer in the small of the back." The car was badly damaged, but a fresh chassis was sent from Maranello overnight.

That wasn't the end of his bad luck. By lap 26 he was up to eighth – "feeling as if my brain would explode with the pain of it all" – when his left front nose fin flew off, bounced on his helmet and smashed into one of the rear wing end plates. That entailed a second pit stop for repairs, after which the F1/86 oversteered violently. "The oil warning light was flickering for most of the time, so I never thought I'd make it to the finish," he shrugged.

Prior to Monza, another intensive Imola test with revised turbos and aerodynamic changes raised the team's hopes, but Alboreto was mysteriously absent for the first day of qualifying. Johansson thus used a qualifying engine earmarked for the Italian, reporting it to be far more powerful than anything he'd previously experienced, while the Italian press went wild with speculation as to Michele's absence.

Their theories ranged from a major row with Enzo Ferrari to food poisoning, but the truth turned out to be far less dramatic. Michele had injured his shoulder in a motorcycle accident, but that did not prevent him from claiming ninth on the grid on the second day. In the race he performed superbly, surging up to third place, hard on the heels of Mansell and Piquet, before his F1/86 snapped into a spin as he exited the first chicane. He kissed the right-hand barriers just hard enough to bend a couple of wheel rims, stopped for repairs, then fought back to fifth before the engine failed. Johansson stalked Gerhard Berger's Benetton all afternoon, breezing by to take a lucky third behind the Williams-Honda duo when the Austrian's car developed a misfire.

Stefan's F1/86 broadside in the middle of the pack at Hockenheim as Teo Fabi's Benetton clips its right front wheel, while the rest of the field streams away from the grid at the start of the 1986 German Grand Prix. The Ferrari got away with it, but the Benetton wasn't so lucky.

A happier moment. Alboreto and Johansson join Prost on the rostrum after finishing 2-3 behind his McLaren-TAG in the 1986 Austrian Grand Prix. The Frenchman was a lap ahead of them both.

Stefan would get even closer to Berger at Estoril during the Portuguese Grand Prix, Ferrari and Benetton pirouetting into a sand trap after Gerhard had rammed the Swede as they battled for fifth place. Stefan resumed with a rumpled right-hand turbo cooling duct, but Michele had nipped past during this fracas, the two Ferraris finishing in fifth and sixth positions.

There was little joy awaiting the team in Mexico or Australia. The return to the Magdalena Mixhuca track saw turbo failures claim both cars, while Michele and Stefan both shunted hard during qualifying at Adelaide, writing off two chassis in the process. Stefan's was by far the worse of these incidents and he was lucky to struggle away with a badly bruised left leg. At least he had the consolation of surviving to third in the race, while Michele finished a disastrous season when he was rammed by Arnoux's Ligier at the start, retiring after a single lap with suspension damage.

Johansson ended up fifth in the World Championship on 23 points, Alboreto a dejected eighth on 14 points, tying with Ligier team-mates Arnoux and Jacques Laffite. But Gerhard Berger had already been signed up to replace the Swedish driver, who would eventually move to McLaren as Alain Prost's partner.

A year later, Stefan would reflect: "I don't think I really got to grips with things at Ferrari, because I didn't know the right channels to use in my dealings with the team. I wanted to test the car in a wind tunnel, for example, but it never happened. Maybe I just went about it all the wrong way."

His frustration was certainly shared by Fiat's senior management, their President, Vittorio Ghidella, becoming very concerned about Ferrari's lack of success. Therefore, back at base, momentous management decisions had been taken with the intention of restoring the Prancing Horse to some semblance of its former glory.

Section VII: The uphill struggle, 1985-88

Chapter 2
Into the Barnard era

By the summer of 1986, the rupture between McLaren International's Ron Dennis and the team's chief designer John Barnard was complete. Their working relationship had deteriorated to the point where it was untenable and Barnard, architect of the superb TAG-turbo-engined machines which had set new standards of F1 performance over the previous two seasons, had to go. Not that John was short of options. He had been discussing an ambitious F1 project with BMW, but was now intrigued to receive an approach from a London-based intermediary, acting for what was described as "a prominent F1 team".

The first potential stumbling block arose when the intermediary inquired of Barnard, "Would you be prepared to relocate to Europe?" The response from Barnard was a very firm negative! Then the intermediary returned to make the formal offer. As John recalls: "I said, 'Yes, that's nice. But I'm not going to live in Europe.' By then I was pretty certain that the offer was coming from Ferrari, and if it wasn't them, then perhaps it might be a French company, either Renault or Peugeot. After some more discussion they came back and said, 'What if you were allowed to be based in England?' So I said we should have a talk on that basis, after which I met Marco Piccinini to discuss the matter in more detail."

Out of this convoluted and apparently unlikely sequence of events was born the Guildford Technical Office or GTO, a somewhat arch title in view of the significance to Ferrari of those initials. This was to be the company's own British-based design studio, situated in new purpose-built premises at Shalford, near Guildford. Barnard had gained plenty of experience of this "arm's length" design process when he had organized the manufacture of the Chaparral 2K Indycar from the UK, designing it at home in Wembley while the chassis was built in Luton by BS Fabrications.

In purely practical terms, there was no reason why such a system should not have worked perfectly, GTO carrying out the design and development of the prototype components, some of which were then manufactured by BS Fabrications, before finalized "production" components were produced for the cars at Maranello. However, to a large extent, realism took something of a back seat to emotion in connection with this project. There is no doubt that many people at Maranello felt affronted that part of Ferrari's F1 design process had been transplanted to England. Of course, that view failed to take account of the fact that the previous two seasons had been pretty dismal, and Barnard's recruitment looked like a positive step.

In his new role as Ferrari's Technical Director, one of John's main briefs was to concentrate on developing the new naturally aspirated machine which would possibly be used in 1988, the final transitional year as F1 turbos were phased out once and for all. He arrived a little too late to exert as much influence as he would have liked on the new F1/87 turbo, the concept of which had originally been devised by former ATS designer Gustav Brunner.

For the revised regulations requiring the use of FISA-supplied control valves limiting boost pressure to 4-bar, in conjunction with a 195-litre fuel capacity maximum, the 1987 car used a brand new 90-degree V6 engine (designated Tipo 033). It transmitted its power through a longitudinal six-speed gearbox, this being one of Barnard's fundamental requirements which he had suggested prior to his official arrival on the Ferrari payroll.

"The only thing I did in connection with the engine programme was to get it torsion-tested, the block being stiffened slightly as a result," John explains. "The overall layout of the chassis had been finalized by the time I came along, so I was only able to change a few things like the top of the fuel cell. I gave them the parameters I wanted from the pull-rod suspension geometry standpoint, designed the uprights myself and had the wishbones manufactured by BS Fabrications. Gustav did the basic layout and I modified it by putting my rear waisting and 'ramps' on the back end."

From the start of the season it was clear that Maranello still couldn't match either TAG/Porsche or Honda for power allied to the required consumption over a race distance. In Rio, once Berger's lanky frame had successfully been installed in a specially tailored cockpit, the Austrian's effervescence enabled him to out-qualify Alboreto, the two Italian cars occupying seventh and ninth places on the grid.

In the race Gerhard made three tyre stops, compared with the victorious Prost's two, while Michele steadfastly ignored his pit signals to come in for a fourth set, desperately staying out on worn rubber in an attempt to beat his team-mate. Eventually Berger hauled back to take fourth place, having dislodged Alboreto, whose undertray had become detached to the accompaniment of a trail of sparks. With three laps to go, the Italian threw it all away with a spin, walking angrily back to the pits to find he'd been classified eighth.

Prior to the San Marino race, the team went testing at Imola, suffering five engine failures as they attempted to improve the V6's power curve and increase its rev range to 12,000rpm. Sleeves were also fitted to the rear shock absorbers to insulate them from heat radiated by the turbos, and one of the internal cockpit bulkheads was slightly modified in Berger's car, giving the Austrian fractionally increased knee room.

The F1/87s qualified 5-6, Gerhard ahead, some 1.7s away from the pole-winning time of Senna's Lotus 99T-Honda (1m 25.826s). Alboreto ran fourth from the start ahead of Berger, the Austrian retiring due to electrical problems only 16 laps into the battle, and as Nigel Mansell moved ahead to win comfortably for Williams-Honda Michele was left battling with Senna for second place. Seven laps from the end, the Italian suddenly lost boost pressure and faded to third, a pipe having become detached from a turbo.

At Spa the F1/87 underbodies were lowered slightly, calling for fillets to close the gap at the rear between the undertray and the chassis. The team was now making reasonable progress with the set-up of its cars, Berger qualifying fourth just ahead of his team-mate. Coming round to complete the opening lap, Gerhard spun his Ferrari at the final tight chicane, wiping out Boutsen's Benetton in the process, but he got a second chance when the race was stopped and restarted following a more serious shunt at *Eau Rouge* involving the Tyrrells of Palmer and Streiff. This time he lasted until lap three, when piston failure intervened.

Alboreto ran well in second place following the restart, between Piquet and Prost, but his transmission broke after nine laps and the team packed up early. A couple of weeks later, in practice at Monaco, he added a few more grey hairs to his curly mane, tangling with Christian Danner's Zakspeed in a fiery, high-speed collision on the climb from *Ste. Devote* to *Massenet*.

It was the sort of incident many people had been dreading at Monaco for years, and it was a miracle that the consequences weren't a lot worse. As Michele attempted to squeeze alongside Danner, his Ferrari's right rear wheel tripped over the Zakspeed's left front, ricocheting the Italian car from barrier to barrier on opposite sides of the circuit. Mercifully, the guard rails contained the debris, but the car was torn apart. The gearbox was wrenched off the back and, more worryingly, the pedal box was ripped out. Understandably, Michele had little sympathy for the German driver, although he did say he felt the organizers were being unnecessarily

Trial by press. The ill-judged 1987 Hockenheim press conference where John Barnard (second from left, between Alboreto and Piccinini) was obliged to waste time which could have been better spent working on the new naturally aspirated car.

harsh when they disqualified Danner from any further participation in the meeting.

Michele still qualified fifth, a full three seconds away from Mansell's pole time, and had moved up to an excellent third at the end of the race, behind Senna and Piquet. Berger was a lapped fourth, looking less convincing than his team-mate on this rare occasion after having his own private shunt during qualifying.

For the rigours of Detroit, the F1/87s experimented with Gleason differentials and Tilton carbon fibre clutches, Alboreto qualifying seventh with Berger 12th after spinning into a wall during second qualifying, a faulty rear upright having caused the F1/87 to become unusually unstable under braking. Berger came home in fourth place, the last runner not to be lapped by Senna's winning Lotus, while Alboreto succumbed to gearbox problems.

As the F1 fraternity headed back to continue the Championship battle in Europe, tensions were building up within the Ferrari camp, fuelled by those on the touchlines who naïvely imagined that John Barnard's arrival on the scene would result in an overnight transformation of the team's fortunes. Further engine development tests were initiated, but neither car finished the French Grand Prix at Paul Ricard, Alboreto's suffering engine problems while Gerhard spun off in the closing stages when a lug on a rear upright fractured. Silverstone brought more frustration in the British Grand Prix where Berger hooked a wheel over a kerb coming through Abbey Curve early in the race, spinning heavily into the guard rail, while Michele retired with damaged rear suspension.

For Barnard, probably the lowest ebb of the season came at Hockenheim. At a time when he should have been back at GTO, pulling out all the stops to develop the new naturally aspirated car, he was diverted to waste time at Hockenheim undergoing what amounted to a "trial by press" in the wake of some comments made by Alboreto in an interview in the French sporting paper *L'Équipe* earlier that same week.

Michele had described the English designer's *modus operandi* as being like "a brain surgeon attempting a complicated operation over the telephone". Marco Piccinini panicked, calling Barnard over from Guildford, and those present can recall the look of thunder on the Englishman's face throughout the weekend. He had a professional respect for Michele's abilities behind the wheel of a Grand Prix car, but was less impressed by what he saw as the Italian's capacity for behind-the-scenes politicking. His mood was not improved when Berger's efforts in Friday qualifying ended in a shunt when his car's left front suspension collapsed.

For his part, Alboreto was fast losing patience with the whole set-up. By the end of 1987 he knew he was a marked man and resolved to leave Maranello when his contract expired at the end of the following year, regardless of whether or not he was asked to stay on. "The tensions built up and I thought to myself that I must have a very quiet winter indeed if I'm going to be able to stand another season driving for them in 1988."

Harvey Postlethwaite was also on the scene in Germany, overseeing a revised aerodynamic package which included changes to the underbody, a narrower chord rear wing with smaller end plates and suspension geometry revisions. Both F1/87s expired with turbo problems in the race, but not before Senna's Lotus had almost forced Michele off the track at 190mph on the straight, leaving the Italian white-faced and speechless with indignation.

This depressing sequence of mechanical unreliability continued at the Hungaroring with two more retirements. However, Berger raised spirits considerably by qualifying alongside Mansell on the front row, shadowing the Williams until transmission problems intervened, after which Michele took over in second place for a while, eventually retiring from third with turbo failure. Maranello's wind tunnel, operational for eight months, was now starting to pay dividends.

It took three attempts to get the Austrian Grand Prix under way after a succession of startline shunts, but no better fortune awaited Maranello on Berger's home ground. Gerhard was out with turbo failure early on and Alboreto succumbed to a broken exhaust after running over Senna's nose cone as the two cars raced for a corner, side by side.

By this stage in the season decisions for 1988 had to be made. Early in the year Barnard had been convinced that the 3.5-litre naturally aspirated route would be the one to take, but as 1987 progressed he became less certain. By the end of the summer, he had changed his mind. "As things stand at the moment," he speculated, "we've got to go for the turbo simply because, even with the rules reducing boost pressure to 2.5-bar with only 150 litres of fuel, it looks as though the turbos will have 100bhp in hand over the atmospheric cars."

The rules for 1988 permitted the use of the previous season's cars, as long as teams nominated them for such use no later than the 1987 Italian Grand Prix. Thus, at Monza, the F1/87s featured certain bodywork alterations around the fuel cell, purely in anticipation of structural changes for the following season. On the engine front the Marelli/Ferrari electronics included a radio-telemetry system to monitor engine data, Maranello making its customary big effort for their home race, and Berger qualified third, a mere half-second slower than Piquet's pole-position Williams-Honda. He ran strongly to finish fourth, but Alboreto retired early with turbo failure.

Berger was now getting the taste for running at the front. Additional engine development work in the break leading up to the Portuguese Grand Prix included new Garrett turbos manufactured so hurriedly that there was insufficient time to produce "handed" pairs. Consequently "left-hand" turbos were used on both banks of the V6, necessitating alterations to the right-hand exhaust to suit the turbo inlets and exits.

Berger timed his fastest run superbly between rain showers, taking pole position with a lap of 1m 17.620s, 0.3s faster than Mansell's Williams, with Alboreto sixth on 1m 18.540s. The race was stopped following a multiple collision at the first corner. On the restart Mansell briefly surged ahead into the first turn, but Berger was tight on the Englishman's tail and slipstreamed past at the end of the opening lap.

Berger dominated the race until Alain Prost's McLaren MP4/3-TAG got through to second place just after half distance. Thereafter the brilliant Frenchman steadily chipped away at Berger's advantage, pressuring the leading Ferrari into a spin just over three laps from the chequered flag. As Gerhard scrambled back into the fray to finish an embarrassed second, Prost surged by to score the record-breaking 28th win of his career. "I spent too much time watching for Alain in my mirrors instead of watching the track ahead," Berger readily admitted.

A week later at Jerez, Ferrari sustained this upsurge in form, Berger and Alboreto qualifying on the second row and running strongly with the leading bunch for much of the distance. Towards the finish Michele over-revved to 14,000rpm, presaging engine failure on the following lap, while Berger slid over a kerb and cracked open the oil tank casting, but it had been fun while it lasted.

Berger had clearly been knocking on the door of success and was ready to profit from any misfortune suffered by McLaren or Williams. That golden moment came at Suzuka, venue for the first Japanese Grand Prix to be staged since 1977. With Mansell having written himself out of the equation in a spectacular practice shunt and Piquet taking it easy now that the Championship was in the bag, only Prost remained as a potential challenger to Gerhard's pole-position F1/87. The Frenchman picked up a puncture on the second lap, so Berger ran out an unchallenged winner, restoring Maranello to the winner's circle for the first time since Alboreto's triumph at the new Nürburgring over two years before.

Not that Michele was without glory on this historic day. His clutch went solid on the grid, the engine stalled and he was last away with the aid of a push start. He drove with all his old fire, climbing through to an eventual fourth behind Senna and Johansson, despite a triple spin, flat in sixth gear, when a back-marker inadvertently moved over on him, and an exhaust tailpipe which was dangling on the track. "I'm pleased that I've made up for Estoril," beamed the winner, "although I was under considerably less pressure today." Nice to listen to a realist...

Then came Adelaide and more of the same. Pole position again fell to Berger, who wrested the lead from Piquet mid-way round the opening lap and blitzed the opposition once more. Alboreto finished third on the road, only to be promoted to second place when Senna's Lotus 99T was disqualified as a result of its additional front brake cooling ducts being found to infringe the permitted maximum dimensions, so the season ended with a glorious 1-2 for Ferrari.

As has happened so frequently in the past, just when Maranello seemed set for

Joy day. Gerhard Berger making the most of his opposition's troubles to head for victory at Suzuka in the 1987 Japanese Grand Prix. Ferrari were back in the winning business after a two-year spell in the wilderness.

28
Agip
Marlboro
HONDA
Marlboro

a competitive streak, some fresh opposition turned up to put them in the shade. Ferrari entered 1988 with a 2.5-bar/150-litre version of the previous year's car, now dubbed F1/87/88C, using a revised Tipo 033B V6 with 81mm × 48.55mm bore and stroke, the rev limit of which had also been raised from 12,000 to 12,500rpm. Dependent on boost pressure, it would produce somewhere in the region of 630-650bhp – around 300bhp less than it had had in 4-bar boost trim the previous year.

Refining the aerodynamic package to produce sufficient downforce with minimal drag was the number one priority with such a modest power output available, so the car was completely revised with new front and rear wings, a much tighter fit for the engine cover and new side pods enclosing intercoolers some 25 per cent smaller, reflecting the reduced amount of heat generated by the muzzled V6.

Berger was highly optimistic about the team's prospects during pre-season testing, although he admitted that the reduction in power output was dramatic and that he had to extract every hundredth from the chassis in an effort to compensate for the loss of engine performance. But all predictions were thrown into disarray when McLaren appeared with the new Honda-engined MP4/4. Ferrari, along with everybody else, simply couldn't compete.

The 1988 season was a quite extraordinary affair, with Senna and Prost winning 15 of the 16 races, Ferrari being left to chase vainly. Berger knew it was all over at Rio when, running second behind Prost towards the end of the Brazilian Grand Prix, he turned in a succession of quick laps in what he thought would be a decisive counter-attack. Prost just speeded up, broke his challenge and won, first time out in the new McLaren, with fuel to spare. "It was obvious that we couldn't compete on power, even at that early stage," said the Austrian.

The F1/87/88Cs collected second and fifth places at Rio, the start of a long summer of frustration. On home ground at Imola, the V6s featured revised engine management programmes set to open the wastegate fractionally before the FISA control valve, thereby preventing an unwanted, sudden surge in boost pressure. But the best result they could manage in the San Marino Grand Prix was a distant fifth, Berger muscling past Nannini's Benetton on the very last lap.

At Monaco only the McLarens were quicker than Berger and Alboreto in practice and, while Senna waltzed away into the distance, Gerhard nosed ahead of Prost on the run to the first corner after the Frenchman missed a gear. Under enormous pressure from the twice World Champion, Berger held him at bay for many laps, but eventually Alain got through, going on to win after Senna crashed. Alboreto finished third after turfing Mansell's Williams FW12-Judd into the barriers on the waterfront.

Whatever Maranello did, McLaren and Honda remained well in control. In Mexico, the Ferraris qualified 3-5 and finished 3-4. They lined up right behind the McLarens at Montreal, but Berger's Canadian GP fuel consumption turned into an appallingly bad joke – "after a dozen laps, the computer said I was already a lap in deficit" – and it turned out that the management system had been incorrectly programmed. Detroit, Prost's personal nemesis, saw Berger make the front row alongside Senna, profiting from the Frenchman's intense dislike of the circuit. But the race produced the same old story, Berger and Alboreto being rammed by the Benetton-Fords, driven by Boutsen and Nannini respectively.

The 1988 Monaco Grand Prix saw Berger performing magnificently as usual, his F1/87/88C staying in second place ahead of Prost's McLaren MP4/4-Honda for many laps. Here the Austrian leads the twice Champion through the tight ess-bend onto the harbourfront.

Back in Europe the Italian V6s occupied the second row of the grid at Paul Ricard and retained their positions behind the McLarens in the race, Michele moving ahead on this occasion, having arrived at a better chassis set-up. John Barnard returned to the pit wall at this race after almost 12 months beavering away on the new atmospheric car, and the following day it was announced that Nigel Mansell would be joining the Maranello line-up for 1989, automatically making Alboreto redundant.

Behind the scenes at Maranello, tensions had been building up for many months. Enzo Ferrari was seriously ill with kidney trouble, no longer in a position to take a day-to-day interest in the operation of the team, and disruptive factions had been developing since the previous year.

Harvey Postlethwaite, who was finding it extremely awkward working under Barnard's regime, decided it was time to leave, moving back to England to join Tyrrell, taking aerodynamicist Jean-Claude Migeot with him. Engine man Jean-Jacques His retraced his path to Renault now that the French company planned an F1 return with Williams for 1989, so Barnard assumed control in the field with former 156 turbo engineer Renzetti overseeing the engine development programme.

The search for ultimate engine power now ceased to be the number one priority and the engine management set-up was totally revised with the object of producing more consistent power over a race distance. At Silverstone, with those engine changes still in the pipeline, Berger and Alboreto managed to qualify together on the front row, but only because McLaren were, relatively speaking, in aerodynamic disarray. Come the rain-soaked race, things were back to normal, even though Gerhard led for 14 gloriously uninhibited, fuel-squandering laps. By the finish he was spluttering out of fuel, trailing home in ninth place. Alboreto was relegated to 17th after timing his tyre stops all wrong.

Hockenheim followed a familiar pattern, Berger and Alboreto taking the chequered flag behind Senna and Prost, while a dramatic lack of grip during practice at the Hungaroring was solved on Berger's car at least when he and John Barnard totally altered the set-up on the morning of the Grand Prix. In the race, Gerhard reported, the chassis was "wonderful, but the engine couldn't have had more than 550bhp to judge by the difficulties I had edging past the slower cars on the straight." He finished fourth while Alboreto stopped when his engine cut out.

Just a week later, Enzo Ferrari finally lost his battle for life at the grand old age of 90, bringing to an end one of the last surviving links with the pioneering days of motor racing. Frail and beset by serious illness, his demise had been expected for some weeks, yet there was still shock and despair at the passing of the man who, for decades, had been regarded almost as a pivotal factor in the continuation of motor racing as a whole, not simply his own team's participation in the sport. The saddest aspect, of course, was that *Il Drake* passed on at a time when the fortunes of his beloved team were at a low ebb, with backs against the wall. Barnard, hitherto directly answerable to the Commendatore, now found himself responsible to Fiat appointee Pier-Giorgio Cappelli.

Maranello's vain pursuit continued at Spa, the McLaren-Hondas running away with the Belgian Grand Prix. Gerhard almost got alongside Prost going into *Les Combes* on the second lap, immediately fading into the pit lane with management system problems. He re-emerged later on, set the fastest lap of the race and then retired when the trouble recurred. Alboreto ran third only for the engine to fail with less than ten laps to go. Michele drove it until it stopped, a smoking wreck, out on the circuit.

It looked as though it would be the same story at Monza, the two F1/87s, now fitted with electrically activated, cockpit-operated front ride height adjusters, retaining their customary occupancy of the second row and the McLarens running away with the race. Until, that is, Prost's Honda V6 suffered piston failure and Senna, marginal on fuel and with Berger closing fast, took a necessary risk lapping Jean-Louis Schlesser's Williams going into the first chicane with just over a lap to go.

The novice Frenchman, by an ironic twist standing in for future *Ferrariste* Mansell, who was unwell, collided with Senna, putting the McLaren out of the race there and then. Berger and Alboreto surged by to inherit an emotional 1-2 success, nine years after Jody Scheckter and Gilles Villeneuve had last put Maranello in the winner's circle in front of an hysterical Monza crowd.

It wasn't easy for Berger, either. "I went badly into deficit with my fuel consumption trying to keep the McLarens in sight during the early stages," he recalled, "so when Michele began to close up, I just had to sit there and let him. He came right up onto my gearbox before I'd got my consumption back on schedule, after which I really had to work hard. He kept me under a lot of pressure."

It was a glorious moment, Ferrari and its drivers profiting by sustaining the pressure on a day when the McLaren steamroller faltered. But there were to be no more glory days in 1988. Ahead lay only a fifth place for Alboreto in Portugal, and a sixth in Spain and a fourth in Japan for Berger. Gerhard pirouetted out of the Portuguese race after activating the cockpit fire extinguisher as his hand reached for the ride height adjustment control. Freezing extinguishant was released into the footwell and Berger's right foot slipped off the brake. The Austrian's Suzuka result was achieved with the assistance of an over-aggressive Alboreto who, having been spun off the road in the early stages by Nannini, a rival who had featured rather too frequently in incidents with Michele in the past, held up the Benetton so badly in the closing stages of the race that Berger was able to catch and overtake him. Later, an animated and unfriendly confrontation ensued between the two Italians in the pit lane.

In Australia, Berger qualified third behind the two McLarens with Alboreto a lowly 12th. On race morning, Alboreto warned Prost that Gerhard was determined to lead this final race of the turbo era, regardless of the consequences for his fuel consumption. Just as at Silverstone, where he knew his car had no hope of running competitively to the finish, the Austrian opted for a spirited display of bravado, going out simply to enjoy himself.

Berger finished the opening lap behind Prost and Senna, taking second place from the newly crowned World Champion mid-way round lap three. He then settled down to reel in Prost's leading McLaren, surging by on lap 14 and immediately pulling away, Alain not wishing to get drawn into what wouldn't really have been a race at all.

The Austrian's strategy was to lead until around three-quarter distance, then to retire with unspecified "brake problems". The plan went wrong two-thirds of the way round lap 26 when Gerhard tripped over Arnoux's wandering Ligier at the end of the back straight. To outsiders, it looked as though René hadn't bothered to look in his mirrors, chopping across the Ferrari's nose as they swung into the hairpin. The unruffled Berger was more charitable, however, conceding that his own brakes were, in truth, fading and that he hadn't been able to stop in time. For Alboreto, his final Ferrari outing could hardly have been worse. At the first chicane he tangled with Alex Caffi's Dallara and found himself bundled very firmly into the guard rail. End of story.

Berger was placed third in the Drivers' Championship, Alboreto fifth. Ferrari were second in the Constructors' table, a massive 134 points behind the matchless McLarens. It had been a two-horse race between the McLaren team-mates all year and, apart from that magical, lucky break at Monza, Ferrari, like the rest, hadn't been in contention.

Barnard and his colleagues could at least console themselves with the fact that the turbo route had been the correct one to follow. One shudders to think what the outcome might have been had they hurried the naturally aspirated Tipo 639, new and untested, into competitive action at the start of 1988.

As it was, Barnard's all-new challenger, originally conceived with 1988 in mind, did not appear for its first tests until June. Outwardly distinguished by its high, narrow side pods, the 639 was powered by a brand new 65-degree V12, its bore and stroke of 84mm × 52.6mm giving a total capacity of 3497.96cc. With a compression ratio of 11.5:1, it was quoted as developing 600bhp at 12,500rpm by the time Gerhard Berger began seriously testing the car at the end of the year.

Equipped with an electrically activated gearchange mechanism for its seven-speed transmission, it performed moderately well in those initial tests, although the pressure of Italian media interest continued to put Barnard's efforts under microscopic scrutiny in a way which the English engineer always found claustrophobic. Concurrent with those tests, he continued work on a definitive Tipo 640, the finalized 1989 race chassis, which reflected the additional aerodynamic input gained with the prototype 639 during the second half of 1988.

Initial signs are that Honda's 3.5-litre V10 cylinder engine, installed in a new chassis, will be good enough to sustain the McLaren team's pre-eminent position into 1989. In many ways, Maranello's latest V12 was Enzo Ferrari's final legacy to the world, for at a time when there was mounting pressure from fellow constructors to restrict F1 power units to a maximum of eight cylinders the Old Man stuck out to retain the 12-cylinder limit.

New generation. Berger with Piero Lardi-Ferrari, the man tipped to take over from his father but ousted from the *Reparto Corse* ***after a typical Maranello internal feud a matter of months before the Commendatore's death.***

In 1986 he offered a deal to FISA, the sport's governing body: "Continue to allow 12-cylinder engines in F1, and I will shelve my Indycar programme." FISA, anxious that the North American CART series should not be allowed to expand beyond its current status as a domestic category lest it threaten Grand Prix racing's international monopoly, acceded to the proposition. They had no desire for CART to benefit from the prestigious presence of Ferrari at Indianapolis. Yet, ironically, now that the Old Man is gone, that Indy engine has been appropriated by Fiat for the Alfa Romeo CART effort and will appear at the Brickyard after all!

Unquestionably, the 1988 season marked the end of an era. The year in which F1 turned its back on turbocharged engines for good was also marked by the death of Enzo Ferrari. What remains is uncertainty, a major question mark as the corporate hand of Fiat now debates how to handle the jewel in its prestigious automotive crown.

As one of the few other car companies with the financial muscle to take on Honda at their own game, Fiat must think long about creating the right engineering environment in which the Ferrari F1 effort can thrive in the future, rather than allow it to wither under a regime of management by committee.

"I don't fear Ferrari, but I do fear Fiat," is how McLaren boss Ron Dennis summed up the future towards the end of the 1988 Grand Prix season.

Italy's national car maker should take its cue from that perceptive remark and do what needs to be done to restore Ferrari as a competitive force within F1 as Grand Prix motor racing goes into the high-technology 1990s.

Hero! Berger in the F1/87/88C breaking the 1988 McLaren-Honda monopoly on his way to a fortuitous victory in the Italian Grand Prix at Monza, a day of celebration in an otherwise barren season of endeavour.

Appendix — Race Results

Note: These results include all Formula A and Formula 1 results, plus Formula 2 results in 1952 and'53 when that category was for the World Championship. It also includes non-title Formula 2 races for those two seasons (since they were for the "Grand Prix cars" of the time), plus the handful of non-title Formula 1 races to the old regulations. I have also chosen to include the formule libre races in South America where they attracted Ferrari representation, plus the 1954 British libre events which attracted the Thinwall Special, because I believe they are of interest and significance. In preparing this data I would like to offer extra thanks to Denis Jenkinson, Doug Nye and Victor Piggot. Chassis numbers are only included where definitely established or proved beyond reasonable doubt.

KEY TO ABBREVIATIONS:

Ret	Retired
DNF	Did not finish
NC	Not classified
DNQ	Did not qualify
DNS	Did not start

1948

Sept 5. ITALIAN GRAND PRIX, Valentino Park, Turin
R. Sommer 125 s/stage 3rd
G. Farina 125 s/stage Ret: accident
B. Bira 125 s/stage Ret: transmission
F. Cortese 166 Ret: engine

Oct 17. Grand Prix Autodrome, Monza
R. Sommer 125 s/stage Ret: driver unwell
G. Farina 125 s/stage Ret: transmission

Oct 24. Circuit of Garda, Salo
G. Farina 125 s/stage 1st
Count Sterzi 166s 2nd
S. Besana 166s 4th
C. Biondetti 166 —

Oct 31. GRAND PRIX OF PENYA RHIN, Pedralbes, Barcelona
G. Farina 125 s/stage(04C) Ret: transmission
B. Bira 125 s/stage(06C) Ret: transmission
J. Pola 125 s/stage(02C) Ret: engine

1949

Jan 30. Juan Peron Grand Prix, Palermo Park, Buenos Aires
G. Farina 125 s/stage DNF

Feb 6. Eva Peron Grand Prix, Palermo Park, Buenos Aires
G. Farina 125 s/stage DNF

Feb 13. Rosario Grand Prix, Argentina
G. Farina 125 s/stage 1st

Feb 27. Mar del Plata Grand Prix, Argentina
G. Farina 125 s/stage DNF

Mar 20. Interlagos, Sao Paulo, Brazil
G. Farina 125 s/stage DNF

Mar 27. Rio de Janeiro Grand Prix, Gavea
G. Farina 125 s/stage 2nd

Apr 3. San Remo Grand Prix, Ospedaletti
F Bonetto 166 s/c 5th
R. Sommer 125 s/stage —
P. Whitehead 125 s/stage(10C) Ret:engine
G. Bracco 166 6th
Count Sterzi 166 8th (heat 1)

Apr 28. Jersey International Road Race, St. Helier
P. Whitehead 125 s/stage(10C) 7th

May 14. BRITISH GRAND PRIX, Silverstone
P. Whitehead/ D. Folland 125 s/stage(10C) 8th
R. Mays/ K. Richardson 125 Thinwall Spl. Ret:accident

June 19. BELGIAN GRAND PRIX, Spa-Francorchamps
A. Ascari 125 s/stage(08C) 3rd
L. Villoresi 125 s/stage(12C) 2nd
P. Whitehead 125 s/stage(10C) 4th

June 26. Grand Premio Autodromo, Monza
A. Ascari 166F2 3rd
C. Landi 166F2 4th
F. Cortese 166F2 5th
L. Villoresi 166F2 Ret.
J.M. Fangio 166F2 1st
F. Bonetto 166F2 2nd
F. Mosters 166F2 Ret.
G. Bianchetti 166F2 Ret.

July 7. SWISS GRAND PRIX, Bremgarten, Berne
A. Ascari 125 s/stage(08C) 1st
L. Villoresi 125 s/stage(12C) 2nd
P. Whitehead 125 s/stage(10C) 9th

July 17. FRENCH GRAND PRIX, Reims-Gueux
L. Villoresi 125 s/stage(12C) 3rd
P. Whitehead 125 s/stage(10C) Ret:brakes

July 31. ZANDVOORT GRAND PRIX, Zandvoort, Holland
A. Ascari 125 s/stage(08C) Ret:stub axle
L. Villoresi 125 s/stage 2nd

Aug 20. Daily Express Trophy, Silverstone
A. Ascari 125 s/stage(08C) 1st
L. Villoresi 125 s/stage(12C) 3rd
P. Whitehead 125 s/stage(10C) Ret:accident

Aug 28. Lausanne Grand Prix, Switzerland
A. Ascari 125 s/stage(08C) 2nd
L. Villoresi 125 s/stage(12C) Ret.
P. Whitehead 125 s/stage(10C) 9th
F. Cortese 166C 4th

Sept 11. GRAND PRIX OF EUROPE, Monza
A. Ascari 125 2-stage(14C) 1st
L. Villoresi 125 2-stage(16C) Ret:gearbox
P. Whitehead 125 s/stage(10C) Ret:transmission
R. Sommer 125 s/stage(12C) 5th
F. Bonetto 125 s/stage(08C) Ret:engine

Sept 25. Czechoslovak Grand Prix, Masaryk, Brno
P. Whitehead 125 s/stage(10C) 1st
F. Cortese 166C —

Dec 18. Peron Trophy, Palermo Park, Buenos Aires
A. Ascari 166FL 1st
J.M. Fangio 166FL 2nd
L. Villoresi 166FL 3rd
B. Campos 166F2 4th
D. Serafini 125 s/stage 8th
P. Whitehead 125 s/stage 10th

1950

Jan 8. Eva Peron Cup, Palermo Park, Buenos Aires
A. Ascari 166FL Ret:accident
J.M. Fangio 166FL 4th
L. Villoresi 166FL 1st
D. Serafini 125GP 2nd
B. Campos 166F2 Rtd.
P. Whitehead 125 s/stage 11th

Jan 15. General San Martin Trophy, Mar del Plata, Argentina
A. Ascari 166FL 1st
J.M. Fangio 166FL Ret:accident
L. Villoresi 166FL Ret:accident
D. Serafini 125GP Ret.
B. Campos 166F2 Ret.

Jan 22. Coppa Accion de San Lorenzo, Rosario, Argentina
A. Ascari 166FL Ret:overheating
J.M. Fangio 166FL Ret:ignition
L. Villoresi 166FL 1st
D. Serafini 125GP DNF
B. Campos 166F2 2nd

Apr 10. Pau Grand Prix, France
L. Villoresi 125 s/stage(16C) 2nd
R. Sommer 125 s/stage(08C) 4th
A. Ascari 166F2 Ret:transmission

Apr 16. San Remo Grand Prix, Ospedaletti
A. Ascari 125 2-stage(14C) Ret:engine
L. Villoresi 125 2-stage(16C) 2nd
D. Serafini 125 s/stage(08C) Ret.
R. Sommer 125 s/stage Ret.
R. Vallone 125 s/stage 4th
P. Whitehead 125 s/stage Ret.

May 21. MONACO GRAND PRIX, Monte Carlo
A. Ascari 125 2-stage(14C) 2nd
L. Villoresi 125 2-stage(16C) Ret:rear axle
R. Sommer 125 s/stage (08C) 4th
P. Whitehead 125 s/stage (10C) DNS

June 4. SWISS GRAND PRIX, Bremgarten, Berne
A. Ascari 125 2-stage(14C) Ret:oil pipe
L. Villoresi 125 2-stage(18C) Ret:axle
R. Sommer 125 s/stage Ret:broken damper
P. Whitehead 125 s/stage(10C) Did not arrive for race.

June 18. BELGIAN GRAND PRIX, Spa-Francorchamps
A. Ascari 275(16C) 5th
L. Villoresi 125 2-stage(14C) 6th

July 2. FRENCH GRAND PRIX, Reims-Gueux
L. Villoresi 275(16C) Did not start
P. Whitehead 125 s/stage(10C) 3rd

July 9. Bari Grand Prix, Italy
D. Serafini 125 (08C) 7th
A. Ascari 125 (14C) Ret: axle
L. Villoresi/ 166 Ret.

A. Ascari
F. Cortese 166s 5th
July 13. Jersey International Road Race, St. Helier
P. Whitehead 125 s/stage(10C) 1st
July 16. Albi Grand Prix, France
A. Ascari Ret.
L. Villoresi Ret.
July 23. DUTCH GRAND PRIX, Zandvoort
A. Ascari 166F2(50/1) 3rd
L. Villoresi 125 s/stage(14C) 2nd
P. Whitehead 125 s/stage(10C) 4th
July 30. Grand Prix Des Nations, Geneva
A. Ascari 340(18C) Ret:engine
L. Villoresi 275(16C) Ret:accident
Aug 12. Ulster Trophy, Dundrod
P. Whitehead 125 s/stage(10C) 1st
Aug 26. Daily Express Trophy, Silverstone
A. Ascari 125 s/stage(14C) Thinwall Spl. Ret:accident
P. Whitehead 125 s/stage(10C) 3rd
Sept 3. ITALIAN GRAND PRIX, Monza
A. Ascari 375/2 Ret:engine
D. Serafini/ 375/1 2nd
A. Ascari
P. Whitehead 125 s/stage(10C) 7th
C. Biondetti Ret: engine
Oct 29. GRAND PRIX OF PENYA RHIN, Pedralbes, Barcelona
A. Ascari 375/2 1st
D. Serafini 375/1 2nd
P. Taruffi 340 3rd
L. Chinetti 125 s/stage(14C) Ret: ignition
Nov 12. City of Parana GP, Parana, Argentina
J.M. Fangio 166FL 1st
J.F. Gonzalez 166F2/FL 2nd
Dec 18. Santiago GP, Chile
J.M. Fangio 166FL 1st

1951
Feb 18. Peron Cup, Costanera, Buenos Aires
J.F. Gonzalez 166FL 1st
O. Galvez 166FL 4th
Feb 25. Eva Peron Cup, Costanera, Buenos Aires
J.F. Gonzalez 166FL 1st
O. Galvez 166FL Ret.
Mar 11. Syracuse Grand Prix, Sicily
A. Ascari 375 Ret:overheating
L. Villoresi 375 1st
D. Serafini 212 2nd
R. Fischer 212 3rd
G. Bracco 166C Ret.
N. Righetti 125(09C) Ret.
P. Staechlin 166C NC
Mar 26. Pau Grand Prix, Pau
A. Ascari 375 Ret:transmission
L. Villoresi 375 1st
D. Serafini 212 Ret:steering probs.
R. Fischer 212 6th
E. Martin 166C DNS: accident
Apr 15. San Remo Grand Prix, Osepdelatti
A. Ascari 375 1st
L. Villoresi 375 Ret:accident
D. Serafini 375 2nd
R. Fischer 212 3rd
P. Whitehead 125 s/stage(114) 13th
Apr 29. Bordeaux Grand Prix
R. Fischer 212 2nd
P. Whitehead 125 3rd
P. Staechlin 166C NC
May 5. Daily Express Trophy, Silverstone
R. Parnell 375 Thinwall Spl. 1st (race abandoned after six laps)
May 14. Festival of Britain Trophy, Goodwood
R. Parnell 375 Thinwall Spl. 1st
May 27. SWISS GRAND PRIX, Bremgarten, Berne
A. Ascari 375 6th
L. Villoresi 375 Ret:accident
P. Taruffi 375 2nd
P. Whitehead 125 s/stage (114) Ret:accident
R. Fischer 212 11th
P. Hirt 166C Ret: fuel pump
June 2. Ulster Trophy, Dundrod
R. Parnell 375 Thinwall Spl. 2nd
P. Whitehead 125 s/stage Ret:piston
June 17. BELGIAN GRAND PRIX, Spa-Francorchamps
A. Ascari 375 2nd
L. Villoresi 375 3rd
P. Taruffi 375 Ret: axle
July 1. EUROPEAN GRAND PRIX, Reims-Gueux
J.F. Gonzalez/ 375 2nd
A. Ascari
L. Villoresi 375 3rd
A. Ascari 375 Ret:gearbox
R. Parnell 375 Thinwall 4th
July 14. BRITISH GRAND PRIX, Silverstone
J.F. Gonzalez 375 1st
A. Ascari 375 Ret:gearbox
L. Villoresi 375 3rd
P. Whitehead 375 Thinwall Spl. 9th
July 22. DUTCH GRAND PRIX, Zandvoort
R. Fischer 212 4th
July 29. GERMAN GRAND PRIX, Nürburgring
A. Ascari 375 1st
L. Villoresi 375 4th
J.F. Gonzalez 375 3rd
P. Taruffi 375 5th
R. Fischer 212 6th
Aug 5. Albi Grand Prix, Les Planques
C. Landi 375 Ret.
G. Comotti 166C Ret.
Aug 15. Pescara Grand Prix, Pescara, Italy
A. Ascari 375 Ret:oil pressure
L. Villoresi/ 375 Ret:rear axle
A. Ascari
D. Murray 125 8th
J.F. Gonzalez 375 1st
P. Whitehead 125 s/stage 5th
Sept 2. Bari Grand Prix, Lungomare
A. Ascari 375 Ret:carburetter fire
L. Villoresi 375 Ret:transmission
J.F. Gonzalez 375 2nd
D. Murray 125 6th
P. Taruffi 625 prototype 3rd
P. Whitehead 125 s/stage 5th
Sept 16. ITALIAN GRAND PRIX, Monza
A. Ascari 375 1st
L. Villoresi 375 2nd
J.F. Gonzalez 375 4th
P. Taruffi 375 5th
F. Landi 375 Ret:transmission
P. Whitehead 125 s/stage Ret:piston
P. Staechlin 166C DNS: accident
Sept 29. Woodcote Cup, Goodwood
R. Parnell 375 Thinwall Spl. 2nd
Daily Graphic Trophy
R. Parnell 375 Thinwall Spl. 2nd
Oct 3. Formule Libre race, Winfield
R. Parnell 375 Thinwall Spl. 1st
Oct 28. SPANISH GRAND PRIX, Pedralbes, Barcelona
A. Ascari 375 4th
L. Villoresi 375 Ret:engine
J.F. Gonzalez 375 2nd
P. Taruffi 375 Ret:lost wheel

1952
Jan 13. Sao Paulo Grand Prix, Interlagos, Brazil
J.M. Fangio 166FL 1st
J.F. Gonzalez 166FL 3rd
F. Landi 166FL 5th
Jan 28. Rio de Janeiro Grand Prix, Gavea
J.M. Fangio 166FL Ret.
F. Landi 166FL 2nd
J.F. Gonzalez 166FL 1st
Feb 3. Boavista Grand Prix, Rio de Janeiro
J.M. Fangio 166FL 1st
F. Landi 166FL 2nd
J.F. Gonzalez 166FL —
Mar 9. 1st Buenos Aires Grand Prix, Parc Almirante Brown
J.M. Fangio 166FL 1st
J.F. Gonzalez 166FL 2nd
F. Landi 166FL 3rd
R. Abrunhosa 125 s/stage 9th
Mar 16. 2nd Buenos Aires Grand Prix, Parc Almirante Brown
J.M. Fangio 166FL 1st
J.F. Gonzalez 166FL —
F. Landi 166FL 3rd
C. Menditeguey 125 s/stage 2nd
Mar 16. Syracuse Grand Prix, Sicily
A. Ascari 500 1st
P. Taruffi 500 2nd
G. Farina 500 3rd
L. Villoresi 500 7th
P. Carini 166 Ret:accident
R. Fischer 500 4th
G. Comotti 166 6th
F. Cortese 166s Ret: engine
P. Whitehead 125 5th
'Tramontana' 125 —
S. Sighinolfi 166C —
V. Marzotto 166C —
G. Bracco 166C DNC
Mar 23. 1st Piriapolis Grand Prix, Uruguay
J.M. Fangio 166 1st
F. Landi 375 2nd
C. Menditeguey 166 4th
L. Rosier 375 10th
Mar 30. 2nd Piriapolis Grand Prix, Uruguay
J.M. Fangio 166 1st
J.F. Gonzalez 166 2nd
L. Rosier 375 3rd
F. Landi 375 —
O. Marimon 125 s/stage 6th
Apr 6. Turin Grand Prix, Valentino Park

L. Villoresi 375 1st
A. Ascari 375 Ret:fuel leak
G. Farina 375 Ret:accident
R. Fischer 212 3rd
P. Taruffi 212 2nd
P. Whitehead 125 s/stage 4th
P. Hirt 166C Ret:engine

Apr 14. Pau Grand Prix, Pau
A. Ascari 500 1st
L. Villoresi 500 Ret:accident
L. Rosier 500 2nd
P. Scotti 500 Ret.
R. Fischer 500 Ret.
M. Trintignant 166C Ret.

Chichester Cup, Goodwood
K. Richardson 375 Thinwall Spl. Ret:accident

3rd Easter Handicap, Goodwood
J.F. Gonzalez 375 Thinwall Spl. 6th

Richmond Trophy, Goodwood
J.F. Gonzalez 375 Thinwall Spl. 1st

Lavant Cup, Goodwood
A. Dobson 125 (10C) 3rd

Apr 19. Ibsley
B. Dobson 125 (10C) 3rd

Apr 27. Marseilles Grand Prix, Parc Borely
A. Ascari 500 1st
L. Villoresi 500 Ret:engine
G. Farina 500 Ret:accident
L. Rosier 500 Ret.
M. Trintignant 166C Ret.

May 10. BRDC International Trophy, Silverstone
P. Whitehead 125(0144) 5th
R. Fischer 500 Ret.
P. Hirt 166 15th
R. Baird 500 Ret.
B. Dobson 125(10C) 12th

May 11. Naples Grand Prix, Posillipo
G. Farina 500 1st
P. Taruffi 500 2nd
G. Comotti 166 3rd
A. Simon 500 —
S. Sighinolfi 166C NC
L. Rosier 500 NC

May 18. SWISS GRAND PRIX, Bremgarten, Berne
P. Taruffi 500 1st
G. Farina 500 Ret:magneto
L. Rosier 500 Ret:accident
R. Fischer 500 2nd
A. Simon/ 500 Ret:magneto
G. Farina
M. Trintignant 166C DNA
P. Hirt 166C 7th

May 25. Eifelrennen, Nürburgring
R. Fischer 500 1st
F. Reiss 166C Ret.

Paris Grand Prix, Montlhery
P. Taruffi 500 1st
G. Farina/ 500 2nd
A. Simon
L. Rosier 500 3rd

June 1. Albi Grand Prix, Albi
L. Rosier 375 1st
G. Comotti 166 7th
F. Landi 375 2nd
P. Whitehead 125 s/stage 5th
R. Fischer 212 6th

June 7. Ulster Trophy, Dundrod
P. Taruffi 375 Thinwall Spl. 1st
L. Rosier 375 4th

June 8. Autodromo Grand Prix, Monza
A. Ascari 500 Ret:engine
L. Villoresi 500 Ret:engine
G. Farina 500 1st
A. Simon 500 2nd
R. Fischer 500 3rd
P. Walker 125 (0114) 6th/4th
P. Carini 166C 11th/Ret
F. Comotti — Ret.
P. Hirt 166C Ret.
C. de Tornaco 500 Ret.

June 18. Aix-les-Bains, France
M. Trintignant 166C Ret.

June 21. Boreham, GB
B. Dobson 125(10C) 3rd

June 22. EUROPEAN GRAND PRIX, Spa-Francorchamps
A. Ascari 500 1st
G. Farina 500 2nd
P. Taruffi 500 Ret:accident
L. Rosier 500 Ret:transmission
C. de Tornaco 500 7th

June 29. Marne Grand Prix, Reims-Gueux
L. Villoresi/ 500 3rd
A. Ascari
G. Farina 500 2nd
L. Villoresi 500 Ret:magneto
L. Rosier 500 5th

F. Comotti 166C Ret.
P. Carini 166C Ret.

July 6. FRENCH GRAND PRIX, Rouen-les-Essarts
A. Ascari 500 1st
G. Farina 500 2nd
P. Taruffi 500 3rd
R. Fischer 500 11th
L. Rosier 500 Ret:engine
F. Comotti 166C DNC
P. Carini 166C Ret.

July 13. Les Sables d'Olonne Grand Prix, Les Sables d'Olonne
A. Ascari 500 Ret:accident
G. Farina 500 Ret:accident
L. Villoresi 500 1st
R. Fischer 500 Ret.

July 19. BRITISH GRAND PRIX, Silverstone
A. Ascari 500 1st
G. Farina 500 6th
P. Taruffi 500 2nd
R. Fischer 500 14th
R. Salvadori 500 8th
P. Hirt 166 Ret:brakes
P. Whitehead 125(0114) 10th

Daily Express Formule Libre Trophy Race, Silverstone
P. Taruffi 375 Thinwall Spl. 1st
L. Villoresi 375 2nd
F. Landi 375 3rd
L. Rosier 375 12th

July 27. Caen Grand Prix, France
L. Rosier 500 3rd
A. Phillippe 125 4th

Aug 3. GERMAN GRAND PRIX, Nürburgring
A. Ascari 500 1st
G. Farina 500 2nd
P. Taruffi 500 4th
R. Fischer 500 3rd
R. Laurent 500 6th
P. Carini 166C Ret:brakes
R. Shoeller 166C Ret:dampers

Aug 2. Formule Libre, Boreham, England
L. Villoresi 375 1st
F. Landi 375 2nd
L. Rosier 375 4th
P. Whitehead 125(0114) 10th
R. Baird 500 8th
F. Cortese 166 16th
B. Dobson 125 (10C) 18th

Aug 10. Comminges Grand Prix, St. Gaudens
A. Ascari 500 Ret:steering
G. Farina 500 2nd
A. Simon/ 500 1st
A. Ascari
L. Rosier 500 Ret:accident

Aug 17. Dutch Grand Prix, Zandvoort
A. Ascari 500 1st
G. Farina 500 2nd
L. Villoresi 500 3rd
C. de Tornaco 500 Ret:engine

Aug 23. Scottish Daily Express National Trophy, Turberry
M. Hawthorn 375 Thinwall Spl. Ret:gear selectors
B. Dobson 166 6th

Aug 24. Le Baule Grand Prix, Le Baule-Escoublac
A. Ascari 500 1st
G. Farina 500 Ret:accident
L. Villoresi 500 2nd
L. Rosier 500 3rd

Sept 7. ITALIAN GRAND PRIX, Monza
A. Ascari 500 1st
G. Farina 500 4th
L. Villoresi 500 3rd
P. Taruffi 500 7th
R. Fischer 500 Ret:engine
A. Simon 500 6th
L. Rosier 500 10th
H. Stuck 166C DNQ
P. Whitehead 125 DNQ
C. de Tornaco 500 DNQ

Sept 14. Modena Grand Prix, Modena
A. Ascari 500 Ret:engine
G. Farina 500 4th
S. Sighinolfi/ 500 3rd
A. Ascari
L. Villoresi 500 1st
R. Fischer 500 5th
H. Stuck 125 9th

Sept 14. Circuit of Cadours, Cadours
L. Rosier 500 1st
C. de Tornaco 500 3rd (heat 1)

Sept 27. Woodcote Cup, Goodwood
G. Farina 375 Thinwall Spl. 2nd

Madgwick Cup, Goodwood
B. Dobson 125 (10C) 11th
R. Salvadori 500 7th

Sept 28. Avus races, Berlin
R. Fischer 500 1st
H. Stuck 125 5th

A. Philippe 125 4th
P. Vignolo 125 Ret.
C. Maneini 166C Ret.
Oct 4. Joe Fry Memorial, Castle Combe
B. Dobson 125 5th
R. Salvadori 500 1st
Oct 11. Daily Record International Trophy race, Charterhall, Scotland
G. Farina 375 Thinwall Spl. Ret:transmission
Newcastle Journal Trophy
R. Baird 500 —
B. Dobson 125 —

1953
Jan 18. ARGENTINE GRAND PRIX, Parc Almirante Brown, Buenos Aires
A. Ascari 500 1st
L. Villoresi 500 2nd
G. Farina 500 Ret:accident
M. Hawthorn 500 4th
Feb 1. Buenos Aires City Grand Prix, Parc Almirante Brown
A. Ascari 375 Ret:engine
L. Villoresi 625 2nd
G. Farina 625 1st
M. Hawthorn 625 3rd
Mar 22. Syracuse Grand Prix, Sicily
A. Ascari 500 Ret:hub failure
L. Villoresi 500 Ret:valve spring
G. Farina 500 Ret:valve spring
M. Hawthorn/ A. Ascari 500 Ret:valve spring
M. Rafaelli 166C 8th
C. de Tornaco 500 6th
Apr 6. Pau Grand Prix, Pau
A. Ascari 500 1st
G. Farina 500 Ret:valve spring
M. Hawthorn 500 2nd
L. Rosier 500 5th
R. Laurent 500 8th
Easter Handicap, Goodwood
P. Taruffi 375 Thinwall Spl. Non-classified
Richmond Trophy, Goodwood
P. Taruffi 375 Thinwall Spl. 2nd
Lavant Cup, Goodwood
R. Baird 500 9th
May 3. Bordeaux Grand Prix, Bordeaux
A. Ascari 500 1st
L. Villoresi 500 2nd
G. Farina 500 Ret:gearbox
L. Rosier 500 ret:gearbox
May 9. Daily Express Trophy, Silverstone
M. Hawthorn 500 1st
L. Rosier 500 10th
T. Cole 500 DNS
R. Baird 500 13th
May 10. Naples Grand Prix, Posillipo
A. Ascari 500 5th
L. Villoresi 500 4th
G. Farina 500 1st
May 16. Ulster Trophy, Dundrod
M. Hawthorn 500 1st
R. Baird 500 3rd
May 24. Grand Prix des Frontieres, Chimay, Belgium
R. Laurent 500 2nd
May 25. Coronation Trophy, Crystal Palace, London
R. Baird 500 Ret:accident
May 30. Snetterton, England
R. Baird 500 3rd
May 31. Eifelrennen, Nürburgring
K. Adolff 500 4th
F. Wacker 500 9th
May 31. Albi Grand Prix, Les Planques
A. Ascari 375 Ret:engine
G. Farina 375 Thinwall. Spl. Ret:oil leak
L. Rosier 500/375 1st
C. de Tornaco 500 6th (heat 1)
June 7. DUTCH GRAND PRIX, Zandvoort
A. Ascari 500 1st
G. Farina 500 2nd
L. Villoresi 500 Ret:engine
M. Hawthorn 500 4th
L. Rosier 500 7th
June 21. BELGIAN GRAND PRIX, Spa-Francorchamps
A. Ascari 500 1st
G. Farina 500 Ret:engine
L. Villoresi 500 2nd
M. Hawthorn 500 6th
L. Rosier 500 8th
June 28. Rouen Grand Prix, Rouen-les-Essarts
G. Farina 625 1st
M. Hawthorn 625 2nd
L. Rosier 375 7th
July 5. FRENCH GRAND PRIX, Reims-Gueux
A. Ascari 500 4th
G. Farina 500 5th
L. Villoresi 500 6th
M. Hawthorn 500 1st
L. Rosier 500 8th
July 12. Avus Races, Berlin
J. Swaters 500 1st
K. Adolff 166 Ret.
July 18. BRITISH GRAND PRIX, Silverstone
A. Ascari 500 1st
G. Farina 500 3rd
L. Villoresi 500 Ret:axle
M. Hawthorn 500 5th
L. Rosier 500 10th
Formule Libre Trophy Race
G. Farina 375 Thinwall Spl. 1st
M. Hawthorn 625 Ret:overheating
July 25. USAF Trophy, Snetterton
R. Baird 500 DNS:fatal practice accident
July 26. Circuit du Lac, Aix-les-Bains
L. Rosier 500 2nd
Aug 2. GERMAN GRAND PRIX, Nürburgring
A. Ascari/ L. Villoresi 500 8th
G. Farina 500 1st
L. Villoresi/ A. Ascari 500 Ret:engine
M. Hawthorn 500 3rd
L. Rosier 500 10th
J. Swaters 500 7th
K. Adolff 166 Ret.
Aug 9. Les Sables d'Olonne Grand Prix
L. Rosier 500 1st
Aug 15. Daily Record International Trophy, Charterhall, Scotland
G. Farina 375 Thinwall Spl. 1st
Aug 23. SWISS GRAND PRIX, Bremgarten, Berne
A. Ascari 500 1st
G. Farina 500 2nd
L. Villoresi 500 6th
M. Hawthorn 500 3rd
L. Rossier 500 Ret:accident
J. Swaters 500 Ret:accident
M. de Terra 500 8th
P. Hirt 500 Ret:water pump
Aug 30. Cadours Grand Prix, France
L. Rosier 500 4th
C. de Tornaco 500 5th
Sept 13. ITALIAN GRAND PRIX, Monza
A. Ascari 500 Ret:accident
G. Farina 500 2nd
L. Villoresi 500 3rd
M. Hawthorn 500 4th
P. Carini 553 2-litre Ret.
U. Maglioli 553 2-litre 8th
L. Rosier 500 16th
Sept 26. Woodcote Cup, Goodwood
M. Hawthorn 375 Thinwall Spl. 1st
Goodwood Trophy
M. Hawthorn 375 Thinwall Spl. 1st

1954
Jan 17. ARGENTINE GRAND PRIX, Autodromo 17 October, Buenos Aires
G. Farina 625 2nd
J.F. Gonzalez 625 3rd
M. Trintignant 625 4th
M. Hawthorn 625 Ret:disqualified
Jan 31. Buenos Aires City Grand Prix, Parc Almirante Brown
G. Farina 625 Ret:rear axle
J.F. Gonzalez/ G. Farina 625 3rd
M. Trintignant 625 1st
M. Hawthorn 625 6th
U. Maglioli 625 8th
Apr 11. Syracuse Grand Prix, Sicily
G. Farina 625/6 1st
J.F. Gonzalez 553 'No.2' Ret:accident, car destroyed by fire
M. Trintignant 625/4 2nd
M. Hawthorn 625/1 Ret:accident
R. Manzon 625 '54/1' 4th
R. Laurent 500 2.5 5th
Apr 19. Pau Grand Prix, France
G. Farina 625/5 5th
J.F. Gonzalez 625/4 Ret:crankshaft
M. Trintignant 625/6 2nd
L. Rosier 500 '186/F2' 6th
R. Manzon 625 '54/1' Ret:gearbox
May 9. Bordeaux Grand Prix, Bordeaux
J.F. Gonzalez 625/4 1st
M. Trintignant 625/6 3rd
L. Rosier 500 '186/F2' Ret:engine
R. Manzon 625 '54/1' 2nd
May 15. Daily Express Trophy Race, Silverstone
J.F. Gonzalez 553 DNS:engine seized whilst being warmed up
M. Trintignant/ J.F. Gonzalez 625 1st
U. Maglioli/ M. Trintignant 625 5th

Driver	Car	Result
L. Rosier	500 '186/F2'	6th
R. Manzon	625 '54/1'	Ret:transmission
R. Parnell	625	Ret:prop shaft
May 23. Bari Grand Prix, Lungomare		
J.F. Gonzalez	625	1st
M. Trintignant	625	2nd
U. Maglioli	625	7th
May 29. Aintree 200, Liverpool		
P. Collins	375 Thinwall Spl.	Ret:ignition
June 6. Rome Grand Prix, Castelfusano		
R. Manzon	625	Ret.
L. Rosier	500 '186/F2'	5th
F. Serena	V12 2-litre	
C. Mancini	V12 '116'	
G. Mancini	500 2-litre	
June 20. BELGIAN GRAND PRIX, Spa-Francorchamps		
G. Farina	553/2	Ret:ignition
J.F. Gonzalez	553/3	Ret:broken oil pipe
M. Trintignant	625/6	2nd
M. Hawthorn/ J.F. Gonzalez	625/7	4th
J. Swaters	625	Ret:engine
July 4. FRENCH GRAND PRIX, Reims-Gueux		
J.F. Gonzalez	553/3	Ret:engine
M. Trintignant	625/6	Ret:engine
M. Hawthorn	553/2	Ret:engine
L. Rosier	500 '186/F2'	Ret:engine
R. Manzon	625 '54/1'	3rd
July 11. Rouen Grand Prix, Rouen-les-Essarts		
M. Trintignant	625/6	1st
M. Hawthorn	625/5	Ret:disqualified
J.F. Gonzalez	553/4	Ret:engine
July 17. BRITISH GRAND PRIX, Silverstone		
J.F. Gonzalez	625	1st
M. Trintignant	625	5th
M. Hawthorn	625	2nd
L. Rosier	500 '186/F2'	Ret.
R. Manzon	625 '54/1'	Ret:engine
R. Parnell	625	Ret.
July 25. Caen Grand Prix, La Prairie		
M. Trintignant	625/2	1st
R. Manzon	625 '54/1'	Ret:timing gears
L. Rosier	500 '186/F2'	5th
Aug 1. GERMAN GRAND PRIX, Nürburgring		
J.F. Gonzalez/ M. Hawthorn	625/7	2nd
M. Trintignant	625/5	3rd
P. Taruffi	625/2	6th
M. Hawthorn	625/6	Ret:axle failure
R. Manzon	625 '54/1'	9th
L. Rosier	500 '186/F2'	8th
Aug 7. Oulton Park Gold Cup		
R. Parnell	625	2nd
Aug 14. Formula 1, Snetterton		
R. Parnell	625	1st
Formule Libre, Snetterton		
P. Collins	375 Thinwall Spl.	1st
Aug 15. Pescara Grand Prix, Italy		
R. Manzon	625 '54/1'	Ret:brakes
L. Rosier	500 '186/F2'	Ret:engine
J. Swaters	625	Ret:gearbox
B. Taraschi	2.5 12-cyl,Spl.	Ret:engine
Aug 22. SWISS GRAND PRIX, Bremgarten, Berne		
J.F. Gonzalez	625/4	2nd
M. Trintignant	625/6	Ret:engine
M. Hawthorn	625/7	Ret:oil pump
R. Manzon	553/2	DNS: after practice accident
U. Maglioli	553/3	7th
J. Swaters	625	8th
Sept 5. ITALIAN GRAND PRIX, Monza		
A. Ascari	625/1	Ret:engine
J.F. Gonzalez	553/2	Ret:gearbox
M. Hawthorn	625/3	2nd
M. Trintignant	625/6	5th
U. Maglioli/ J.F. Gonzalez	625/2	3rd
R. Manzon	625	Ret:engine
Sept 19. Avus Races, Berlin		
J. Swaters	625	5th
Sept 25. Formule Libre Race, Goodwood		
P. Collins	375 Thinwall Spl.	1st
Oct 2. Daily Telegraph Trophy, Aintree		
R. Parnell	625	Ret.
Formule Libre Race, Aintree		
P. Collins	375 Thinwall Spl.	Ret:ignition
Oct 24. SPANISH GRAND PRIX, Pedralbes, Barcelona		
M. Hawthorn	553	1st
M. Trintignant	625	Ret:gearbox
R. Manzon	625	Ret:engine
J. Swaters	625	Ret:engine
1955		
Jan 16. ARGENTINE GRAND PRIX, Autodromo 17 October, Buenos Aires		
G. Farina/	625	3rd
U. Maglioli/ M. Trintignant		3rd
J.F. Gonzalez/ M. Trintignant/G. Farina	625	2nd
M. Trintignant	625	Ret:engine
Jan 30. Buenos Aires City Grand Prix, Parc Almirante Brown		
J.F. Gonzalez/ M. Trintignant	625	3rd
G. Farina/ J.F. Gonzalez M. Trintignant	625	10th
M. Trintignant	625	Ret:engine
U. Maglioli	625	11th
C. Bucci	625	9th
Mar 27. Turin Grand Prix, Valentino Park		
G. Farina	625/No.8	Ret:gearbox
M. Trintignant	625/No.2	Ret:engine
H. Schell	625/No.6	5th
A. de Portago	625 '540'	Ret:engine
B. Taraschi	V12	7th
Girard	500 '0184'	Ret.
Apr 17. Pau Grand Prix, Pau		
A. de Portago	625 '540'	8th
J. Lucas	625	9th
L. Rosier	625 '54/1'	7th
Apr 24. Bordeaux Grand Prix, Bordeaux		
G. Farina	555	Ret:gearbox
M. Trintignant	555	Ret:brakes
A. de Portago	625 '540'	Ret:overheating
May 8. Naples Grand Prix, Posillipo		
G. Scarlatti	500 '210F2'	5th
B. Taraschi	V12	6th Non-classified
May 22. GRAND PRIX OF EUROPE, Monte Carlo		
G. Farina	625	4th
M. Trintignant	625	1st
H. Schell	555	Ret:engine
P. Taruffi/ P. Frere	555	8th
May 29. Albi Grand Prix		
P. Levegh	625 '54/1'	Ret.
June 5. BELGIAN GRAND PRIX, Spa Francorchamps		
G. Farina	555	3rd
M. Trintignant	555	7th
P. Frere	555	4th
June 19. DUTCH GRAND PRIX, Zandvoort		
M. Trintignant	555	Ret:gearbox
E. Castellotti	555	5th
M. Hawthorn	555	7th
J. Claes	500/625	11th
July 16. BRITISH GRAND PRIX, Aintree		
M. Trintignant	625/No.2	Ret:engine
M. Hawthorn/ E. Castellotti	625/No.6	6th
E. Castellotti	625/No.4	Ret:transmission
Sept 11. ITALIAN GRAND PRIX, Monza		
M. Trintignant	555	7th
E. Castellotti	555	3rd
M. Hawthorn	555	Ret:gearbox
U. Maglioli	555	6th
(Lancia-Ferrari D50s withdrawn following practice)		
Sept 24. Daily Despatch Gold Cup, Oulton Park		
M. Hawthorn	D50	2nd
E. Castellotti	D50	7th
A. de Portago	625 '540'	Ret:accident
1956		
Jan 22. ARGENTINE GRAND PRIX, Autodromo 17 October, Buenos Aires		
J.M. Fangio	D50	Ret:engine
L. Musso/ J.M. Fangio	D50	1st
P. Collins	555	Ret:collision
O. Gendebien	555-V8	5th
E. Castellotti	D50	Ret:gearbox
Feb 5. Mendoza Grand Prix, Argentina		
J.M. Fangio	D50	1st
E. Castellotti	D50	Ret:oil pipe
L. Musso	D50	Ret:engine
P. Collins	555	5th
O. Gendebien	555-V8	6th
Apr 14. Syracuse Grand Prix, Sicily		
J.M. Fangio	D50/0007	1st
L. Musso	D50/0001	2nd
P. Collins	D50/0008	3rd
E. Castellotti	D50/0003	Ret:accident
B. Taraschi	2.5 V12 Spl.	Ret.
G. Scarlatti	500 2-litre	Ret.
May 5. Daily Express International Trophy, Silverstone		
J.M. Fangio	D50	Ret:clutch
P. Collins/ J.M. Fangio	D50	Ret:clutch
May 6. Naples Grand Prix, Posillipo		
E. Castellotti	D50	Ret:engine
L. Musso	D50	Ret:engine
B. Taraschi	2.5 V12 Spl.	6th
G. Scarlatti	500 2-litre	4th

May 13. MONACO GRAND PRIX, Monte Carlo
J.M. Fangio/ E.Castellotti D50/0002 4th
P. Collins/ J.M. Fangio D50/0007 2nd
E. Castellotti D50/0001 Ret:clutch
L. Musso D50/0003 Ret:accident
G. Scarlatti 500 2-litre DNS
June 3. BELGIAN GRAND PRIX, Spa-Francorchamps
J.M. Fangio D50 Ret:transmission
P. Collins D50 1st
E. Castellotti D50 Ret:transmission
P. Frere D50 2nd
A. Pilette D50 6th
July 1. FRENCH GRAND PRIX, Reims-Gueux
J.M. Fangio D50 4th
P. Collins D50 1st
E. Castellotti D50 2nd
A. de Portago D50 Ret:gearbox
O. Gendebien D50 Ret:clutch
July 14. BRITISH GRAND PRIX, Silverstone
J.M. Fangio D50 1st
P. Collins D50 Ret:engine
A. de Portago/ P. Collins D50 2nd
E. Castellotti/ A. de Portago D50 10th
Aug 5. GERMAN GRAND PRIX, Nürburgring
J.M. Fangio D50 1st
P. Collins D50 Ret:fuel leak
E. Castellotti D50 Ret:magneto
L. Musso/ E. Castellotti D50 Ret:accident
A. de Portago/ P. Collins D50 Ret:accident
Aug 26. Caen Grand Prix, France
J. Lucas 500 '186/F2' 5th
A. Pedini 500 2-litre 7th
Sept 2. ITALIAN GRAND PRIX, Monza
J.M. Fangio D50 Ret:broken steering arm
P. Collins/ J.M. Fangio D50 2nd
E. Castellotti D50 8th
L. Musso D50 Ret:broken steering arm
A. de Portago D50 Ret:damaged steering
W. von Trips D50 DNS

1957

Jan 13. ARGENTINE GRAND PRIX, Autodromo 17 October, Buenos Aires
J.F. Gonzalez/ A. de Portago D50 5th
W. von Trips/ P. Collins/C. Perdisa D50 6th
P. Collins D50 Ret:clutch
M. Hawthorn D50 Ret:clutch
E. Castellotti D50 Ret:lost wheel
A. de Tomaso 500 9th
Jan 27. Buenos Aires City Grand Prix, Autodromo 17 October
P. Collins/ M. Gregory D50 3rd
M. Hawthorn D50 4th
E. Castellotti D50 5th
L. Musso D50 Ret:clutch
Apr 7. Syracuse Grand Prix, Sicily
P. Collins D50 1st
L. Musso D50 2nd
Apr 22. Pau Grand Prix, France
M. Rozier/ M. Trintignant 625 Ret:engine
Apr 29. Naples Grand Prix, Posillipo
P. Collins D50 1st
M. Hawthorn D50/0005 2nd
L. Musso V6 Dino F2 3rd
B. Taraschi 1.5 V12 Ret:split fuel tank
May 19. MONACO GRAND PRIX, Monte Carlo
M. Trintignant D50/0006 6th
P. Collins D50/0008 Ret:accident
M. Hawthorn D50/0005 Ret:accident
W. von Trips D50/0009 Ret:accident
July 7. FRENCH GRAND PRIX, Rouen-les-Essarts
L. Musso D50/0010 2nd
P. Collins D50/0008 3rd
M. Hawthorn D50/ 4th
M. Trintignant D50/ Ret:magneto
July 14. Reims Grand Prix, Reims-Gueux
L. Musso D50/0001 1st
M. Hawthorn D50/0009 Ret:engine
P. Collins D50/0007 Ret:engine
O. Gendebien D50/0005 Ret:engine
July 20. BRITISH GRAND PRIX, Aintree
L. Musso D50/0010 2nd
P. Collins D50/0008 Ret:radiator leak
M. Hawthorn D50/0009 3rd
M. Trintignant D50/0006 4th
July 28. Caen Grand Prix, France
M. Rozier 625 Ret:ignition
Aug 4. GERMAN GRAND PRIX, Nürburgring
M. Hawthorn D50/0009 2nd
P. Collins D50/0008 3rd
L. Musso D50/0010 4th
Aug 18. PESCARA GRAND PRIX, Pescara, Italy
L. Musso D50/0008 Ret:oil tank worked loose
Sept 8. ITALIAN GRAND PRIX, Monza
W. von Trips D50/0006 3rd
M. Hawthorn D50/0009 6th
P. Collins D50/0008 Ret:engine
L. Musso D50/0010 8th
Sept 22. Modena Grand Prix, Italy
L. Musso Dino F2/0011 2nd
P. Collins Dino F2/0012 4th
Oct 27. Moroccan Grand Prix, Ain Diab, Casablanca
M. Hawthorn Dino F2/0011 Ret.
P. Collins Dino F2/0012 Ret.

1958

Jan 19. ARGENTINE GRAND PRIX, Autodromo 17 October, Buenos Aires
L. Musso 246/0011 2nd
M. Hawthorn 246/0001 3rd
P. Collins 246/0012 Ret:rear axle
Feb 2. Buenos Aires City Grand Prix, Autodromo 17 October
L. Musso 246/0011 2nd
M. Hawthorn 246/0001 Non-classified
P. Collins 246/0012 Non-classified
W. von Trips 246/0002 Ret:accident
Apr 7. Glover Trophy, Goodwood
M. Hawthorn 246/0003 1st
Apr 27. Syracuse Grand Prix, Sicily
L. Musso 246/0001 1st
May 4. BRDC International Trophy, Silverstone
P. Collins 246/0002 1st
May 18. MONACO GRAND PRIX, Monte Carlo
L. Musso 246/0001 2nd
P. Collins 246/0002 3rd
M. Hawthorn 246/0003 Ret:fuel pump
W. von Trips 246/0011 Ret:engine
May 25. DUTCH GRAND PRIX, Zandvoort
M. Hawthorn 246/0003 5th
P. Collins 246/0002 Ret:gearbox
L. Musso 246/0001 7th
June 16. BELGIAN GRAND PRIX, Spa-Francorchamps
M. Hawthorn 246/0003 2nd
P. Collins 246/0002 Ret:overheating
L. Musso 246/0004 Ret:accident
O. Gendebien 246/0011 6th
July 6. FRENCH GRAND PRIX, Reims-Gueux
M. Hawthorn 246/0003 1st
P. Collins 246/0001 5th
L. Musso 246/0004 Fatal accident
W. von Trips 246/0002 3rd
July 19. BRITISH GRAND PRIX, Silverstone
M. Hawthorn 246/0003 2nd
P. Collins 246/0002 1st
W. von Trips 246/0001 Ret:engine
Aug 3. GERMAN GRAND PRIX, Nürburgring
M. Hawthorn 246/0003 Ret:clutch
P. Collins 246/0002 Fatal accident
W. von Trips 246/0004 4th
P. Hill F2 156/0011 5th in F2 class
Aug 28. PORTUGUESE GRAND PRIX, Oporto
M. Hawthorn 246/0003 2nd
W. von Trips 246/0007 5th
Sept 7. ITALIAN GRAND PRIX, Monza
M. Hawthorn 246/0005 2nd
W. von Trips 246/0006 Ret:accident
P. Hill 246/0004 4th
O. Gendebien 246/0007 Ret:rear axle
Oct 19. MOROCCAN GRAND PRIX, Ain Diab, Casablanca
M. Hawthorn 246/0005 2nd
P. Hill 246/0004 3rd
O. Gendebien 246/0007 Ret:accident

1959

Apr 18. Aintree 200, Liverpool
J. Behra 256/0004 1st
T. Brooks 246/0003 2nd
May 2. BRDC International Trophy, Silverstone
T. Brooks 246/0003 Ret:misfire
P. Hill 246/0002 4th
May 10. MONACO GRAND PRIX, Monte Carlo
J. Behra 246/0004 Ret:engine
T. Brooks 246/0003 2nd
P. Hill 246/0002 4th
C. Allison F2 156/0011 Ret:accident
May 31. DUTCH GRAND PRIX, Zandvoort
J. Behra 246/0011 5th
T. Brooks 246/0002 Ret:oil leak
P. Hill 246/0003 6th
C. Allison 246/0004 9th
July 3. FRENCH GRAND PRIX, Reims-Gueux

J. Behra 246/0011 Ret:overheating
T. Brooks 246/0002 1st
P. Hill 246/0003 2nd
O. Gendebien 246/0004 4th
D. Gurney 246/0007 Ret:damaged radiator

Aug 2. GERMAN GRAND PRIX, Berlin
T. Brooks 246/0002 1st
P. Hill 246/0003 3rd
D. Gurney 246/0007 2nd
C. Allison 246/0004 Ret:clutch

Aug 23. PORTUGUESE GRAND PRIX, Monsanto Park, Lisbon
T. Brooks 246/0002 9th
P. Hill 246/0003 Ret:accident
D. Gurney 246/0007 3rd

Sept 13. ITALIAN GRAND PRIX, Monza
T. Brooks 246/0002 Ret:clutch
P. Hill 246/0003 2nd
D. Gurney 246/0007 4th
C. Allison 246/0004 5th
O. Gendebien 246/0011 6th

Dec 12. UNITED STATES GRAND PRIX, Sebring
T. Brooks 246/0004 3rd
W. von Trips 246/0002 6th
C. Allison 246/0003 Ret:clutch
P. Hill 246/0006 Ret:clutch

1960

Feb 7. ARGENTINE GRAND PRIX, Autodromo 17 October, Buenos Aires
C. Allison 246/0001 2nd
P. Hill 246/0007 8th
W. von Trips 246/0005 5th
J.F. Gonzalez 246/0004 10th

May 14. BRDC International Trophy, Silverstone
P. Hill 246/0003 5th
C. Allison 246/0004 8th

May 29. MONACO GRAND PRIX, Monte Carlo
P. Hill 246/0004 3rd
R. Ginther 246'P'/0008 6th
W. von Trips 246/0011 8th
C. Allison 246/0003 Practice accident DNS

June 6. DUTCH GRAND PRIX, Zandvoort
P. Hill 246/0005 Ret:engine
W. von Trips 246/0004 5th
R. Ginther 246/0006 6th

June 19. BELGIAN GRAND PRIX, Spa-Francorchamps
P. Hill 246/0007 4th
W. von Trips 246/0004 Ret:clutch
W. Mairesse 246/0005 Ret:engine

July 3. FRENCH GRAND PRIX, Reims-Gueux
P. Hill 246/0007 12th not running at finish
W. von Trips 246/0004 11th not running at finish
W. Mairesse 246/0005 Ret:transmission

July 16. BRITISH GRAND PRIX, Silverstone
P. Hill 246/0007 7th
W. von Trips 246/0005 6th

Aug 1. Silver City Trophy, Brands Hatch
P. Hill 246/0004 4th
R. Ginther 246/0006 9th

Aug 14. PORTUGUESE GRAND PRIX, Oporto
P. Hill 246/0004 Ret:clutch
W. von Trips 246/0005 5th

Sept 4. ITALIAN GRAND PRIX, Monza
P. Hill 246/0007 1st
R. Ginther 246/0003 2nd
W. Mairesse 246/0006 3rd
W. von Trips 156'P'/0008 5th

1961

Apr 25. Syracuse Grand Prix, Sicily
G. Baghetti 156/0008 1st

May 14. MONACO GRAND PRIX, Monte Carlo
P. Hill 156/0003 3rd
W. von Trips 156/0002 4th
R. Ginther 156/0001 2nd

Naples Grand Prix, Posillipo
G. Baghetti 156/0008 1st

May 22. DUTCH GRAND PRIX, Zandvoort
P. Hill 156/0003-2 2nd
W. von Trips 156/0004 1st
R. Ginther 156/0001 5th

June 18. BELGIAN GRAND PRIX, Spa-Francorchamps
P. Hill 156/0003 1st
W. von Trips 156/0004 2nd
R. Ginther 156/0001 3rd
O. Gendebien 156/0002 4th

July 2. FRENCH GRAND PRIX, Reims-Gueux
P. Hill 156/0003 9th
W. von Trips 156/0004 Ret:overheating
R. Ginther 156/0001 Ret:engine(15th)
G. Baghetti 156/0008 1st

July 15. BRITISH GRAND PRIX, Aintree
P. Hill 156/0003 2nd
W. von Trips 156/0004 1st
R. Ginther 156/0001 3rd
G. Baghetti 156/0008 Ret:spun off

Aug 6. GERMAN GRAND PRIX, Nürburgring
P. Hill 156/0003 3rd
W. von Trips 156/0004 2nd
R. Ginther 156/0001 8th
W. Mairesse 156/0002 Ret:spun off

Sept 10. ITALIAN GRAND PRIX, Monza
P. Hill 156/0002 1st
W. von Trips 156/0004 Fatal accident
R. Ginther 156/0001 Ret:engine
G. Baghetti 156/0003 Ret:engine
R. Rodriguez 156/0006 Ret:engine

1962

Apr 1. Brussels Grand Prix, Heysel
W. Mairesse 156/0006 1st

Apr 24. Pau Grand Prix
R. Rodriguez 156/0003 2nd
L. Bandini 156/0006 5th

Apr 28. Aintree 200, Liverpool
P. Hill 156/0007 3rd
G. Baghetti 156/0001 4th

May 12. BRDC International Trophy, Silverstone
I. Ireland 156/0001 4th

May 20. DUTCH GRAND PRIX, Zandvoort
P. Hill 156/0004 3rd
G. Baghetti 156/0007 4th
R. Rodriguez 156/0003 Ret:accident

Naples Grand Prix, Posillipo
W. Mairesse 156/0001 1st
L. Bandini 156/0006 2nd

June 3. MONACO GRAND PRIX, Monte Carlo
P. Hill 156/0007 2nd
L. Bandini 156/0001 3rd
W. Mairesse 156/0004 7th

June 17. BELGIAN GRAND PRIX, Spa-Francorchamps
P. Hill 156/0009 3rd
R. Rodriguez 156/0003 4th
G. Baghetti 156/0001 Ret:ignition
W. Mairesse 156/0004 Ret:accident

July 21. BRITISH GRAND PRIX, Aintree
P. Hill 156/0007 Ret:ignition

Aug 5. GERMAN GRAND PRIX, Nürburgring
P. Hill 156/0002 Ret:suspension
R. Rodriguez 156/0006 6th
L. Bandini 156/0008 Ret:spun off
G. Baghetti 156/0007 10th

Aug 19. Mediterranean Grand Prix, Enna-Pergusa
L. Bandini 156/0009 1st
G. Baghetti 156/0003 2nd

Sept 16. ITALIAN GRAND PRIX, Monza
P. Hill 156/0002 11th
L. Bandini 156/0006 8th
W. Mairesse 156/0008 4th
R. Rodriguez 156/0007 Ret:ignition(14th)
G. Baghetti 156/0003 5th

1963

May 11. BRDC International Trophy, Silverstone
J. Surtees 156/0001 Ret:oil leak
W. Mairesse 156/0002 Ret:spun off

May 26. MONACO GRAND PRIX, Monte Carlo
J. Surtees 156/0001 4th
W. Mairesse 156/0003 Ret:clutch

June 9. BELGIAN GRAND PRIX, Spa-Francorchamps
J. Surtees 156/0003 Ret:fuel system
W. Mairesse 156/0002 Ret:engine

June 23. DUTCH GRAND PRIX, Zandvoort
J. Surtees 156/0003 3rd
L. Scarfiotti 156/0002 6th

June 30. FRENCH GRAND PRIX, Reims-Gueux
J. Surtees 156/0003 Ret:fuel pump
L. Scarfiotti 156/0002 DNS:practice accident

July 20. BRITISH GRAND PRIX, Silverstone
J. Surtees 156/ 2nd

Aug 4. GERMAN GRAND PRIX, Nürburgring
J. Surtees 156/0002 1st
W. Mairesse 156/0003 Ret:accident

Aug 18. Mediterranean Grand Prix, Enna-Pergusa
J. Surtees 156/0002 1st

Sept 8. ITALIAN GRAND PRIX, Monza
J. Surtees 156/0004(Aero) Ret:engine
L. Bandini 156/0002 Ret:gearbox

Oct 6. UNITED STATES GRAND PRIX, Watkins Glen
J. Surtees 156/0003 Ret:misfire
L. Bandini 156/0002 5th

Oct 27. MEXICAN GRAND PRIX, Mexico City
J. Surtees 156/0003(Aero) DIS
L. Bandini 156/0001(Aero) Ret:misfire

Dec 14. Rand Grand Prix, Kyalami
J. Surtees 156/0003(Aero) 1st
L. Bandini 156/0001 2nd

Dec 28. SOUTH AFRICAN GRAND PRIX, East London
J. Surtees 156/0001(Aero) Ret:engine
L. Bandini 156/0003(Aero) 5th

1964

Race / Driver	Car	Result
Apr 12. Syracuse Grand Prix, Sicily		
J. Surtees	158/0005	1st
L. Bandini	156/0003(Aero)	2nd
May 2. BRDC International Trophy, Silverstone		
J. Surtees	156/0003(Aero)	Ret:fuel pump
May 10. MONACO GRAND PRIX, Monte Carlo		
J. Surtees	158/0005	Ret:gearbox
L. Bandini	156/0003(Aero)	10th
May 24. DUTCH GRAND PRIX, Zandvoort		
J. Surtees	158/0006	2nd
L. Bandini	158/0005	Ret:fuel injection
June 14. BELGIAN GRAND PRIX, Spa-Francorchamps		
J. Surtees	158/0006	Ret:engine
L. Bandini	158/0005	Ret:oil leak
June 28. FRENCH GRAND PRIX, Rouen-les-Essarts		
J. Surtees	158/0006	Ret:oil pipe
L. Bandini	158/0005	9th
July 11. BRITISH GRAND PRIX, Brands Hatch		
J. Surtees	158/0006	3rd
L. Bandini	156/0004	5th
July 17. Solitude Grand Prix, W.Germany		
J. Surtees	158/0006	2nd
L. Bandini	156/0003(Aero)	Ret:accident
Aug 2. GERMAN GRAND PRIX, Nürburgring		
J. Surtees	158/0005	1st
L. Bandini	156/0004(Aero)	3rd
Aug 23. AUSTRIAN GRAND PRIX, Zeltweg		
J. Surtees	158/0005	Ret:suspension
L. Bandini	156/0004(Aero)	1st
Sept 6. ITALIAN GRAND PRIX, Monza		
J. Surtees	158/0006	1st
L. Bandini	158/0005	3rd
L. Scarfiotti	156/0003(Aero)	9th
Oct 4. UNITED STATES GRAND PRIX, Watkins Glen		
J. Surtees	158/0005	2nd
L. Bandini	1512/0007	Ret:engine
Oct 25. MEXICAN GRAND PRIX, Mexico City		
J. Surtees	158/0005	2nd
L Bandini	1512/0001	3rd
P. Rodriguez	156/0004(Aero)	6th

1965

Race / Driver	Car	Result
Jan 1. SOUTH AFRICAN GRAND PRIX, East London		
J. Surtees	158/0005	2nd
L. Bandini	1512/0007	Ret:ignition
Mar 13. Race of Champions, Brands Hatch		
J. Surtees	158/0005	Ret:engine
Apr 4. Syracuse Grand Prix, Sicily		
J. Surtees	158/0005	2nd
L. Bandini	1512/0007	3rd
May 15. BRDC International Trophy, Silverstone		
J. Surtees	158/0006	2nd
L. Bandini	1512/0007	7th
May 30. MONACO GRAND PRIX, Monte Carlo		
J. Surtees	158/0006	4th
L. Bandini	1512/0007	2nd
June 13. BELGIAN GRAND PRIX, Spa-Francorchamps		
J. Surtees	158/0006	Ret:engine
L. Bandini	1512/0007	9th
June 27. FRENCH GRAND PRIX, Clermont-Ferrand		
J. Surtees	158/0005	3rd
L. Bandini	1512/0007	Ret:accident(8th)
July 10. BRITISH GRAND PRIX, Silverstone		
J. Surtees	1512/0007	3rd
L. Bandini	158/0006	Ret:engine
July 18. DUTCH GRAND PRIX, Zandvoort		
J. Surtees	1512/0007	7th
L. Bandini	158/0006	9th
July 31. GERMAN GRAND PRIX, Nürburgring		
J. Surtees	1512/1118	Ret:gearbox
L. Bandini	158/0006	6th
Sept 12. ITALIAN GRAND PRIX, Monza		
J. Surtees	1512/0009	Ret:clutch
L. Bandini	1512/0008	4th
N. Vaccarella	158/0006	12th
Oct 3. UNITED STATES GRAND PRIX, Watkins Glen		
L. Bandini	1512/0009	4th
P. Rodriguez	1512/0007	5th
R. Bondurant	158/0006	10th
Oct 24. MEXICAN GRAND PRIX, Mexico City		
L. Bandini	1512/0009	8th
P. Rodriguez	1512/0008	7th

1966

Race / Driver	Car	Result
May 1. Syracuse Grand Prix, Sicily		
J. Surtees	312/0010	1st
L. Bandini	246/0006	2nd
May 14. BRDC International Trophy, Silverstone		
J. Surtees	312/0010	2nd
May 22. MONACO GRAND PRIX, Monte Carlo		
J. Surtees	312/0010	Ret:transmission
L. Bandini	246/0006	2nd
June 12. BELGIAN GRAND PRIX, Spa-Francorchamps		
J. Surtees	312/0010	1st
L. Bandini	246/0006	3rd
July 3. FRENCH GRAND PRIX, Reims-Gueux		
L. Bandini	312/0010	Non-classified
M. Parkes	312/0011	2nd
July 24. DUTCH GRAND PRIX, Zandvoort		
M. Parkes	312/0011	Ret:accident
L. Bandini	312/0010	6th
Aug 7. GERMAN GRAND PRIX, Nürburgring		
L. Bandini	312/0010	6th
M. Parkes	312/0011	Ret:engine
L. Scarfiotti	246/0006	Ret:battery
Sept 4. ITALIAN GRAND PRIX, Monza		
L. Bandini	312/0010	Ret:ignition
M. Parkes	312/0011	2nd
L. Scarfiotti	312/	1st
G. Baghetti	246/0006	10th
Oct 2. UNITED STATES GRAND PRIX, Watkins Glen		
L. Bandini	312/0010	Ret:engine

1967

Race / Driver	Car	Result
Mar 12. Race of Champions, Brands Hatch		
L. Bandini	312/	2nd
L. Scarfiotti	312/	4th
C. Amon	312/	DNS
Apr 29. BRDC International Trophy, Silverstone		
M. Parkes	312/0011	1st
May 7. MONACO GRAND PRIX, Monte Carlo		
L. Bandini	312/0001	Fatal accident
C. Amon	312/0003	3rd
May 21. Syracuse Grand Prix, Sicily		
M. Parkes	312/	dead heat for 1st
L. Scarfiotti	312/	
June 4. DUTCH GRAND PRIX, Zandvoort		
C. Amon	312/0003	4th
M. Parkes	312/0011	5th
June 18. BELGIAN GRAND PRIX, Spa-Francorchamps		
C. Amon	312/0003	3rd
M. Parkes	312/0011	Ret:accident
L. Scarfiotti	312/0005	Non-classified
July 2. FRENCH GRAND PRIX, Bugatti circuit, Le Mans		
C. Amon	312/0003	Ret:throttle cable
July 15. BRITISH GRAND PRIX, Silverstone		
C. Amon	312/0003	3rd
Aug 6. GERMAN GRAND PRIX, Nürburgring		
C. Amon	312/0003	3rd
Aug 27. CANADIAN GRAND PRIX, Mosport Park		
C. Amon	312/0005	6th
Sept 10. ITALIAN GRAND PRIX, Monza		
C. Amon	312/0007	7th
Oct 1. UNITED STATES GRAND PRIX, Watkins Glen		
C. Amon	312/0007	Ret:engine
Oct 22. MEXICAN GRAND PRIX, Mexico City		
C. Amon	312/0007	9th(not running)
J. Williams	312/0003	8th
Nov 12. Spanish Grand Prix, Jarama		
A. de Adamich	312/	9th

1968

Race / Driver	Car	Result
Jan 1. SOUTH AFRICAN GRAND PRIX, Kyalami		
C. Amon	312/0007	4th
J. Ickx	312/0003	Ret:oil tank
A. de Adamich	312/0005	Ret:spun off
Mar 17. Race of Champions, Brands Hatch		
C. Amon	312/0007	4th
J. Ickx	312/0003	8th
A. de Adamich	312/0005	DNS:practice accident
Apr 27. BRDC International Trophy, Silverstone		
C. Amon	312/	3rd
J. Ickx	312/	4th
May 12. SPANISH GRAND PRIX, Jarama		
C. Amon	312/0007	Ret:fuel pump
J. Ickx	312/0009	Ret:ignition
June 9. BELGIAN GRAND PRIX, Spa-Francorchamps		
C. Amon	312/0007	Ret:damaged oil radiator
J. Ickx	312/0003	3rd
June 23. DUTCH GRAND PRIX, Zandvoort		
C. Amon	312/0007	6th
J. Ickx	312/0009	4th
July 7. FRENCH GRAND PRIX, Rouen-les-Essarts		
C. Amon	312/0011	10th
J. Ickx	312/0009	1st
July 29. BRITISH GRAND PRIX, Brands Hatch		
C. Amon	312/0011	2nd
J. Ickx	312/0009	3rd
Aug 4. GERMAN GRAND PRIX, Nürburgring		
C. Amon	312/0011	Ret:differential
J. Ickx	312/0015	4th
Aug 17. Gold Cup, Oulton Park		
C. Amon	312/0011	2nd
J. Ickx	312/0015	Ret:electrical
D. Bell	312/0007	Ret:engine
Sept 8. ITALIAN GRAND PRIX, Monza		
C. Amon	312/0011	Ret:accident
J. Ickx	312/0015	3rd
D. Bell	312/0009	Ret:fuel feed
Sept 22. CANADIAN GRAND PRIX, Ste. Jovite		
C. Amon	312/0009	Ret:transmission

J. Ickx 312/0015 DNS:practice accident
Oct 6. UNITED STATES GRAND PRIX, Watkins Glen
C. Amon 312/0009 Ret:water pump
D. Bell 312/0007 Ret:engine
Nov 3. MEXICAN GRAND PRIX, Mexico City
C. Amon 312/0009 Ret:transmission
J. Ickx 312/0003 Ret:ignition

1969
Mar 1. SOUTH AFRICAN GRAND PRIX, Kyalami
C. Amon 312/0009 Ret:engine
Mar 30. BRDC International Trophy, Silverstone
C. Amon 312/0017 10th
D. Bell 312/0009 9th
May 4. SPANISH GRAND PRIX, Barcelona
C. Amon 312/0017 Ret:engine
May 18. MONACO GRAND PRIX, Monte Carlo
C. Amon 312/0019 Ret:transmission
June 21. DUTCH GRAND PRIX, Zandvoort
C. Amon 312/0017 3rd
July 6. FRENCH GRAND PRIX, Clermont-Ferrand
C. Amon 312/0017 Ret:engine
July 19. BRITISH GRAND PRIX, Silverstone
C. Amon 312/0017 Ret:gearbox
P. Rodriguez 312/0009 Ret:engine
Sept 7. ITALIAN GRAND PRIX, Monza
P. Rodriguez 312/0019 6th
Sept 20. CANADIAN GRAND PRIX, Mosport Park
P. Rodriguez 312/0017 Ret:engine
Oct 5. UNITED STATES GRAND PRIX, Watkins Glen
P. Rodriguez 312/0017 5th
Oct 19. MEXICAN GRAND PRIX, Mexico City
P. Rodriguez 312/0017 7th

1970
Mar 7. SOUTH AFRICAN GRAND PRIX, Kyalami
J. Ickx 312B/001 Ret:oil leak
Apr 18. SPANISH GRAND PRIX, Jarama
J. Ickx 312B/002 Ret:accident
May 10. MONACO GRAND PRIX, Monte Carlo
J. Ickx 312B/001 Ret:driveshaft
June 7. BELGIAN GRAND PRIX, Spa-Francorchamps
J. Ickx 312B/003 8th
I. Giunti 312B/002 4th
June 21. DUTCH GRAND PRIX, Zandvoort
J. Ickx 312B/001 3rd
G. Regazzoni 312B/003 4th
July 5. FRENCH GRAND PRIX, Clermont-Ferrand
J. Ickx 312B/003 Ret:engine
I. Giunti 312B/002 14th
July 19. BRITISH GRAND PRIX, Brands Hatch
J. Ickx 312B/003 Ret:transmission
G. Regazzoni 312B/002 4th
Aug 2. GERMAN GRAND PRIX, Hockenheim
J. Ickx 312B/003 2nd
G. Regazzoni 312B/001 Ret:transmission
Aug 19. AUSTRIAN GRAND PRIX, Österreichring
J. Ickx 312B/001 1st
G. Regazzoni 312B/003 2nd
I. Giunti 312B/002 7th
Sept 6. ITALIAN GRAND PRIX, Monza
J. Ickx 312B/001 Ret:clutch
G. Regazzoni 312B/004 1st
I. Giunti 312B/002 Ret:engine
Sept 20. CANADIAN GRAND PRIX, Ste Jovite
J. Ickx 312B/001 1st
G. Regazzoni 312B/004 2nd
Oct 4. UNITED STATES GRAND PRIX, Watkins Glen
J. Ickx 312B/001 4th
G. Regazzoni 312B/004 13th
Oct 25. MEXICAN GRAND PRIX, Mexico City
J. Ickx 312B/001 1st
G. Regazzoni 312B/004 2nd

1971
Mar 6. SOUTH AFRICAN GRAND PRIX, Kyalami
J. Ickx 312B/001 8th
G. Regazzoni 312B/004 3rd
M. Andretti 312B/002 1st
Mar 21. Race of Champions, Brands Hatch
G. Regazzoni 312B/5 1st
Mar 28. Questor Grand Prix, Ontario Motor Speedway, Calif.
J. Ickx 312B/001 Ret:damaged wheel
M. Andretti 312B/002 1st
Apr 18. SPANISH GRAND PRIX, Barcelona
J. Ickx 312B/003 2nd
G. Regazzoni 312B/004 Ret:engine
M. Andretti 312B/002 Ret:engine fire
May 23. MONACO GRAND PRIX, Monte Carlo
J. Ickx 312B2/006 3rd
G. Regazzoni 312B2/005 Ret:accident
M. Andretti 312B/002 DNQ
June 13. Jochen Rindt Memorial Race, Hockenheim
J. Ickx 312B/003 1st
G. Regazzoni 312B/004 13th
June 20. DUTCH GRAND PRIX, Zandvoort
J. Ickx 312B2/006 1st
G. Regazzoni 312B2/005 3rd
M. Andretti 312B/003 Ret:fuel system
July 4. FRENCH GRAND PRIX, Paul Ricard
J. Ickx 312B2/006 Ret:engine
G. Regazzoni 312B2/005 Ret:accident
July 17. BRITISH GRAND PRIX, Silverstone
J. Ickx 312B2/006 Ret:engine
G. Regazzoni 312B2/005 Ret:engine
Aug 1. GERMAN GRAND PRIX, Nürburgring
J. Ickx 312B2/006 Ret:accident
G. Regazzoni 312B2/005 3rd
M. Andretti 312B2/007 4th
Aug 15. AUSTRIAN GRAND PRIX, Österreichring
J. Ickx 312B2/006 Ret:engine
G. Regazzoni 312B2/007 Ret:engine
Sept 5. ITALIAN GRAND PRIX, Monza
J. Ickx 312B/004 Ret:engine
G. Regazzoni 312B2/005 Ret:engine
Sept 19. CANADIAN GRAND PRIX, Mosport Park
J. Ickx 312B2/006 8th
G. Regazzoni 312B2/005 Ret:accident
M. Andretti 312B2/007 13th
Oct 3. UNITED STATES GRAND PRIX, Watkins Glen
J. Ickx 312B/004 Ret:electrics/oil leak
G. Regazzoni 312B2/005 6th

1972
Jan 23. ARGENTINE GRAND PRIX, Autodromo 17 October, Buenos Aires
J. Ickx 312B2/006 3rd
G. Regazzoni 312B2/005 4th
M. Andretti 312B2/007 Ret:engine
Mar 4. SOUTH AFRICAN GRAND PRIX, Kyalami
J. Ickx 312B2/006 8th
G. Regazzoni 312B2/005 12th
M. Andretti 312B2/007 4th
May 1. SPANISH GRAND PRIX, Jarama
J. Ickx 312B2/006 2nd
G. Regazzoni 312B2/008 3rd
M. Andretti 312B2/005 Ret:engine
May 14. MONACO GRAND PRIX, Monte Carlo
J. Ickx 312B2/006 2nd
G. Regazzoni 312B2/005 Ret:accident
June 4. BELGIAN GRAND PRIX, Nivelles-Baulers
J. Ickx 312B2/006 Ret:engine
G. Regazzoni 312B2/005 Ret:accident
July 4. FRENCH GRAND PRIX, Clermont-Ferrand
J. Ickx 312B2/005 11th
G. Galli 312B2/007 13th
July 17. BRITISH GRAND PRIX, Brands Hatch
J. Ickx 312B2/005 Ret:split oil cooler
A. Merzario 312B2/007 6th
Aug 1. GERMAN GRAND PRIX, Nürburgring
J. Ickx 312B2/005 1st
G. Regazzoni 312B2/007 2nd
A. Merzario 312B2/008 11th
Aug 13. AUSTRIAN GRAND PRIX, Österreichring
J. Ickx 312B2/005 Ret:fuel system
G. Regazzoni 312B2/007 Ret:fuel system
Sept 10. ITALIAN GRAND PRIX, Monza
J. Ickx 312B2/005 Ret:electrics
G. Regazzoni 312B2/007 Ret:collision
M. Andretti 312B2/008 7th
Sept 24. CANADIAN GRAND PRIX, Mosport Park
J. Ickx 312B2/005 12th
G. Regazzoni 312B2/007 5th
Oct 8. UNITED STATES GRAND PRIX, Watkins Glen
J. Ickx 312B2/005 5th
G. Regazzoni 312B2/007 8th
M. Andretti 312B2/006 6th

1973
Jan 28. ARGENTINE GRAND PRIX, Autodromo 17 October, Buenos Aires
J. Ickx 312B2/005 4th
A. Merzario 312B2/008 8th
Feb 11. BRAZILIAN GRAND PRIX, Interlagos, Sao Paulo
J. Ickx 312B2/005 5th
A. Merzario 312B2/008 4th
Mar 3. SOUTH AFRICAN GRAND PRIX, Kyalami
J. Ickx 312B2/006 Ret:accident
A. Merzario 312B2/005 4th
Apr 29. SPANISH GRAND PRIX, Barcelona
J. Ickx 312B3/010 10th
May 20. BELGIAN GRAND PRIX, Zolder
J. Ickx 312B3/010 Ret:engine
June 3. MONACO GRAND PRIX, Monte Carlo
J. Ickx 312B3/010 Ret:driveshaft
A. Merzario 312B3/011 Ret:oil pressure
June 17. SWEDISH GRAND PRIX, Anderstorp
J. Ickx 312B3/010 6th
July 1. FRENCH GRAND PRIX, Paul Ricard
J. Ickx 312B3/010 5th
A. Merzario 312B3/012 7th

July 14. BRITISH GRAND PRIX, Silverstone
J. Ickx 312B3/010 8th
Aug 19. AUSTRIAN GRAND PRIX, Österreichring
A. Merzario 312B3/011 7th
Sept 9. ITALIAN GRAND PRIX, Monza
J. Ickx 312B3/010 8th
A. Merzario 312B3/012 Ret:accident
Sept 22. CANADIAN GRAND PRIX, Mosport Park
A. Merzario 312B3/011 15th
Oct 7. UNITED STATES GRAND PRIX, Watkins Glen
A. Merzario 312B3/011 16th

1974

Jan 13. ARGENTINE GRAND PRIX, Autodromo 17 October, Buenos Aires
N. Lauda 312B3/012 2nd
G. Regazzoni 312B3/011 3rd
Jan 27. BRAZILIAN GRAND PRIX, Interlagos, Sao Paulo
N. Lauda 312B3/012 Ret:engine
G. Regazzoni 312B3/011 2nd
Mar 17. Race of Champions, Brands Hatch
N. Lauda 312B3/012 2nd
G. Regazzoni 312B3/011 5th
Mar 30. SOUTH AFRICAN GRAND PRIX, Kyalami
N. Lauda 312B3/012 Ret:electrics
G. Regazzoni 312B3/011 Ret:engine
Apr 28. SPANISH GRAND PRIX, Jarama
N. Lauda 312B3/015 1st
G. Regazzoni 312B3/014 2nd
May 12. BELGIAN GRAND PRIX, Nivelles-Baulers
N. Lauda 312B3/012 2nd
G. Regazzoni 312B3/011 4th
May 26. MONACO GRAND PRIX, Monte Carlo
N. Lauda 312B3/010 Ret:ignition
G. Regazzoni 312B3/014 4th
June 9. SWEDISH GRAND PRIX, Anderstorp
N. Lauda 312B3/015 Ret:suspension
G. Regazzoni 312B3/011 Ret:gearbox
June 23. DUTCH GRAND PRIX, Zandvoort
N. Lauda 312B3/015 1st
G. Regazzoni 312B3/014 2nd
July 7. FRENCH GRAND PRIX, Dijon-Prenois
N. Lauda 312B3/012 2nd
G. Regazzoni 312B3/014 3rd
July 20. BRITISH GRAND PRIX, Brands Hatch
N. Lauda 312B3/015 5th(awarded on appeal)
G. Regazzoni 312B3/014 4th
Aug 4. GERMAN GRAND PRIX, Nürburgring
N. Lauda 312B3/012 Ret:accident
G. Regazzoni 312B3/016 1st
Aug 18. AUSTRIAN GRAND PRIX, Österreichring
N. Lauda 312B3/015 Ret:engine
G. Regazzoni 312B3/014 5th
Sept 8. ITALIAN GRAND PRIX, Monza
N. Lauda 312B3/015 Ret:engine
G. Regazzoni 312B3/014 Ret:engine
Sept 22. CANADIAN GRAND PRIX, Mosport Park
N. Lauda 312B3/015 Ret:accident
G. Regazzoni 312B3/016 2nd
Oct 6. UNITED STATES GRAND PRIX, Watkins Glen
N. Lauda 312B3/014 Ret:engine
G. Regazzoni 312B3/011 11th

1975

Jan 12. ARGENTINE GRAND PRIX, Autodromo 17 October, Buenos Aires
N. Lauda 312B3/020 6th
G. Regazzoni 312B3/014 4th
Jan 26. BRAZILIAN GRAND PRIX, Interlagos, Sao Paulo
N. Lauda 312B3/020 5th
G. Regazzoni 312B3/014 4th
Mar 1. SOUTH AFRICAN GRAND PRIX, Kyalami
N. Lauda 312T/018 5th
G. Regazzoni 312T/021 16th
Apr 13. BRDC International Trophy, Silverstone
N. Lauda 312T/022 1st
Apr 27. SPANISH GRAND PRIX, Barcelona
N. Lauda 312T/022 Ret:accident
G. Regazzoni 312T/021 9th
May 11. MONACO GRAND PRIX, Monte Carlo
N. Lauda 312T/023 1st
G. Regazzoni 312T/018 Ret:accident
May 25. BELGIAN GRAND PRIX, Zolder
N. Lauda 312T/023 1st
G. Regazzoni 312T/022 5th
June 8. SWEDISH GRAND PRIX, Anderstorp
N. Lauda 312T/023 1st
G. Regazzoni 312T/021 3rd
June 22. DUTCH GRAND PRIX, Zandvoort
N. Lauda 312T/022 2nd
G. Regazzoni 312T/021 3rd
July 6. FRENCH GRAND PRIX, Paul Ricard
N. Lauda 312T/022 1st
G. Regazzoni 312T/024 Ret:engine
July 19. BRITISH GRAND PRIX, Silverstone
N. Lauda 312T/023 8th
G. Regazzoni 312T/024 13th
Aug 3. GERMAN GRAND PRIX, Nürburgring
N. Lauda 312T/022 3rd
G. Regazzoni 312T/021 Ret:engine
Aug 17. AUSTRIAN GRAND PRIX, Österreichring
N. Lauda 312T/022 6th
G. Regazzoni 312T/024 7th
Aug 24. Swiss Grand Prix, Dijon-Prenois
G. Regazzoni 312T/021 1st
Sept 7. ITALIAN GRAND PRIX, Monza
N. Lauda 312T/023 3rd
G. Regazzoni 312T/024 1st
Oct 5. UNITED STATES GRAND PRIX, Watkins Glen
N. Lauda 312T/023 1st
G. Regazzoni 312T/024 Withdrawn after dispute with race officials

1976

Jan 25. BRAZILIAN GRAND PRIX, Interlagos, Sao Paulo
N. Lauda 312T/023 1st
G. Regazzoni 312T/024 7th
Mar 6. SOUTH AFRICAN GRAND PRIX, Kyalami
N. Lauda 312T/023 1st
G. Regazzoni 312T/022 Ret:engine
Mar 14. Race of Champions, Brands Hatch
N. Lauda 312T2/025 Ret:brake pipe
G. Martini 312T/021 Accident on warm-up lap
Mar 28. UNITED STATES GRAND PRIX WEST, Long Beach, Calif.
N. Lauda 312T/023 2nd
G. Regazzoni 312T/024 1st
Apr 11. BRDC International Trophy, Silverstone
G. Martini 312T/021 10th
May 2. SPANISH GRAND PRIX, Jarama
N. Lauda 312T2/026 2nd
G. Regazzoni 312T2/025 11th
May 16. BELGIAN GRAND PRIX, Zolder
N. Lauda 312T2/026 1st
G. Regazzoni 312T2/025 2nd
May 30. MONACO GRAND PRIX, Monte Carlo
N. Lauda 312T2/026 1st
G. Regazzoni 312T2/027 Ret:accident
June 13. SWEDISH GRAND PRIX, Anderstorp
N. Lauda 312T2/026 3rd
G. Regazzoni 312T2/027 6th
July 4. FRENCH GRAND PRIX, Paul Ricard
N. Lauda 312T2/026 Ret:engine
G. Regazzoni 312T2/027 Ret:engine
July 18. BRITISH GRAND PRIX, Brands Hatch
N. Lauda 312T2/028 1st(awarded on appeal)
G. Regazzoni 312T2/026 Excluded from results
Aug 1. GERMAN GRAND PRIX, Nürburgring
N. Lauda 312T2/028 Ret:accident
G. Regazzoni 312T2/025 9th
Aug 29. DUTCH GRAND PRIX, Zandvoort
G. Regazzoni 312T2/027 2nd
Sept 12. ITALIAN GRAND PRIX, Monza
N. Lauda 312T2/026 4th
G. Regazzoni 312T2/027 2nd
C. Reutemann 312T2/025 9th
Oct 3. CANADIAN GRAND PRIX, Mosport Park
N. Lauda 312T2/026 8th
G. Regazzoni 312T2/027 6th
Oct 10. UNITED STATES GRAND PRIX, Watkins Glen
N. Lauda 312T2/026 3rd
G. Regazzoni 312T2/027 7th
Oct 24. JAPANESE GRAND PRIX, Mount Fuji
N. Lauda 312T2/026 Driver withdrew
G. Regazzoni 312T2/027 5th

1977

Jan 9. ARGENTINE GRAND PRIX, Autodromo 17 October, Buenos Aires
N. Lauda 312T2/026 Ret:metering unit
C. Reutemann 312T2/029 3rd
Jan 23. BRAZILIAN GRAND PRIX, Interlagos, Sao Paulo
N. Lauda 312T2/026 3rd
C. Reutemann 312T2/029 1st
Mar 5. SOUTH AFRICAN GRAND PRIX, Kyalami
N. Lauda 312T2/030 1st
C. Reutemann 312T2/027 8th
Apr 3. UNITED STATES GRAND PRIX, Long Beach, Calif.
N. Lauda 312T2/030 2nd
C. Reutemann 312T2/029 Ret:collision damage
May 8. SPANISH GRAND PRIX, Jarama
N. Lauda 312T2/030 DNS/driver injury
C. Reutemann 312T2/029 2nd
May 22. MONACO GRAND PRIX, Monte Carlo
N. Lauda 312T2/030 2nd
C. Reutemann 312T2/029 3rd
June 5. BELGIAN GRAND PRIX, Zolder
N. Lauda 312T2/030 2nd
C. Reutemann 312T2/029 Ret:spun off
June 19. SWEDISH GRAND PRIX, Anderstorp
N. Lauda 312T2/030 Driver withdrew
C. Reutemann 312T2/029 3rd
July 3. FRENCH GRAND PRIX, Dijon-Prenois
N. Lauda 312T2/031 5th

C. Reutemann 312T2/029 6th
July 16. BRITISH GRAND PRIX, Silverstone
N. Lauda 312T2/031 2nd
C. Reutemann 312T2/029 14th
July 31. GERMAN GRAND PRIX, Hockenheim
N. Lauda 312T2/031 1st
C. Reutemann 312T2/029 4th
Aug 14. AUSTRIAN GRAND PRIX, Österreichring
N. Lauda 312T2/031 2nd
C. Reutemann 312T2/029 4th
Aug 28. DUTCH GRAND PRIX, Zandvoort
N. Lauda 312T2/030 1st
C. Reutemann 312T2/029 6th
Sept 11. ITALIAN GRAND PRIX, Monza
N. Lauda 312T2/031 2nd
C. Reutemann 312T2/029 Ret:spun off
Oct 2. UNITED STATES GRAND PRIX, Watkins Glen
N. Lauda 312T2/031 4th
C. Reutemann 312T2/030 6th
Oct 9. CANADIAN GRAND PRIX, Mosport Park
C. Reutemann 312T2/029 Ret:fuel pressure
G. Villeneuve 312T2/030 Ret:driveshaft
Oct 23. JAPANESE GRAND PRIX, Mount Fuji
C. Reutemann 312T2/029 2nd
G. Villeneuve 312T2/030 Ret:accident

1978
Jan 15. ARGENTINE GRAND PRIX, Autodromo 17 October, Buenos Aires
C. Reutemann 312T2/031 7th
G. Villeneuve 312T2/027 8th
Jan 29. BRAZILIAN GRAND PRIX, Autodromo Riocentro, Rio
C. Reutemann 312T2/031 1st
G. Villeneuve 312T2/027 Ret:spun off
Mar 4. SOUTH AFRICAN GRAND PRIX, Kyalami
C. Reutemann 312T3/033 Ret:accident
G. Villeneuve 312T3/032 Ret:spun off
Apr 2. UNITED STATES GRAND PRIX WEST, Long Beach, Calif.
C. Reutemann 312T3/032 1st
G. Villeneuve 312T3/034 Ret:accident
May 7. MONACO GRAND PRIX, Monte Carlo
C. Reutemann 312T3/032 8th
G. Villeneuve 312T3/034 Ret:accident
May 21. BELGIAN GRAND PRIX, Zolder
C. Reutemann 312T3/033 3rd
G. Villeneuve 312T3/034 4th
June 4. SPANISH GRAND PRIX, Jarama
C. Reutemann 312T3/033 Ret:accident
G. Villeneuve 312T3/034 10th
June 17. SWEDISH GRAND PRIX, Anderstorp
C. Reutemann 312T3/036 10th
G. Villeneuve 312T3/034 9th
July 2. FRENCH GRAND PRIX, Paul Ricard
C. Reutemann 312T3/036 18th
G. Villeneuve 312T3/035 12th
July 16. BRITISH GRAND PRIX, Brands Hatch
C. Reutemann 312T3/033 1st
G. Villeneuve 312T3/034 Ret:driveshaft
July 30. GERMAN GRAND PRIX, Hockenheim
C. Reutemann 312T3/033 Ret:fuel system
G. Villeneuve 312T3/035 8th
Aug 13. AUSTRIAN GRAND PRIX, Österreichring
C. Reutemann 312T3/036 Disqualified
G. Villeneuve 312T3/034 3rd
Aug 27. DUTCH GRAND PRIX, Zandvoort
C. Reutemann 312T3/036 7th
G. Villeneuve 312T3/034 6th
Sept 10. ITALIAN GRAND PRIX, Monza
C. Reutemann 312T3/035 3rd
G. Villeneuve 312T3/034 7th
Oct 1. UNITED STATES GRAND PRIX, Watkins Glen
C. Reutemann 312T3/035 1st
G. Villeneuve 312T3/034 Ret:engine
Oct 8. CANADIAN GRAND PRIX, Ile Notre Dame, Montreal
C. Reutemann 312T3/035 3rd
G. Villeneuve 312T3/034 1st

1979
Jan 21. ARGENTINE GRAND PRIX, Autodromo 17 October, Buenos Aires
J. Scheckter 312T3/035 Ret:accident
G. Villeneuve 312T3/036 Ret:engine
Feb 4. BRAZILIAN GRAND PRIX, Interlagos, Sao Paulo
J. Scheckter 312T3/035 6th
G. Villeneuve 312T3/034 5th
Mar 3. SOUTH AFRICAN GRAND PRIX, Kyalami
J. Scheckter 312T4/038 2nd
G. Villeneuve 312T4/037 1st
Apr 8. UNITED STATES GRAND PRIX WEST, Long Beach, Calif.
J. Scheckter 312T4/038 2nd
G. Villeneuve 312T4/037 1st
Apr 15. Race of Champions, Brands Hatch
G. Villeneuve 312T3/033 1st
Apr 29. SPANISH GRAND PRIX, Jarama
J. Scheckter 312T4/039 4th
G. Villeneuve 312T4/037 7th
May 13. BELGIAN GRAND PRIX, Zolder
J. Scheckter 312T4/040 1st
G. Villeneuve 312T4/039 7th
May 27. MONACO GRAND PRIX, Monte Carlo
J. Scheckter 312T4/040 1st
G. Villeneuve 312T4/039 Ret:transmission
July 1. FRENCH GRAND PRIX, Dijon-Prenois
J. Scheckter 312T4/040 7th
G. Villeneuve 312T4/041 2nd
July 14. BRITISH GRAND PRIX, Silverstone
J. Scheckter 312T4/039 5th
G. Villeneuve 312T4/038 Ret:handling probs.
July 29. GERMAN GRAND PRIX, Hockenheim
J. Scheckter 312T4/040 4th
G. Villeneuve 312T4/041 8th
Aug 12. AUSTRIAN GRAND PRIX, Österreichring
J. Scheckter 312T4/040 4th
G. Villeneuve 312T4/041 2nd
Aug 26. DUTCH GRAND PRIX, Zandvoort
J. Scheckter 312T4/040 2nd
G. Villeneuve 312T4/041 Ret:tyre failure
Sept 9. ITALIAN GRAND PRIX, Monza
J. Scheckter 312T4/040 1st
G. Villeneuve 312T4/038 2nd
Sept 30. CANADIAN GRAND PRIX, Ile Notre Dame, Montreal
J. Scheckter 312T4/040 4th
G. Villeneuve 312T4/041 2nd
Oct 7. UNITED STATES GRAND PRIX, Watkins Glen
J. Scheckter 312T4/040 Ret:tyre burst
G. Villeneuve 312T4/041 1st

1980
Jan 13. ARGENTINE GRAND PRIX, Autodromo 17 October, Buenos Aires
J. Scheckter 312T5/042 Ret:engine
G. Villeneuve 312T5/043 Ret:steering failure, accident
Jan 27. BRAZILIAN GRAND PRIX, Interlagos, Sao Paulo
J. Scheckter 312T5/042 Ret:engine
G. Villeneuve 312T5/045 Ret:jammed throttle(16th)
Mar 1. SOUTH AFRICAN GRAND PRIX, Kyalami
J. Scheckter 312T5/046 Ret:engine
G. Villeneuve 312T5/042 Ret:transmission
Mar 30. UNITED STATES GRAND PRIX WEST, Long Beach, Calif.
J. Scheckter 312T5/046 5th
G. Villeneuve 312T5/045 Ret:driveshaft
May 4. BELGIAN GRAND PRIX, Zolder
J. Scheckter 312T5/046 8th
G. Villeneuve 312T5/045 6th
May 18. MONACO GRAND PRIX, Monte Carlo
J. Scheckter 312T5/046 Driver withdrew
G. Villeneuve 312T5/045 5th
June 1. SPANISH GRAND PRIX, Jarama
J. Scheckter 312T5/046)Entries withdrawn following sanctioning dispute
G. Villeneuve 312T5/044)regarding race's status.
June 29. FRENCH GRAND PRIX, Paul Ricard
J. Scheckter 312T5/046 12th
G. Villeneuve 312T5/045 8th
July 13. BRITISH GRAND PRIX, Brands Hatch
J. Scheckter 312T5/046 10th
G. Villeneuve 312T5/048 Ret:engine
Aug 10. GERMAN GRAND PRIX, Hockenheim
J. Scheckter 312T5/046 13th
G. Villeneuve 312T5/048 6th
Aug 17. AUSTRIAN GRAND PRIX, Österreichring
J. Scheckter 312T5/044 13th
G. Villeneuve 312T5/043 8th
Sept 14. ITALIAN GRAND PRIX, Dino Ferrari Autodrome, Imola
J. Scheckter 312T5/043 8th
G. Villeneuve 312T5/048 Ret:accident
Sept 28. CANADIAN GRAND PRIX, Ile Notre Dame, Montreal
J. Scheckter 312T5/044* DNQ(*practice only)
G. Villeneuve 312T5/044 5th
Oct 5. UNITED STATES GRAND PRIX, Watkins Glen
J. Scheckter 312T5/044 11th
G. Villeneuve 312T5/043 Ret:accident

1981
Mar 15. UNITED STATES GRAND PRIX WEST, Long Beach, Calif.
G. Villenueve 126CK/051 Ret:transmission
D. Pironi 126CK/050 Ret:engine
Mar 29. BRAZILIAN GRAND PRIX, Autodromo Ricentro, Rio
G. Villeneuve 126CK/051 Ret:turbo wastegate
D. Pironi 126CK/050 Ret:accident
Apr 12. ARGENTINE GRAND PRIX, Autodromo 17 October, Buenos Aires
G. Villeneuve 126CK/051 Ret:driveshaft
D. Pironi 126CK/050 Ret:engine
May 3. SAN MARINO GRAND PRIX, Dino Ferrari Autodrome, Imola
G. Villeneuve 126CK/052 7th
D. Pironi 126CK/050 4th
May 17. BELGIAN GRAND PRIX, Zolder
G. Villeneuve 126CK/052 4th
D. Pironi 126CK/050 8th

May 31. MONACO GRAND PRIX, Monte Carlo
- G. Villeneuve 126CK/052 1st
- D. Pironi 126CK/050 4th

June 21. SPANISH GRAND PRIX, Jarama
- G. Villeneuve 126CK/052 1st
- D. Pironi 126CK/053 15th

July 5. FRENCH GRAND PRIX, Dijon-Prenois
- G. Villeneuve 126CK/052 Ret:electrics
- D. Pironi 126CK/053 5th

July 18. BRITISH GRAND PRIX, Silverstone
- G. Villeneuve 126CK/054 Ret:accident
- D. Pironi 126CK/053 Ret:engine

Aug 2. GERMAN GRAND PRIX, Hockenheim
- G. Villeneuve 126CK/054 10th
- D. Pironi 126CK/053 Ret:engine

Aug 16. AUSTRIAN GRAND PRIX, Österreichring
- G. Villenueve 126CK/050B Ret:accident
- D. Pironi 126CK/051B 9th

Aug 30. DUTCH GRAND PRIX, Zandvoort
- G. Villeneuve 126CK/050B Ret:accident
- D. Pironi 126CK/051B Ret:accident damage

Sept 13. ITALIAN GRAND PRIX, Monza
- G. Villeneuve 126CK/053 Ret:turbo
- D. Pironi 126CK/049B 5th

Sept 27. CANADIAN GRAND PRIX, Ile Notre Dame, Montreal
- G. Villeneuve 126CK/052 3rd
- D. Pironi 126CK/049B Ret:engine

Oct 17. LAS VEGAS GRAND PRIX, Caesars Palace
- G. Villeneuve 126CK/051B Excluded for start line infringement
- D. Pironi 126CK/049B 9th

1982

Jan 23. SOUTH AFRICAN GRAND PRIX, Kyalami
- G. Villeneuve 126C2/055 Ret:turbo
- D. Pironi 126C2/056 18th

Mar 21. BRAZILIAN GRAND PRIX, Autodromo Riocentro, Rio
- G. Villeneuve 126C2/057 Ret:accident
- D. Pironi 126C2/056 6th (after disq. of 1st and 2nd place cars)

Apr 4. UNITED STATES GRAND PRIX WEST, Long Beach, Calif.
- G. Villeneuve 126C2/058 Disqualified
- D. Pironi 126C2/056 Ret:accident

Apr 25. SAN MARINO GRAND PRIX, Dino Ferrari Autodrome, Imola
- G. Villeneuve 126C2/058 2nd
- D. Pironi 126C2/059 1st

May 9. BELGIAN GRAND PRIX, Zolder
- G. Villeneuve 126C2/058 Fatal practice accident
- D. Pironi 126C2/059 Withdrawn after practice

May 23. MONACO GRAND PRIX, Monte Carlo
- D. Pironi 126C2/059 2nd

June 6. UNITED STATES GRAND PRIX (DETROIT), Detroit, Michigan
- D. Pironi 126C2/056 3rd

June 13. CANADIAN GRAND PRIX, Ile Notre Dame, Montreal
- D. Pironi 126C2/059 9th

July 3. DUTCH GRAND PRIX, Zandvoort
- D. Pironi 126C2/060 1st
- P. Tambay 126C2/057 8th

July 18. BRITISH GRAND PRIX, Brands Hatch
- D. Pironi 126C2/060 2nd
- P. Tambay 126C2/061 3rd

July 25. FRENCH GRAND PRIX, Paul Ricard
- D. Pironi 126C2/060 3rd
- P. Tambay 126C2/061 4th

Aug 8. GERMAN GRAND PRIX, Hockenheim
- D. Pironi 126C2/060 DNS:Practice accident
- P. Tambay 126C2/061 1st

Aug 15. AUSTRIAN GRAND PRIX, Österreichring
- P. Tambay 126C2/061 4th

Aug 29. SWISS GRAND PRIX, Dijon-Prenois
- P. Tambay 126C2/ Withdrew after practice owing to driver unwell

Sept 12. ITALIAN GRAND PRIX, Monza
- P. Tambay 126C2/062 2nd
- M. Andretti 126C2/061 3rd

Sept 25. LAS VEGAS GRAND PRIX, Caesars Palace
- P. Tambay 126C2/062 Withdrew after practice owing to driver unwell
- M. Andretti 126C2/061 Ret:suspension

1983

Mar 13. BRAZILIAN GRAND PRIX, Autodromo Riocentro, Rio
- P. Tambay 126C2B/065 5th
- R. Arnoux 126C2B/064 10th

Mar 27. UNITED STATES GRAND PRIX WEST, Long Beach, Calif.
- P. Tambay 126C2B/065 Ret: accident
- R. Arnoux 126C2B/064 3rd

Apr 17. FRENCH GRAND PRIX, Paul Ricard
- P. Tambay 126C2B/062 4th
- R. Arnoux 126C2B/064 7th

May 1. SAN MARINO GRAND PRIX, Dino Ferrari Autodrome, Imola
- P. Tambay 126C2B/065 1st
- R. Arnoux 126C2B/064 3rd

May 15. MONACO GRAND PRIX, Monte Carlo
- P. Tambay 126C2B/065 4th
- R. Arnoux 126C2B/064 Ret:accident

May 22. BELGIAN GRAND PRIX, Spa-Francorchamps
- P. Tambay 126C2B/065 2nd
- R. Arnoux 126C2B/062 Ret:engine

June 5. UNITED STATES GRAND PRIX (DETROIT), Detroit, Michigan
- P. Tambay 126C2B/065 Ret:stalled at start
- R. Arnoux 126C2B/064 Ret:electrics

June 12. CANADIAN GRAND PRIX, Ile Notre Dame, Montreal
- P. Tambay 126C2B/065 3rd
- R. Arnoux 126C2B/064 1st

July 16. BRITISH GRAND PRIX, Silverstone
- P. Tambay 126C3/067 3rd
- R. Arnoux 126C3/066 5th

Aug 17. GERMAN GRAND PRIX, Hockenheim
- P. Tambay 126C3/067 Ret:engine
- R. Arnoux 126C3/066 1st

Aug 14. AUSTRIAN GRAND PRIX, Österreichring
- P. Tambay 126C3/067 Ret:engine
- R. Arnoux 126C3/068 2nd

Aug 28. DUTCH GRAND PRIX, Zandvoort
- P. Tambay 126C3/067 2nd
- R. Arnoux 126C3/066 1st

Sept 11. ITALIAN GRAND PRIX, Monza
- P. Tambay 126C3/069 4th
- R. Arnoux 126C3/066 2nd

Sept 25. GRAND PRIX OF EUROPE, Brands Hatch
- P. Tambay 126C3/069 Ret:slid off
- R. Arnoux 126C3/066 9th

Oct 15. SOUTH AFRICAN GRAND PRIX, Kyalami
- P. Tambay 126C3/069 Ret:turbo
- R. Arnoux 126C3/066 Ret:engine

1984

Mar 25. BRAZILIAN GRAND PRIX, Autodromo Riocentro, Rio
- M. Alboreto 126C4/072 Ret:brake caliper
- R. Arnoux 126C4/073 Ret:electrical

Apr 7. SOUTH AFRICAN GRAND PRIX, Kyalami
- M. Alboreto 126C4/072 Ret:fuel system
- R. Arnoux 126C4/073 Ret:fuel system

Apr 29. BELGIAN GRAND PRIX, Zolder
- M. Alboreto 126C4/074 1st
- R. Arnoux 126C4/073 3rd

May 6. SAN MARINO GRAND PRIX, Dino Ferrari Autodrome, Imola
- M. Alboreto 126C4/074 Ret:exhaust
- R. Arnoux 126C4/073 2nd

May 20. FRENCH GRAND PRIX, Dijon-Prenois
- M. Alboreto 126C4/074 Ret:engine
- R. Arnoux 126C4/073 4th

June 3. MONACO GRAND PRIX, Monte Carlo
- M. Alboreto 126C4/074 7th
- R. Arnoux 126C4/075 4th

June 17. CANADIAN GRAND PRIX, Ile Notre Dame, Montreal
- M. Alboreto 126C4/076 Ret:fuel pump drive
- R. Arnoux 126C4/075 5th

June 24. UNITED STATES GRAND PRIX (DETROIT), Detroit, Michigan
- M. Alboreto 126C4/076 Ret:engine
- R. Arnoux 126C4/075 Ret:spin damage

July 8. DALLAS GRAND PRIX, Fair Park, Dallas, Texas
- M. Alboreto 126C4/076 Ret:accident
- R. Arnoux 126C4/075 2nd

July 22. BRITISH GRAND PRIX, Brands Hatch
- M. Alboreto 126C4/075 5th
- R. Arnoux 126C4/076 6th

Aug 5. GERMAN GRAND PRIX, Hockenheim
- M. Alboreto 126C4/073 Ret:electrics
- R. Arnoux 126C4/074 6th

Aug 19. AUSTRIAN GRAND PRIX, Österreichring
- M. Alboreto 126C4/073 Ret:electrics
- R. Arnoux 126C4/074 7th

Aug 26. DUTCH GRAND PRIX, Zandvoort
- M. Alboreto 126C4/076 Ret:engine
- R. Arnoux 126C4/075 Ret:electrics

Sept 9. ITALIAN GRAND PRIX, Monza
- M. Alboreto 126C4/076 2nd
- R. Arnoux 126C4/077 Ret:gearbox

Oct 7. GRAND PRIX OF EUROPE, Nürburgring
- M. Alboreto 126C4/074 2nd
- R. Arnoux 126C4/077 5th

Oct 21. PORTUGUESE GRAND PRIX, Estoril
- M. Alboreto 126C4/074 4th
- R. Arnoux 126C4/077 9th

1985

Apr 7. BRAZILIAN GRAND PRIX, Autodromo Riocentro, Rio
- M. Alboreto 156/85/079 2nd
- R. Arnoux 156/85/080 4th

Apr 21. PORTUGUESE GRAND PRIX, Estoril
- M. Alboreto 156/85/079 2nd
- S. Johansson 156/85/080 8th

May 5. SAN MARINO GRAND PRIX, Dino Ferrari Autodrome, Imola
- M. Alboreto 156/85/081 Ret:electrics
- S. Johansson 156/85/079 6th

May 19. MONACO GRAND PRIX, Monte Carlo
M. Alboreto 156/85/081 2nd
S. Johansson 156/85/079 Ret:collision
June 16. CANADIAN GRAND PRIX, Ile Notre Dame, Montreal
M. Alboreto 156/85/081 1st
S. Johansson 156/85/082 2nd
June 23. UNITED STATES GRAND PRIX (DETROIT), Detroit, Michigan
M. Alboreto 156/85/081 3rd
S. Johansson 156/85/082 2nd
July 7. FRENCH GRAND PRIX, Paul Ricard
M. Alboreto 156/85/079 Ret:turbo
S. Johansson 156/85/081 4th
July 21. BRITISH GRAND PRIX, Silverstone
M. Alboreto 156/85/081 2nd
S. Johansson 156/85/079 Ret:collision
Aug 4. GERMAN GRAND PRIX, Nürburgring
M. Alboreto 156/85/080 1st
S. Johansson 156/85/079 9th
Aug 18. AUSTRIAN GRAND PRIX, Österreichring
M. Alboreto 156/85/080 3rd
S. Johansson 156/85/079 4th
Aug 25. DUTCH GRAND PRIX, Zandvoort
M. Alboreto 156/85/080 4th
S. Johansson 156/85/079 Ret:engine
Sept 8. ITALIAN GRAND PRIX, Monza
M. Alboreto 156/85/085 Ret:engine
S. Johansson 156/85/083 5th
Sept 15. BELGIAN GRAND PRIX, Spa-Francorchamps
M. Alboreto 156/85/085 Ret:clutch
S. Johansson 156/85/083 Ret:engine/spin
Oct 6. GRAND PRIX OF EUROPE, Brands Hatch
M. Alboreto 156/85/085 Ret:turbo
S. Johansson 156/85/086 Ret:engine
Oct 19. SOUTH AFRICAN GRAND PRIX, Kyalami
M. Alboreto 156/85/083 Ret:turbo
S. Johansson 156/85/086 5th
Nov 3. AUSTRALIAN GRAND PRIX, Adelaide
M. Alboreto 156/85/083 Ret:gear linkage
S. Johansson 156/85/086 5th

1986
Mar 23. BRAZILIAN GRAND PRIX, Autodromo Riocentro, Rio
M. Alboreto F1/86/088 Ret:fuel pump
S. Johansson F1/86/087 Ret:spun off
Apr 13. SPANISH GRAND PRIX, Jerez
M. Alboreto F1/86/088 Ret:wheel bearing
S. Johansson F1/86/087 Ret:accident
Apr 27. SAN MARINO GRAND PRIX, Dino Ferrari Autodrome, Imola
M. Alboreto F1/86/088 10th
S. Johansson F1/86/090 4th
May 11. MONACO GRAND PRIX, Monte Carlo
M. Alboreto F1/86/088 Ret:turbo
S. Johansson F1/86/090 10th
May 25. BELGIAN GRAND PRIX, Spa-Francorchamps
M. Alboreto F1/86/089 4th
S. Johansson F1/86/090 3rd
June 15. CANADIAN GRAND PRIX, Ile Notre Dame, Montreal
M. Alboreto F1/86/092 8th
S. Johansson F1/86/091 Ret:accident
June 22. UNITED STATES GRAND PRIX (DETROIT), Detroit, Michigan
M. Alboreto F1/86/092 4th
S. Johansson F1/86/086 Ret:electrics
July 6. FRENCH GRAND PRIX, Paul Ricard
M. Alboreto F1/86/092 8th
S. Johansson F1/86/093 Ret:turbo
July 13. BRITISH GRAND PRIX, Brands Hatch
M. Alboreto F1/86/092 Ret:turbo
S. Johansson F1/86/093 Ret:engine
July 27. GERMAN GRAND PRIX, Hockenheim
M. Alboreto F1/86/092 Ret:transmission
S. Johansson F1/86/093 11th
Aug 10. HUNGARIAN GRAND PRIX, Hungaroring
M. Alboreto F1/86/092 Ret:collision
S. Johansson F1/86/090 4th
Aug 17. AUSTRIAN GRAND PRIX, Österreichring
M. Alboreto F1/86/092 2nd
S. Johansson F1/86/089 3rd
Sept 7. ITALIAN GRAND PRIX, Monza
M. Alboreto F1/86/092 Ret:engine
S. Johansson F1/86/093 3rd
Sept 21. PORTUGUESE GRAND PRIX, Estoril
M. Alboreto F1/86/092 5th
S. Johansson F1/86/093 6th
Oct 12. MEXICAN GRAND PRIX, Mexico City
M. Alboreto F1/86/092 Ret:turbo
S. Johansson F1/86/093 12th
Oct 26. AUSTRALIAN GRAND PRIX, Adelaide
M. Alboreto F1/86/089 Ret:collision
S. Johansson F1/86/094 3rd

1987
Apr 12. BRAZILIAN GRAND PRIX, Autodromo Riocentro, Rio
M. Alboreto F1/87/096 8th
G. Berger F1/87/095 4th
May 3. SAN MARINO GRAND PRIX, Dino Ferrari Autodrome, Imola
M. Alboreto F1/87/096 3rd
G. Berger F1/87/097 Ret:electrical
May 17. BELGIAN GRAND PRIX, Spa-Francorchamps
M. Alboreto F1/87/096 Ret:transmission
G. Berger F1/87/097 Ret:turbo
May 31. MONACO GRAND PRIX, Monte Carlo
M. Alboreto F1/87/098 3rd
G. Berger F1/87/097 4th
June 21. UNITED STATES GRAND PRIX (DETROIT), Detroit, Michigan
M. Alboreto F1/87/098 Ret:gearbox
G. Berger F1/87/097 4th
July 5. FRENCH GRAND PRIX, Paul Ricard
M. Alboreto F1/87/098 Ret:engine
G. Berger F1/87/099 Ret:suspension
July 12. BRITISH GRAND PRIX, Silverstone
M. Alboreto F1/87/098 Ret:suspension
G. Berger F1/87/099 Ret:spun off
July 26. GERMAN GRAND PRIX, Hockenheim
M. Alboreto F1/87/098 Ret:turbo
G. Berger F1/87/099 Ret:turbo
Aug 9. HUNGARIAN GRAND PRIX, Hungaroring
M. Alboreto F1/87/100 Ret:engine
G. Berger F1/87/098 Ret:transmission
Aug 16. AUSTRIAN GRAND PRIX, Österreichring
M. Alboreto F1/87/100 Ret:exhaust
G. Berger F1/87/097 Ret:electrics
Sept 6. ITALIAN GRAND PRIX, Monza
M. Alboreto F1/87/100 Ret:turbo
G. Berger F1/87/098 4th
Sept 21. PORTUGUESE GRAND PRIX, Estoril
M. Alboreto F1/87/097 Ret:transmission
G. Berger F1/87/098 2nd
Sept 27. SPANISH GRAND PRIX, Jerez
M. Alboreto F1/87/095 Ret:engine (15th)
G. Berger F1/87/098 Ret:engine
Oct 18. MEXICAN GRAND PRIX, Mexico City
M. Alboreto F1/87/101 Ret:engine
G. Berger F1/87/098 Ret:engine
Nov 1. JAPANESE GRAND PRIX, Suzuka
M. Alboreto F1/87/101 4th
G. Berger F1/87/098 1st
Nov 15. AUSTRALIAN GRAND PRIX, Adelaide
M. Alboreto F1/87/101 2nd
G. Berger F1/87/098 1st

1988
Apr 3. BRAZILIAN GRAND PRIX, Autodromo Riocentro, Rio
M. Alboreto F1/87/88C/103 5th
G. Berger F1/87/88C/104 2nd
May 1. SAN MARINO GRAND PRIX, Dino Ferrari Autodrome, Imola
M. Alboreto F1/87/88C/103 Ret:engine (18th)
G. Berger F1/87/88C/102 5th
May 15. MONACO GRAND PRIX, Monte Carlo
M. Alboreto F1/87/88C/103 3rd
G. Berger F1/87/88C/104 2nd
May 28. MEXICAN GRAND PRIX, Mexico City
M. Alboreto F1/87/88C/103 4th
G. Berger F1/87/88C/104 3rd
June 12. CANADIAN GRAND PRIX, Ile Notre Dame, Montreal
M. Alboreto F1/87/88C/103 Ret:engine
G. Berger F1/87/88C/104 Ret:electrics
June 19. UNITED STATES GRAND PRIX (DETROIT), Detroit
M. Alboreto F1/87/88C/103 Ret:accident
G. Berger F1/87/88C/104 Ret:puncture
July 3. FRENCH GRAND PRIX, Paul Ricard
M. Alboreto F1/87/88C/103 3rd
G. Berger F1/87/88C/104 4th
July 10. BRITISH GRAND PRIX, Silverstone
M. Alboreto F1/87/88C/103 17th
G. Berger F1/87/88C/104 9th
July 24. GERMAN GRAND PRIX, Hockenheim
M. Alboreto F1/87/88C/103 4th
G. Berger F1/87/88C/104 3rd
Aug 7. HUNGARIAN GRAND PRIX, Hungaroring
M. Alboreto F1/87/88C/103 Ret:engine cut
G. Berger F1/87/88C/104 4th
Aug 28. BELGIAN GRAND PRIX, Spa-Francorchamps
M. Alboreto F1/87/88C/103 Ret:engine
G. Berger F1/87/88C/104 Ret:electrics
Sept 11. ITALIAN GRAND PRIX, Monza
M. Alboreto F1/87/88C/103 2nd
G. Berger F1/87/88C/102 1st
Sept 25. PORTUGUESE GRAND PRIX, Estoril
M. Alboreto F1/87/88C/103 5th
G. Berger F1/87/88C/104 Ret:spun off
Oct 2. SPANISH GRAND PRIX, Jerez
M. Alboreto F1/87/88C/103 Ret:engine
G. Berger F1/87/88C/104 6th
Oct 30. JAPANESE GRAND PRIX, Suzuka
M. Alboreto F1/87/88C/103 11th
G. Berger F1/87/88C/104 4th
Nov 13. AUSTRALIAN GRAND PRIX, Adelaide
M. Alboreto F1/87/88C/103 Ret:accident
G. Berger F1/87/88C/104 Ret:collision